GESTALT THERAPY

GESTALT INSTITUTE OF CLEVELAND PRESS

THE NEUROTIC BEHAVIOR OF ORGANIZATIONS
Uri Merry and George Brown

BODY PROCESS: A GESTALT APPROACH TO WORKING
WITH THE BODY IN PSYCHOTHERAPY
James I. Kepner

ORGANIZATIONAL CONSULTING: A GESTALT APPROACH
Edwin C. Nevis

BECOMING A STEPFAMILY: PATTERNS OF
DEVELOPMENT IN REMARRIED FAMILIES
Patricia Papernow

GESTALT THERAPY: PERSPECTIVES AND
APPLICATIONS
Edwin C. Nevis, Editor

GESTALT RECONSIDERED: A NEW APPROACH
TO CONTACT AND RESISTANCE
Gordon Wheeler

Gestalt Therapy

Perspectives
and
Applications

Edited by
Edwin C. Nevis, Ph.D.

The Gestalt Institute of Cleveland Press

Published and Distributed by
GARDNER PRESS, INC.
New York ● London ● Sydney ● Toronto

  GARDNER PRESS, INC.
  19 Union Square West
  New York, New York 10003

Gestalt Institute of Cleveland Press
Published and Distributed by Gardner Press

Library of Congress Cataloging-in-Publication Data

Gestalt therapy : perspectives and applications / edited by Edwin C. Nevis.
  p. cm.
 Includes bibliographical references.
 ISBN 0-89876-143-3
 1. Gestalt therapy. I. Nevis, Edwin C..
 [DNLM: 1. Psychotherapy. WM 420 G384]
KC489.G4G485 1990
616.89'143—dc20
DNLM/DLC
for Library of Congress   90-3080
                       CIP

10 9 8 7 6 5 4 3 2 1

Printed in Mexico

Design by Publishers Creative Services

CONTENTS

v

GESTALT   THERAPY

Introduction

EDWIN C. NEVIS, Ph.D.

This volume attests to the continuing richness of Gestalt therapy as a conceptual and methodological base from which helping professionals can craft their practice. The contributors are a diverse group with varied backgrounds and ways of working. They represent all generations of those influenced by the founders of Gestalt therapy, and include four new voices of students of the students of Fritz Perls, Laura Perls, Paul Goodman, and Isadore From. Moreover, the volume reflects the freedom that Gestalt therapy allows for practitioners to express their individuality of style. From Bob Goulding's unique sharing of his "wise old man's insights," through Joseph Zinker's often poetic, metaphorical emphasis, to the intellectual sharpness of Joel Latner and Gordon Wheeler, and on to Ilana Rubenfeld's personal and caring way of working and sharing of her process—and to the other voices herein—we see the full measure of this diversity.

To set this volume in perspective, it may be helpful to take a brief look at the history of publication of works on Gestalt therapy. The first books by the founders, *Ego, Hunger, and Aggression* (Perls, 1947) and *Gestalt Therapy* (Perls, Hefferline, & Goodman, 1951), were essentially revolutionary treatises with a different way of looking at things. These books, and the workshops and seminars conducted by the authors of these books, generated a profound interest on the part of both seasoned psychotherapists and students and other beginners. As Fritz Perls, Laura Perls, Isadore From, Paul Goodman, and their associates found themselves in great demand to provide training workshops, institutes were formed in New York, Cleveland, and Los Angeles, and a "movement" was fully under way to actualize this new therapy.

What is interesting to note is that for almost 20 years no new books on Gestalt therapy were published. There were articles here and there, brief monographs, and presentations at various meetings, but no full-length volumes. And what did appear concerned itself largely with explaining what Gestalt therapy was and with extolling its virtues.

Beginning in 1970 this changed dramatically and numerous books appeared, most of them written by the first students of the New York group and some students of these students. It would appear that serious practitioners had spent years developing themselves to the point where they had something to say to others. I do not list all the books of that period, but noteworthy are Fagan and Sheperd's (1970) *Gestalt Therapy Now*, Polster and Polster's (1973) *Gestalt Therapy Integrated*, Latner's (1973) *Gestalt Therapy Book*, Smith's (1976) *The Growing Edge Of Gestalt Therapy*, and Zinker's (1978) *Creative Process in Psychotherapy*. In 1978 the *Gestalt Journal* was founded to provide a forum for the growing number of serious papers that began to appear.

Viewed as a whole, this body of work made it clear that Gestalt therapy had taken its place as a psychotherapeutic approach of broad appeal. Moreover, these books displayed the stamp of their authors and went beyond repeating what the founders had laid down in their early writings and teachings. The authors concentrated on the basic issues of Gestalt individual psychotherapy, but they added to our understanding and our practice.

As a result of these publications and the work of the Gestalt therapy postgraduate training institutes throughout the world, new generations have become influenced by Gestalt therapy and have applied it to situations beyond individual therapy. We now have training programs for working with couples and families, for working with groups, for working with organizations, and so on. Although some people, notably Isadore From and Joel Latner, have questioned the applicability of Gestalt therapy beyond its model of individual growth and development, significant numbers of people who work in arenas other than the individual therapy, private practice setting have been adopting Gestalt therapy concepts and methods as a means of improving the effectiveness of their work. In short, the past 15 years may be viewed as the "Age of Applications," and this book is an attempt to bring together under one cover a discussion of some of the more important of these. It is one of several applications books being published by the Gestalt Institute of Cleveland Press, for whom the applied focus is a major objective.

The focus on application does not mean that there is little interest in examination and revision of the basic concepts of Gestalt therapy. Indeed, as a group of third- and fourth-generation students have matured they have revisited the basic concepts and looked at how confusions or weak points may be clarified. In addition, we now have some well-developed integrations of Gestalt therapy with other approaches to therapy and self-development. These broaden the perspective of the practitioner and enrich the ground between theory and application. Some of these are discussed in this book.

The book is divided into two parts. Part 1, on perspectives, begins with an excellent statement of the theory of Gestalt therapy. In his usual articulate, succinct, and knowledgeable way, Joel Latner walks us through the core aspects of Gestalt therapy. He conveys the power of the approach and also calls our attention to some of the soft spots in our theory and to the need to address these weaknesses. This chapter can serve as an introduction for beginning readers and as a pungent refresher for the more experienced. Latner conveys a great deal of useful material with grace and clarity.

Following this chapter is a conception of diagnosis from a Gestalt point of view. Joseph Melnick and Sonia Nevis deal here with an issue that Gestalt therapists tended to ignore or play down in the early years. The here-and-now, process emphasis of Gestalt therapy led many practitioners to believe that it was not necessary to engage in traditional diagnostic exercises or that the typical nosological entities made little sense in a Gestalt framework. Melnick and Nevis make a convincing case that clinical diagnosis not only is compatible with a Gestalt approach, but is very useful to the therapeutic undertaking. In particular, their presentation of the borderline personality in terms of sensory awareness malfunctioning is a real contribution.

The third chapter presents a model for looking at therapy over the entire span of the relationship. This model emphasizes an initial phase that is particularly useful with populations other than the typical Gestalt therapy clients, such as reasonably aware, generally professional class people. Norman Shub points out that the more or less unstructured awareness work of typical Gestalt therapy is not always suitable; many clients, such as borderline cases, have to be prepared for it in what he calls the ''initial phase'' of therapy. (We will be seeing more on this important area; a recent book by John Masterson (1988) deals with the same issue from the point of view of psychoanalytic object relations theory.) Following this, Shub deals with the middle phase of therapy, which he sees largely as a task of dealing with introjects.

The next chapter raises a critical, yet relatively neglected issue in recent times, that of values or ethics in Gestalt therapy. Gordon Wheeler, a fresh voice writing with fine literary skill, addresses the question by saying that we have emphasized the ethics of process and have shied away from taking stances on the substance of content. He shifts the emphasis from the ethics of good figure formation to the definition of Gestalt ethics in terms of the structure of the ground. He concludes that all figures or processes are not equal. He takes us through a Socratic-like dialogue around some of the most difficult issues in defining an ethical stance, concluding that the key to the dilemma lies in relatedness of figure and ground.

Bob Goulding's chapter reflects the ease and power available to a wise, talented master therapist. His work is supported by the conceptual and methodological bases of both Transactional Analysis and Gestalt therapy. The resulting perspective is one of fluidity in the service of keen attention to a few firmly held principles. Moreover, we get a glimpse of how the power of Goulding's presence seems to energize the client. It appears easy, but his work has an underlying foundation of pliable steel rods that were forged over years of development.

Ilana Rubenfeld's personal and often moving account shows the power in the integration of Gestalt therapy with sophisticated approaches to body work. Anyone who has ever worked with Laura Perls knows that attention to the body was part of Gestalt therapy from the very beginning; we were taught to pay attention to what we were doing to and with ourselves physically. Likewise, Fritz Perls made sure that we were familiar with the work of Wilhelm Reich and how the muscular theory of repression was an important cornerstone of his model. Now we have new generations of practitioners who have done years of painstaking study and training in the Alexander Technique, the Feldenkreis Method, Polarity therapy, and so on, moving us further along in methodology to work with a true integration of mind and body. Ilana Rubenfeld is a prime example and one of the pioneers in this movement. This chapter gives us a detailed look at how she works and at the potential in this approach.

Janette Rainwater, one of the early people trained by Fritz Perls, discusses psychosynthesis, a powerful approach that was quite popular some years ago but does not now receive the attention it deserves. Partly because of the quiet style of its founder, Robert Assagioli, and the relative lack of proselytizing by him and his adherents, a significant movement did not develop in the United States. Some students of the approach studied at the Gestalt Institute of Cleveland in the 1960s, and the work with fantasy by the Cleveland group was much influenced by exposure to guided imagery. It may be that with the passage of time action-oriented methods have become more popular than the patient, inward-directed method of psychosynthesis. Also, as Maslow pointed out years ago, much of the value of psychosynthesis comes in dealing with higher level growth and development—as opposed to treating deficiency needs—and it may be most useful in expanding awareness and higher order insights rather than in symptom reduction. Hopefully, the perspective advanced herein by Rainwater will inspire others to study psychosynthesis and to integrate its methods and concepts into their work.

Part II turns its attention to applications, and discusses six areas in which experienced Gestalt therapists have enhanced their work through use of Gestalt concepts and methods. The authors identify for us the characteristics or requirements of these special situations and then show how they deal with them from the perspective of Gestalt therapy. Three of the chapters focus on the individual level and deal with difficult populations: alcoholics, psychotics, and children. The other three deal with people in units of more than one, reflecting the substantial interest in going "beyond the one": groups, couples, and milieu therapy.[1]

Carlock, Glaus, and Shaw present an extensive and sensitive discussion of issues in working with alcoholics. They lay out their treatment strategy in great detail, sharing their assumptions and concerns at each step of the way. The Gestalt cycle of experience serves as a foundation for looking at alcoholism as a disorder in self-regulation. Also noteworthy in this presentation is the way they include the use of Alcoholics Anonymous as an integral aspect of the therapy with alcoholics. The chapter is rich with ideas and examples; indeed, this work serves as an encyclopedic summary on its subject.

Cynthia Harris's chapter on working with psychotics places psychotherapeutic work in the context of an understanding of the care for the mentally ill and shows how it fits with overall treatment. She makes a case for the importance of medication, and considers psychotherapy to be an adjunct to use of psychotropic drugs. Having said that, she then shows how a Gestalt orientation enhances the work with this population. She deals with issues of contact and awareness, laying out a truly humanistic and noncondescending approach that serves to help the patient maintain a sense of personhood. Among the useful ideas presented is a discussion of the difference between "glue" and "solvent." Neurotics may need solvent to help them become "unstuck," but Harris makes a good case for focusing on glue with psychotics. Thus, she points out the need to work carefully with awareness with psychotics, and the value of reassurance and comforting interventions.

The chapter on working with children has been provided by Violet Oaklander, one of the foremost practitioners in this area. While many Gestalt therapists have worked with children at some point in their career, today most of them work with children only as part of family therapy. Oaklander has developed an approach that centers on the child, and brings in parents as adjuncts. Here she deals with negative introjects and the expression of anger, among the most difficult issues in work with children. The detailed presentation of therapist–child dialogue shows us the power of her approach and tells us that there is a place for work with the child that may supplement or take the place of work with the family that includes the child.

Next we have a chapter on working with couples, written by Joseph Zinker. This summarizes some of the research and practice done by Zinker, Sonia M. Nevis, and their associates at the Center for the Study of Intimate Systems of the Gestalt Institute of Cleveland. Highlighted are the concepts of fusion, differentiation, and the creative notion of complementarity and middle ground. The approach helps couples see the things that hold them together, as well as focus on the difficulties that may be driving them apart. In his inimitably lyric style, Zinker presents a framework to produce awareness about health, and a way of dealing with despair that enables people to come to better resolution of their difficulties.

The chapter by Huckabay on working with groups shows how this area of endeavor can meld the concepts of general systems theory, group dynamics, and Gestalt therapy into a more flexible and powerful approach than that provided by any one of these schools of thought alone. All three disciplines came into prominence simultaneously about 50 years ago, and ever since that time practitioners who have been exposed to them have worked toward an integration. The late Richard Wallen deserves mention here as being both one of the early members of the National Training Laboratories (NTL) and a founder of the Gestalt Institute of Cleveland in 1954. He taught many of us the power of these approaches in combination. By the time of the early 1960s, Gestalt-trained people were doing NTL workshops at Bethel, Maine and people trained in group dynamics were studying and teaching at various institutes for Gestalt therapy and other centers.

Huckabay's tightly woven paper summarizes in a succinct and provocative way the major accomplishments of these years of study and application. She makes it clear that we have now broadened our approach to groups and can work at all the levels of intervention that make for truly enriching learning experiences. In reading this chapter I realized how much I miss the work with groups that was a large part of my professional life for a 20-year period.

The book concludes with a chapter on the application of "Gestalt thinking" to the therapeutic milieu by Claire Stratford, who spent several years in organizing and helping to direct a highly innovative and successful milieu program. Stratford starts by redirecting us to see the patterns of interaction that the environment offers, rather than the individual, as the figure. From this perspective she outlines a way to look at what is required to provide a healthy environment as the main cornerstone of effective therapy. We see that the teaching and support of skills of everyday living become a central part of the repertoire of the milieu setting. As with the British version of halfway houses, individual psychotherapy takes a subordinate position. We do not hear much about milieu therapy these days, possibly because of deinstitutionalization of much of the care of the mentally ill, yet I am convinced that the powerful way of thinking discussed by Stratford is applicable to all kinds of settings. We still have many institutions that care for groups as diverse as the physically disadvantaged, the mentally retarded, and the elderly. The management of all of these can benefit much from this approach.

Here then is a book of diverse and rich offerings. The perspectives and applications presented are those of active, current practitioners who show us the power of Gestalt therapy in many arenas. What is even more noteworthy than the range of applications are the modifications and extensions that are reported: We are not just introjecting what we were taught; we are adding and changing as we continue to learn. This book tells us that Gestalt therapy is alive and well as we enter the last decade of the 20th century.

Note

1. Other areas where Gestalt therapy has been applied are work with families and with educational and business organizations. These are covered by Brown (1971) in the field of education; by Herman and Korenich (1977), Nevis (1987), and Merry and Brown (1987) in the organizational realm; and by Kempler (1974), Papernow (1992), and Zinker and Nevis (in press) in the area of family therapy.

REFERENCES

Brown, G. I. (1971). *Human teaching for human learning: An introduction to confluent education.* New York: Viking Press.

Fagan, J., & Sheperd, I. (1970). *Gestalt therapy now.* Palo Alto, CA: Science and Behavior Books.

Herman, S. M., & Korenich, M. (1977). *Authentic management.* Reading, MA: Addison-Wesley.

Kempler, W. (1974). *Principles of Gestalt family therapy.* Oslo: Nordahls Taykkeri.

Latner, J. (1973). *The Gestalt therapy book.* New York: Julian Press.

Masterson, J. F. (1988). *The search for the real self.* New York: Free Press.

Merry, U., & Brown, G. (1987). *The neurotic behavior of organizations.* Cleveland: Gestalt Institute of Cleveland Press. Published and distributed by Gardner Press.

Nevis, E. C. (1987). *Organizational consulting: A Gestalt approach.* Cleveland: Gestalt Institute of Cleveland Press. Published and distributed by Gardner Press.

Papernow, P. (1992). *Becoming a step family: Stages of development in remarried families.* Cleveland: Gestalt Institute of Cleveland Press.

Perls, F. S. (1974). *Ego, hunger and aggression.* New York: Random House, 1969.

Perls, F. S., Hefferline, R. F., & Goodman, P. (1951). *Gestalt therapy.* New York: Dell.

Polster, E., & Polster, M. (1973). *Gestalt therapy integrated.* New York: Brunner/Mazel.

Smith, E. L. (1976). *The growing edge of Gestalt therapy.* New York: Brunner/Mazel.

Zinker, J. (1977). *Creative process in Gestalt therapy.* New York: Brunner/Mazel, 1977.

Zinker, J., & Nevis, S. M. (In press). *Changing small systems: Gestalt theory of couple and family therapy.* Cleveland: Gestalt Institute of Cleveland Press. Published and distributed by Gardner Press.

Part I

Perspectives

1

The Theory of Gestalt Therapy

JOEL LATNER, Ph.D.

We believe that the Gestalt outlook is the original, undistorted, natural approach to life.
—Perls, Hefferline, and Goodman, *Gestalt Therapy*

THE THEORY OF GESTALT THERAPY takes as its centerpiece two ideas. The first is that the proper focus of psychology is the experiential present moment. In contrast to approaches which look at the unknown and even unknowable, our perspective is the here and now of living. The second idea is that we are inextricably caught in a web of relationship with all things. It is only possible to truly know ourselves as we exist in relation to other things.

These twin lenses, here-and-now awareness and the interactive field, define the subject matter of Gestalt therapy. Its theory provides a system of concepts describing the structure and organization of living in terms of aware relations. Its methodology, techniques, and applications, which are the subject of the remaining chapters of this book, link this outlook to the practice of Gestalt therapy. The result is a psychology and method with a rich and unique view of everyday life, the depths and difficulties which life encompasses, and "the high side of normal," the ennobling and most creative heights of which we are capable. Gestalt therapists believe their approach is uniquely capable of responding to the difficulties and challenges of living, both in its ability to relieve us of some measure of our misery and by showing the way to some of the best we can achieve.

ORIGIN AND DEVELOPMENT
OF GESTALT THERAPY

The theory of Gestalt therapy has three major sources. First is psychoanalysis, which contributed some of its major principles concerned with the inner life. Humanistic, holistic, phenomenological and existential writings, which center on personal experience and everyday life, constitute a second source. Gestalt psychology, the third source, gave to Gestalt therapy much more than its name. Though Gestalt therapy is not directly an application or extension of it, Gestalt psychology's thoroughgoing concentration on interaction and process, many of its important experimental observations and conclusions, and its insistence that a psychology about humans include human experience have inspired and informed Gestalt therapy.

Gestalt therapy emerged from the clinical work of two German psychotherapists, Frederick Salomon Perls, M.D., and Lore Perls, Ph.D. F.S. Perls, known to many of his students as Fritz, was trained as a psychiatrist. He worked with Kurt Goldstein, a principal figure of the holistic school of psychology, in his inquiries into the effects of brain injuries on veterans of the first World War. Later, in the 1920s, he trained in psychoanalysis with Karen Horney and Wilhelm Reich. Laura Perls—she adopted the anglicized spelling after she came to the United States—studied with the existential philosopher Martin Heidegger and was awarded a doctorate in psychology for her graduate studies. The most important of her teachers was the Gestalt psychologist Max Wertheimer. F. S. and Laura Perls fled Western Europe in 1933 ahead of the onslaught of Nazism to Johannesberg, South Africa, where they practiced until the termination of hostilities in 1945.

Ego, Hunger and Aggression was written during this period. The book, published under F. S. Perls's name in London in 1947, is subtitled *A Revision of Psychoanalysis*. It included chapters reevaluating the analytic viewpoint on aggression. They suggested that Freud and his followers had underestimated the importance of the development of teeth, eating, and digestion, and that this developmental watershed was as important as the others noted by Freud. These suggestions constitute an early contribution to the development of ego psychology. The book also contained chapters from holistic and existential perspectives and chaptes describing therapy exercises. These exercises were designed to promote physical awareness rather than insight, and were called concentration therapy.

With the end of the war, the Perlses emigrated to the United States. They settled in New York City, in a community of artists and intellectuals versed in philosophy, psychology, medicine, and education. Several years of collaboration with members of this group resulted in the training of the first generation of Gestalt therapists, a comprehensive formulation of the theory, methodology, and practice for this new approach, and a book describing it. Published by the Julian Press in 1951, the volume was entitled *Gestalt Therapy: Excitement and Growth in the Human Personality*. Authorship was credited to F. S. Perls, along with Ralph Hefferline, a professor of psychology at Columbia University, and the writer Paul Goodman, perhaps best known for his subsequent best-seller, *Growing Up Absurd* (1963). Half the book consisted of reports of the results of exercises in awareness which Hefferline administered to his students. The other half was their statement of their new approach. Goodman wrote this section, basing his work on a manuscript by F. S. Perls and reflecting the common ground achieved by the collaborators. Goodman's keen and prolific mind—he wrote more than 30 books and hundreds of shorter pieces (novels, plays, poems, articles, short stories, and books of shorter essays in the fields of literature, psychology, philosophy, and social and educational criticism)—is reflected in the volume. His special respect for the many contributions to psychology of Otto Rank, perhaps especially the importance of art and the artist in understanding daily life, for Reich, and for communitarian philosophers like Kropotkin also find a place in *Gestalt Therapy*, and he is responsible for a large measure of its completeness and power. *Gestalt Therapy* remains the basic book of the theory and practice of Gestalt therapy, a cornerstone of the Gestalt approach.

AWARE RELATIONS

Here and Now: Primacy of the Present Moment

In its theory, is methodology, its practice, and its applications, Gestalt therapy is a present-centered approach. Both of the central concepts upon which Gestalt therapy is based—awareness, and the field—have meaning only in terms of the present moment. All of the important strains of philosophical, spiritual, political, scientific, and psychological thought which underpin Gestalt therapy's concentration on the phenomenology and problems of awareness share this, though some simply take it for granted while others put it front and center.

Gestalt psychology, for example, is concerned with the nature and structure of perceptual experience. This work is unavoidably present centered: By definition it is about what is perceived in the present moment. Many areas of inquiry and knowledge are present-centered in this same way: physics, chemistry, biology, architecture, and nursing are examples. In contrast, others such as astronomy, sociology, anthropology, and political science, look to a significant extent at the past, while another group—history itself, of course, but also geology, paleontology, the law, archeology—turn their attention as much or more to the past as to the present. Holism, akin to Gestalt psychology, is another scientific and philosophical field which has made an important contribution to both the central ideas of Gestalt therapy. It is present centered in the same way as Gestalt psychology, because it is impossible to conceive of the holistic perspective without its present-centered focus.

This is also true of phenomenology. Phenomenology takes as its subject matter the study of the objects and events we perceive and the development of thorough and comprehensive methods for observing and examining them. The philosophical school called existentialism takes as its main concern modern (and present-centered) questions about the nature and meaning of living, death, and personal relations, and the nature of our relation to authorities, including God. Even psychoanalysis betrays a recognition of the importance of the here and now, in concepts such as transference and countertransference, which are ways of characterizing phenomena in the psychotherapeutic present moment, and in its current interest in what they call "the real relationship" in therapy. Reich's seminal analytic work on character analysis, where the therapy centers on the body and bodily experience in the present moment, was a step further forward in that same direction.

What does this mean, "present centered"? In essence, it means that what is important is what is actual, not what is potential or what is past, but what is here, now. What is actual is, in terms of time, always the present; in terms of location, it is what is here, in front of us. Hence this familiar phrase: the here and now. Behind this idea is the conviction that studying, describing, and observing what is available to us now will allow us to comprehend it satisfactorily. In Kierkegaard's famous phrase, "Life is not a problem to be solved, but a reality to be experienced." A present-centered approach is distinguished from a historical one, in which the present is seen as a consequence of past causes. The historical point of view stands inevitably in the present, looking backward to the past. A present-centered approach stands in the present and looks at it, here and now.

For a historical perspective the critical animating force is the question, Why? What caused these present conditions? The answers have to do with past events. This necessarily turns one's eyes away from the present moment. "To understand," wrote Poulet, "is almost the opposite of existing." A present-centered approach raises different questions: How? What? What is this? What is the experience of this? Of what does it consist? How is this for me? How is this organized? From this point of view, the past is here, now. It is embedded in the present. The present contains everything. Memories, dreams, reflections are all present activities. They take place in the now. They concern events which occurred at some other time, as do anticipating, planning, preparing. But remembering is done in the present, planning is done in the present, reflecting is done in the present. It cannot be otherwise.

In the Gestalt present-centered approach, our interest is as much or more in the experience and awareness of remembering as it is in what is remembered. A present-centered approach leads more to attempts to embrace the present, to encompass it, and to appreciate it than it does to questions about the past (even the past in the present). A present-centered psychotherapy almost inevitably becomes a way of making it possible to better embrace the present moment, as well as a way of illuminating how we manage to miss so much of the present. Some present-centered philosophies come to despair in the recognition that our present lives are all there is. It is perhaps an article of faith in Gestalt therapy—or maybe just a profound commitment to its conception of our own human nature—that the present moment, should we be fully attuned to it and absorbed in it, is sufficient. It will allow us to make lives that are not only the best that can be lived in the circumstances, but also, granting some measure of decent circumstances, good enough.

The Nature and Shape of Awareness: Awareness as Creation

We usually think awareness is an indiscriminate, random, and passive process—that waves of light touch our eyes, that waves of sound touch our ears, that our awareness of events and people is controlled by the way they capture our attention. In our view, this is only a partial description of the character of awareness. It is a description of its passive aspect. Gestalt therapists consider awareness as an interplay in which both the individual and the environment participate. Each is both active and passive in turn.

Take this example. You are beginning to lose interest in your work, having become aware that you are hungry. Your textbooks and papers, your desk and chair fade out of your awareness as you begin thinking about the things in the refrigerator and whether the local pizza delivery place is still open. Opening the refrigerator door, you sort out its contents with your hands and eyes, shifting bottles and containers. Notice how your awareness is shaped by what is important to you, and how you shape your reality accordingly. You see what is interesting and important to you now, at this moment—this hungry moment—reaching out into the field with your eyes: you seek out and see the refrigerator, not the dishwasher, the cans of beans, not furniture wax. Conversely, the things that are not important at this moment—your studies, your family, your sexual appetites—are phenomenologically insignificant. For the moment, they do not exist; you have caused them to disappear.

Or take this different example. It is early morning. You have been up late last night past the hour when you can count on having a good night's sleep. Sure enough, when your alarm goes off, it interrupts your sound sleep and wrenches you awake. From your point of view, your awareness is suddenly awakened by the sound of your alarm clock, as though the clock has thrust itself under your nose or shaken you by your collar. Here, the environment is active—vigorously so—from the phenomenological point of view. You, on the other hand, are positively pushed around by the force of the interruption in this particular interplay of individual and environment.

What Is Awareness?

Awareness has five distinct qualities. They are contact, sensing, excitement, figure formation, and wholeness.

Contact is the meeting of differences. For us—that is, from the point of view of our own experience—it is coming up against the other, what is different from what we think of, or feel, or experience as us. (This is discussed in the next section.)

Sensing determines the nature of awareness. *Close* sensing is sensate, touching or feeling; *far* sensing is visual and auditory perception. Although these last two are functions of our organs, they are experienced at a distance. Although most close and far sensing occurs outside us, sensing can also occur within us, where it is called "proprioception." Thoughts and dreams are included here, as well as body sensations and emotions.

Excitement covers the range of emotional and physiological excitation from the most diffuse hum of well-being through the sharper alertness and interest to the most shrill and concentrated. If we turn to see someone on the street who reminds us of a close friend, our awareness includes contacting the person we see, the stranger in the environment. It also includes our memories, the proprioceptive contacting of ideas and feelings. Our interest, a form of excitement, might be just a mild murmur of attentiveness or it might be an arresting swell, felt as deep breathing or pleasure, tingling or flushing, or an impulse toward action. When we speak of our experience, it is usually these qualities, awareness, sensing, and excitement, and figure formation to which we are referring.

Figure formation refers to the way awareness is shaped and developed. In this example of seeing a stranger, a central focus of interest has emerged. This is characteristic of the second phase of figure formation. Figure formation will be discussed in the section after contact.

The final fundamental quality of awareness is wholeness. The statement for which Gestalt psychology is perhaps best known, "the whole is greater than the sum of its parts," embodies holistic principles. The word "greater" is meant qualitatively, not quantitatively. The whole is different from, more encompassing than what you can conclude by adding the parts together. Looking at the functioning of the components of our hands—the five digits, the palm, the back—is not sufficient to tell us what the totality is. A hand is a unity, a whole, which, while composed of elements, can be understood fully only in its entirety. In fact, it cannot be understood essentially at all except as a whole.

What is a whole? First, it is a loose translation of the German word "gestalt," meaning something which is experienced as a singularity although it is composed of distinct elements. The word "gestalt" suggests much more in its German context than do the words which are used in English as equivalents: whole, configuration, and figure. As a consequence, it is used in our own language even outside Gestalt therapy and Gestalt psychology to refer to these wholes of experience.

Anything which is experienced as a whole may be a gestalt. A person may be a whole, though he or she has a heart, a mind, a history. Yet, at another time, a person may be a part of a whole, part of a marriage or a class or a team or a music group. In these instances, each aggregate is the whole, and the individuals themselves are elements. Gestalts can be composed of any elements in the field. A hand is a grouping of physical elements; so is a body. Wholes may be groupings of ideas: The Rights of Man is one example; women's rights is another. Wholes may be composed of past events, such as a history of the Middle Ages, or of the American Revolution. Wholes may combine different kinds of elements; America, love, Buddhism, and evolution are examples.

These examples also illustrate how these wholes are given in the nature of our experience. In fact, it is basic to Gestalt thinking (brought over from Gestalt psychology) that wholes are existentially intrinsic to us. We cannot live without forming wholes of experience. Gestalt therapy is concerned with wholeness in other ways as well: with wholeness as a defining quality of healthy living; with the unity of mind, body, and spirit (the wholeness of the individual); and with ecological wholeness, the oneness of ourselves and our environment.

The Field Perspective

There are other principles which underlie Gestalt psychology and also serve as a basis for the theoretical structure of Gestalt therapy. They come from modern physics and are part of what is known as field theory. The field perspective views all phenomena as inextricably linked, part of a vast network of interaction which is called the field.

The field perspective makes the interactive nature of the field primary. From this point of view, particular things, be they objects, animate life, ideas, exist first by virtue of the interplay with each other and their relation to the entire field. Of course, their particular qualities are to be known as well, but these are never considered abstractly, by themselves, in isolation, but always in the context of the field.

As this applies to Gestalt therapy, the authors of *Gestalt Therapy* put it this way:

> In any psychological investigation whatever, we must start from the interacting of the organism and its environment. Every human function is an interacting in an organism/environment field, socio-cultural, animal and physical. No matter how we theorize about impulses, drives, etc., it is always to such an interacting field that we are referring, and not to an isolated animal. [Perls, Hefferline, & Goodman, 1951, p. 228]

The interactive grounding of Gestalt therapy inevitably focuses its psychotherapy on the interactions which occur in the here and now of the therapy meeting. By definition, the relation of the persons in therapy is a major focus of the therapeutic work, whether the therapy is individual, couple, group, or family therapy, or working with larger groups such as agencies, work groups, organizations, cities, or nations.

The field includes those who study or observe it. Since all the aspects of the field are related, there is no way to know a field except within it, as a part of it. Thus, studying the field means including yourself in your study. Elements of the field can be known only in terms of their relation to us, our relation to them, and of course in terms of the tools, instruments and sensibilities with which we meet and study them. There is no objectivity in field theory, because there is nothing you can objectify, nothing you can stand outside. You are related to everything; everything is different because you exist in relation to it. Since there is no objectivity, there is no subjectivity, either—you cannot have one without the other. Instead, there are only different perspectives, different positions.

Research in a field includes the researcher's own tools and perspective. Therapy includes the therapist. What takes place in therapy is created by both the therapy and the person or persons who come to therapy, and the therapeutic work is the work done by all the individuals in the room. These principles underlie the conviction shared by Gestalt therapists that technical and theoretical knowledge is not sufficient for the thorough training of Gestalt therapists. Intensive personal therapy is required as well. Since the therapist is part of the therapeutic work, effective psychotherapy demands the therapist's fullest measure of self-knowledge, so that his or her contribution to the therapy can be fully known.

In the 20th century, the field perspective has begun to replace the Newtonian or mechanistic scientific perspective which emerged in Western civilization at the onset of the Enlightenment. It is useful to contrast them. The Newtonian universe is a universe composed of subjective experience and reality, consisting of objects which are connected in the way billiard balls are connected, the ways the parts of a machine are connected. They are connected by contrivances and collisions which move them without changing them in any other way. Reality in this perspective exists independently of our experience, outside us. It is objective reality, the pool players' place, God's viewpoint—outside of things. Because reality is objective, facts—right and wrong—and objective truth are possible in this universe.

In contrast, in the relativistic universe—the term comes from the relativity theories which first defined the new physics—"facts" are replaced by probabilities dependent on context. Objectivity disappears, since there are no independent objects, no view outside the field.

Elements of the field are altered by their position in relation to other things. Nothing is independent. In a relativistic universe, we are part of what we are observing, describing, or measuring. In the Newtonian universe, the emphasis is on objects and their properties. In the relativistic one, the emphasis is on interaction, and objects and their properties are inseparable and known only in the different contexts in which they are found, as wholes and parts of whole events.

Although the older mechanistic approach has been replaced in modern science, the reader will recognize that the peoples of most Western cultures, including our own, still see the world in this way. Naturally, most psychological theories are also of this type. They look for the individual and the individual's psychological properties, ego states, cognition, tendencies to self-realization or to individuation. These are objects, the equivalents of the planets in a Newtonian universe. Alternatively, the new perspective looks at the dimensions of interplay in time and space, the effects of relatedness over time. Its terminology reflects relatedness. Important wholes in the field, for example, are characterized as vague or pervasive, looming or far reaching, concentrated or diffused, directly or complexly related. This contrasts with the equivalent mechanistic terms, which include ''core,'' as in core neurosis; ''deep''; ''early,'' as in early trauma; ''low'' and ''high,'' and as in higher functioning, for instance. The model of the latter is historical rather than present centered, and three or even two dimensional rather than four dimensional (the fourth dimension is time, which in this context is process), as well as object oriented.

A principal conclusion of the Gestalt psychologists shows how the interactive field perspective and a phenomenological, awareness orientation are unified. Their experiments demonstrated that organizing our experience is intrinsic to our nervous systems. In the very moment we perceive or sense, we organize what we experience. Life as we live it is already organized.

If what exists is shaped, created as it is apprehended, the field is part of our awareness; our awareness is part of the field. The interaction is primary. Reality and experience are inseparable. It is impossible to separate the two. This is not the same as saying we structure reality, for that suggests that reality exists, out there, and we structure it. Rather, there is only the reality we know, the organized reality of our experience. The field is ourselves, too; we and the environment. It is a whole composed of us and the environment. The Gestalt psychologists sought to define the principles by which our experience is structured in our interplay with the rest of the field. Gestalt therapy works to attune each individual to the organizing principles themselves, by concentrating on awareness, the primacy of relations, and their unity.

CONTACT

The Gestalt therapy interest in awareness in the field leads to a focus on the relation of the elements of the field. Seen from our individual point of view, rather than another position in the field, it is a focus on our relation to the environment. We call this encounter, or meeting, or even dialogue, but primarily we call it contact.

Contact can be described in terms of its distinguishing characteristic, its location, and its primary dimension. Its distinguishing quality is the meeting of differences. Its location we call the contact boundary, and the fundamental organizing quality of contact we call figure/ground. The following sections describe the nature, organization, intentions, creative dimensions, and experience of contact.

The Meeting of Differences

Ordinarily, "contact" means to connect, to meet, or to join. We say, "3-2-1-contact," and we say that a person makes good contact with another person. We say, as in this savvy and bellicose song, "Do you take me for such a fool / To think I'd make contact / With the one who tries to hide what he don't know to begin with?" Gestalt therapists use contact in a way which includes this meaning of meeting and refines it.

Contact is a quality of awareness which involves the meeting of differences. From the phenomenological, first-person perspective, contact is the experience of difference. Without difference, there is no contact. If you touch your own fingers, you will feel in one finger the pressure of the other. If you do not, you will not feel the meeting—there is no contact. For contact, there must be the experience of difference. Think of this as a perspective on personal relations: In order for people to meet, they must touch where they are different. Without knowing how we are different, there is no relationship, because relating must involve two. (An application of this: A couple in which each partner is trying to be like the other is avoiding contact, avoiding relationship.)

There are times when the field is not divided in this way, into disparate meaningful elements—in the kind of landscape in which sea merges into sky and nothing stands out, for instance. If there is no difference, no contact, no meeting, what is there? What is left besides contact? What is left is the awareness of the undifferentiated field, the experience that nothing is different—or, since these formulations are experiential ones, that nothing makes a difference: Nothing matters. Sometimes it is the experience of oneness, belonging, being a part of a whole. Before the field is separated into foreground and background, it is called undifferentiated. There is no focus. If we contact the other, we experience the difference between us. (The difference is between us, and it also joins us. Actually, it is more accurate to say there is no *between* at all, only differences touching.) If we do not experience the difference, we do not meet. We may instead feel part of the other, or we may feel indifferent.

The hallmark of contact is excitement. It accompanies the encounter in the same way the heat and light of the sun accompany each other. The relation is not causal. Excitement is an aspect of the contact. It implies feeling and concern, energetic response or action, perhaps pleasure, curiosity, and mobilization. It stands opposite to indifference. It is not the same as pleasure, and figure formation should not be confused with pleasure seeking. Even when enjoyment is present, it is not the point of figure formation. "Enjoyment is not a goal," wrote Goodman, "it is a feeling that accompanies important ongoing activity" (1960).

The Contact Boundary: The Venue of Contact

"Scarborough Fayre" is an English folk song with its roots going back nearly a thousand years, but it remains alive in cultures where English is spoken. It surfaced once again, in the 1960s, as a popular song. It is a beautiful, bitter song of love betrayed.

> Are you going to Scarborough Fayre?
> Parsley, sage, rosemary, thyme—
> Remember me to one who lives there
> He once was a true love of mine.

But he is no longer a true lover. He was untrue. He will not remember the singer as the singer remembers him. In a succeeding verse, the singer sets a task for the faithless lover. The task illustrates the singer's bitterness and the impossibility of the situation.

> Tell him to buy me an acre of land—
> Parsley, sage, rosemary, thyme—
> Between the salt water and the sea shore
> And he will be a true love of mine.

He will never be true, because there is no land at all where the salt water meets the seashore. There is nothing at all between the water and the sand. And yet, what happens here, at this juncture of sea and sand, is central to Gestalt therapy. Let us look and see what does exists here.

There is nothing—no *thing*—in between, nothing between the water and the sand. There is no physical entity, as the sand is and the sea is. There is nothing additional to the sea and the land. But there is the shoreline, at this point where the salt water is meeting the seashore.

What is the shoreline, though, if it is not a physical entity? The shoreline is an encounter, a meeting, a venue—"the locale of a gathering," according to *Webster's Dictionary*, from the Middle French and Latin "to come."

When the ocean's waters are lapping the beach, the sand taking in the waters, they are meeting. If the shoreline is not a physical entity, what is it? It is a "whole of experience," the kind of interplay we discussed under field theory. We usually call this actuality of occurrence an event, or a process. (Look carefully. We do not see the shoreline. We see the joining. It is a joining without a joint.)

We find the shoreline whenever and wherever water touches sand. The existence of the shoreline requires sea and sand, and it requires that they meet. Without these, there is no event called a shoreline. If sand touches sand, we call it sand, or sand dunes, or sometimes a beach. If water touches water, we call it an ocean, a lake, a river. Only if sand touches water can we call it a shoreline. (Sometimes we use the word ''beach'' to describe the unity of sand and water, but that is a different whole altogether—not a meeting at all. Not all gestalts are meetings.)

This meeting consists of the touching of two things which are different: water and sand. In Gestalt therapy, the meeting of differences is called contact. So, this meeting of sand and sea is contact. The event that is created by this meeting of differences is called the contact boundary. In this example, the contact boundary is the shoreline.

The contact boundary takes into account both the differences between the elements which are meeting and also the unity of their meeting, the whole created by it. The contact boundary always has this duality within it: One, it acknowledges the differences, without which there would be no contact. Two, it acknowledges what unifies them, without which there would be no gestalt, no whole of experience. This is a special use of the word ''boundary,'' which most often suggests only separation. In Gestalt therapy, it suggests union as strongly.

The boundary does not belong to one side or to the other. It is not the sand's boundary or the sea's. It is a collaborative effort created by the meeting. The boundary belongs to itself, to the meeting, not to either of the elements, the sand or the sea. In Gestalt therapy, we say it is a *function* of the meeting. Other psychologies use concepts and phrases involving the term boundary: ego boundary, for instance. Or we say, ''He tried to push past my boundaries.'' The contact boundary is not that kind of boundary. It belongs to the encounter, not the individual or the ego. Another difference is that the boundary belongs to all meetings in the field, even those which do not involve persons—the salt water and the seashore, for instance. Still another difference is that contact boundary exists only as long as the boundary event itself. It is dissolved when the meeting ends. And, to repeat, the boundary is an event, a venue, not an entity.

The special qualities of the contact boundary are captured in this old story.

A Zen master, the seventeenth in a direct line of teachers of the Dharma from Gotama Buddha, when walking with his disciple, asked about the wind bells suspended from the four corners of the temple roof. ''What is ringing,'' he said, ''the wind or the bells?'' The disciple said, ''The wind is not ringing, the bells are not ringing, the mind is ringing.''
Dogen, a later master who first taught Zen in Japan, commented on this story, ''It is the wind ringing, it is the chimes ringing, it is the blowing ringing, it is the ringing ringing.''

Foreground and Background: Contact's First Differentiation

Experientially, the field is usually organized into a center and a periphery. The center is the foreground, the figure or gestalt; the periphery is called the background, or the ground; and this primary structure is known as figure/ground. the foreground contains what is central, important, focal, meaningful to the present moment. The background contains what is irrelevant, unimportant, immaterial to the present moment. Because contact requires difference, figure/ground is a function of contact. When there is no contact, the field is not differentiated; there is no figure and no background.

The field is organized in this way according to our interests and the interests of other elements of the field. It is organized in this way because our nervous systems can do nothing other than this. This is how we experience. When we become interested, background and foreground appear. As the figure develops, with each change, each passing moment, the field—foreground and background together—is continuously reorganized. This process is called figure formation. It will be described in the next section.

At this very moment, you, the reader, have probably formed a figure that includes the book you are reading, the words on the page, related psychological concepts that you have studied, perhaps also the notes you are taking and the scratching sound your pen makes. Perhaps you are also aware, though probably less centrally, of your sitting position and the quality of the light which illuminates this book. Most of this is figural awareness, the center of your attention. Perhaps some of it—the lighting, maybe, or the sound of your pen, or your posture—is in the near background, along with such aspects of your present contact as the gravitational field in which you are adjusting your posture and the nature and quality of your breathing (slow or fast, deep or shallow, anxious or tense or relaxed, and so on). They may become figural as you read these words.

Farther yet into the background are a host of assimilated and partly assimilated experiences and undeveloped capabilities, from the earliest days of your life to recent times, from school learning to personal relations, including feelings about yourself, the place you live in, ideas about your future, your ability to understand your native tongue and perhaps other languages, musical and physical talents. This part of the background includes ideas, conclusions, memories, attitudes, feelings and beliefs. These may be true or false, accurate or not; our experience will likely include distortions of what we have heard or seen, and will surely include entirely fictitious elements (from books, plays, movies as well.) At any given time, these constitute a substantial part of the background.

Some of these elements remain continuously in the background, virtually irretrievable: memories of learning to speak, or of coming to love your parents, perhaps, or the way you developed your feelings about your native country or city, for instance. They are so thoroughly embedded throughout the farthest reaches of the ground that they will be brought to awareness only if the very ground of your being is challenged. This was the case for the allegiance of many Americans in the 1960s, as a consequence of the Vietnam War, and it is typically the case in a thoroughgoing psychotherapy.

The background is, for the most part, what is outside our awareness. In Gestalt therapy, it replaces most of what is usually termed ''the unconscious'' in other psychologies. The background, the elements of the field of which we are presently unaware, is dynamic and organized. The background is a field concept, not an individualistic one, as the unconscious is. It is a unification of the parts of oneself and the parts of the environment which are not in the present figure.

The background also has none of the connotations of the unconscious which suggest malevolence, nor those which suggest the unknown and unknowable. To the contrary, the background is always present as the foundation for contact, framing and supporting our present experience. It holds the figure together and is available to awareness as figures emerge and develop. We are continually in contact with aspects of the background, out of awareness. This can be seen in the way sleepers adjust their postures, taking into account the size of the bed and the overlay of blankets. A more vivid example occurs when the background thrusts itself into the foreground in emergencies, as when we wake bolt upright in the middle of the night, hearing an untoward noise in the house, or when a mother wakes out of the deepest sleep because her baby's breathing pattern has changed.

Creative Adjustment: The Design of Contact

Contacting is the way we change and grow. It is how we come to grips with our lives, organizing the field to make possible the best achievements and solutions it will support. At the same time, contacting is the way in which the environment, the rest of the field, adjusts us to it. We call this interplay, all of it, creative adjustment, because the result is assimilation and growth and because the process of adjustment is mutual. In creative adjustment, our achievements and solutions are made by us and given to us both in the give and take of our creative partnership with the rest of the field. Adjustment is creative as well because it cannot follow a formula. It must be accomplished uniquely, according to each opportunity. Our achievements and solutions must be novel if they are to be the best each situation can produce.

This creative activity is a given for us as we live. It *is* living. Out of our needs and appetites, our wishes and desires, our curiosity, we encounter the environment and work and rework it to suit our own interests. And, out of the needs and appetites, wishes and desires of the environment, it encounters and molds us. The result is a true universal ecology.

From our first-person perspective, creative adjustment is organismic self-regulation, the way we use the abilities inherent in us to make the best of any situation. Conceiving of our lives in this way, as creative achievements, while unusual in psychology, is not unique to Gestalt therapy. Psychologists from Freud onward have been fascinated with the creative life of artists. Otto Rank, an intimate of Freud and an important earlier contributor to the growth of psychoanalysis, was singularly important in recognizing the kinship of the creative process of the artist and the everyday activities of ordinary people. For this reason, and others, his was a major influence on the development of Gestalt therapy.

All contact is creative adjustment, not only contact which results in new solutions and vistas. All of it is organismic self-regulation, the best we can do in the present circumstances—though some of it is not very good at all. The vitality of free functioning is worlds away from the dullness of apathy and indifference and the peculiar urgency, the driven quality which accompanies so much unsatisfying behavior. But each individual, even the one who continually avoids other possibilities in life—someone, for example, who has the reverse Midas touch, and can turn anything into dross—is, even so, doing the best he or she can. Though the lively, uniquely varied responses and reactions of free functioning are lacking, replaced by contacting that is routinized and stereotypic, this is creative adjustment. (Surely you know someone who insists on steering a destructive course, turning all possibilities to the same conclusion.) Creativity can serve many ends.

Creative adjustment replaces the conventional term ''resistance'' in the vocabulary of Gestalt therapy. Resistance is the usual psychological characterization for the individual's seeming unwillingness to change or grow, or to accept the therapist's direction. Implied in it is the conviction that the person in therapy being resistant should stop doing so. But resistance is creative adjustment, and organismic self-regulation. It is integral to the individual's way of being in the world, and no approach driving at holistic solutions can ask a person to set aside parts of themselves. The goal in Gestalt therapy, and any holistic approach, is integration—or, in this case, reintegration—not amputation.

According to this principle, and as will be seen in the succeeding chapters of this volume, Gestalt therapy practice replaces the conventional emphasis on overcoming, breaking through, or ignoring resistances with procedures which encourage and explore these creative adjustments. By taking them seriously, by bringing them into awareness, individuals can wrestle with their own conflicts and discover their own way to integrate these seemingly opposed desires into new wholes.

GESTALT FORMATION

Figure Formation: The Shape of Contact

Contacting, the way we work with the environment to create the most satisfying solutions, has a special organization and structure. Influenced again by Gestalt psychology, Gestalt theory describes in detail the way in which experience and action in the world are inevitably and inherently structured. It is an organization which shapes our phenomenology. It is called gestalt formation, or figure formation, or, more fully, gestalt or figure formation and destruction.

The Gestalt psychologists identified many characteristics governing the formation of visual figures in their attempts to understand figure formation. One researcher was able to find 114 of these laws, but there are perhaps a dozen basic ones. These include good organization, definite outlines, satisfying (good) form, closure, stability, balance, and proportion. These formulations are essentially aesthetic in character. Gestalt therapists have adapted and modified them in order to be able to characterize the entirety of experience, not only the perceptual aspect. Therefore, Gestalt therapists speak as well of figures which have power, liveliness, vigor, unity, and clarity, figures which are rich, compelling, satisfying, complete. Good figures have these qualities sufficiently or abundantly, bad ones have them less, or lack them entirely. At a certain point, the dearth of these characteristics turns poor figures into nonexistent ones. Perhaps these illustrations will clarify this point.

Any group of people—a class, a therapy group, a professional association, a nation—linked richly and often by interactions and interchange, with strong feelings among the members or a task which engages them all, is a good figure: clearly defined, lively, well organized, cohesive. An apathetic group, without much common purpose, is not. At the extreme, an apathetic group is no group at all, but simply an aggregate of individuals—elements in the field, but no figure at all. Acting as though an aggregate is a group—perhaps because you think you should be involved with them, though you do not care to be—makes for a bad figure.

If you do not like the movie you are seeing and lose interest in it, the accompanying experiential figure will be diffuse, lacking clear outlines and vitality. Perhaps it will lack a sense of coherence altogether. You begin to think of walking out or slip into reveries of other situations or things you would rather do. Making yourself pay attention is no solution; it forces the figure, a contradiction in terms (a split figure, not a unified one).

The concept of marriage is a good figure, well defined and vital, though the outlines are not always clear, and for many it is not a figure of interest. A particular marriage may be a good or a bad figure. A "bad" marriage may be a bad figure: ill defined, dull, and at the same time rigid, but even with an abundance of antagonism and difficulty, it may be full of excitement, vitality, definition, good outlines, and so on.

Figure Formation: Health and Its Absence

In nature a repulsive caterpillar turns into a lovely butterfly. But with human beings, it is the other way round: a lovely butterfly turns into a repulsive caterpillar.

—Chekhov

We consider the ability to form and destroy good figures paramount to health. The ability to create lively, well-formed, clearly defined figures which make the most adequate use of the resources of the field *is* health itself. This is called free functioning. It is called *free* functioning because we can range anywhere in the field, through all of our abilities and knowledge and experience and everything present in the environment, to find those things which will make the most apt contributions to emerging figures. Our freedom consists not in being free to choose whatever suits us individually, because it is not only our personal needs, wishes, desires, and interests that control how figures best emerge and grow. The figure's needs determine the best figure. Free functioning is the freedom to seek out anything which will contribute to what is emerging, freedom to contribute whatever the figure requires, and freedom to follow the figure wherever it takes us, giving ourselves over entirely to its working.

Ill health, by contrast, is functioning which is not free. It is figure formation in a field so impoverished that good figures become impossible; or, it is figure formation in a promising field—but one in which we cannot partake freely, because we must avoid or are ignorant of elements in it which are at the same time essential to emerging figures. Instead of being whole, we are cut off from our essentials. We become split in two, into the parts of ourselves we can acknowledge, and those parts we suppress and disown. And we see the world in the same way. There is good and there is bad, heaven and hell, moral and immoral, us and them, body and mind, black and white, round eyed and pure, Jew and Arab. And then we reinforce this fragmentation so as to maintain it, ignoring what does not fit our conception of things and fabricating sometimes intricate deceptions which support it. If we are clever, we end up not seeing what is right in front of us. The author Saul Bellow expressed the paradox of this wonderfully, saying, "A great deal of intelligence can be invested in ignorance when the need for illusion is deep."

The result is figures which are incomplete. Either they do not complete themselves because the requirements of each phase are not met—they are skipped over or ignored—or because field elements which would make adequate figures are not available. The result is unfinished figures, unfinished business. If health is the wholeness signalled by the creation and destruction of good figures, then its absence is the loss of our wholeness and the presence of these splits, poor figures, and unfinished business.

Our understanding of figure formation gives us a standard for judging the depth and reality of experience which, while not isolated from social values, is also not determined by them. We exist in a field which is social and cultural, but when the figure is weak, dull, graceless, confused, we know there is some difficulty. On the other hand, figures which display the qualities of good figures—definition, coherence and cohesiveness, vitality, grace, and the rest—signal health. We do not need to look elsewhere—to social mores or biblical injunctions, for instance—to reach this conclusion.

This autonomous criterion, making good figures, provides a counter weight to the other ways we determine who is well and who is sick. Normality as defined by psychologists or other experts is not necessarily the same as health; nor is social adjustment as defined by legislators, your teachers or your children's teachers, or religious or political authorities. And conversely, deviations from what is socially or politically or morally acceptable to others do not necessarily mean there is something wrong with us.

Other, related dimensions of the Gestalt perspective need to be mentioned in this discussion of health. We think they have equally profound and far-reaching implications. The impairments of free functioning are called variously illness (dis-ease), neurosis, sickness, craziness, and also spiritual hunger, anomie, madness, and sometimes normality. These disabilities interrupt, inhibit, and constrain our creative abilities, the workings of free functioning in the field. We are willing to label this area of investigation and clinical work abnormal psychology if it is entirely clear to the reader that the field perspective prevails here, as elsewhere. These interruptions, inhibitions, and constraints are field phenomena, in the same way that free functioning is.

None are entirely of our own making, even though they may come to be predominantly our own doing.

We are embedded in the field, but are not its creation. We exist in it along with the environment in an interplay of creative forces which allows certain possibilities and forecloses others. We are more likely to function freely in circumstances in tune with us than in straitened ones. Ranging widely over the riches of the field requires bounteous possibilities. In impoverished circumstances, our figures may be impoverished—both the best that can be achieved and unsatisfactory as well. Crazy times make it difficult, though not impossible, to be clear-headed; they will, however, make it impossible to be fulfilled or contented.

It is possible to be disabled and troubled in a generous setting and there is certainly a limit to the extent to which we can be fulfilled in a disturbed one. In any setting, it is essential to have a criterion for health which gives adequate weight to our native structures. These observations are vital to Gestalt therapy because they flow directly out of its deepest concerns; because therapists journey frequently in the dark, roiling waters of our unrecognized and unfulfilled selves, which lie beyond the mainstream; because we see how common it is to notice only the landscape above ground, pretending there is nothing underground; and because psychotherapy is all too easily and too often a handmaid of the dominant groups in any culture. If the reader thinks of "sick societies" such as Nazi Germany and the Communist oligarchies, where the honest and innocent are imprisoned and the thugs run the government, he or she may well find it easy to understand and accept this. But the dull emptiness, conformity, emotional subjection, covert violence, indifference to both feeling and intelligence, shallow excitements, and materialistic excesses of everyday life in the United States are more what we have in mind.

How is free functioning lost? Given the creative tendencies which are our birthright, how does it happen that we make poor figures, living out lives of quiet desperation or ruinous destructiveness, or sleepwalking through it all?

The discussion above suggests an important part of the answer—the largest part. We learn to lose touch with it. "How is it that little children are so intelligent and men so stupid?" asked Alexandre Dumas, *fils*. "It must be education that does it." We teach our young and ourselves ways of living which ignore the imperatives of figure formation and avoid important parts of ourselves and the environment. Sometimes our feelings are the first to go ("Don't cry; you're not hurt"), and our integrity ("Don't fight with Julie; share your toys") is besieged soon after. Sometimes our creative tools are attacked directly ("Make up your mind—right now!"). While figure formation is a given for us, even at birth, our ability to form adequate figures must have the opportunity to develop as we grow. If it does not, we do not mature to meet the challenges which larger vistas provide, and we come to lack the gifts we need to make the most of what is available.

Perls, Hefferline and Goodman put it this way, emphasizing the personal fragmentation and self-estrangement which make free functioning and good figures impossible:

> The average person, having been raised in an atmosphere full of splits, has lost his Wholeness, his Integrity. To come together again he has to heal the dualism of his person, of his thinking and of his language. He is accustomed to thinking of contrasts as though they were opposing entities. The unitary outlook which can dissolve such a dualistic approach is buried. [1951, p. viii]

This attack on our ability to participate in figure formation undermines our willingness to experience the loss of our sense of ourselves which is an essential part of the creation of good figures. This phenomenon, which will be described in the sections on figure formation and the self, becomes an attack on the ground of our being. It creates doubt and fear in us, and we universally try to counter this by insisting upon our own existence. Dedicated to creating the experience that we exist, we become pervasively willful and thus willful at the wrong moments, and we do our best to avoid those aspects of figure formation in which the loss of our sense of ourselves is paramount. As a result, we become disabled. Amiel put it well: "At the bottom of the modern man there is always a great thirst for self-forgetfulness, self-distraction . . . and therefore he turns away from all those problems and abysses which might recall to him his own nothingness".

But why? Do we believe parents are monsters and the society in which we live is inhumane? We know parents are often responsible for the disaffection of their children; they are usually the single most important influence on a child's development. We know the values which cultures encourage are often substituted for finding our own compass. It is possible, even, that there is an irreconcilable conflict between our species' newly developed and increasing requirements for social harmony and individual fulfillment. All these contending requirements are exceedingly difficult to reconcile.

On the other hand, our native gifts for creating meaningful wholes include the capacity to adjust these demands in the course of finding our own best solutions. Some ways of raising children are infinitely better than others. They allow us to come closer to our own best impulses. And some ways of treating each other and living together make it much more likely that our promise will be realized. At the same time, even the best situations we have been able to create have their share of an unhappiness which never seems inevitable, though it often seems unavoidable. Our magnificent abilities leave us far from perfection. Neurosis appears to be as much our human condition as figure formation, and greatly more than does free functioning.

All of us will be unhappy, disappointed, and aggrieved in the course of our lives, more than we would wish. The condition is an existential one for us; it is part of being alive. We will choose to love, for instance, although we will suffer the loss of those we love—unavoidably. And beyond this, we believe that each of us will bear another large measure of disappointment, pain, and sorrow in our lives, well beyond what our human condition seems to warrant. This seems an inescapable conclusion, based on the evidence of human life on this planet. Expecting more than this is probably paradisal longing, composed of one part yearning for the realization of our potential and one part recognition of the immensity of the loss we all suffer because our potential will, all too often, not be realized. Perhaps it is enough, though, to ask that the world we live in support us enough that our wounds heal, that the loss of our gifts is not irretrievable, and that all of us have it within our power to pursue our fulfillment with passion and diligence.

The Phases of Gestalt Formation

Gestalt or figure formation and destruction proceeds in a manner which is probably best thought of as a spiral. While the phases of figure formation circle back on each other—the last phase is followed by the first—the end of any specific cycle of figure formation and destruction is growth, something novel which has been assimilated. Because of this, the actual starting place for another new figure is different from anything that has existed previously. And, it is not simply the individual which is changed by the growth. The field is a web of linked elements; change in any of its aspects means that the entire organism/environment field is new.

The four phases of figure formation are forecontact, contact, final contact, and postcontact. In forecontact, while the elements of the field are present, there is no figure. It is not correct to say that all is background, for background implies foreground. Rather, the field is not differentiated into figure and ground. Contact, with its inevitable division of the field into what is relevant to the emerging figure and what is not, is missing. There is no focus of interest, and in that sense, because nothing matters, nothing exists.

In the next phase, the contact phase, the figure begins to form and then to develop. The undifferentiated field falls out into the primal polarity, figure/ground. Some elements of the field become identified with the coming center of interest and are included in it, contributing their energy to the forming figure. Other elements, alien to the forming figure, stay in the background, the remainder of the organism/environment field.

Characteristic of the contact phase is a mounting excitement, the thunder which accompanies the lightning of the emerging gestalt. Novelty initiates the phase. It provokes the emergence of the figure by initiating contact and awareness. Generally, what is novel are needs, urges, appetites, curiosities, pains, desires, wishes, requirements, circumstances. They may originate anywhere within the field, in the individual or the environment.

The momentum of the creative synthesis which is forming culminates in the phase called final contact. Here, the figure attains its mature form. The characteristics which define it are fully realized. In recognition of this, the phase is sometimes called full contact—but it is the figure which is full, not the contact. It is the final phase of contacting, hence its name. In this phase, as the figure develops, the background becomes less important. It recedes, sometimes disappearing entirely, experientially. At this time, we are fully absorbed in the figure, and our sense of ourselves recedes or even disappears.

The fourth phase is postcontact. It is the phase where the figure is destroyed. New growth is integrated, what is used up is discarded, and the field adjusts to the new situation. This is assimilation. On the metabolic level, it is ingestion, assimilation, and elimination, turning what has been experienced and achieved into nourishment. The early part of this phase may include a certain amount of aware savoring and reevaluation, but most of postcontact goes on unawares; hence its name. It is a time when excitement ebbs and generally when activity ebbs as well. Much of postcontact is vegetative. Let me sleep on it, we say, knowing that our inner intelligence will be integrating what has been experienced and give us the fresh perspective born of growth and learning. While the entirety of figure formation is concerned with learning, it is in this phase that we begin to realize what we have learned. The course of the figure was, perhaps, thrilling, consuming; now, in this fourth phase, it is seen in its context, as significant but not the total picture. At the same time, the ending of a figure may have pathos or tragedy. If the figure that is being destroyed is a relationship with someone just recently dead, the mourning (itself its own figure) may be wrenching; the vegetative reworking of the ground of being may spill into awareness.

It is useful and apt to think of figure formation and destruction as a process of birth and death, akin to the turning of the seasons. There is a distinct continuity to it, and at the same time, each season has a quality all its own. Sometimes it is hard to know when one season ends and another begins. Spring leads to summer, seeding to fruiting, the phases sometimes overlapping—yet the sense of new birth characteristic of spring is entirely different from verdant, lush summer. Some years it seems that summer never came at all, or it was hard to tell if December was autumn, or winter coming in. In some climes it is hard to find winter at all, and summer seems to last forever.

The workings of figure formation are closer to enlightened play than they are to problem solving. "To be surprised, to wonder, is to begin to understand." Spontaneity, adventure and playfulness are its hallmarks. Though it eventuates in growth, figure formation is not directed toward any end. Rather, as Kant so well put it, we proceed "with a sense of purpose, without a purpose." In forming and destroying figures, we bring the entirety of our being to it. Not just our brains, but all of ourselves: heart, body, soul, mind, intellect. Perhaps it can be conceived of as thinking with the whole body.

Each phase of figure formation is itself a figure, and is composed of many figures, each with its own forecontact, contact, final contact and postcontact phases. A life is a figure, and within it are larger figures, such as adventures, creative acts, and a career; and smaller ones, such as a day, a concert, and an encounter—figures within figures.

CONTACT BOUNDARY DISTURBANCES

The Creativity of Contact. We do not passively meet the environment. We pick and choose and at the same time are picked and chosen. Although this interplay is a complex one, it is only part of the way that we participate in organizing our experience. Another important way we structure our experience is by altering our experience by manipulating the contact boundary. This can be done in many ways. Its location can be altered, so that the meeting is somewhere else than where it appears to be. The nature of the boundary itself can be changed, its characteristics altered or the boundary dissolved or ignored. These are the contact boundary disturbances.

Confluence and Projection. An instance of confluence was described earlier, in the discussion of the first, forecontact phase of figure formation. The reader will recall that the field in that phase is not differentiated, meaning that while the elements of the field are distinct, no element or elements stand out in front of the rest. In that case, there is no contact, no figure, and no boundary. When the boundary does not exist, the elements are confluent.

Another instance was mentioned in the description of the third, contact phase of figure formation. There, the individual is absorbed in the figure, not (as in the first phase) in the field. The boundary disappears when the absorption is total. We generally prefer to say that the boundary has been dissolved as a function of that phase of figure formation.

This confluence is the experience of no difference, no contact, and no meeting (because no difference). It is even so an experience. In fact, some of our most important experiences have this boundaryless dimension. Confluence is the contact boundary involved in experiences we call oceanic, when we feel at one with the universe or with God or our beloved. The boundary is dissolved in this experience of inseparability; the dissolution of the boundary provides the condition for the experience of inseparability. It is a frequent occurrence in infancy, when the child's ability to experience a meeting of differences is more occasional than it is for us. Later on, it is the characteristic contact boundary disturbance in empathic experiences, when we know another's experience because we are experiencing it as well, and perhaps, in the background, it contributes to the fellow feeling we have at those times when our relations with others are most human and special.

If we create confluence by dissolving the contact boundary without knowing we are doing so, we create a situation in which we will confuse another with ourselves. We may not be able to distinguish our own thoughts or attitudes or feelings from something or someone else. This phenomenon underlies the psychology of crowds and mobs, and it is commonplace in personal relations as well. We may think we are in contact, but we are not.

Projecting, we do not dissolve the boundary; instead, we relocate it. For example, looking at a landscape, a sunny hillside, we typically make the boundary meeting between the scene and ourselves. But, if the hillside is bare and we imagine the house we might like to build on it, we see what is in our mind's eye projected onto the hillside. Projecting, we change the location of the boundary. We are looking at our own wishes against the background of the hillside, instead of looking at the bare hillside. At the boundary, we meet our own thought or feeling, something within us. If we can see that we are doing this, it is awares projection; if not, if we believe the house is out there, we are unaware that we are not just making the boundary but manipulating it.

Whereas in confluence we are indistinct and the boundary is absent, in projection, we are on both sides of the boundary we have created. We make an environment of an element of ourselves, and then we meet it. If at some time in the past, you became angered by a friend and did not recognize your feeling, you may run into your friend subsequently and, looking at the friend, believe he or she is mad at you. In doing so, you disturb the contact boundary between you, relocating it so you are seeing your own anger. You project your own feeling onto the friend. Though it appears to you that the boundary joins the friend and you, it does not. You are only meeting yourself. (Of course, you will see other salient parts of the friend at the same time; the boundary disturbance concerns only the anger you have that you are projecting.)

Introjection and Retroflection. As creative synthesis, figure formation reorganizes the field according to the requirements of the present situation, in the service of growth. Using the example of our metabolism, we transform the field by choosing and taking in something from the environment and subjecting it to the digestive process. Introjection treats digestion differently. It avoids it. In introjection, we take in an element of the environment without digesting it. Since we have not digested it, it is still in its original form (though it is in a new context).

If we imitate a gesture we have seen in a movie, we introject it. We have not made it ours—we have merely swallowed it. If we try to be the kind of person our parents wanted us to be—a dutiful husband, say, who acts responsibly and does what his wife, bosses, and peers expect—without making our own choices about these goals and attitudes so they are our own, we are acting on the basis of what we have introjected.

Introjecting is swallowing whole; introjects are what we swallow. Awares introjecting is trying something out; unawares introjecting is playing a role without knowing we have taken it on. Faintly sensing our introjects, we are like Pretty Nurse in "Penny Lane," "And though she feels as if she's in a play / She is, anyway."

When we are introjecting, as when we are projecting, we retain the nature of the boundary as a meeting of differences, but we place it farther away. What belongs to the environment—these values, or that gesture—seems to be within us. Thus, we avoid the aggressive digestive labor, the tearing and separating and destroying which is an important part of our way of making things our own. We slip out of the obligation to assess what we encounter in the light of our own values, needs, and circumstances. Instead, we swallow them just as they are given, hook, line, and sinker. As with projection, introjection sets the boundary not between ourselves and the environment, but between one part of ourselves and another.

If our lives are based on what we have introjected, our behavior may well be vague and colorless, our figures lacking in the incisiveness and definition which come from using our own compasses to guide ourselves. We will seem inauthentic to others, and we are. We are almost believable; what we say and do is nearly heartfelt, but not quite. (To the extent that what is termed "the superego" represents values which are incorporated in this fashion, we see it as a constellation of introjects.)

If we bite our tongue to keep from sniping at someone who has offended us, if we titillate or masturbate ourselves because it seems inappropriate to us to act sexually toward another person, we are retroflecting. Similarly, if we control and channel the excitement of a high-powered tennis match into our strokes and strategy, resisting the impulse we feel to hit the ball too hard or throw our racquet in the air, we are retroflecting. When we chew on the inside of our cheek and do not reognize that we are angered by someone and unwilling to chew them out, we are retroflecting unawares. In all these cases of retroflecting, we allow the boundary to retain its properties—it is not dissolved, for instance—but we disturb it by changing its location so as to alter what is being met. The boundary, typically between us and the environment—to that person who has irritated us, or turned us on—is placed instead so that we are our own environment. Then, we do something to ourselves. We are on both sides of the boundary, doing to ourselves what is intended for the other.

Egotism, Deflection, and Other Contact Boundary Disturbances. You have surely met someone who talks to hear herself speak, or to let you know how smart she is. Or someone who, while seeming to listen to you, is listening only to prepare his next response, or to convince you of his sincerity or concern for others. These interpersonal events involve the contact boundary disturbance which Gestalt therapists call egotism. Egotism is a boundary disturbance of a different order than any we have described thus far. In egotism, the boundary is not relocated, nor is it dissolved. Instead, something which is characteristic of contact boundaries is eliminated: the interplay of the meeting.

The contact boundary is the location of a meeting of differences, where the interaction of the elements which are meeting contributes to the forming of the figure. In egotism, there is a contact boundary event, a meeting. The person making the figure is intent only on his or her own contribution to the meeting. Mutuality is absent or exceedingly diminished here, the boundary seemingly one-sided because the concern here is almost exclusively with one's sense of oneself. Thus, there is no interplay, no give and take. Egotists are so tuned to their own voice, thoughts, actions, or feelings that they proceed without full knowledge of who or what they are meeting.

We may manipulate the boundary in this way, with awareness, in insisting on our right to be heard in a situation where we are being made unwelcome, for instance, or in restraining ourselves during a lengthy period of preparation and maturation during which premature commitment is invited. But egotism as a contact boundary disturbance substitutes looking at oneself for a more embracing focus upon the entirety of the meeting. The result is that you are out of touch with the part of the field which is outside oneself.

For the most part, egotism in contacting makes for stiffness and rigidity in figure formation, the quality of figures, and personal demeanor. Abandon, or just flexibility, requires a keener sense of the other that is being met than egotism allows. Nor is true spontaneity possible, because that also requires contact, not just an impulse. The only thing possible is the impulse itself without any contact, which is impulsivity.

These five contact boundary disturbances, which the authors of *Gestalt Therapy* described, do not exhaust the ways in which the contact boundary can be manipulated. Primary among the others which have been proposed is deflection, in which the individual relocates the boundary so that the contact is with some other individual or topic or idea or feeling—some other element of the field. If you are annoyed by your employer and come home and kick the dog, you turn the action meant for your boss to the dog by creating a boundary meeting between your dog and yourself. If you do not allow yourself to know you have been irritated by your boss and believe instead that your dog's insistent jumps onto your leg are the sole reason you are kicking him, you are deflecting outside awareness. If you bite your tongue when your boss is bawling you out unfairly and then come home and kick your dog out of frustration at the boss, your retroflecting (the biting) and deflecting (the kicking) are awares. In deflection, the impulse is directed toward a substitute in the environment. You may substitute an object, as in the example of the hapless canine (object deflection), or you may substitute a subject, as happens when a child complains about the way in which her day will be spent, "Mom, I don't want to go see those stupid people today," and Mom replies by changing the subject to the way she expresses herself, "Honeybunch, don't talk about your Aunt and Uncle that way" (subject deflection).

This listing of the contact boundary disturbances is no doubt incomplete. As Gestalt therapists continue to look at the events at the contact boundary, new structures will undoubtedly be recognized. For instance, an additional boundary disturbance, provisionally named conflection, consists of doing to yourself what you wish for yourself. An example is the kind of idle caressing—rubbing their face or arm or fingers with their own hands—which people do sometimes while talking about themselves. Here the desire is not to caress someone else; that would be retroflecting. Rather, it is to have another caress you. In this instance, the boundary is relocated as it is in retroflection, transferred from its intended place where you and the other meet and placed instead so you meet yourself. You have made an environment, an other, of yourself. Some forms of masturbation are instances of this, as is the action of a woman who says to the person to whom she is making love, by way of instruction, "Here, touch me like this," and touches herself to illustrate her words.

Boundary disturbances play an important role in the formation of good figures, as tools in the service of the creative imagination and healthy, free functioning. When the boundary is disturbed unawares, however, these creative energies become implicated in the disabilities and miseries which beset us. They allow us to avoid aspects of the field and thus make it possible for us to construct the inadequate and unsatisfying, painful and destructive solutions and achievements which typify those miseries and disabilities. The use of the term "disturbance" in contact boundary disturbance, however, is intended to suggest only which the normal boundary functions have been interrupted or altered, not that the individual is disturbed.

THE SELF

The Wholeness of Contact

Much of the practice of Gestalt therapy consists of a careful examination of contact, the creation and destruction of figures (creative adjustment), and the experiential dimensions of these. The part of Gestalt theory which concerns itself with these as attributes of the individual is called the theory of the self.

The self is the agent of change. It is the organism as a whole making contact in the present moment, being aware in the process of creative adjustment throughout the stages of figure formation and destruction over time, and growing. The term "self" refers to the system of contacts in any present situation and the way our experience is organized by us. These different systems of organization are called structures or aspects of the self. The self exists wherever contact occurs, not as an additional object of the psyche (as it might in conventional psychology) but as the process of figure formation in the individual. When we are not referring to any particular boundary contact but only to a generalized present or present, as in this discussion, the self is felt only as an experiential potentiality or a memory. The authors of *Gestalt Therapy* put it this way, "The self is not to be thought of as a fixed institution; it exists wherever and whenever there is in fact a boundary interaction. The self *is* the figure/ground process in contact-situations" (p. 373).

This seems to be a "six blind men and the elephant" situation, with no sighted person in view, where the aspects of the self correspond to the different experiences of the blind men as they grasped the tail, the legs, the trunk, the hide. The self is the integrative force, though, the sighted person who can see the whole.

The self is often discussed in terms of the forms it takes in the different phases of figure formation and in different situations. These forms are called structures. They are partial constructs of the self, similar to the ways that we are each different in different kinds of situations. We are thoughtful and receptive when listening to something which interests us, animated and active when we are responding. These structures of the self are the id functions, the ego functions, and the personality functions—and one additional construct of a different nature, the middle mode.

Though the first three may have familiar names, they have been recast in the phenomenological spirit, as aware structures which the self creates according to the particular purposes and circumstances of creative adjustment. They are the major stages of figure formation, from the vantage point of the individual, the aware organism.

Ego Functions and Id Functions

The second phase of figure formation is characterized by the ego functions, by the individual's accepting elements of the field which need to join the emerging figure and rejecting others which do not belong. More often, there are not only the spontaneous dominances of interest that determine these inclusions and exclusions but also more deliberate choice exercised by the individual in the making of the figure. The second phase is the time par excellence when the individual feels himself or herself to be the doer, the figure maker. You are not only attentive, you pay attention; you concentrate, you organize materials and time, you put things in order. The workings of this phase, especially, call for healthy deliberation, restricting certain activities and concentrating exclusively on others.

Experientially, the ego functions give the individual a sense of being instrumental in the figure's forming. You feel yourself to be the one who is making things happen. In this phase, you approach the environment aggressively, using and mastering the elements of the field rather than merely cooperating with them. Phenomenologically, this gives you a sense that you make the figure, whereas at other times you are less instrumental, more a partner in the enterprise, participating along with other elements in its formation. Because of this, there is in the ego functions a feeling of being separate and different from the elements you are controlling and ordering. The contact boundary's role as divider is clearly felt; differentiation is foremost; joining is less noticed.

Counterposed to this are the id functions, wherein we experience ourselves as passive, moved by things outside us. Our experience of our emotions is of this kind, as are rest and relaxation, situations which are vaguely organized and not problematic, and many of those situations as well in which we are in touch with ourselves physically, sensing proprioceptively. This experience of the id functions is of course a familiar one at certain times—in sleep and sleepiness, at certain times in lovemaking, rest, being massaged. The language of the id functions says it all: We are fondled, we are moved to tears, we are tired, we are touched, we are excited, we fall asleep.

This description is typical of the experience of the first phase of figure formation and the end of it as well. Though they exist throughout the phases of figure formation, the id functions predominate at those times. If there is contact and interplay, for instance, the ego functions alternate with the responsive id functions in the second, contact phase, in order that the effects of our actions may be felt and in order that whatever is beyond our control may be noticed. The self-awareness of the id functions is unengaged, diffuse, acted upon. The boundary here may hardly be felt at all when all the world is at rest, or it may be clearly felt, when we are not only receptive but receiving.

Middle Mode and Personality

Middle mode is a term inspired by the study of languages. It refers to a voice, the middle voice, which lies in between the active and passive voices and has qualities of both. The active voice is the voice of the ego functions, and the passive voice is the voice of the id functions. There is no middle voice in English (the intransitive is not quite the same), but it is suggested, perhaps, by locutions such as "We are taking a walk" (different from the active voice of "We are walking"). Or, "I would not have kept myself from . . . ," or "I am having a good time." The reader may find this description of middle mode obscure, but the experience of the middle mode is a common one. The middle mode is spontaneity. It is what we experience when activity and passivity are balanced, when we let go and give ourselves over to an activity we care about and are deeply involved in. It is making love once we are past technique and expectations. It is reading with absorption, giving ourselves over to the experience. It is playing music or cards, or animated conversation, when we are beyond our worries about our performance or the impression we are making, and when the mental static of second-guessing ourselves has disappeared.

It is the experience which athletes these days are coming to call "the zone," when everything goes well, easily. We feel unified, balanced, whole, thoroughly attuned to what we are doing, what we are involved with. The ego and id functions are balanced; we are neither doing it nor being done to, and at the same time we are doing, and we are being done to. It is somewhere in the middle, encompassing both. The result is a new gestalt, not the sum of the ego and id functions, but a new function with a character all its own: the middle mode. In terms of engagement, we might call the result impartiality, or use the Oriental term "nonattachment," or the old-fashioned term "disinterested," passionate but not biased. The feeling is not loss of self, but self in interplay; immediate, concrete, thoroughly present. "A player's effectiveness is directly related to his ability to be right there, doing that thing, in the moment," wrote the veteran professional quarterback John Brodie. "He can't be worrying about the past or the future or the crowd or some other extraneous event. He must be able to respond in the here and now."

The middle mode has a special standing in relation to the self. While the other special aspects of the self, the id and ego functions and the personality, are separate and distinct aspects of the self, the middle mode is this and more. On the one hand, it is a distinct aspect of the self, with experiential qualities which markedly set it apart from the others. On the other hand, it partakes of qualities of both the id and ego functions. Beyond this, the middle mode is a less partial, more pervasive quality of the self which encompasses both the id and ego functions.

Perls, Hefferline, and Goodman term the middle mode "the unity prior (and posterior) to activity and passivity, containing both" (1951). In part, they are suggesting what its name, middle mode, also suggests, that the middle mode balances the manipulative disengagement of the ego functions with the accommodating engagement of the id functions, the aggressiveness of the ego functions and the receptiveness of the id functions, creating something else entirely. They are also pointing to another special quality of the middle mode: its pervasiveness. Middle mode is both a particular quality of experience in which the id and ego functions are balanced and also spontaneous free functioning itself, encompassing and subsuming most of what we feel as the ego and id functions.

The personality functions, as a structure of the self, consist of the system of attitudes, beliefs, convictions, and assumptions about ourselves and the workings of the world to which we refer when we are asked to explain ourselves. It is also being aware of oneself, studying oneself, reflecting upon oneself in the present moment, as well as referring to oneself. The personality is both a reproduction of ourselves in words—"a verbal replica of the self," Perls, Hefferline, and Goodman wrote—and the self-conscious activity of studying and replicating ourselves.

The personality involves speaking of oneself; therefore it exists in terms of our relations to others because speaking is a social act: We speak to others. (Of course, we also speak to ourselves; this is interpersonal, as well, since we make an object of ourselves.) When we are out of touch with aspects of ourselves and the world, the personality is replete with mistaken ideas, distortions, and introjects. We think we know ourselves, but we do not. In health, when there is nothing hidden, it is accurate (as far as it goes; its limits are our inventiveness, and what can be verbal). The personality is responsible—we feel we can be responsible for what we know—for we can commit ourselves to something if we know ourselves through and through. We can say, "Yes, I would like to try white water rafting; I like things like that."

We refer to our ideas of ourselves and the world in the course of forming figures, especially in the second phase of figure formation, as a way of facilitating the figure's emergence and development. At the same time, liking the idea of white water rafting because we like other similar things is eating the menu, not the dinner. It is not *it,* it is only thinking about it. The personality is sometimes a menu, a shortcut to creative synthesis, but it is not creative synthesis itself.

As "consciousness," awareness of oneself, the personality function of the self is a part of healthy living. For the most part, however, it is important only in those times when especial difficulties in figure formation occur, and those which involved reconsiderations of ourselves—including psychotherapy. In general, we consider the personality a minor aspect of the self in healthy, free functioning. In fact, Gestalt therapists believe the importance of thinking in daily life is overrated. Most of what we call thinking is not considered thought at all, but subvocal speech, talking to oneself. Nearly all useful mental activity goes on out of awareness, necessarily, where it can best function as an instrument of the requirements of the present figure and stand out of the way of the rest of our abilities when it is not needed. It is a disease of humans, perhaps especially of educated people, to believe that persistent and aware mental activity is important. The belief plays a large part in the excessive reliance on logic and the mental which keeps us from being fulfilled. The uniqueness of each present moment requires the kind of flexibility which is usually precluded by the personality. Relying on it as a substitute for the uncertainty and even mystery of the creative process is painting by numbers. And this habit of mind keeps us from becoming thoroughly absorbed in the here and now of our lives. "We should take care," Einstein wrote, with this in mind, "not to make the intellect our god; it has, of course, powerful muscles, but no personality." Or, as the oft-quoted Yankee philosopher has said, "How can you think and hit at the same time?"

We end with a conception of the self in which there is almost no constancy or regularity, except as the force for growth. And, differently from the way the self is usually thought of, there is frequently little or no sense of ourselves at all. Paradoxically, in health we often forget ourselves. At bottom, we could say, we are virtually nonexistent, virtually selfless, because of the variety of our qualities and experience. "The true value of a human being," Einstein said, "is determined primarily by the measure and sense in which he has attained liberation from the self." It is this quality of the self which was referred to earlier in the section on health and its absence: the fear of experiences which do not assure us that we exist. The threat here is that without the solid ground of confidence in our ability to make and destroy figures we will die. And yet, we must die, in a way. We must take no thought for ourselves or for the morrow. We must efface ourselves in figure formation if we are to participate in it fully. A multitude of artists, spiritual figures, and others attest to this. "In every part and corner of our life, to lose oneself is to be gainer; to forget oneself is to be happy."

CHARACTER, PSYCHOPATHOLOGY, AND DEVELOPMENT

The conception of character in Gestalt therapy was inspired by the work of Wilhelm Reich, a leading figure in German psychoanalysis in the 1920s and 1930s, and a teacher of F. S. Perls. Reich developed character analysis when it had become apparent that examining the mental life of those in psychoanalysis was not enough to effect significant changes in their lives. Reich concluded that the body needed analysis in the same way the psyche did. Although this was entirely in keeping with Freud's emphasis on psycho-somatic unity, Reich was much more interested in how the body is tied to the psychic life or mind than the other way around.

Character analysis is a way of paying attention to the physical dimensions of the individual—the body: movement, breathing, musculature, speech, posture—in the therapy. As holists, Gestalt therapists consider the body/mind a unity, and involve ourselves with the physical dimensions of the individual with the same avid interest we bring to the emotional, spiritual, and cognitive dimensions. Reich's method, with its present-centered focus on the individual in the therapy room, has been adopted and adapted by Gestalt therapists.

From the Gestalt perspective, character is what we do characteristically. That is, it is the typical ways in which we function emotionally, physically, intellectually, spiritually. Each of us has a characteristic way of walking, of talking, of responding to fatigue and sleeplessness, of becoming sexually aroused, of meeting new people, of using our eyes and voice, of understanding a problem. Character is what is characteristic of us.

This conception of character is a present-centered one. It is true, of course, that what is characteristic of us is what we have learned in context and interplay with what we are given—that is, it is something we have grown to. At the same time, we are not saying that character is something inside us that makes us act a certain way. That is mechanistic thinking, the engine which is needed to drive the machinery. It creates an extra part of the individual, "character," which makes us act. On the contrary, in Gestalt therapy, what we are and what we do are inseparable. Character is what we are, what we do regularly.

In health, there is very little character, just as there is very little personality. A hallmark of free functioning is flexibility. No matter how similar to a past situation the present one is, the present moment is unique. You are not the person you were then—you cannot be—and the situations are therefore never identical, even if the other conditions appear to be identical. In contrast, habitual behavior is out of touch. To be responsive to unique situations is to respond differently than you have done before. This is free functioning, and it suggests that character restricts our responsiveness.

In another way of speaking, taken from everyday language, character connotes integrity and distinctiveness. In this sense, character is plenteous in health. Integrity and distinctiveness are important dimensions of free functioning, because free functioning requires that we find *our* unique responses to the present circumstances, the ones which most exactly fulfill them.

Gestalt therapists work with a theory of psychopathology based on figure formation and the contact boundary disturbances. When the contact boundary is disturbed outside awareness, we become unable to distinguish the field as fully as we would be able to if the boundary had not been altered; we may mistake one thing for another and miss certain other things altogether. A careful and thorough description of how this occurs as figures emerge, develop, and are destroyed in each single instance constitutes an understanding of what is amiss and what is right from the Gestalt point of view. It is an understanding of figure formation; it can be applied in a multitude of circumstances because it is the structure of these situations, of our everyday lives as well as the remarkable special moments. This is what Van Gogh had in mind when he wrote, "If one is master of one thing and understands one thing well, one has at the same time insight into and understanding of many things."

Though Gestalt therapists are informed about current conceptions of psychopathology, they are out of step with them, for several reasons. Our emphasis, in Gestalt therapy, on the necessarily unique events occurring in the present moment and on individual solutions to individual problems has led to a concentration on enhancing the particulars of psychotherapy—in method, a focus on learning to be fully in the present moment, for instance—and not to the kind of generalizing which would result in a theory of psychopathology. Gestalt therapists are inclined by their training to consider pathology as emergent in the therapeutic process, to be encountered as it appears, not before. This way of doing things—in contrast to the usual method, where estimates are made about the individual at the beginning of therapy on the basis of tests and interviews—reduces the value of developing a theory of psychopathology. Finally, we believe that human beings, virtually all of us, are both the architects of our own misfortune and the ministers of our own healing. Psychopathology itself, with its attendant connotations of disease (afflictions from outside) and treatment (also, in the medical model that spawns psychopathology, applied from outside) is foreign to our point of view.

Our preference, instead, is for a careful, moment-by-moment examination of the way in which the person creates figures in the therapy situation. This is done utilizing the conceptual structure of the contact boundary disturbances and figure formation. If we examine any figure as it is being created and destroyed, we can see if the creative process is interrupted or impaired in any phase, and also how the contact boundary is manipulated in order to do this.

There are a multitude of possibilities. Perhaps a person avoids the uncertainty inherent in the forecontact phase and forces the figure/ground differentiation instead, without taking the time to find out what is available in the field and what interests him or her. Perhaps the person does this by deducing appetites rather than feeling them: "I must be hungry—it's time to eat," or "Of course I love you! I wouldn't have married you if I didn't love you." Perhaps she acts on principle, whether it applies in this situation or not: "Of course I trust you, doctor—you are a professional person." Perhaps he proceeds without even the illusion of an appetite: "I know I need to be here. My wife and all my friends say so."

In contacting, in the second phase, is she clumsy and grabby or penetrating or insufficiently curious or afraid of the aggression required by the acts of tearing things apart and grinding them up: "I don't want to cause anyone any pain. I wouldn't want to say what I think; it might hurt him." Can he bite things off and tear them away from what they are a part of while staying in touch with them and the experience of dividing the element? "I know I need to talk to him. He's been working for me for 2 years and can't do the job, but I can't bear to fire him.'' Or, "Yes, I'm not very happy with the way things are going, but I am afraid to speak up. I don't want to make any trouble.''

In the final contact phase of figure formation, is he afraid to let go, afraid of really getting his teeth into it, afraid to go beyond what we can control? Is she nonorgasmic? Does he always have to be in charge when he gets together with his friends? Conversely, is she unwilling to wait until passions are high enough? Does she plunge into new romances without making sure he is worthy of her love?

In the penultimate postcontact phase, does she allow enough time for contemplating the end of the figure, or does she distract herself immediately after the job is completed? In therapy, for instance, does she cry a bit and then reach for the tissues, saying "That's enough, now. I know why I'm crying.'' Does he hold on to what is dying or dead, an old girlfriend or college days or the 1950s: "I suppose I should go find someone else, but honestly, I try. No one else interests me. I would rather think about her.'' Or, its opposite, does she rush into a new activity as soon as the old one shows signs of ending ("Sorry—I've got to get back to work''), though it is still not concluded?

Each of these observations is based on our understanding of figure formation. We start by observing where the phases do not coincide with what will create the best figure. We will be able to notice where important elements of the field are being avoided. Sometimes these elements are aspects of the self, as when a woman avoids asserting herself because she does not want to experience taking charge of a situation. Subsequently, our knowledge of the contact boundary disturbances guides our observations as we learn to see *how* these interferences with free functioning are achieved. If you do not have an orgasm, how do you achieve this? Do you sense the rising wave of release and resist it by tightening your vaginal muscles or sphincter, or do you check out, beginning to think about something else? If you eat when you are not hungry, are you avoiding your anxiety or even anger about the job your teacher is doing, chewing your food with a ferocity which is intended for chewing her out?

Anxiety, a difficulty of these first two phases, warrants especial mention both for the frequency with which it occurs and for Gestalt therapy's remarkable approach to it. It arises in this contact phase and sometimes earlier, in the forecontact phase, when the emerging figure cannot develop further because it is divided. Instead of figure/ground emerging out of the undifferentiated field, the differentiation takes the form of two elements which are both significant but which cannot join in a single figure. Since figure formation requires that a single figure emerge and develop, the process remains stuck at this point. The figure divides when one's interests are split or unclear or, as in this case, when the important elements which enter the foreground are at odds with each other.

Anxiety is a special case of this. When the individual is anxious, the emerging figure is being divided by the tension which occurs at the same time as the mounting excitement which normally accompanies (or even sometimes announces) the gestalt. This tensing of the musculature is often experienced as labored breathing or rapid, shallow breathing, alert tunnel vision, self-consciousness, tingling in the soft inside of the arm, and an overall tension in the superficial muscles. Emotionally, the main experience is fear or a feeling related to it: restlessness, dread, panic. The reader will recognize that these physical reactions are symptoms of fear. Perls et al. (1951) called anxiety the fear of one's own daring, and it now becomes possible to understand this. Anxiety is the conflict which arises when we are caught between our interest in something and our fears of it. We want to speak up in class because we have something to say, but we are afraid to say something stupid. We want to introduce ourselves to someone in the room, but we do not want to appear vulnerable. The paradigm for anxiety is stage fright: We want to go on stage, we are ready to go on stage—but the curtain does not go up for another hour. So we are anxious, at odds with ourselves.

Eating and its ancillary functions—the development of appetite, seeking out food, taking it in, tasting and chewing it, and the subsequent digestion and elimination—is a familiar and penetrating instance of figure formation. F. S. Perls, in *Ego, Hunger and Aggression*, developed and extended it beyond its immediate circumstances into a conceptualization called the mental metabolism. Some of the examples in the preceding paragraphs utilize it. We have appetites for companionship, for sleep, for meaningful work, for recognition, for honesty. The folk wisdom of our culture already recognizes this, in phrases such as, "Let me chew on that for a while," "I need something more substantial to do—something I can get my teeth into," "You make me sick," and "Do you expect me to swallow that?"

The mental metabolism discloses an important developmental dimension to Gestalt theory. It suggests that the ability to deal aggressively and creatively with the world, which is a given in the infant, takes a leap forward with the acquisition of teeth in the last half of the first year. From the onset of baby teeth, children are not limited to what can be gummed and swallowed and require less of the predigestion on the part of the environment which milk and then mashed and ground-up foods represent. Children have a more varied and skilled way to deal with their environment and turn it to their own interests. Young children can encounter more of the field, since their teeth can tear and bite off a piece more alien and process difficult aspects of it and chew them completely before it is swallowed. This conclusion has been seconded by recent research in child psychology and amendments to analytic theory which give infants a more central role in creating their life experiences. As Gestalt therapists, it obliges us to see how active even the youngest children are in shaping their own experience, and it supports our conviction that we are intimately involved in creating for ourselves the lives we lead.

DREAM THEORY IN GESTALT THERAPY

Gestalt therapists look at dreams in several ways. F. S. Perls, expressing a viewpoint first explicated in *Gestalt Therapy*, characterized them as projections. The dreamwork he developed, where the dreamer enacted the elements of the dream, was designed to allow the dreamer to reintegrate what had been projected. Later on, he considered them "existential messages," summary statements about the present or general state of the dreamer's life. Here, the dream enactments were intended to clarify these summations.

Many Gestalt therapists approach dreams as he did. Others have suggested that dreams can be retroflections of reactions within therapy sessions—reactions to the therapist, for the most part—or to events of the previous day. An example is a dream in which a woman turns her back on the man dreaming about her. His therapist might ask if the dreamer felt dismissed by her and did not say so, or if the dreamer felt dismissive of her, and did not say so. When the understanding of the figure/ground process described by Gestalt psychologists has been applied to dreams, they have been treated as reversals of organization that permit background material to become foreground. (In the best known reversal picture, an ornate goblet can be visually reversed so it becomes two silhouetted profiles, face to face.) Dreams have also been considered unsatisfactory attempts to complete figures initiated earlier—attempts which are unsatisfying because the figures cannot be satisfactorily completely in the context of sleep. In this case, the dream work consists of continuing the dream while the dreamer is awake, as the dreamer's creative fantasy.

The idea that dreams are existential messages, it has been rightly pointed out, is out of tune with Gestalt therapy. It points us away from the actual, away from the phenomenology of dreams and in the direction of something to which it is supposed to refer. Also, as an interpretation, it forecloses discovering the dreamer's intention in making this dream in favor of introjecting a preexisting conclusion about the dream.

It is for these reasons and others that interpretation is generally avoided in Gestalt therapy. It encourages unaware introjection. It also encourages a relationship between the therapist and the individual in therapy in which the former encourages introjection in the latter. This arrangement promotes the authority of the therapist and the submission of the person in therapy and works against the stated intention of the therapy: to foster the individual's growth. Finally, interpretation short-circuits the process whereby the individual will discover for himself or herself the exact nature of every particular and unique dream.

These reservations apply to all these characterizations of the nature of dreams and dreaming. But these characterizations can be, and are, enormously useful in therapeutic work if they are instead considered as potentially fruitful hypotheses about the nature of a particular dream, to be tested and explored in therapy or outside it. Beyond this, Gestalt therapists are generally united in regarding dreams as quintessential instances of the spontaneous play involved in creative living, more adequate perhaps than most of the figures we are able to create while awake. Though good figures are perhaps easier to form in the context which dreams inhabit, it is also true that they therefore speak to us with a clarity and power which convince us of the virtuosity and richness of the creative capacities of our native intelligence.

CURRENT TRENDS IN GESTALT THEORY

The strands of ideas and individuals that have been woven together into Gestalt therapy coalesced into a defined theory and practice in 1951 with the publication of *Gestalt Therapy*. Within 20 years, it had become the most frequently named alternative to psychoanalysis among psychotherapy professionals in the United States. The statements and writings of its best known practitioners, preeminent among them F. S. Perls, and a narrow sampling of its techniques were familiar not only to professionals but to many others as well.

In the ensuing years, the spotlight of public attention has swung away from Gestalt therapy, as it has generally swung away from the psychological preoccupations of the 1960s and early 1970s. Yet, as Gestalt therapy enters its fifth decade, it continues to grow. Some of the enthusiasm which greeted it in the United States can be seen in Central and Eastern Europe, in Canada, and in Latin America, where dozens of institutes are training Gestalt therapists.

At the same time, some facets of the outlook and practices of Gestalt therapy have been assimilated into the work of psychotherapists of many persuasions. Chief among these are the greater emphasis on the present moment and a readiness to open the therapeutic process to examination. Gestalt therapists were involved in some of the earliest aural and visual recordings and transcripts of sessions, which are increasingly common today, and they have done a preponderant number of them. Significant, also, is a greater understanding of field concepts, recognizing that the therapeutic process includes the environment outside the therapist's office, an increased willingness on the part of the therapist to take a more prominent role in the therapy, and a commensurate willingness to ask the individual in therapy to be more active on behalf of his or her own growth. The subsequent interest in strategic and family therapies, the growth of psychology self-help books, and the pervasiveness of workshops and other activities intended to promote personal growth are reflections of different influences from Gestalt therapy.

The greatest single trend in the development of the theory of Gestalt therapy is away from a virtually singular reliance on the person, utterances, and work of Frederick S. Perls to a more thorough and rigorous adherence to the theory created by him and others in *Gestalt Therapy*. F. S. Perls, the most visible of Gestalt therapists until his death in 1970 and an enormously effective and charismatic teacher, was of course a central figure in Gestalt therapy's gestation and growth. During the late 1960s and until the early 1980s, he had become preeminent, determining Gestalt therapy's tone, practices, and framework almost single-handedly. But his writings, talks, teaching workshops, and therapy demonstrations were designed for promotional as well as didactic purposes. The simplifications almost unavoidable in such circumstances promoted distortions or misunderstandings of Gestalt theory or principles at odds with it as well as therapeutic practices which were inconsistent with it.

For instance, F. S. Perls's "workshop method" for doing psychotherapy, in which one individual works with a therapist while both are being observed by others, was suited to demonstrations but virtually ignored interactional field phenomena, and it abetted the notion that Gestalt therapy was a psychotherapy for individuals only, inapplicable to group and family work. Another example is Perls's claim that healthy people had "lost their minds and come to their senses." This ran directly counter to Gestalt therapy's holistic commitment to embracing everything the individual could contribute to the emerging figure: the intellectual and spiritual as well as the physical and the emotional. In the contexts and ways in which this claim was offered, it also became part of a commonplace conviction of the time, which Perls both fostered and refuted, that significant and enduring growth could be attained quickly and easily.

Though Perls was himself widely read and keenly sensitive to intellectual influences in tune with his interests, his antipathy to intellectualizing extended sometimes to discouraging serious thought altogether. His manner and actions sometimes encouraged his students to imitate him, emulate his methods, and repeat his words thoughtlessly, introjecting him at the expense of finding their individual, considered responses to his teachings. At the same time, also following his example, others decided for themselves what constituted Gestalt therapy without distinguishing ideas from slogans.

It would not be accurate to attribute these attitudes within Gestalt therapy to antiintellectualism, personal foibles, and misunderstandings alone. It also reflects some things which are basic to it. Gestalt therapists have always mistrusted orthodoxies and encouraged each individual to find his or her own way of doing things. These attitudes, closely linked to its theory, work against whatever impulse exists within Gestalt therapy to set standards for its theory and practice. Far more important, though, is a paradox which lies at the heart of Gestalt therapy. On the one hand, it is a psychology consisting of a theory, methods, and practice which stands upon a foundation built on important psychological perspectives and material from philosophy and the sciences. These sources are reflected directly in the language in which it is couched and the influences it acknowledges. At the same time, it is based on something more than these important progenitors, something which exists parallel to them and to which access can be gained without even understanding the theory or practice of Gestalt therapy.

The authors of *Gestalt Therapy* acknowledged this in its introduction.

> Indispensable—for the writing and the thorough understanding of this book—is an attitude which as a theory actually permeates the content and method of the book. . . . The authors have not invented such a mentality. On the contrary, we believe that the Gestalt outlook is the original, undistorted, natural approach to life; that is, to man's thinking, acting, feeling. . . . The unitary outlook . . . is buried but not destroyed and, as we intend to show, can be regained with wholesome advantage. [p. viii]

They are referring to the intrinsic processes of figure/ground, figure formation, the contact boundary disturbances, and the self. In his last years, F. S. Perls often spoke to the same effect. "Gestalt is as ancient and old as the world itself," he remarked. "The world, and especially every organism, maintains itself, and the only law which is constant is the forming of gestalts—wholes, completeness."

But if the Gestalt approach is the original, natural approach to life, it need not be spoken about in the terms which Perls, Hefferline, Goodman, and their collaborators developed. There are texts written before "*gestalt*" could be pronounced—the *Tao Te Ching*, the Taoist scripture, comes to mind—which demonstrate and even teach this approach. Gestalt therapy, then, is a particular manifestation of this original, ancient approach. In *Gestalt Therapy*, Perls, Hefferline, and Goodman produced a comprehensive statement of it in terms which were sophisticated and contemporary at the time it was written, drawing upon a vocabulary and concepts from modern psychology and modern philosophy. Their statement spoke to an educated, thoughtful audience, and for the most part a professional one.

In the 40 years since the publication of *Gestalt Therapy*, the constituency for books about psychology has changed dramatically as values and standards for popular, general, and professional education have changed. Many professionals find the book is beyond them. But those for whom the book is inaccessible can claim a different authority than *Gestalt Therapy* for understanding the Gestalt approach, based on a direct apprehension of the original approach. Though unmediated by Perls, Hefferline, and Goodman's text, they still call what they understand Gestalt therapy, perhaps because it is a modern home for this original approach within psychology. Some Gestalt therapists would characterize F. S. Perls himself in this way. Others within Gestalt therapy have used these same principles over the years, albeit sometimes, it seems, with less clarity and precision than they were used in *Gestalt Therapy*, and without convincingly demonstrating that they fully comprehend the book or even the approach. The result has been both the diversity which Gestalt therapists value and also conflict, contradictions, and confusion. The gestalt of Gestalt therapy has become diffused, something less than the vibrant, vigorously outlined figure Gestalt therapists would prefer.

A major trend in the last 10 years has been directed toward recognizing, remedying, and resolving this situation. Many Gestalt therapists have become convinced that Gestalt therapy, its practitioners, and the people who work with them, would benefit from the rigor, focus, and precision which a better knowledge of Gestalt theory would permit. This is a basic lesson about figures, of course: Any whole has added impact and vitality when it is consistent, clear, and coherent.

The consequences of this trend have included more discussion of the nature of Gestalt theory itself, and clearer demarcations between different ways of looking at Gestalt therapy. A significant number of the articles which have appeared in the past half-dozen years in the professional journal of Gestalt therapy in the United States, *The Gestalt Journal*, deal with theory or the relation of theory to practice, demonstrating how Gestalt therapists are attempting to come to grips with their theoretical underpinnings. (This chapter itself is a reflection of this trend, including the likelihood that some Gestalt therapists would take exception to some of its formulations.)

Another consequence of this trend has been more discussion among Gestalt therapists about Gestalt psychotherapy in relation to theory, and attempts to augment and refine both theory and practice. Chief among these last are projects intended to create a diagnostic nomenclature consistent with the Gestalt outlook and attempts to flesh out the developmental theory suggested by the concepts of figure formation and destruction and the mental metabolism.

REFERENCES

Goodman, Paul. *Growing Up Absurd*. New York: Random House, 1960.

Kohler, Wolfgang. *Gestalt Psychology*. New York: NAL Books, 1975.

Latner, Joel. *The Gestalt Therapy Book*. New York: The Julian Press, 1973. Highland, New York: The Center for Gestalt Development, Inc., 1988.

Perls, F. S. *Ego, Hunger and Aggression: A Revision of Psychoanalysis*. London: Allen and Unwin, 1947; New York: Random House, 1969.

————. *Gestalt Therapy Verbatim*. Lafayette, California: Real People Press, 1969; Highland, New York: The Center for Gestalt Development, Inc., 1988.

————, R. Hefferline, P. Goodman. *Gestalt Therapy: Excitement and Growth in the Human Personality*. New York: The Julian Press, 1951.

Polster, Erving, and M. Polster. *Gestalt Therapy Integrated*. New York: Brunner/Mazel, 1973.

Rank, Otto. *Truth and Reality*. New York: W. W. Norton Co., 1964.

Reich, Wilhelm. *Character Analysis*. New York: Farrar, Straus, and Giroux, 1949.

Winokur, Jon. *Zen To Go*. New York: NAL Library, 1989.

2

Diagnosis: The Struggle for a Meaningful Paradigm

JOSEPH MELNICK, Ph.D.,
and SONIA MARCH NEVIS, Ph.D.

T HE WORD DIAGNOSIS conjures up complex feelings and images for most psychotherapists. For some it implies a powerful form of assessment that predicts the dos and don'ts of treatment, whereas for others it indicates a prejudicial label that reveals more about the biases of the diagnostician than about the diagnosed. Yet, irrespective of one's beliefs concerning the efficacy of formal diagnosis, one is continuously assessing. To say it simply, one cannot not diagnose.

Furthermore, there are compelling influences outside the realm of theoretical and personal considerations that are forcing psychotherapists to diagnose in a more formal way. These forces include the insistence of medical insurance companies on formal diagnoses from the revised third edition of the *Diagnostic and Statistical Manual of Mental Disorders* (*DSM-III-R*), treatment plans, and predicted treatment outcomes. In addition, the proliferation of health maintenance organizations (HMOs) and professional provider organizations (PPOs) is threatening the autonomy of psychotherapy. By requiring diagnostic criteria similar to that required by the insurance companies, these organizations are forcing therapists of all professional and theoretical persuasions to grapple with the dilemma of diagnosis.

This chapter is an attempt to explore this dilemma from the theoretical perspective of Gestalt therapy. First, diagnosis will be defined and a rationale for its utility will be presented. Second, a comparison between other systems of diagnosis and Gestalt therapy will be made. Third, the Gestalt therapy "experience cycle" (cf. Polster & Polster, 1973; Zinker, 1977) will be presented as the basis of a diagnostic system (see Fig. 2.1). And finally, specific diagnostic formulations from *DSM-III-R* (borderline, phobia, histrionic, and post-traumatic stress syndrome) will be analyzed and intervention strategies will be articulated. Because the withdrawal phase of the experience cycle has received only minimal attention by Gestalt theorists, it will be given special emphasis here.

WHAT IS DIAGNOSIS?

Diagnosis is first and foremost a descriptive statement that articulates what is being noticed in the moment. Yet it also means going beyond the moment, implying a pattern as well as a prediction, no matter how minimal. In addition, diagnosis may or may not include a concept of causality. Thus to diagnose is to attempt to enlarge the picture, to move from what is observable to what is difficult to notice. It includes a schema not only of what is to be noticed but also of *how* it is to be observed.

One major difference between how Gestalt therapists and others diagnose centers around the concept of causality. Gestalt theory does not imply a system of cause. Gestalt therapists believe in causation, but perceive it as inherently unknowable. As systems proponents, they are aware that the number of influences that impinge on any given system is so vast that a full and meaningful description of cause is improbable, if not impossible.

In summary, diagnosis is an attempt to make sense out of limitless experience—to impose a pattern on something fundamentally unknowable. In this sense, to diagnose is to play a game with oneself. It is acceptable to play this game only if one does not forget that it is illusory.

WHY DIAGNOSE?

If diagnosis is "only a game," one is forced to grapple with the question, Why diagnose? Actually, this is, in fact, a pseudo question since one must diagnose in order to organize the impinging data. One constantly derives meaning after first making patterns out of unorganized experience. Yet, as

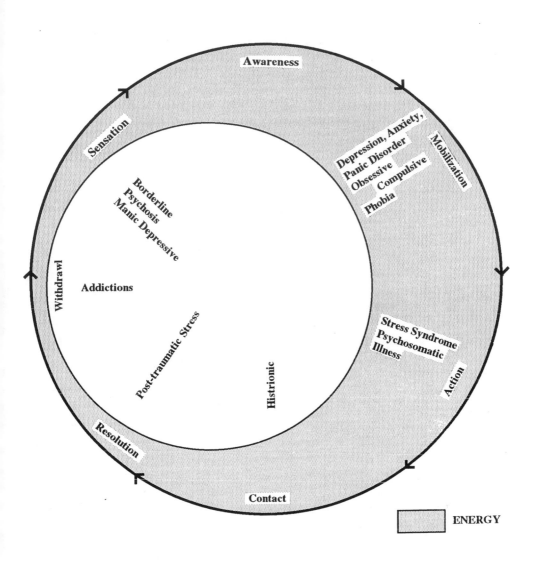

Figure 2-1 Gestalt Cycle of Experience

systems therapists, Gestaltists know that this "derivation of meaning" is arbitrary since it is selective and incorporates, along with the patient's behavior, both the diagnostician and the environmental field.

Given the fact that one has to diagnose, a more fruitful question becomes, Why diagnose in a formal systematic manner? There are several reasons. First, diagnosis gives one a map and describes possibilities of how a person can evolve. Therefore the therapist benefits from a structure—that is, a compass to help organize the information and provide clues to a direction, and to navigate through the vast field of data.

Second, the process of diagnosing allows the therapist to control anxiety. By removing oneself from the data, the therapist may remain calm while waiting for a figure to emerge. Thus the process of diagnosing is grounding and keeps the therapist from jumping precipitously into the infinite while waiting. Simply stated, it gives one something to do.

A third reason to diagnose in a more formal way is that it is economical. By linking Gestalt theory to other systems of diagnosis, a vast array of research and theory opens to the clinician. Furthermore, it is also efficient in that the therapist can make predictions without having to wait each time for the data to emerge from immediate experience.

Fourth, Gestalt therapists in particular need to be grounded in a wider perspective that includes the past and the future. This is because their orientation, which is to stay close to the patient's immediate experience, can lead to a sense of discontinuity. Moments, no matter how powerful, must be linked with others in order for an enduring picture to be formed (Miller, 1985).

Finally, diagnosing prevents the Gestalt therapist from becoming isolated from others with different theoretical orientations. Consequently, Gestalt theorists, even while debating issues concerning process versus structure, still use traditional diagnostic labels such as schizophrenia, narcissism, and borderline (cf. From, 1984; Tobin, 1985). Thus, although the use of diagnostic categories may not be totally congruent with our theory, we still employ them in communicating with others.

HOW DOES GESTALT THERAPY DIFFER FROM OTHER SYSTEMS?

Although Gestalt therapists may utilize the terminology of more traditional diagnosis, they approach diagnosis from a fundamentally different perspective. Gestalt diagnosis is gleaned essentially from the moment and thus provides the key to intervention, interpersonal process, and change. Because of this viewpoint, it is important to note at the outset that Gestalt theory encompasses the therapist in the assessment process and thus makes the therapist part of the diagnosis.

This implies not only that the therapist does influence what is seen but also that what is seen evokes reactions in the therapist that help create a unique systemic experience. Gestalt theorists Perls, Hefferline, and Goodman (1951) believed that the self is in fact the "system of contacts," and that contact is the meeting of the organism and the environment. Therefore, much of what will be said about the patient (the observed) is equally true of the diagnostician (the observer) and the environmental field.

Despite this process orientation and the acknowledgment of the therapist's role, the Gestalt therapist, in diagnosing, nonetheless makes a formalized statement relating to the patient alone. The therapist therefore makes a choice to deal with only one part of the organism/environment equation as if the clinician and environmental components could be frozen and the patient isolated from the interaction. Although this perspective is admittedly limited and incomplete, it is fairly consistent with the way people experience and interpret the world.

In diagnosing one of the primary differences between the Gestalt system and other systems is its focus on the fluctuating process of the moment as opposed to the labeling of long-term, ongoing, and fixed characteristics. Gestalt therapists pay attention to blocks in one's process (i.e., avoidance of awareness or contact) and describe them as disturbances or neurotic self-regulation—projection, confluence, retroflection, retrojection, and deflection. This assessing in the here and now is a therapeutically optimistic stance that supports change in people who might have been restricted by the more traditional, historical, and permanent forms of diagnosis. Diagnosis in the here and now keeps one open to seeing possibilities and provides clues to new meanings and changes in the patient system. The negative implication of this philosophical approach is that the therapist may fail to recognize or acknowledge, as the more traditional diagnostician might, the degree to which people are locked into a pattern of behavior. The patient may consequently be destined for disappointment by this optimism and omission.

Consistent with the here-and-now focus on change is the Gestalt tendency to diagnose with verbs and not nouns. Seeing the world in an active and therefore potentially changing way, the clinician chooses words that emphasize behavior. Thus, the description is of "bear trapping" rather than "bear trapper"; "obsessing" rather than an "obsessive." Once a noun is used, the person and not just the behavior is characterized and a bit of hope is lost, for diagnosis is not only a description of the moment but also a subtle prediction of the future. Therefore, Gestalt therapy's approach to identifying behavior patterns as opposed to character deficiencies has served as an appropriate and optimistic counterpoint to Freudian determinism.

Because of Gestalt therapy's process orientation, the individual is seen as continually moving through overlapping series of experiences that have beginnings, middles, and ends. Because of the complexity of these phenomena, one can become stuck at many different points along the experience continuum. Therefore, the value of a diagnostic tool is to help the clinician discover the point of difficulty for the patient and intervene at the correct level (e.g., sensation, awareness, mobilization of energy, action) with appropriate and suitable techniques.

Other therapeutic disciplines tend to target only one place in the cycle for intervention. For example, body approaches focus on unblocking sensations so that awareness can be heightened and thus lead to mobilization, contact, withdrawal, and resolution. Behavioral orientations often emphasize action in the hope that repertoire expansion will lead to improved contact. Lastly, in psychoanalytic systems, therapy is often focused on withdrawal, where old experience is chewed over, digested, and integrated in order for a new figure to form (Melnick & Nevis, 1987).

Gestalt therapists, because of their process perspective, risk overlooking that their in-the-moment assessments are in fact diagnoses. To avoid this oversight, what is needed is a recognition of the nature of diagnosis within the Gestalt framework and a healthy inclusion of aspects of more traditional diagnostic approaches. This latter recommendation addresses the pitfall mentioned earlier of the therapy being too fixed in the here and now without an acknowledgment of the patient's habitual behavior patterns. Therefore, it is useful to broaden the Gestalt diagnostic perspective by borrowing from other therapeutic disciplines. Ultimately, however, regardless of how one defines diagnosis, it is crucial to remember that it is merely a tool for change. Its purpose is not to burden the patient or therapist with constricting and irremediable labels but to facilitate the patient's awareness, growth, and health.

HOW DO GESTALT THERAPISTS DIAGNOSE?

Traditionally, Gestalt therapists have diagnosed by paying attention to the phenomenon in the moment. At some point an aspect of behavior becomes interesting, something stands out, and a pattern emerges. This pattern might lead to a diagnostic statement such as, ''The patient appears to be retroflecting.'' The remaining therapeutic work in the session might be focused on that retroflection. This form of diagnosis is valuable for a number of reasons. First, the behavior is readily observable. Second, the techniques outlining how to work with retroflections are clearly articulated and straightforward. And third, the diagnosis defines a piece of therapeutic work that can often be satisfactorily completed in one therapy session. It should be pointed out that Gestalt therapists do not have a single way to deal with the phenomenon of someone who characteristically—that is, more often than is normal—retroflects energy when faced with stressful situations. Furthermore, we do not have a theory for predicting if the constant work on retroflections will result in some enduring change by affecting the ground of the individual. The ground consists of the traces of experience, history, and physiology contained in larger, deeper grooves out of which lively figures spring forth. This ground must ultimately be affected if a person is to experience a more permanent change.

Gestalt writers have paid much attention to enhancing figure formation but have virtually ignored the more difficult task of the integration of here-and-now experience into more enduring patterns. Figures can be changed and manipulated relatively easily as research on LSD, weight reduction programs, encounter groups, and charismatic religious movements has indicated. However, long-term change is more subtle and more difficult to achieve. Gestalt therapists must attend to ground formation and learn to maximize the incorporation of healthy figures into a richer, more vibrant, responsive, and supportive field.

Furthermore, an overemphasis on quick-forming figures has led people to become less likely to accept who they are, and more likely to believe that if only they might find the right approach or the right therapist, radical change would be possible. The increasing number of lawsuits against therapists by patients who feel they have been misled and deceived is one unfortunate outcome of this naive promise of hope. A second sad result of this promise is that people are less willing to struggle to accept themselves as they are, as good enough. Thus, self-acceptance, one of the primary goals of psychotherapy, is struggled with in a misleading context of patients' believing that they can become whomever they wish to be. Unfortunately, clinicians have formulated as many fad therapies as fad diets, which often result in poor long-term results.

EXPERIENCE CYCLE AND CHARACTER

Healthy, organized functioning can be defined by breaking down figure formation and destruction into an "experience cycle" (Zinker, 1977). The cycle has been used historically to describe a unit of experience. It should be pointed out that the experience cycle is a limited metaphor describing figure formation and destruction that involves the meeting of the individual and the environment only from the perspective of the individual. Despite this limit, the remainder of this paper will be utilized to stretch this metaphor even further—to describe the concept of character.

Character is derived from the Greek word for engraving and is traditionally defined as consisting of "those pervasive features of behavioral thinking that are deeply etched and relatively unchanging throughout life" (Milan, 1981, p. 81). In essence, this definition presents character as the distinctive ways in which individuals organize their experience. Thus, character is the equivalent of a person's psychological signature; it is what makes one recognizable. And like one's signature, there are infinite variations.

In relation to the experience cycle, healthy functioning involves moving through the individual phases with ease, that is, without either too much blockage or too much speed. Poor functioning involves either redundant stuckness or recurrent, too rapid movement through the cycle, resulting in a lack of completeness and satisfaction as defined by the individual or others.

GESTALT CYCLE OF EXPERIENCE

In this section our assumptions will be stated regarding the utility of the cycle, after which the individual stages will be outlined. Then a *DSM-III-R* diagnosis will be listed that reflects poor functioning at certain phases. Finally, an approach to treatment will be described that will appear consistent and congruent with our analysis. This is done in an exploratory way with no intention of implying a cookbook approach to psychotherapy. Instead, it is posited that a theory of psychotherapy based on the experience cycle can imply both an assessment component and a treatment form, which are consistent with each other.

Utility of the Cycle

We make the following assumptions about the Gestalt cycle of experience:

1. The stages of the cycle of experience are in fact artificial demarcations of a continuous, flowing unit of experience; thus, the phases are overlapping.

2. Competence is directly related to the skills and abilities needed to articulate and complete each stage satisfactorily (Zinker & Nevis, 1981).

Ultimately, being able to complete a cycle, to create and destroy a figure with clarity, defines healthy functioning (Wallen, 1957).

3. Although the cycle was originally intended to describe momentary experience, it can be extended to encompass larger periods of time.

4. The stages of the cycle reflect a developmental progression. The earlier in the cycle the disturbance occurs, the more the experience tends to (a) consist of very old ingrained patterns, (b) be primarily physiologically as opposed to behaviorally influenced, and (c) be less observable to others, and thus less amenable to therapeutic change.

5. A disturbance at one stage of the cycle will affect all remaining stages.

6. An understanding of the cycle is adequate to articulate therapeutic strategies and interventions. Utilizing other theories to explain causality, although possibly useful, is not necessary.

7. Although one might intervene at later stages of the cycle with some success, character can be affected ultimately only by intervening at the phase where the disturbance originally occurred.

8. The intervention(s) must occur many times before any long-lasting changes can occur.

Individual Phases of the Cycle

Sensation/awareness. The first stage of the cycle, sensation/awareness involves all experiences taken in by the senses. The individual must be able to sort out an awareness from the vast array of internal and external stimuli impinging on the senses. Sensations consist of everything one sees, touches, hears, smells, and tastes and include all of the physiological, proprioceptive, and kinesthetic sensations. They also can include such influences as values, languages, and desires. Completion of this phase results in the ability to articulate a clean awareness, that is, one upon which to accurately build as well as one that reflects with accuracy the sensual experience of the individual.

Energy/mobilization. The second phase is energy/mobilization. As an awareness is defined, an individual's interest and energy begin to grow, ultimately organizing a want, a desire. Thus, competing figures recede into the background as energy is invested in a dominant content (Zinker & Nevis, 1981). The task of this phase is to form a sharply delineated figure out of a rich and varied ground.

Movement or action. The movement or action stage is built on sensation/ awareness and mobilization/energy. Since this is the first stage that is clearly obvious to others, blockage in the first two stages will most likely be evident here. This stage involves the ability to move toward an attractive object or away from an unattractive one.

Contact. The fourth phase of the cycle is contact. According to Zinker and Nevis (1981), contact "is the fruit of the energy/action phase. Wants or concerns have been melded into a newly created whole—a whole which is different from its parts" (p. 10). Strong contact is based on a clear awareness supported by ample energy. Contact also produces and enhances energy arousal. This stage continues the sharpening of a compelling figure. The contact phase, too, is largely observable to others.

Resolution/closure. The resolution/closure phase involves review, that is, a summarizing, reflecting, and savoring of one's experience. It involves both an appreciation of what has been and a regretting of what could not be. This is a slow stage because most of the energy has been drained from the figure and the person is psychologically positioning himself or herself to let go, to withdraw, and ultimately to turn to a new sensation.

Withdrawal. The final stage marking the end of a cycle before a new one begins is withdrawal. It is a period during which one's boundaries are drawn closer, and energy used in contacting the environment is minimal. Many in our action-oriented society might perceive this phase as boring and thus miss the significance of this integrating stage. Both resolution/closure and withdrawal are primarily internal in nature and not easily observed by others.

Figure 2-1 illustrates the cycle of experience. The energy builds from sensation to contact and then recedes. Individual phases are placed around the inside of the circle and various disorders are plotted near the phase reflecting their hypothesized origins. It should be noted that this schema is a beginning attempt at integrating the cycle and diagnostic categories.

Sensation/Awareness Stage: Borderline Personality Disorder

Borderline personality disorder as described in *DSM-III-R* is an example of blockage at the sensation/awareness level. Diagnostic criteria include:

A pervasive pattern of instability of mood, interpersonal relationships, and self-image, beginning by early adulthood and present in a variety of contexts, as indicated by at least *five* of the following:
1. a pattern of unstable and intense interpersonal relationships characterized by alternating between extremes of overidealization and devaluation

2. impulsiveness in at least two areas that are potentially self-damaging, e.g., spending, sex, substance use, shoplifting, reckless driving, binge eating (Do not include suicidal or self-mutilating behavior covered in [5].)
3. affective instability: marked shifts from baseline mood to depression, irritability, or anxiety, usually lasting a few hours and only rarely more than a few days
4. inappropriate, intense anger or lack of control of anger, e.g., frequent displays of temper, constant anger, recurrent physical fights
5. recurrent suicidal threats, gestures, or behavior, or self-mutilating behavior
6. marked and persistent identity disturbance manifested by uncertainty about at least two of the following: self-image, sexual orientation, long-term goals or career choice, type of friends desired, preferred values
7. chronic feelings of emptiness or boredom
8. frantic efforts to avoid real or imagined abandonment (Do not include suicidal or self-mutilating behavior covered in [5].) [p. 347]

As one can summarize from the above diagnostic criteria, the borderline patient has little sensorial stability. To use Gestalt terminology, the ground available to the borderline patient is nonsupportive, resulting in an inability to tolerate little more than minimal stimulation. Individuals who are unable to accurately organize sensations are often labeled as schizophrenic or borderline and suffer from sensory distortions such as hallucinations and delusions. Whether it is the distorted intake of sensations, the inability of an individual to code sensory stimuli into a manageable form, or the overloading of stimuli that interferes with figure formation is of much theoretical debate. What is certain is that some individuals cannot easily tolerate, manage, or translate these sensory stimuli into acceptable and manageable forms and figures.

It should be pointed out that sensations are difficult for all of us. Most of our sensory appetites are too large for what is organismically acceptable, and thus we have to learn management techniques. However, most people do not have to deal with the variability, largeness, and enormous distortion of sensation with which people who are characteristically bound in this phase must contend.

The therapeutic work with a borderline patient is to help with the management of sensations by lowering and limiting them at both an internal and external level. Once sensation is manageable, awareness can emerge and movement through the cycle can continue. The traditional primary interventions have been drugs that minimize internal stimulation and various forms of institutionalization that structure and narrow external experience.

In psychotherapy, the task is to teach these patients to manage sensations by lowering input, or when this is impossible and stimulus overload occurs, by draining the mobilized energy through supportive and nondestructive forms of expression. The first task involves learning to slow down the input in order for the individual to run less of a risk of being flooded. Sensations need to be made smaller in order to form a figure that can be satisfactorily completed. This is accomplished by helping patients focus on and label their experience.

Techniques that increase sensations, such as the use of the empty chair, are potentially dangerous (From, 1984), as are confrontational, behavioral, and paradoxical interventions that tend to produce added or ambiguous sensory input. Another major therapeutic mistake would be to teach borderline patients management or repertoire expansion techniques that assume that their sensory mechanisms are working properly. The basic problem is not one of inadequate behavioral repertoire.

When flooding occurs, the therapeutic work involves teaching the patient to drain energy in a nondestructive way. Stimulus overload can be minimized in this instance by a therapeutic stance of "soft, clean contact." It is here that the concept of soothing is important. If the therapist becomes upset—for example, becomes mobilized or increases his or her sensations—it will add to the patient's already excessive stimulation. The therapist must learn to keep internal stimulation low by self-soothing and ultimately by teaching the patient soothing techniques. (It is interesting that this approach to the treatment of borderlines is consistent with that articulated by the self-theorists and outlined by Tobin [1982] and Yontef [1983]. However, unlike these theorists, and as stated in assumption 5, Gestalt theorists do not believe it is necessary to hypothesize a cause, e.g., a specific form of inadequate mothering, in order to prescribe an intervention.)

Mobilization Energy: Simple Phobia

The second phase of the experience cycle occurs with the generation of energy around sensation. If the energy gets trapped in the body and there is no muscle release, anxiety occurs. The way that the individual deals with this trapped energy has historically been labeled psychoneurosis and, more recently, anxiety disorder. *DSM-III-R* lists within this category such disorders as obsessive-compulsive, panic disorder, and various phobias such as agoraphobia and simple phobias. One can also add to these a vast array of psychosomatic problems that result from this chronic blocking of energy.

To illustrate mobilization/energy dysfunction, simple phobia has been chosen. The characteristics include:

A. A persistent fear of a circumscribed stimulus (object or situation) other than fear of having a panic attack (as in Panic Disorder) or of humiliation or embarrassment in certain social situations (as in Social Phobia).
Note: Do not include fears that are part of Panic Disorder with Agoraphobia or Agoraphobia without History of Panic Disorder.

B. During some phase of the disturbance, exposure to the specific phobic stimulus (or stimuli) almost invariably provokes an immediate anxiety response.
C. The object or situation is avoided, or endured with intense anxiety.
D. The fear or the avoidant behavior significantly interferes with the person's normal routine or with usual social activities or relationships with others, or there is marked distress about having the fear.
E. The person recognized that his or her fear is excessive or unreasonable.
F. The phobic stimulus is unrelated to the content of the obsessions of Obsessive Compulsive Disorder or the trauma of Post-traumatic Stress Disorder. [p. 244–245]

Phobias involve either the investment of too much energy around an appropriate figure (a person will not visit the South because of a fear of poisonous snakes) or the mobilization of energy around a wrong awareness (a person avoids all heights but has no experience of trauma connected with them). In the second case the sensation is given the incorrect meaning because the individual's system cannot tolerate the correct labeling of the sensation. Labeling of a sensation is one way to define "meaning." Phobia involves the avoidance of the accurate meaning that could lead to a completion of the cycle that is appropriate to the sensation. Instead, a distorted (symbolic) or incorrect meaning is given to the sensation.

Phobias are maladaptive because they do not lead to satisfactory completion. They do, however, often serve to discharge or deflect the energy, thus temporarily controlling it so that the individual can tolerate it. For example, as stated above, one may label certain sensations (increased heartbeat, tightness in the chest, sweaty palms, etc.) as "fear of heights." This incorrect attribution of meaning allows the individual to function in a relatively anxiety-free manner as long as heights are avoided. However, if therapy produces the understanding that these sensations are attached to an avoidance of intimacy then the patient is faced with a conflicting duality. Now it is possible to move toward emotional closeness with another, but only with an awareness of the heightened tension that such intimacy may create.

The two major manifestations of phobias are a distorted or exaggerated response to an appropriate object to be feared (e.g., a poisonous snake) that is generalized well beyond the object and a distorted or exaggerated response to a metaphorical, symbolic, or psychologically linked object that has little or no correlation with the appropriate sensation. Treatment involves the symbolic or in vivo matching of the correct figure with the stimulus so that completion can occur. Since much of what we call psychotherapy deals with the above, it might be best to categorize the approaches briefly.

Certain techniques lead to diminution of anxiety so that the person can reexperience the situation and attach the correct meaning to the sensation. These include many desensitization and cognitive approaches. Others, such as meditative and breathing techniques, help the individual to tolerate the sensations so that a less distorted meaning can emerge. Still other approaches provide support so that people do not have to bear their pain and anxiety alone, thus helping them complete the cycle. The financial, psychological, and ideological support that our society is beginning to provide for Vietnam veterans and victims of sexual and psychological abuse are examples of this support. It should be noted that if a specific meaning emerges, then the patient may be diagnosed as suffering from post-traumatic stress, which is described in the last section.

In summary, to move through the mobilization stage of the cycle means to discharge the trapped energy so that a contactful figure that may lead to completion can be created. As with the other stages, the work must be done over and over again in order for the energy to be available for the generation of appropriate and adequate contact.

Contact Phase: Histrionic Personality Disorder

The fourth stage of the experience cycle occurs when awareness, supported by appropriate energy, results in a flexible and meaningful meeting of the self and the environment, usually in the form of an other. To meet phenomenologically implies that not only do I see, but also I am seen; that not only do I speak in order to reach you, but also I am heard. In the moment, each notices that there is a "we" that is different from either alone.

Disturbance of contact results in experiences that do not fit within the range of "good enough," but rather are too little or too much for a specific environmental context. An example is a hug that either has too little energy and is not warm enough or is inappropriately passionate given the environmental situation. Either extreme is jarring and incompatible and does not result in a joining experience. Both extremes are contextual disturbances in that the evaluation of too little or too much is made in relation to the other as well as to the total phenomenological field. The expression "too little energy," which typically involves the pulling back from another, has been historically labeled as retroflection, whereas "too much energy" has been traditionally called hysterical or histrionic.

It should be noted that disturbances of contact, rather than reflecting characterological issues, might instead be a function of inadequate behavioral repertoires. Traditionally, inadequate repertoires have been analyzed and increased through educational channels, including behavior modification. Furthermore, the increasing of repertoires has, until recently, generally not been considered as falling within the domain of psychopathology or psychotherapy. However, if the therapeutic dilemma is not one of inadequate but, instead, one of fixed repertoires that limit and narrow a person's ability to make contact with the environment, then the behaviors do fall within the diagnostic guidelines of disorders.

Histrionic personality disorder is an example of disturbance of the contact boundary, as described by *DSM-III-R*. Diagnostic criteria include:

> A pervasive pattern of excessive emotionality and attention-seeking beginning by early adulthood and present in a variety of contexts, as indicated by at least *four* of the following:
> 1. constantly seeks or demands reassurance, approval, or praise
> 2. is inappropriately sexually seductive in appearance or behavior
> 3. is overly concerned with physical attractiveness
> 4. expresses emotion wth inappropriate exaggerations, e.g., embraces casual acquaintances with excessive ardor, uncontrollable sobbing on minor sentimental occasions, has temper tantrums
> 5. is uncomfortable in situations in which he or she is not the center of attention
> 6. displays rapidly shifting and shallow expression of emotions
> 7. is self-centered, actions being directed toward obtaining immediate satisfaction; has no tolerance for the frustration of delayed gratification
> 8. has a style of speech that is excessively impressionistic and lacking in detail, e.g., when asked to describe mother, can be no more specific than, "She was a beautiful person." [p. 349]

The stereotypic model of histrionic functioning is that of the flamboyant actor. Unfortunately, this stereotype is often true for the histrionic character wishes to be seen, heard, appreciated, and applauded and is not very interested in others in more deep complex ways. Thus, if a therapist attempts to prematurely create for the patient a more contactful experience, the therapist may run into indifference at best and difficulty at worst.

The energy in histrionic patients is inner determined, undisciplined, and exaggerated and does not keep pace with the environmental field. They are perpetually in action without benefit of a broad awareness. Thus, the existential work with histrionic people is to help them bear the truth of their overly large existence. They are fated to take up a lot of room, to say a lot, and to do a lot. Even though they may suffer from an energy disturbance, it would be a mistake to attempt directly to teach them to be aware of or change their energy. Histrionic people are only minimally interested in awareness for it complicates life and makes it less exciting.

Thus the dilemma for the therapist is how to help these patients slow down as well as become interested in the environmental field. Experiments that deal directly with slowing down the action, such as reading a menu completely before ordering food or counting to 10 before acting, may be utilized. Further, having the patient learn to go inward before acting heightens the probability that the forthcoming action may be truly contactful. Thus directing the patient to notice tension, breathing and so on might ultimately lead to a slowing down of movement.

To help these patients trade in their wish for simplicity for a more complex orientation to the world is difficult at best. However, experiments that teach them to notice environmental contexts, including other people, are beneficial. Examples include having the patient ask the therapist questions as well as notice and articulate physical and psychological boundaries.

Demobilization Phase: Post-Traumatic Stress Disorder

The last stage will be labeled demobilization as it incorporates both the resolution/closure and withdrawal stages of the experience cycle previously discussed. The purpose of demobilization is to allow for the absorption of an experience into the ground of the individual so that it will not be elicited inappropriately.

As with other stages of the cycle, when there is a synergy between the experience of the individual and the individual's capacity to deal with it, demobilization proceeds in a smooth and graceful manner. The person is able to disengage from the experience to chew it over, and absorb and digest it. Ultimately, the individual becomes somehow different and wiser in a subtle way. If the experience is too large to be easily absorbed into the ground, then a form for expelling or using up the excess energy must be initiated. If this is not done, then the old figure will not be properly integrated and will have a perpetually distorting and disproportionate effect on the current and future experience of the individual.

This need to demobilize is a complex process that has been largely ignored by society as well as by Gestalt therapists. Society supports a cultural bias against demobilization by teaching people to believe in Horatio Alger stories and characters like "The Little Engine That Could." To move toward objects and goals is a Western ideal. One who moves away or gives up risks being labeled in a myriad of negative ways. Furthermore, as a culture we do not value aloneness and movement inward. When one mobilizes, it is movement outside the skin toward contact. However demobilization involves a movement inward to a nonpublic place where one is alone.

Gestalt therapists, too, have ignored and had difficulty in articulating the demobilization process. In the past it has been taught as a smaller part of the experience cycle than in fact it is. The difficulty in understanding this process is connected with its largely intrapsychic nature. It is harder for others to see. Thus, like the sensation stage of the experience cycle, the process of the individual must be inferred rather than actually observed.

Furthermore, demobilization is often unpleasant. When the event is large and negative, the experience is a grief reaction. Thus, demobilization is associated with death, illness, divorce, and defeat. However, demobilization can also be a positive process, such as falling off to sleep, dreaming, fantasizing, and celebrating.

Hypothetically, demobilization can be broken down into four substages: turning away, assimilation, encountering the void, and acknowledgment. By describing the experience cycle as reflecting larger experiences in the life of the individual, one expands beyond the original definition of the cycle as a description of momentary experiences. Hopefully, describing demobilization in terms of substages is useful despite the distorting and stretching of the cycle experience.

The first substage involves either a turning away from (e.g., stopping drinking) or a being turned away from a figure in which energy is still invested (e.g., death of a spouse). The need of parents in our society to diminish their interest in their children as the children grow older is a common experience of turning away. The relationship begins in confluence and progresses into the stage where the child introjects the parents' ideas and values. In some cultures children may continue to introject for much of their lives, but in our society, which values autonomy and independence, an increasing psychological separation between parent and child is preferred. For children to develop integrity—that is, to experience boundaries cleanly and clearly—they must detach from parents and create other interests. As a child leaves, so must the parents distance themselves, or they will be faced with one of two equally sad alternatives: either a hard rupturing of the child–adult boundary resulting in mutual trauma or a type of deadly confluence that restricts developmental maturation. One aspect of maturity is the capacity to move away from a boundary gently.

To turn away when one still has energy requires much support. It can come in many ways, in the form of either self-generated or external support. To be self-supportive, to rely only on one's own resources, is difficult and runs contrary to the natural inclination to move toward energized objects in the environment. Not only does self-support incorporate an intellectual and emotional introjection of values, it also includes an invoking of an internalized rhythm sadly absent for many in our society. For to have faith, to hold one's hand, to gently rock and talk softly to oneself, ultimately involves the introjection of good nourishing parenting.

The generation of external support often involves placing oneself within a structure that provides highly detailed procedures for leading one's life while in the process of turning away. Therefore choice, as well as temptation, is minimized. Examples of this type of structure are Alcoholics Anonymous and similar organizations that deal with addictive behaviors. These organizations articulate both the techniques for and the potential pitfalls in the turning-away process.

Another external option utilized in turning away involves the creation of a large and compelling figure to which to transfer unspent energy. Love on the rebound and some born again religious conversions are examples of this unfortunate type of figure substitution. The problem with moving quickly toward something large and captivating is that it does not allow for the next substage of the demobilization process, assimilation, to occur. Consequently, little is ultimately learned, and the person may be doomed to skip from one love or religious experience to another.

Assimilation involves a chewing over of the experience in order to drain the energy. The process is difficult for many therapists in that the work may appear redundant and boring. Furthermore, because our society underestimates the amount of time necessary to chew over experience, patients may be faced not only with doing the hard work but also with having to deal with the embarrassment engendered by the intensity of feelings and the surprisingly long time that their interest remains. It is the therapist's task to normalize the experience and support the process. However, if a patient's restlessness with the duration and intensity of feelings is joined by the therapist's boredom, blockage may ensue.

The third substage, encountering the void, can be terrifying. Our society does not value or provide much training for the experience of feeling emptied of interest, of caring, of figures. The void consists of a segment in time when nothing matters. Often we avoid it by creating artificial engagements such as self-talk and noncontactful activities. Ultimately, it is the fear of the unknown that keeps many locked into either painful or nonnourishing figures. And it is this inability to turn from the old, the painful, and the nonnourishing to the unknown that is a precondition for many of the ''addictions'' so prevalent in our society today such as workaholism, love addiction, and codependency.

The fourth substage, acknowledgment, involves a soft, low energy and an owning of how the experience has changed the individual. It is during this time that individuals are able to articulate the learnings, both good and bad, from the experience as well as to express and live out the changes in their lives. Thus the patients have gained a piece of wisdom and are able to interact with the environment in a fresh and more profound manner.

An example of an inability to demobilize can be found in post-traumatic stress disorder (PTSD). Criteria include:

A. The person has experienced an event that is outside the range of usual human experience and that would be markedly distressing to almost anyone, e.g., serious threat to one's life or physical integrity; serious threat or harm to one's children, spouse, or other close relatives and friends; sudden destruction of one's home or community; or seeing another person who has recently been, or is being, seriously injured or killed as a result of an accident or physical violence.

B. The traumatic event is persistently reexperienced in at least one of the following ways:

1. recurrent and intrusive distressing recollections of the event (in young children, repetitive play in which themes or aspects of the trauma are expressed)
2. recurrent distressing dreams of the event
3. sudden acting or feeling as if the traumatic event were recurring (includes a sense of reliving the experience, illusions, hallucinations, and dissociative [flashback] episodes, even those that occur upon awakening or when intoxicated)
4. intense psychological distress at exposure to events that symbolize or resemble an aspect of the traumatic event, including anniversaries of the trauma

C. Persistent avoidance of stimuli associated with the trauma or numbing of general responsiveness (not present before the trauma), as indicated by at least three of the following:

1. efforts to avoid thoughts or feelings associated with the trauma
2. efforts to avoid activities or situations that arouse recollections of the trauma
3. inability to recall an important aspect of the trauma (psychogenic amnesia)
4. markedly diminished interest in significant activities (in young children, loss of recently acquired developmental skills such as toilet training or language skills)
5. feeling of detachment or estrangement from others
6. restricted range of affect, e.g., unable to have loving feelings
7. sense of a foreshortened future, e.g., does not expect to have a career, marriage, or children, or a long life

D. Persistent symptoms of increased arousal (not present before the trauma), as indicated by at least two of the following:

1. difficulty falling or staying asleep
2. irritability or outbursts of anger
3. difficulty concentrating
4. hypervigilance
5. exaggerated startle response
6. physiologic reactivity upon exposure to events that symbolize or resemble an aspect of the traumatic event (e.g., a woman who was raped in an elevator breaks out in a sweat when entering any elevator)

E. Duration of the disturbance (symptoms in B, C, and D) of at least one month.

Specify delayed onset if the onset of symptoms was at least six months after the trauma. [*DSM-III-R*, 1987, pp. 250–251]

The first therapeutic task in the demobilization of PTSD involves helping patients accept that a turning away must occur. Once this acknowledgment takes place, then the work of draining the interest can begin. However, since

trauma can be mesmerizing and addicting, we must help patients acknowledge both sides: that they both wish to lose interest and wish to stay interested
in the traumatic event.

A second therapeutic task involves helping patients find forms through
which they can express their feelings in a small way. These forms usually
involve repetitive actions that cause no harm. Talking is the primary method
utilized as a form of ''doing'' without a large mobilization. The patient must
feel supported in the expression of a feeling without an external outcome or
without an aim to change anything.

When demobilization from powerful events associated with PTSD is
dealt with, sadness is often elicited naturally as the seasons of the year and
anniversaries trigger affect-laden memories and sensations. When the sadness
is evoked, the task is then to softly talk through the events. However, the
therapist may get stuck and experience difficulty in helping patients move
beyond the traumatizing event. There are several possible reasons for this.
The first is pacing. Demobilization is a slow process that must be supported.
The therapist must struggle to not become impatient or judgmental regarding
the redundancy and amount of time involved. Second, patients will sometimes become frightened by the emotions that are engendered. It is the
therapist's job to foster the development of adequate support for the patient
to tolerate the emotional arousal as well as to help keep the emotions at a
level that can be absorbed into the individual's ground. Third, patients may
have an inadequate repertoire with which to drain the energy. To ''sing the
blues,'' protest, light a candle, or plant a flower are rituals that are socially
sanctioned for dealing with trauma and can be used to expand patients'
repertoire.

Lastly, the therapist must carefully monitor his or her own interest. One
must learn to be interested just enough. Too little interest will not provide
enough support and too much on the part of the therapist will generate
energy that fuels the patient's attachment and prevents demobilization. When
demobilization is being worked on, a real danger is created if the therapist
is more interested than the patient.

It should be pointed out that we are describing an ideal, for one can never
demobilize fully. If one is lucky, most figures will naturally be assimilated
into background and the remaining energy will be used in a productive way.

The last substage of demobilization is an acknowledgment of the process.
If patients have learned well, they will know something that they never knew
before. If demobilization has proceeded correctly, patients will be able to
answer the question, How am I different?

In sum, the work in dealing with problems in demobilization is to help
the individual create small experiences to soften the energy. The danger is

in creating a remobilization experience. It should be pointed out that as with other stages of the cycle of experience, an inability to demobilize might be a function of the person's inability to experience or integrate sensations, to mobilize, or to make contact. If this is the case, then the work must include dealing with these other aspects of the cycle.

SUMMARY

In this chapter a basic human dilemma is posed: How is one to know and describe another? To answer that query, the issues faced by Gestalt therapists in attempting to meaningfully diagnose and assess patients and the Gestalt experience cycle and its utilization for describing character have been discussed. Finally an effort has been made to fit a few common *DSM-III-R* diagnoses into the paradigm of the cycle of experience as well as to prescribe appropriate methods of intervention.

Diagnosis is an art as well as a science, for its purpose, after all, is to provide a useful model of experience. As Gleick (1987) so aptly writes:

> The choice is always the same. You can make your model more complex and more faithful to reality, or you can make it simpler and easier to handle. Only the most naive scientist believes that the perfect model is the one that perfectly represents reality. Such a model would have the same drawbacks as a map as large and detailed as the city it represents, a map depicting every park, every street, every building, every tree, every pothole, every inhabitant, and every map. Were such a map possible, its specificity would defeat its purpose: to generalize and abstract. Mapmakers highlight such features as their clients choose. Whatever their purpose, maps and models must simplify as much as they mimic the world. [p. 279]

In retrospect, this attempt at mapmaking is but a rough beginning filled with contradictions and exceptions. But this is how it should be, for Gestalt psychotherapy is a phenomenologically based theory grounded in the celebration of the uniqueness of the individual.

ACKNOWLEDGMENT

We gratefully acknowledge the editorial contributions of Gloria Melnick, Ph.D., M.S.W.

REFERENCES

American Psychiatric Association. *Diagnostic and statistical manual of mental disorders* (3rd ed.-rev.). (1987). Washington, DC: Author.

From, I. (1984). Reflections on Gestalt therapy after thirty-two years of practice: A requiem for Gestalt. *The Gestalt Journal, VII*, 4–12.

Gleick, J. (1987). *Chaos*. New York: Viking.

Latner, J. The kingdoms of experience. *The Gestalt Journal, VII*, 84–109.

Melnick, J., & Nevis, S. (1987). Power, choice and surprise. *The Gestalt Journal, IX*, 43–51.

Milan, T. (1981). *Disorders of personality, DSM III: Axis II*. New York: Wiley.

Miller, M. J. (1985). Some historical limitations of Gestalt therapy. *The Gestalt Journal, VIII*, 51–54.

Perls, F. S., Heifferline, R. F., & Goodman, P. (1951). *Gestalt therapy*. New York: Julian Press.

Polster, E., & Poster, M. (1973). *Gestalt therapy integrated*. New York: Brunner/Mazel.

Tobin, S. (1982). Self-disorder, Gestalt therapy & self psychology. *The Gestalt Journal, V*, 3–44.

Tobin, S. (1985). Lacks and shortcomings in Gestalt therapy. *The Gestalt Journal, VIII*, 65–71.

Wallen, R. (1957). *Gestalt therapy and Gestalt psychology*. Paper presented at the Ohio Psychological Association meeting 1957.

Yontef, G. (1983). The self in Gestalt therapy: Reply to Tobin. *The Gestalt Journal, VI*, 55–70.

Zinker, J. (1977). *Creative process in Gestalt therapy*. New York: Brunner/Mazel.

Zinker, J., & Nevis, S. M. (1981). *The Gestalt theory of couple and family interactions*. Working paper, Center for the Study of Intimate Systems, Gestalt Institute of Cleveland.

3

Gestalt Therapy Over Time: Integrating Difficulty and Diagnosis

NORMAN SHUB, M.S.W., B.C.D

AN INTRODUCTION
TO A LONGITUDINAL MODEL

"THE PRESENT IS A PASSAGE OUT OF THE PAST TOWARD THE FUTURE, AND THESE ARE THE STAGES OF AN ACT OF SELF AS IT CONTACTS THE ACTUALITY." *(Perls, 1951.)*

GESTALT THERAPY IS A PRESENT centered experience, so why the need for a longitudinal model? The answer lies in the observation that too many times the Gestalt therapist is fixed upon the present Gestalt, and its qualities and can't see beyond to the deeper patterns of behavior. The purpose of a longitudinal model is to attempt to create a generalized road map, one shared in part by the client. A road map in which the way towards the future seems visible in dim outline form yet continues to be shaped and changed by the present. The need for this model doesn't mitigate the theory of causality central to the Gestalt theory. (See Perls, 1951, ch. V, p. 2.) The model merely broadens the viewpoint of the therapist to take into account more of the ground of their past therapeutic experiences.

There are OTHER factors that must be considered in understanding the need for this model. They include:

1. *Providing a new common language to discuss process over time.* The model provides a general framework for understanding our common experiences as therapists over longitudinal time. Having such a model would provide a definite common language for Gestalt therapists to speak about their ongoing experience during the progress of the therapeutic encounter. This language is particularly helpful in talking about goals, experiences and problems as the therapist moves through parts or phases over the longitudinal time of the psychotherapeutic process.

2. *Enhancing the internal integrity of the therapist.* As we have noted, above, a frequent trap for Gestaltists is to become preoccupied with the intricacies of the present figure and to view, in a superficial way, the more complex dilemmas of the client. Having internal guideposts, as dim and illusory as these are, helps to remind the therapist to look deeper into the process of the present to see larger patterns, to make those patterns important and to STICK with the ongoing attempt to change patterns.

3. *To teach boundaries for what is essentially boundariless.* Having a model with distinct phases allows the therapist to learn to maximize and contain the energy of the process and to economize the therapeutic experience over time. In this day of insurance companies, limits of coverage, etc., it is in the client's best interest to be able to limit work in a particular area if possible and maximize the therapeutic benefits over time.

4. *To enhance and heighten our awareness of patterns.* As we have noted above, looking for the deeper pattern, the broader perspective has been somewhat of a problem for Gestaltists. To avoid the superficial, the unimportant, the therapist must train him or herself to see, evaluate, explore and ENLARGE patterns without losing the creative power of the present—the moment. Thinking longitudinally *encourages pattern awareness* and adds to the therapeutic ground.

5. *The need for repetitive and systematic work.* One of the most important implications of longitudinal thinking is the importance of dealing with difficult phenomena in a systematic and repetitive manner. Too often the excitement of the moment wins out over the need for repetitive work with the deeper or more embedded patterns of behavior. Having a map or even illusory guideposts helps keep in mind that we need to be going somewhere. To move forward we must work systematically to integrate the deeper blocks, and that requires patient effort. In the case of a strong introject or in

the example of a rigid character, systematic, repetitive therapeutic experiences are absolutely necessary to loosen what is deeply lodged.

Finally, the longitudinal view of therapy over time can seem to quiet the anxiety of a new therapist by providing an opportunity to use a form until that form or model is no longer needed.

A PHASIC APPROACH

This developing longitudinal model of therapy over time is divided into three phases: early, middle and late. Each phase includes general themes for work in that specific phase. These themes also point to specific patterns which might be present and require systematic work in that phase. Having specific phases promotes intellectual honesty about what is going on and where one is. It also serves to focus therapeutic emphasis.

INITIAL PHASE

The early phase has to do with evaluation, teaching awareness and contact skills, working at the interpersonal boundary and developing the beginning themes of the therapeutic process. In diagnostic phenomena where blocks to the development of awareness and contact skills are great, (as in character problems, borderline phenomena fragment personality and psychosis) the initial phase requires long term systematic emphasis as the blocks to the development of those skills are dealt with. (See chapter 9 on Gestalt therapy with psychotics.)

MID PHASE

In the mid phase, the therapeutic context is developed and family of origin or identity/alienation (Perls, 1947) issues are paramount. In diagnostic phenomena, where the introject/projection system is the strongest impediment to enhancing contact, systematic work is highlighted and necessary. The mid-phase focus is upon expansion of SELF, reowning lost or disowned parts and creating an approach to life which underscores the need for constant expansion.

LATTER PHASE

In a situation where there is no initial phase block or strong introject system, the latter or growth phase is emphasized. This phase is especially important for those individuals who come to therapy for learning and growth. The latter phase also highlights relationships with others and issues of self support (termination).

These phases are meant as road maps to be used in conjunction with diagnostic information, to measure one's own progress and highlight the need for more systematic approaches. While the phases are illusory markers along the way of an unchartable journey, they can be helpful in setting up changeable models of the present. (See Figure 3-1.)

While we describe these phases as equal segments on a horizontal line: beginning ———→ middle ———→ latter, they are more clearly visualized as three giant balloons whose shape and forms are incredibly malleable.

Visualizing each phase as a balloon of various size allows the therapist to take into account

1. Time
2. Effort
3. The need for systematic work
4. The realistic qualities of one phase as it compares and relates to another
5. Constant attention to the shape of the phase being changed by the unfolding present experience

This conceptualization of the phases of this model discourages recipe ways of looking at therapy over time, yet provides the therapist an opportunity to create a *unique* one-time only internal model to help keep him or her on track. While we believe that each therapeutic experience over time includes all phases, the actual duration of the phase is completely varible.

INITIAL PHASE

The initial phase of therapy (see Figure 3-2) includes evaluation, teaching awareness and contact skills and formulating a therapy contract. The initial phase in cases where there are deeply embedded patterns (such as in one example below) require a commitment to making oneself fully available and to prepare oneself for a long term systematic effort.

In cases where the blocks to contact are more primitive, (Zinker, 1977), relating to a specific disruption of the contact cycle) much more time is spent

Therapy with a schizoid personality might look like this:

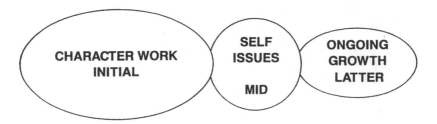

while a borderline personality might appear like this:

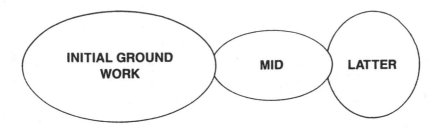

and a phobic individual like this:

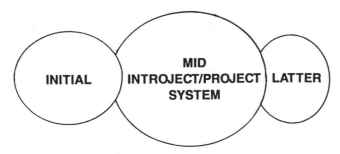

You will notice from these diagrams that the shape and relative size of the balloons are not uniform.

Figure 3-1

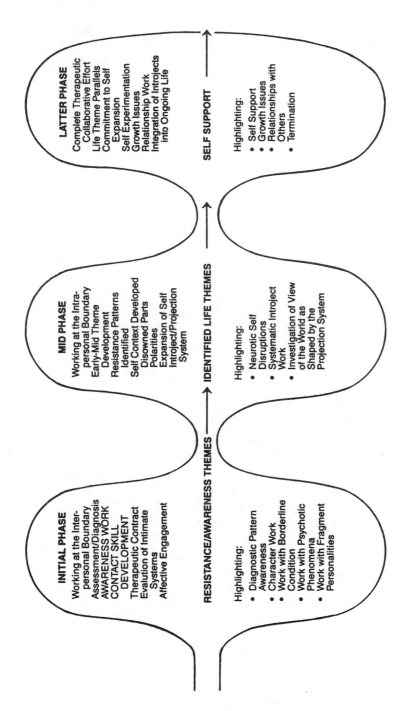

Figure 3-2
The Phases of Ongoing Therapy Over Time

in preparing the individual for awareness work. In the case of a borderline individual, the initial stage may and will encompass a large portion of the therapy over many years. As we explore the interface of specific diagnostic phenomena with this model the nature and duration of the phase and sub-phases will become clearer.

The model presented here uses the construct of diagnoses to give some direction and structure to the Gestalt process over time. Melnick and Nevis in Chapter 2 present an excellent introduction to using the cycle of experience to develop a diagnostic paradigm. As Latner, (see Chapter 1) points out, this search for a diagnostic nosology is one of the most important challenges that face Gestalt therapists today. It is clear that any attempt at a diagnostic paradigm must be centered upon understanding the disruptions in the contact cycle and translating these into terms which can interface with the general therapeutic community. Using the developing diagnostic nosology in conjunction with this model clearly demonstrates the theoretical comprehensiveness and power the Gestalt therapy brings to the arena of human behavior.

To have validity, a theoretical system (Kuhn, 1971) must be applicable to the set of individuals being covered by the theory. Clearly these attempts are moving the Gestalt approach much more powerfully in the direction of comprehensiveness. An example of this interface between model and diagnostic paradigm is the treatment of a difficult long term personality (which we will call character from this point forward) problem. This type of phenomena is a particularly apt example because of the degree of difficulty required in promoting change over time.

In his pioneering book on the treatment of personality disorders, Lion (1978, p. 337) notes, "There are several factors a student should keep in mind when studying personality disorders, first and foremost are personality disorders that are characterized by deeply *ingrained maladaptive* patterns of lifelong behavior . . .".

Lion (1978), Milan (1981) and others are somewhat pessimistic about the POSSIBILITIES for treatment of some character disorders. In our phase one work with character disorders, we have discussed an approach which demonstrates positive approaches for the treatment of character issues and is in keeping with Gestalt philosophy.[1]

THE INITIAL PHASE BEGINS

We have found that most of our patients come to Gestalt therapy with *little or no understanding* of the therapeutic process. They may have heard something about Gestalt therapy (often something theatrical and superficial) but many times in no way understand THEIR ROLE in the Gestalt process.

Preparing a patient to work on AWARENESS, preparing him intellectually to understand his/her role in the process, and deciding mutual expectations, are all part of the initial stage of Gestalt work. Therefore, in the early stages of therapy, there must be a strong, strong *commitment* to teaching patients basic awareness skills so they can begin their work on the continuum of awareness.

Learning contact skills describes the overall universe of skill development an individual uses to meet and experience the environment. Contact skills are the active expression of contact functions (see Polster & Polster, 1973). Contact skill development includes such examples as:

Learning to listen
Developing an enhanced ability to see clearly
Allowing yourself greater mobility
Exploring the skill of responding in different ways
Touching and kinesthetically sensing more deeply and fully
Being more aware of the taste of an object
Moving towards something rather than away from it.

Teaching basic AWARENESS/CONTACT skills is a critical yet sometimes underemphasized part of the Gestalt therapy process. As a supervisor and trainer of therapists, I have seen many clients perform *Phony Work*, going through the motions of therapy without genuinely owning, experiencing or exploring the process. The reason for phony work usually is the absence of emphasis by the therapist on learning basic contact and awareness skills. We cannot stress enough the necessity for focusing on these skills so that the "work" doesn't go on to be pointlessly circular.

The Gestalt literature is replete with various examples, explorations, and demonstrations of the initial teaching of the awareness process. Part one of Perls, Hefferline and Goodman (1951), clearly sets the stage for careful, precise experimental teaching of awareness.

In addition to teaching awareness skills, the beginning of the initial phase encompasses the following:

1. Initial evaluative contact is begun.

2. Awareness training begins. A contract is developed and the patient is *affectively engaged*.

3. General present centered diagnostic impressions and systemic impressions are formulated.

4. Diagnostic ideas formed are integrated into the phasic model in the present.

5. Awareness training and contact work continues and themes emerge.

It is intrinsic to the Gestalt process that all work begins with awareness, so that any opening experience always deals with the *current ability* of the patient to be aware. During the initial session (and this is true in an agency, hospital, and private practice) we use the current ability of the client as a diagnostic tool to determine a therapeutic direction. The patient comes in and sits down . . .

P: I am Jean Smith. Nice to meet you.

T: I am Norman Shub. Welcome. How are you feeling being here today (or right now)?

P: I am nervous. I don't know what to expect.

T: I am aware of your hands shaking.

P: . . . (doesn't answer)

T: (repeats statement) Your lips!

P: I just feel nervous, that's all!

T: Your heart . . .

P: (interrupts) Yes, my heart is beating very quickly.

Several things have already happened. I am clearly telling the patient that:

1. I am interested in what is happening now; and
2. I want you to pay attention to yourself.

This is my expectation. Awareness training and contact skill development has begun.

This brief description of an ongoing dialogue is but one of many ways to begin present centered work. This observation as a diagnosis tool is designed for more fully functioning individuals and is obviously too invasive for borderline or more fragile individuals, for example. The Gestalt literature is replete with examples of opening experiences which are designed to sensitively meet the client at the level they can comfortably begin at (Zinker, 132–133, 1977). Evaluation and diagnosis of present phenomena coupled with early phase work models such as those defined by Polster and Zinker (Polster, 1977; Zinker, 1978) encourages a clear, beginning awareness of the individual's boundaries. This evaluation process is a part of the internal road map described above.

This work can be done in any setting and within any framework. Our trainees who work in agencies and hospitals many times complain that they must take a history. Awareness training can be done while taking a history by beginning to call the patient's attention to what he or she is experiencing at any moment during the history.

T: While you told me about your income level, I noticed your jaw tightening.
P: Yeah, well, that boss of mine is a jerk.
T: Now your jaw seems to be tightening again.

The special present centered work of the early phase is a great strength of the Gestalt approach and one of its major contributions to the therapeutic world. Zinker (1977) has elaborated on specific approaches to working with individuals during the opening phases of therapy. Zinker suggests the therapists begin by:

> "Look at the person the way you would look at a sunset or at mountains. Take in what you see with pleasure. Take in the person for his own sake. After all, you would do that with the sunset also. Chances are you wouldn't say 'This sunset should be more purple' or 'These mountains should be taller in the center.' You would simply gaze with wonder. So it is with another person. I look without saying, 'His skin should be more pink' or 'His hair should be cut shorter.' The person is. The creative process begins with one's appreciation of what is there—the essence, the clarity, and the impact of what is around us."
> (Zinker, 1977, page 22.)

Tracking, grading, contact/awareness experiments including the plethora of those developed in Perl's early work provide a wonderful framework and many early phase openings for ongoing therapy. The process of moving from awareness/contact training to early theme development involves beginning where the person is and identifying and starting to weave the strands that make up the therapeutic tapestry. That is an art in itself. The more intense acting out or enactment experiments tend to be the property of mid-phase work while the wonderfully creative unfolding created by early awareness experiments is part of the unique contribution of the Gestalt approach to a historical early phase therapeutic work.

The example we will use here illustrating early phase work, is not illustrative of a typical therapeutic beginning. This example is illustrative of a more difficult characterological interior and is used to demonstrate the breadth of the Gestalt approach.

Jim comes to therapy at the request of his wife Marsha. He relates that she is never happy with him because he is so 'distant'. After doing some initial awareness work with Jim, I determine that he has a schizoidal character structure. Jim reports not 'feeling bad' and he really doesn't know why he came in except to get his wife off of his back. Jim is not in pain and seems to have little interest in cooperating or being in the session. He doesn't 'feel much' and thinks this 'therapy stuff is a waste of money'.

As we have noted above, in the cases where there is deeply embedded patterned behavior, the individual is continually stuck in a primitive position on the cycle of experience. In order to engage Jim and encourage his participation in the therapeutic process, we shift over to what we call systematic character work. This approach is designed, through repetitive experiences, to help individuals to experience his/her character structure in the present.

The treatment of character problems requires as a first stage the AWARE-NESS of the character structure. When a client comes in to therapy who: 1) lies, 2) is insensitive and 3) is highly manipulative (sociopathic, for example) our first goal is to help him/her become aware of the impact of this character structure on themselves, others, and the world at large.

As we confront the character of the individual, they then begin to see how rigid and limiting their way of life is. As Perls has noted (Perls, 1947), "In a rigid character we see that the Ego-Functions cease almost completely as the personality has become conditioned to habits and behavior automatically."

As we work specifically to bring the character structure into awareness, the individual begins to realize that they are dealing with the world over and over again in the same negative way. For them, this approach to life is causing them to be optionless and possibly causing others great pain. Out of this creative awareness comes the desire to be different and move forward to do the type of work Nevis and Melnick propose in Chapter 2 with the histrionic character.

It is important to note here that in our Character Treatment Program, we differentiate between:

1) character disorders;
2) borderline condition;
3) fragmented personalities.

The description of work here relates to the category of phenomena we define as character disorders. Each character structure is different and requires different degrees of sensitivity, relationship and awareness for the character picture to become clear to the individuals.

In situations where the individual is more fragile, where for example, the character structure overlays a terrified view of the world, appropriate ground work, attention to boundaries, grading and tracking (Zinker, 1977, 132–133) are all important considerations in designing the character work intervention. The word "confrontation" does not necessarily imply intensity or aggression. The character confrontation, like all Gestalt work, is done with sensitivity, gentleness and the greatest respect for the integrity of the individual's boundaries.

Each character phenomena—histrionic, obsessive compulsive, infantile, avoidant, etc., has its unique core traits, including a specific view of the world, and the concommitant character picture is developed understanding these limitations and concerns.

In order to make Jim aware of these deeply embedded lifelong patterns the therapist must see beyond the present figure and become aware of and bring to the present the client's character picture before anything else can happen. Since this chapter is not about character work per se, we will only briefly discuss this first stage process to heighten awareness of the character structure and to encourage experimentation with the rigid core traits.

We have to this point:

1. Made some therapeutic contact with Jim;
2. Evaluated the contact and awareness skill and developed a feeling about where this work needs to go;
3. We have done a systems evaluation and decided that the character work needed to pre-date any marital experiences;
4. We have begun awareness training and;
5. Are attempting to use the development of the character picture as the early themes and a contract to work.

Out of the here and now encounter, I began to explore the part of the character structure which is the most rigid.

Jim was:
1. insensitive
2. ungiving
3. 'emotionally dead'—lack of feeling (by wife and self description)
4. disinterested in others

I began to draw the character picture by helping him to see what it is like to be in a relationship with a person who interacts with the world in this rigid manner. Only by helping Jim become aware of his character structure through repetitive, systemic work, can he begin to get the picture of himself and the impact of his behavior on others and as a result begin to want to learn new ways of relating with the world.

Throughout the process of character work, we see each trait on a continuum of experience, insensitive ——————— sensitive, ungiving ———————— giving. (We explore, through systematic experimentation, the development of greater flexibility of options for being at any of these points between the poles.) The focus here is on the rigidity of the character structure—not good or bad traits. The goal is to promote flexibility and more options on each continuum through systemic experimentation. Once Jim is engaged, has made a contract to work on his character, and owned the character picture, we begin systematically to experiment with each trait individually to allow him to explore being different in the world.

Character work includes:

A. Identification of the general character picture;
B. Trait identification;
C. Intensification of the character picture—feeling the impact on others more profoundly;
D. Trait polarization—seeing the continuum;
E. Trait experimentation and expansion—exploring different parts on the continuum through systemic experimentation;
F. Greater flexibility;
G. Transition to traditional process.

Once Jim and I "opened up" his rigid character somewhat, we were ready to move on towards the mid-phase of therapy (issues regarding self, self esteem, self approval, that were emerging from his work in the present moment).

The character work with Jim took several years of consistent, patient, systematic work. At the end of the initial phase, Jim had a whole new set of themes regarding himself that he wanted to work with. As in the example of the borderline client in Chapter 2 and the psychotic client in Chapter 9, as well as with Jim, the first phase of treatment, developing contact and awareness, can be immensely difficult and have many subtexts and substages.

As the character structure becomes more flexible the client's own self-identification issues (the neurotic phase) tend to emerge and thus the transition to the mid phase of therapy begins.

MOVING TOWARDS MID PHASE

As Jim's first phase character work ends, he moves on to new work as other themes begin to emerge for the first time:
—Yeah, I am angry with my boss and I can't tell him.
—I am always nervous in new situations. I am scared of people.
—I still don't know what I feel most of the time.

In a non-modified Gestalt process over time these themes become part of the contract to work in the therapeutic situation. They provide an initial framework for the client *to come to terms with an unstructured situation* and have some understanding of where he or she is going. In the model presented here, our diagnosis would lead to a modification which structures the work.

The therapeutic contract is a clear agreement between the therapist and patient that he/she wants to engage in Gestalt work based on: 1.) the experience of the first sessions; 2.) the general themes which have emerged; and, 3.) the feeling the patient has about the therapist.

The last item is extremely important. Gestalt therapy is an encounter between a patient and therapist, and the therapeutic relationship is the medium for growth. There must be some affective recognition of this relationship in order to really engage the patient in the therapeutic process. We define affective engagement as an ability to sense the growing contact possibilities between the patient and the therapist. If there isn't this kind of potential for transactions, then the patient isn't engaged and little will happen. This is what I mean by development of a contract based on good contact between therapist and patient.

In the course of getting general diagnostic and systematic impressions and in negotiating a contract, the therapist determines the nature of the possible relationship between therapist and patient. On the one hand the therapist points out and encourages anxiety producing experiences, and on the other, the patient must feel safe enough to venture forth into new unexplored territory.

Much of the early phase work is working at the contact skill/awareness training, interpersonal boundary level. The experiments and experiences explored during this phase may create a framework for more intensive interpsychic exploration or may become the framework for intensive work as in the example of the characterologic phenomena presented here.

This, then, is the early phase of Gestalt work. In every case, a contract has been developed based on themes that naturally emerge or upon themes generated from the directed identification of the diagnostic phenomena. As a part of this process, the patient and I begin to see the therapy in the context of present life, past experiences, and future aspirations. The next phase of the model, the middle phase, begins the process of exploration of self expansion so powerful in the traditional Gestalt approach. Movement into the middle phase of therapy presupposes the individual's ability to work on awareness, as described above, and this is not possible without the work in the early phase.

MIDDLE PHASE

For some clients, the initial stages of therapy can be brief. Assuming no major diagnostic phenomena requiring interpersonal, intense phase one work, the client quickly moves into "the work" of Gestalt therapy, exploring and experimenting with the boundaries of his/her ability to deal with the world. It is here that the creative process of the Gestalt approach is again evident as the client begins to experience feeling, behaviors, and parts of self that have been put aside during previous times. It is here that the client begins to see him—herself more clearly and to experiment with new ways of experiencing the self in the world.

The structure, function and use of the experiment and/or experimental thinking (trying the novel) is an integral part of the Gestalt approach. It is and can be used from the first moment onward. Zinker (1977), Polster (1973) and others have beautifully described the creative power of the methodology involved. The spontaneous, and limitless store of experiments cannot be described or quantified. Suffice it to say, by the mid phase of therapy the therapist and patient can become partners in designing and carrying out experiments which continue the process of mid phase exploration of self. In simple terms, the initial phase looks at "how am I?" and the mid phase at taking the "how am I?" and figuring out my way of expressing that "how?" in the environment, the self. The mid phase is also concerned with the primary and intrapsychic blocks to that expression of self in the world.

During this phase, the "ongoing themes related to self", become clear. I begin to see myself more clearly as I am now, the introjected beliefs from the past that are getting in the way are evidenced. It is this author's belief that the introject/projection system always needs to be explored during the course of therapy. This usually takes place during the middle phase.

Theme development is the process by which the several strands of the initial phase grow into the complex picture of seeing and experiencing myself as I am now. As the theme unfolds, the self picture becomes more and more clear until the self context begins to be developed. As I begin to experience myself more clearly and profoundly, I also begin to see the process by which the blurred spots in the therapeutic tapestry (Perls worksheet of roles in the personality) become clearer and a fuller tapestry emerges. This unsystematic process of theme exploration and experimentation underlies the early part of the mid phase.

Jerry comes into therapy complaining of being slightly depressed and concerned regarding his upcoming marriage. During the early phase work with him, we create the following:

1. Jerry developed better contact skills, particularly around listening.
2. No major diagnostic problems present themselves.
3. During some of the preliminary early phase work, the following themes *BEGAN* to emerge:

    a. Jerry "has trouble getting angry".
    b. He never feels "good enough".
    c. Jerry took his present job because his father told him to and is "resentful" of that fact. Jerry has his own ideas about jobs.
    d. Jerry loves his fiancee but doesn't want to disappoint her the way he feels he has many other significant people in his life.

These themes become the contract to continue his therapeutic work with me.

During the early phase work, much effort was made to improve basic contact skills, attention was paid to enhancing contact functions while the context of Jerry's concerns were defined in some way as themes for mid-phase work. As Jerry's awareness increased and his ability to work at the interpersonal boundary improved, we began to move into the mid phase of his therapy.

As the therapeutic process unfolded, deeper themes began to emerge from regained awareness. As contact functions were restored, major patterns of resistance became even clearer than they were during first phase work.

T: What are you aware of now?
J: (looking sad) I am feeling sad. My father really was like that.
T: Go on.
J: (looking sadder—eyes beginning to tear) I am remembring a time when he grabbed me by the shirt and threw me down. (Jerry now deeply sighs—his tears stop and he turns to me.)
T: You don't look sad anymore.

Some retroflections, (see Latner, Chapter 1) were observed during early phase work but as we began to experimentally move into the mid phase, retroflective patterns began to emerge. Whenever we approached working on an important theme, Jerry constantly retroflected (Perls, 1947) to deaden his affect, block deeper contact, and slow down the work. Together, we found that this major resistance pattern emerged over and over again when we tried to develop sensitive themes. This resistance pattern was owned and worked with by Jerry and integrated more fully into the self, thus facilitating better contact between us.

The ability to develop and identify strong themes is an integral part of the Gestalt process. Some themes are brief and are only played once; some are repeated again and again in variation throughout the course of therapy. These major themes we call life themes and will discuss them further below.

As the work with Jerry progressed and he became more aware of himself, he began to realize how difficult it was for him to express anger due to the beliefs about anger and his fears about the impact of his anger on others.

J: I saw my father yesterday and he started up on that same old thing about my marrying Paula—not Jewish—this and that. I told him that really makes me mad. (Jerry explained this in a very monotonic voice—little affect).

T: Your voice, Jerry . . . It sounds . . .

J: Dead.

T: Yeah, and your hand . . .

J: (squirming and opening his hand) I am making a fist. I'd like to squeeze a little of that self-righteousness out of him. (Jerry's voice gradually rising . . .)

T: Out of . . .

J: My dad! (swallowing) I am sick of him telling me what to do and not to do. I hate it when he talks about Paula, but I just can't fight him.

T: But . . .

J: But . . . but . . . I know your buts! (voice really rising now) But nothing! I am angry!

T: I am angry at . . .

J: (gulping air then . . . all of a sudden calming down . . . flat again . . .) I am angry at my dad; but I won't be disrespectful to him.

At this point, Jerry and I began to work with the retroflective pattern which was blocking deeper contact with his anger. Working with a theme is frequently like attempting to unravel a ball of yarn. One never knows where it will stop, get stuck, or lead to.

In the example we have given above regarding Jerry's anger, the exploration of this theme leads to several other strands of yarn tied up in the anger theme.

T: You want to be angry with your father . . .

J: I am going to tell you something I have never told anyone else. When I was eleven years old, I caught my father having sex with someone who works for him. I saw him in the basement of our plant, and I ran upstairs. He never said a thing about it, but he knows that I saw. I felt like killing him, really. Many times after that I knew what he was doing . . . I never said a thing.

As the retroflection becomes less of a block and Jerry's anger begins to emerge in the session, it becomes clear that his *BELIEF* about expressing his anger and the hurt it will cause is interfering with his ability to be angry in the world.

As the anger emerges, the therapeutic tapestry begins to become more clear. The belief system interfering with the development of a more beautiful, full tapestry also becomes more clear.

As Jerry's work continued, he began to see and experience himself in the world more and more clearly in both positive and negative ways. The theme development allows the unfinished Gestaltan (see Chapter 1) of the past to emerge and become a part of the past in the present picture.

Jerry began to explore these themes and he began to see more clearly his self context in the present.

MID PHASE—SELF WORK I
THE CONTEXT

"Identification" as described by Perls in *Ego, Hunger and Aggression*, 1947, is explored in mid phase. According to Perls, "The Ego (self) for instance, as I intend sharing later, should not be a conglomerate of introjections, but a *FUNCTION*. To achieve a proper functioning of the personality, one has to dissolve these introjects."

Perls rightfully points out that Freud didn't recognize this important ego function. "Thus, I agree with Freud that the Ego is closely related to identification. Freud, however, overlooks the one fundamental difference between the healthy and the pathological Ego. In the healthy personality, identification is an Ego-function, whereas the pathological "Ego" is built up of introjections (substantial identifications) which determine the personality's actions and feelings, and limit their range. Super-Ego and Ego-Ideals invariably contain a number of permanent, partly unconscious, identifications. But the Ego becomes pathological if its identifications are permanent instead of *functioning* according to the requirements of different situations, and *disappearing* with the restoration of the organismic balance."

The process of developing self then has to do with the need for introjection and assimilation. If the introject system becomes rigid or fixed, this is a pathological ego. It is this process which is more thoroughly explored in the mid phase.

If integration has to do with the developing sense of self (Perls, et al, 1951, page 341), projection has to do with the way we see the world. Like introjects, projections can be positive or negative. However, the projection system which results from the introject group helps to shape one's view of the world. This hand-in-glove fit, beginning awareness of the way we see the world as it relates to the emergence of our beliefs, is the ground for the mid phase. By projecting we change our view of the world, possibly based upon negative beliefs (Perls, et al, 1951, page 237). The introjection/projection system then requires not only the integration of unassimilated introjects, but the assimilations of projection, which color the experiential field.

By the mid phase of therapy, enough work has been done, enough awareness restored and contact encouraged that the therapist and patient can become the partners in designing and carrying out experiments to further this exploration of self. Both therapist and patient use the philosophy of experimental thinking to define the process to move forward.

Understanding what we call the "context" is also an aid to exploring the projection/introjection system. The context or self picture is made up of the environment and people from which the introject system developed and is developing in. This includes the family of origin, early influential institutions and all other significant people (parents), events, experiences, etc. It also includes the projected view of the world which is a reflection of the introjected self and the unassimilated parts of the personality in the negative sense.

This unsystematic unfolding gives the patient and the therapist a chance to build together and explore the self context in the *PRESENT*. As the initial themes identified in the early mid-phase of therapy are explored, they lead to a fuller understanding of how a patient is currently experiencing his life and what unfinished material exists.

The development of this context is not a deliberate process, but evolves naturally and slowly out of the earlier theme work. As the reader can see from an examination of Figure 3-3, the development of therapeutic self context is the transitional phase to deeper introject/project work—and happens concurrently as themes are explored and deeper work begins. However, a full and clear exploration of the self context maximizes the therapeutic experience.

As we have noted above, the context develops gradually out of the theme work and provides the affective network to support the deeper introject/project work.

MID PHASE—SELF WORK II INTROJECT/PROJECT SYSTEM

A central issue in the process of restoring contact skills in order to have a fuller life is removing the major blocks to the development of awareness. In the model we are presenting here, one of the essential elements of this

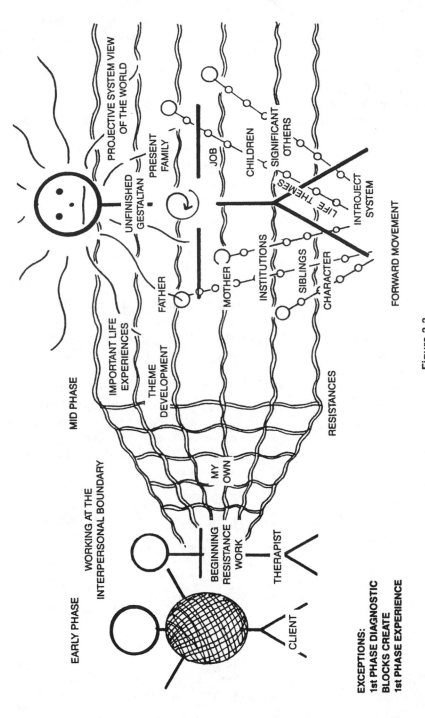

Figure 3-3

SELF CONTEXT SEEING AND EXPERIENCING MYSELF IN A DIFFERENT WAY

process is to more fully integrate the introject/project system, which is alive in the self and can continually block expansion into the environment and thus inhibit the process of identification and *self-development*.

Gestalt therapy began as a serious attempt to move away from the normative process of psychoanalysis and, as Goodman (1977) states, to ''Be yourself, instead of know yourself.'' The goal was to allow the natural organismic process to be the healing needed for the individual to regain, naturally, disowned parts of his/her personality. The second important factor in the equation is the restrictive nature of the social forces on our own ability to live freely in society.

A negative introject is, for our purposes, more operationally identified as a belief, idea, or feeling in relation to the self (or the self in relationship to others) which interferes with the individual's ability to positively and freely contact the environment. Obviously, all of us have an introject system whose manifestations are projections into the world which help organize our behavior and structure our lives. This model of Gestalt therapy over time hypothesizes that the collective phenomena which develops as a result of negative introjects form the core of the neurotic's misery and inhibit the ability to freely contact the environment. Thus, integration and control of this introject system becomes crucial in work with neurotic patients and in promoting greater freedom in and for society as a whole.

Understanding the projected view of the world is also vitally important in working with the neurotic self. This view is made up of both positive and negative introject/projections which help to form the perceived view of the experimental field. The concept of 'view of the world' we identify as having five sources:

1. perception of what is and what was
2. projection of unacceptable parts of self
3. projection of acceptable parts of self (including wishes, thoughts, etc.)
4. projection of *strong, powerful negative introjects*
5. projection of positive introjects.

As Perls has noted (*Ego, Hunger, Aggression*, p. 241), ''After the first step of realizing the existence of projections and secondly of recognizing them as belonging to your own personality, you have to assimilate them . . . if you merely introject the project, you only increase the danger of becoming a paranoic. Therefore, you must get to the nucleus—the source of the projection.''

It is clear from our discussion of introjection that a part of the process of developing one's own view of the world is the introjected view of the family of origin. When the view of world becomes fixed, rigidified, then the negative projections are predominately causing the individual to see the world over and over again in the same way. The goal here is to identify and assimilate these powerful negative projections which rigidify the view of the world.

As the fixed view becomes more open, 1.) the individual can see the external world more clearly 2.) the patient can express his/her self more clearly 3.) the unacceptable parts of the personality comes more into awareness 4.) and the introjects that are the source of some projections emerge.

The rigid view of the world can be the veil which shrouds the therapeutic self context. In the neurotic self, the projected part of the project/introject system obfuscates the self. The projections that make up the veil are like strings in a ball of yarn, and as each is worked back (or through) and assimilated more and more is learned about the self and the therapeutic context.

As we noted above, the projection system can obscure the individual's seeing and experiencing his/her true self and obscure deeply introjected beliefs. Learning to work with projection is a part of the art of psychotherapy, especially Gestalt psychotherapy.

The difficulty in identifying projections is discussed by Perls in *Ego, Hunger and Aggression* (p. 239). Here, Perls strives to describe in Gestalt terms the complex types that projections can manifest. The process of work with projections includes:

1. identification of the projection
2. supporting it (allowing it to fully emerge)
3. exploring the differences between what is self and what is other
4. owning it (emotionally and intellectually)
5. assimilation

Many examples of this type of work are described in the existing Gestalt literature and will not be further described here. The reader is particularly encouraged to examine (or re-examine) Perls, Hefferline and Goodman (Part I, Chapter VIII) for numerous examples of the work. Finally, learning to work with projections is many times like finding the thread that begins to unwind a complicated spool which seemed at first too tangled to straighten out, but all of a sudden becomes clear.

Sally is a forty-two year old woman who comes to therapy because she is depressed about her twenty year old son who is constantly in trouble with the police and still lives at home. Sally reported being raised in a family where her mother was very nervous. "I always was careful not to upset her and give her a headache.'' (Projection of unassimilated introject.) Sally's father told Sally, ''Your responsibility is to make sure that you don't upset your mother, and further, to make sure that your sisters and brothers don't either.'' Sally felt responsible for her mother's well being and during most of her childhood worked hard at being a good girl and taking care of her mother.

Sally spent her childhood years acting out the projected/introjected message she got from her father, 'It is your job in life to be responsible for the health and happiness of others' (an impossibility, as we all know). She continually projected upon others her preoccupation with their physical and mental well being. She was unaware of her own deep concern for her own well being.

Sally got married at 18 years of age to escape the trap of her home life and started taking care of her husband. He eventually separated from her and divorced her, leaving Sally with a young son to take care of. At the time Sally entered therapy the son was acting out, attempting to emancipate from his mother who was trying to take care of his physical and mental well being and ignoring her own. Sally's significant relationships and contact experiences were distorted by the powerful introject she took in from her father. In a supervision session with Sally's therapist, I pointed out that until the introject was fully dealt with, Sally would continue to repeat the same behaviors. I also pointed out that Sally has never experienced being taken care of, asking for support and getting it. (A projected wish.) The reality of the introject colored all of Sally's relationships and kept her isolated and lonely. Sally needed to understand, experience her own introject/projection, as well as their deeper manifestations.

As Sally and her therapist began to work at a deeper level on the introjected/projected material Sally became aware of:

1. her projected anger and other feelings toward her mother for being an ''emotional cripple and never mothering her'', i.e., being preoccupied with her emotional and physical health;

2. her anger at her father for casting her in the role of the caretaker;

3. once the projections were more assimilated, her sadness over the presumed absence of her childhood; and the excitement regarding the possibility of experiencing these childhood feelings in the present and regaining that part of self which was disowned;

4. her pain/joy relating to her loneliness and isolation resulting from her unwillingness to take and, therefore, never really feeling safe.

In Sally's attempt at dealing with this introject, she arrived at a point where she felt totally alone and unattached in the world. This occurred once she began to assimilate her projections regarding the need for care from her. At that point Sally was able to reach out to her therapist, ask for and receive support, attention, etc., and for the first time in her life feel moderately safe and cared for. She was also able to experience and appreciate the love and caring she did and did not feel from her parents, especially her mother.

As we move along with Sally, we can see the context of the therapy emerge and her excitement about the potential for expanding her boundaries into the environment. As the introjection/projection system becomes more clear and controlled the world ''opens up'' and Sally's view of the world begins to change.

SELF WORK III
INTROJECTS

As we have noted, an introject is a powerful message about a person or his/her life which was taken in unassimilated into the personality and is highly affectively charged and floating free in the self. Since the introject is unassimilated and highly affectively charged, it constantly emerges in contact episodes and directs the nature of the contact by limiting or structuring interactions.

As Sally attempts to develop a relationship with her son, the highly charged introjected/projected message (you must care for others) emerges and structures her contact experiences. The flexibility of the Gestalt therapeutic relationship allows the self to experience or re-experience in the deepest sense, these life themes in new ways (as the toxic introjects are integrated).

Of course, all of us have many introjects, most of which do not have a toxic effect on our lives by greatly prohibiting important contact experiences. In our model of Gestalt therapy we conceptualize three levels of introjects and concommitant projections.

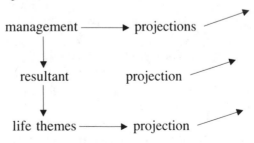

The management introjects are the ones which structure the day to day management of our lives.

—don't eat with your fingers
—drink fluids when you are sick
—be on time
—wear boots or rubbers when you go out in the snow
—be polite

These introjects influence our contact experiences and are considered *negative* only if they block full contact. Always feeling the need to "be on time" could, of course, produce problems in free flowing contact experiences.

Resultant introjects are developed as a result of *life themes* (life themes are the most powerful, most affectively charged and deepest of the introjects). These messages either enhance contact, have no effect, or become toxic inhibitors, depending on their nature, the degree of charge or the context they emerge within. In Sally's case the life theme of taking care of others produced many resultant introjects:

a. having fun isn't important
   (I take other people seriously)
b. life is very serious
   (I care a great deal about people's lives)
c. I always have to be careful not to hurt anyone
d. never say negative things, etc.
e. I must work hard

The resultant introjects make up a complicated system of rules which govern our emotional lives. The same introjected system which prompts Sally to take in stray animals also encourages her to interfere in the lives of the children of her friends. The parameters of these systems, when fully integrated, provide a kaleidoscope of life experiences—constantly changing. When parts are disowned or unassimilated, the kaleidoscope gets stuck at one configuration.

These resultant introjects provide the therapeutic access to the life theme in the Gestalt process. As the life theme surfaces, the patient regains behaviors and feelings which were disrupted by the potency of the introject and the projections in the present life. Life themes are the central core introjects which can block the individual's attempt to expand into the environment and grow. These introjects affect an individual's life, from physical appearance, posture and breathing, to the nature of their interpersonal relationships.

Sally's negative/positive life theme we are examining in this example are:

1. I need to take care of everyone else.
2. I will never be taken care of.
3. Concern for others is paramount in my life, my work, etc.

During the initial therapy sessions, Sally's therapist remarked that her patient (Sally) reminded her (therapist) of a penitent waiting for absolution. Sally sat in her therapist's office with her hands folded prayerfully on her lap, sitting in an upright, rigid manner, discussing how she takes responsibility for others.

At work, Sally took responsibility for other employees, always being the one to stay late (and feeling secretly angry, of course). At home, she spent her time trying to take care of her son. In her relationships with men Sally always, as she noted, "tried hard to be nice but never seemed to get what she wanted".

As the introjected material was dealt with and the affect discharged, Sally began to feel freer to expand into the environment, by saying and doing things she felt prohibited from doing previously. FREEDOM as Paul Goodman (1977) would say.

The middle phases of the Gestalt process include: 1.) the development of themes which create the context and 2.) the work on the deeper introjected problems. We have found in our work with all patients where a significant neurotic introject/projection system exists, that the creativity and power of the therapeutic process is stunted.

In most unstructured therapeutic experiences, the introjects emerge naturally because of their impact on the therapeutic process. Our model over time tries to deal with situations where introjects are not an obvious part of the process. The model also helps to underscore the value of systematically working on introjects after the early phase of therapy has been adequately handled. In this way, the patient may be helped to gain a measure of control over his introjects and foster further integration. We have found that many times, powerful life theme introjects are *TOUCHED ON BUT NOT DEALT WITH IN A SYSTEMATIC ENOUGH MANNER TO ALLOW PATIENTS TO REALLY BEGIN THE INTEGRATION PROCESS ON THEIR OWN.*

In this model of Gestalt therapy over time, working with the life theme introject is one of the pivotal experiences in the therapeutic process. While it is clear that the life theme introjects will naturally emerge over and over in the process, it is not clear that they will be given the priority they deserve.

In Sally's work she became aware that she felt the need to keep rigidly to a time schedule, when during a therapy session she got up to leave in the midst of dealing with an intensely, emotional experience. When her therapist asked her if she was finished, she said no, but her time was up and she didn't want to infringe on anyone else's time.

T: Do you want to stay?
S: Yes, but my time is up—I should go.
T: Right now you feel . . .
S: Very, very sad; but, you have someone waiting out there, don't you?
T: What about you, Sally?
S: I can wait. I'll be O.K.
T: Is there anything you want before you leave?
S: Yes, but . . .

As Sally began to gain awareness of how she limited herself, she was eventually able to identify the life themes in question.

Sally has now gained some awareness of her life theme (responsibility for others). She is a full partner in the therapy as she has owned this theme and desires to move with it. The next stage of the work—helping her to integrate this more fully into her personality so she can gain control over it—is a difficult one.

Experiments of all types, visualizations, two-chairs work, acting out roles, small dramas, story telling, etc., all have and are being used in the process of integrating the life themes. Since these deeper introjects cover great pain, anger, etc., creative therapeutic approaches to their undoing are essential. Each patient's contact boundary configuration is different, and they consequently respond in different ways. The general guidelines presented below form a basis upon which the creative therapist can work these life themes.

I. STATE AND IDENTIFY THE INTROJECT AND DECIDE TO CHANGE OR GIVE IT UP

As in theme development, the patient must clearly identify the introject, be responsible for it, and express a desire to amend or change the life situation. Sally was eventually able to say, "I don't want to feel responsible for anyone else anymore."

II. IDENTIFY THE SOURCE OF THE INTROJECT/PROJECTION

We have found that it can be extremely important to frame work in terms of the source of the introject. Bringing the source of the introject into the present allows the affect connected with the source of the introject (and the resulting life experiences caused by it) to emerge. This ultimately allows the discharge of some of the affect surrounding the introject.

III. FRAMING AND WORKING THROUGH THE INTROJECT

In the case of Sally, the introject regarding responsibility was framed and worked through with the source—her father.

Sally eventually was able to imagine her father and deal directly in the present with the introject (visualizations in this case). By working with the introject framed by her father, she was ultimately able to direct the rage and sadness (engendered by the toxic introject) towards her father.

S: (with her eyes closed imagining her father) ''Dad, I am angry with you and hurt.'' (quietly crying) I am angry that I've lived all these years trying to do the impossible. Damn! Look where it's gotten me! I can't even take care of myself yet!

T: How do you feel now, Sally?

S: Angry, angry, angry! Goddammit! I am sick of taking care of him! (Rob, her son)

T: Tell your father that.

S: Dad, I am sick of taking care of Rob! I am sick of Mom! I am sick of you! I want to take care of myself for once!

T: Tell him what you are going to do now.

S: I am not going to listen to you anymore when I hear that voice (the identified introject) telling me to take care of him! I am going to ignore it! YOU HEAR? IGNORE IT!

T: Where are you now, Sally?

S: (Calming a bit—after a minute or two) I feel a little relieved.

Framing and working with the introject in terms of its source allows the maximum potency for discharging affect and gaining control over the life theme. Since it is very hard for all of us to confront parents, authorities and important institutions in our lives, this process is difficult. Working with the life themes also allows other discarded polar feelings, i.e. appreciation, tenderness, affection to be recognized, re-engaged and re-arranged.

It is important to identify and work with one introject at a time to allow the patient to have a clear experience. Many times as you approach the deeper life themes, all sorts of unintegrated material and affective experiences emerge, and it is easy to get lost and overwhelmed. The clearer and sharper the introject is, the more integrated it will become.

IV. EXPERIENCING THE EMERGENCE OF THE INTROJECT OUT-
SIDE OF THE THERAPEUTIC ENVIRONMENT

The goal of all introject work is to help the patient to begin to sense, on his/her own, when the introject in question begins to emerge in the self. Through the therapeutic work, the patient begins to be able to sense when the introject is emerging in his/her outside life. This happens naturally (or can be encouraged through experimentation, experiential homework and other forms of therapeutic experimentation not discussed here) as the patient begins to be aware of the emergence of the introject outside the therapuetic environment. As the individual becomes more fully aware of the introject, his/her feelings regarding that experience may intensify. The patient begins to see (introject), as Sally eventually did, how much the feeling arises and interferes with daily living and the projections which arise as a result of it.

As the individual becomes more fully aware of the emergence of the introject, he/she begins to experience it as something alien to *themselves*. This feeling becomes connected with the past external environment and is not connected to their present life experience. They begin to wonder:

1. why don't they feel good enough, since their grades are excellent; or
2. why don't they feel pretty, even though they receive a lot of attention from the opposite sex; or
3. why don't they trust, even though their friends have been there for them time and time again.

The introject comes to be seen as 1.) alien to the self, 2.) having come from some external experience, and 3.) having less power over the self.

As the individuals gain greater control over the introject, they can begin to make choices as to whether or not they want to listen to that alien voice in their head and control the projections which are manifest as a result of that voice.

We, many times, can give our patients' introjected voices names:

"Oh, the dummy is emerging again."

"It's time to be Superman."

"Your Scrooge is coming out."

We tend to nickname our introjects toward the latter phases of introject work when just the evocation of the name is enough to allow the patient to become aware of the introject and to gain control over its integration again. Choosing to ignore your Scrooge or Superman or Mr. Perfect is the process of integrating this alien concept into the self.

SELF WORK IV
INTROJECTION—INTEGRATION OF LIFE PARALLELS

As in theme development, it is essential that the patient emotionally and cognitively understands and experiences the parallel of the introjected message to his/her present life. As the introject becomes more integrated, the patient can anticipate the situation—in Sally's words, "My father's voice again, but this time I know what to do."

As Sally becomes more aware of her introject, she can:

1. become sensorily more aware when it emerges;
2. decide for herself on a moment to moment basis whether she will listen to "that voice again."
3. Sally can also begin to *understand* and come to terms with how the existence of this unassimilated introject/projection system affected and affects her life. After the brief piece of work presented above, Sally began to talk with her therapist about the life parallels to the work she had just completed. Sally gradually, over time, began to understand how the introjected experiences engendered numerous parallel experiences in her life. Understanding and exploring these life parallels helps the patient to integrate the introject more fully into the personality by being more fully aware of and anticipating potential situations where the weakened introject might interfere.

The working through of a life theme introject is a primary part of the therapeutic process and happens gradually over time. Many times, once identified, the life theme emerges again and again; each time the patient gains more control through awareness. These introjects are, of course, never eradicated (since nothing is ever given up) but ultimately come to play a much smaller part in an individual's contact experiences.

In summary then, the integration process of a life theme from the patient's point of view involves:

1. affective discharge;
2. sensorial awareness of the introject's effect on the patient's life situation;
3. understanding the scope of the introject's effect on the patient's life situation;
4. awareness of parallels from past experiences to present reality.

As the introject work continues, and the introject becomes weakened and more in Sally's control, the therapeutic work continues in the latter phase of therapy.

Thus the mid-phase guideposts have to do with the continued expansion of the self and maintaining this process by dealing with the introject/projective system. Once the therapist/client relationship has moved past that, the door is open to the latter or growth stage.

LATTER PHASE OF THERAPY

The line between middle and latter phases of therapy is difficult to define. As the introject/projection system is more fully integrated, excitement regarding the patient's future freedom of existence emerges and motivates curiosity about the latter phases of the therapeutic process.

As the middle phase winds down many individuals choose to leave therapy. This situation can reflect the absence of a commitment to the humanist/existential idea of unlimited potential of an individual to grow. If we can look at this process in somewhat of a systematic way, once the major blocks to awareness are more fully integrated, there is no limit to what can be explored or done in a rich Gestalt therapy relationship. To be fair, many clients see therapy as a way to reverse pain, "or do better in relationship", etc., and do not see Gestalt therapy as a medium for the growth of self. It is the commitment of the therapist and his/her integration of this ideal that makes this more possible.

Successfully working through the deeper life themes allows the therapeutic process to proceed to what I find to be the most exciting part of the Gestalt therapy-unlimited creative growth and experimentation. While growth and experimentation have been taking place throughout the work to this point, the integration of the toxic life themes really allows fuller growth experiences as the notion of greater freedom becomes more real.

As the introjects and deeper themes are dealt with, the patients usually find themselves in a somewhat confused and disorganized state since their view of what was possible was greatly limited. The rules (introjects) they have lived by for so long are not as powerful a force in their lives, and they usually report feeling a little lost.

In Sally's case once she had integrated the deeper introjects, she told her therapist, "Well, if I don't spend my life taking care of everyone else, what am I going to do, to be?" Thus, the dawning of the humanistic notion of unlimited choices.

Some of the major roadblocks to a fuller life have been somewhat removed, and now the door is open for fuller expansion into the environment. Changing the rules of what is allowed in one's life is a frightening experience. The therapeutic relationship developed in Gestalt work provides a place to experiment with new rules and to try out and get support for new experiences.

As Sally's work progressed she returned to some of the major themes that she had identified in the initial phase of her work. Since she felt more energetic and alive, she became excited about the feeling that she *could and would* move forward with the themes she chose to work on.

Sally chose to work on: 1. her personal power; 2. the development of her career; 3. her relationships with men; 4. her spirituality.

As she began to creatively explore her potential, her excitement and confidence grew and she felt more in control of her life.

The latter stage of therapy is one of "no limits." Since the Gestalt approach is a creative/experimental process, then anything can be experimented with or upon. Many times this phase of therapy is the longest and most rewarding to the patient. Both Zinker (1977) and Polster (1973) and others do a wonderful job exploring the powerfully creative potential of Gestalt therapy. Therapist and client become even more fully partners in the therapeutic process during the latter stage as many clients track, monitor, grade, and propose their own work and their own experiments.

Much of the present Gestalt literature is descriptive of work in this stage of the process, which is vitally important. Numerous examples of boundary expansion work are to be found. The notion of the experimental thinking, not explored here, is, of course, one formula for trying things differently. The experiment and experimental thinking and acting becomes a way of life for the patient in the latter phase of therapy as the client takes an experimental attitude towards life, looking forward to experiencing the novel.

Since the client is constantly learning and changing, the length of therapy is not at issue here. Rather than providing a solution to a problem, Gestalt therapy provides a way of looking at and discovering life as well as the tools to attempt this freedom from neurotic/limiting misery. In this era of "brief", "short term", problem related therapy, we must not lose sight of the fact that our goals, point of view, and methodology are very different. We are teaching freedom through awareness.

LATTER PHASE II
TERMINATION

Ending therapy, like beginning, can be difficult as well as exciting and liberating. For many patients the Gestalt therapy relationship has been one where they experienced and experimented with things they hadn't done in their lives to that point.

As we have discussed in the beginning of this chapter, the relationship between the patient and therapist in Gestalt work is a special one, and many times, an extremely intense one. Letting go of this relationship can be difficult/exciting for both patient and therapist.

In the model we are presenting here of Gestalt therapy over time, the patient and therapist many times arrive at the point of termination together. The patient feels that he/she has:

1. increased awareness;
2. more awareness and control of projection;
3. more control over introjects;
4. less unfinished business;
5. greater access to the changing environment;
6. greatly expanded many of their contact boundaries;
7. developed a new attitude and excitement towards living;
8. increased curiosity and desire to experiment with the novel and the confidence to do so.

At this point, Sally wanted to "try her wings and go off experimenting on her own"; and, Sally was able to say goodbye to her therapist.

Termination is unusually important in the latter stage of therapy because of the ending of a significant relationship rather than the fears of dependence in coping. We are working towards self-support, the ability to assimilate the novel and continue to take care of oneself. Therefore ending (which we are always aware of throughout the process) is the loss of a friend rather than removal of a necessary prop.

Termination in this model *doesn't* imply the end of therapy. It implies the end of this current relationship. The goals of the Gestalt approach include:

a. developing the skills to continually expand your ability to contact the environment.

b. developing an experimental view of the world where you feel free to continue to experiment with new ways of being and living.

c. developing continuing self-support, the inner ability to take care of oneself in a day to day life.

Therefore, in the truest sense, therapy doesn't end with end of therapy. The process continues just as the therapist continues to learn, change and grow.

This, then, is the model we use in our work with individuals over time. Of course, the therapeutic experience rarely unfolds as neatly and clearly as in this model, however, I find that many times in looking back on my work with someone, the work I have done generally follows the model presented here. Models are developed to learn, assimilate and then make one's own. Hopefully, this model will be used in those uniquely personal ways which make Gestalt therapists so different, yet operating from a common theory base.

BIBLIOGRAPHY

1. Davidove, Douglas Martin. *Theories of Introjection and Their Relation to William James' Concept of Belief: An Application of the Unitary Approach of Gestalt Therapy. New York University. 1980.*
2. Davidove, Douglas (1985). The Contribution of Paul Goodman. *The Gestalt Journal*, VIII, 1, 72–77.
3. Ferenczi, Sandor. "Freud's Group Psychology and the Analysis of the Ego", FINAL CONTRI-BUTIONS, 1955. New York: Basic Books, p. 371–376.
4. Goodman, Paul. NATURE HEALS, 1977, p. 48–50. New York: Free Life Editions.
5. Kuhn, Alexander. *The Structure of the Scientific Revolution*. Random House, 1971.
6. Lion, John R. *Personality Disorders: Diagnosis and Management*. Williams & Wilkins Co., 1974.
7. Masterson, J. F. *The Search for the Real Self*. New York: Free Press, 1988.
8. Milan, T. (1981). *Disorders of Personality, DSM-III: Axis II*. New York: John Wiley & Sons.
9. Perls, F. S. *Ego, Hunger and Aggression*. New York: Random House. 1947, 1969.
10. Perls, F. S., Hefferline, R. F., and Goodman, P. (1951). *Gestalt Therapy*. New York: Julian Press.
11. Polster, E. & Polster, M. (1973). *Gestalt Therapy Integrated*. New York: Brunner/Mazel.
12. Smith, E. L. *The Growing Edge of Gestalt Therapy*. New York: Brunner/Mazel, 1976.
13. Sussman, Henry. *The Hegelian Aftermath*. Baltimore, London: John Hopkins University Press, 1982.
14. Zinker, J. (1977). *Creative Process in Gestalt Therapy*. New York: Brunner/Mazel.

[1]*The Hegelian Aftermath*, Readings in Hegel, Kierkegaard, Freud, Proust, and James, by Henry Sussman, the Johns Hopkins University Press, 1982.

4

Gestalt Ethics

GORDON WHEELER, Ph.D.

I'm me and you're you. I'm not in this world to live up to your expectations, and you're not in this world to live up to my expectations. —Fritz Perls

Spontaneous dominances are . . . an immediate ethics, not infallible, and yet in a privileged position . . . —Paul Goodman

Man does not strive to be good; the good is what it is human to strive for. —Paul Goodman

Evil is simply error. —Socrates, as quoted by Paul Goodman

CLARIFYING FIGURE, DEVELOPING GROUND

WHAT IS A GESTALT ETHICS, a Gestalt system of values? Can we even speak meaningfully of such a thing, in a process methodology such as the Gestalt model, with its emphasis on questions of how, as opposed to what and why? Goodman and Perls explicitly sought a therapy that would "establish a norm as little as possible," preferring to draw on "the structure of the actual situation, here and now," for evaluative/diagnostic criteria of health and dysfunction (Perls, Hefferline, & Goodman, 1951, p. 329).[1] Does this mean, from a Gestalt theoretical point of view, that we are completely indifferent to questions of content, as long as certain healthy process criteria are satisfied? That is, are all processes equal, in the Gestalt view, as far as their intentions and outcomes are concerned? If and when we do bring our own value positions and concerns to bear on a clinical or other problem of intervention for change, is this something we do from some domain completely outside of and unrelated to Gestalt theory? If so, what is the nature of the boundary between those two domains, process and content? And what is it about that boundary that makes it so impermeable?

Or do we rather believe that certain contents, certain value positions, are incompatible by their very nature with healthy process as we understand it under the Gestalt model? And then that other stances, other ethical positions, or ranges of possible ethical positions, perhaps, are inherently favored in the Gestalt view, or even implicitly or explicitly contained in the Gestalt process model itself? In other words, can evaluative content criteria be somehow derived from process criteria (or conceivably vice versa)? And if so, then where in our theory should we look for such content implications, and such limiting (or joining) boundary conditions? How would we go about accounting for them, and what would they look like if we found them?

Now by ethics we simply mean any organized or systemic set ("systemic" meaning that the various parts are affected by each other, and by the whole) of *values*—where "value" is understood to mean an *established preference* for particular behaviors, or sets of behaviors, under some given range of circumstances, *without regard for immediate outcome of the behavior or considerations of personal satisfaction or pleasure*, other than the resolution or satisfaction of that ethical gestalt itself. Such a pattern, or predisposing tendency, which is the structured residue of past figure or past organizations of experience, is itself a ground condition or *ground structure*, which enters into the shaping and selection of new figure in an ongoing and interactive way. Thus in Gestalt theory, experience (or "reality," in Goodman's term) is always a new creative engagement, involving and integrating current felt urgencies, current perceived environmental conditions (internal and external), *and the organized accumulation of past experience*, which is in (or which is) the *structured personal ground*. The quality of this integration, this organization of figure *and ground*, is the quality of the experience, in both the momentary and ongoing sense. In the words of Sonia March Nevis (1988), a weak or chaotic organization leads to (or is) a chaotic experience, and an absence or low level of satisfaction: This is the particular insight and the crux of the Gestalt model itself.

Now clearly there are many such established preferences, or evaluative behavioral patterns, in the life and ground of any person (or any organization), by which certain outcomes and certain contact styles (or "resistances") will tend to be preferred over others, across time and across situations. Indeed, the sum or system of these preferences or predispositions is what we mean in Gestalt, or in any other system for that matter, when we speak of *personality*—that is, all the relatively stable or predictable ways in which one person will behave differently from another, under the same external conditions. One person is easily combative; another more able to function confluently. One person is sensitively empathic; another lacks this projective faculty. One likes crowded restaurants; another lacks the ability to modulate his or her boundary permeability, and so prefers a quiet place, and so on. But obviously not all such preferential patterns are what we mean when we are thinking of "values" or "ethical choices." On the contrary, most of them are simply instrumental choices, made with greater or lesser awareness, in relation to the anticipated outcome of the behavior, or perhaps just by habit (whether understood in a dynamic or a learning theory sense). When we speak of *values*, or the organization of values into ethical systems, we specifically mean those habitual preferences which are *not* governed by perceived outcome, and may quite possibly run counter to some desired outcome state.[2] Thus the qualifier in the definition above—"without regard for . . . outcome" and so on. Rather, by the use of the words "ethical issue" or "matter of principle," we are signaling that we feel a pull, at least, from some consideration other than practical outcome or personal desire in the ordinary sense, and that that pull has to do with the satisfaction or resolution of issues of the *organization of the personal ground*, the structured relationship of figures with other figures, and with ground structures themselves. And thus the final qualifier, "other than." Certainly value preferences, like other established preferences in the ground, are governed by considerations of outcome. But the outcome considerations are significantly different in kind from those involved in most behavioral choices, or most behavioral choice patterns. This is what we mean when we speak of values.

But note that this means, almost by definition, that when we speak of values we are always or nearly always speaking of a situation of *conflict*, or *competition for dominance* (spontaneous or otherwise), of one figure, one desire, over others. "I would do it," we hear ourselves saying, "but I don't believe in it" or "it goes against my principles," or just plain, "it's wrong." In other words, conflicting desires,[4] or a felt desire that brings disharmony, or a threat of destructuring, to some satisfying organization of ground, and of particular ground structures. It may be possible to imagine some ethical stance, some cohesive organization of values, which would never bring one into conflict with one's various other needs and desires, other figural possibilities of the given moment; but in such a case we would have no occasion to speak of values or ethics: the subject would simply never come up. If the subject does come up—becomes figural—then by definition there has to be some tension, some contrast accompanying and accounting for our investment of attention ("tension," "attention," from the same Latin root *tendere*, ''to stretch or stress''). This again is the very crux of the Gestalt perceptual/attentional model of experience itself, on which our understanding of human process and change is based (see discussion in Koffka, 1935). To *speak* of ethics, again almost by definition, is to talk about the conflict of figures, or of figure with ground-structural constraints, vying as it were for figural energy. Thus when we hear the word ''ethical,'' we naturally expect it to be followed by words like ''problem,'' ''decision,'' or perhaps most commonly, ''dilemma.''[5] Now conflict, perhaps in an oversimplified interpersonal version, is something the Gestalt process model is thought to be particularly adept at handling. But is it? Do we really have much more to say about the processes of conflict resolution or integration, intrapersonal or interpersonal, than ''spontaneous dominance''? What of the conditions of this dominance, spontaneous or not, and the ground structures, values and other valences alike, which in interaction with other urgencies account for the shape and boundaries of that new integration, and the structure of the new contact organization that results? Where, again, in our theory do we look for discussion of issues of this kind, and what shape can that discussion take once we find it?

And note too how this exploration of values and valuing, as necessarily involving structures of figure *and ground*, throws light on the particular usefulness of the Gestalt model as a framework for understanding conservation *and* change, and the relationship between them, as the inherent polar conditions of life, both of which must be taken into account in any useful descriptive model of life processes. Thus in the Gestalt system the defining characteristic of life is growth (contact = ''the structure of growth,'' see Perls et al., 1951, vol. 2, chap. 1), where growth is not just change but the integration of the two poles, change and preservation, which in their union define life itself (change without preservation is not life, but decomposition, or rotting). And thus the Gestalt system, as a ground for containing/understanding value questions, is inherently both conservative/preservationist *and* radical/progressive at the same time. Conservative in its recognition that all behavior, all experience, is by definition *organized*—which is to say, coherently related to the accumulating structural residue of past experience, past figure now become worked into the structured ground. And radical/progressive in its insistence that in order to live, the organism (again, by definition) shows an inherent drive to make contact with (i.e., achieve a new organization of) the *new*, or some element of the new: that which ''is unlike,'' in Goodman's phrase, ''that can become like'' (Perls et al., 1951, p. 270; cf. Piaget, 1947, on assimilation and accommodation, or structural change). This is the crucial ''difference in outlook,'' as Goodman says, between the older Freudian notion of ''adjustment,'' in which the subject learns to conform to (possibly to some extent to work around) immutable societal ground structures (including especially the given values and value systems), and the Goodman concept of "creative adjustment," under which the subject is understood to be continually creating (and critiquing) his or her own world, interactively with the environment, in the process of living.

By the same token, a Gestalt definition of health (or dysfunction) could then be constructed around this notion of the flexible interactive process and influence between and among current, momentary structures of figure, and ongoing, relatively more stable *structures of ground*—a definition which might then have important implications for our exploration of value structures here, since the question of whether there can be such a thing as "healthy values" is, after all, where we began. Too rigidly structured a ground, with correspondingly constricted, impoverished figure, yields the hypervigilant, socially "overadjusted" personality of the type Goodman and Perls had in mind in their critique of Freudian methodology, where the structures of intrapersonal and social ground alike are taken as largely given and unalterable (relationships among the immutable ground structures of psychic life may be somewhat correctively adjusted, in classical analysis; see Perls et al., 1951, pp. 278ff., for discussion of the "neurosis of normalcy"). On the other hand, and what has been relatively neglected in some Gestalt writing, too malleable or unstructured a ground, a ground which is itself impoverished through a lack of well-differentiated and well-related structures for retention and evaluation, goes with a figure formation process that is episodic and flat, a restless quest for "peak experiences" in place of passion itself—and a personality that remains impulsive, consumerist (because never satisfied), and ultimately not "grounded" in community or meaning (and here likewise see Perls et al., 1951, pp. 475ff. on "creativity without . . . adjustment"). Here as elsewhere in the Gestalt model, the challenge of full, healthy living would then be seen to lie not in the glorification one or another of these polar extremes, but in the integration/organization of the polarities themselves, which is the process of growth.

And finally, it is this view of figure and ground structures in interaction that gives the Gestalt model its theoretical emphasis on *experiment*—not only in therapy, but in process in general. By this view, all living process is by definition experimental in nature, in the sense of always involving the testing of established structures against the stimulus of the new, and vice versa ("experience"/"experiment," both from the same Latin root, *experiri*, "to put to the test or try"). Figure is not figure, after all, until it is organized, made "real," as Goodman says, by subjective structure—which is to say, by relating it to some established features of personal ground. And ground, as Lewin pointed out, is only potential, or unknown, unless and until its structure is revealed by contact/accommodation with the new.[6] Here again, a full Gestalt definition of dysfunction (and possibly of dysfunctional value systems) would focus on the failure or interrruption, not just of figure formation alone, but of this ongoing, structurally interactive, *experimental* stance in living, by which structures of figure and ground are continually tested against and with one another, in the ongoing process that is creative adjustment, or growth.[7] The failure to test ground, by introducing/incorporating the new, means, again, the rigid and unpassionate personality Goodman derided as "normal," the person who cannot be "moved" by the reorganizing force of contact itself. On the other hand, the failure to test figure, by doing the work of integration of the new into ongoing ground structures of meaning *and value*, surely yields the anomie, uncertain commitment, and other failures of the heart of so many psychotherapeutic clients today. "Reality and value," Goodman argues, "emerge as a result of self-regulation whether healthy or neurotic" (Perls et al., 1951, p. 320). Does this mean that we can, after all, speak of "healthy (or neurotic) values"? Can ground structure then, not just figure alone, be judged as healthy or otherwise? If so, then we might find ourselves part of the way, at least, on the road to the link we were looking for, between process and content. But by what criteria do we arrive at such judgments? And what would be their implications for then moving from process criteria to content criteria in the domain of values?

This brings us full circle, in this preliminary excursion, back to the questions we started with. With the ground of inquiry thus "mapped out" (to use another Lewinian metaphor)—and with figure, the questions themselves, thus located in the ground and amplified, at least in a preliminary sort of way ("fattened," in the rich terminology of Sonia March Nevis)—let us now turn to experiment, by way of seeing where this more energized contact with the new terrain may lead us.

EXPERIMENT

Since the Gestalt model teaches us to appreciate the experimental nature of experience itself, let us construct and consider a series of thought experiments, new organizations of contact in imagination, by way of laying bare or putting to the test, as Lewin suggests, the ground structures of theory itself (and remembering here too Lewin's dictum that there is "nothing so practical as a good theory," or, we would add, so theoretically enlightening as good practice; see Marrow, 1969). Imagine yourself, for a first experiment, in private practice of Gestalt psychotherapy. And imagine as your client some despicable fascist—the deposed or aspiring dictator, let us say, of some benighted foreign country, out of office or in exile or otherwise passing a period of career setback in your city (so as to enjoy the tolerant bourgeois political climate he or she is at pains to restrict or eliminate in his or her own land). Since Gestalt theory also teaches us the value of extreme cases, or clear polarities for consideration, let us say that the moment is the 1920s, still the formative years of Gestalt psychology, and the height of the psycho/political influence of Nietzsche (and Nietzsche's critique of bourgeois society was after all a principal philosophical influence on Perls's critique of Freud, perhaps the principal philosophical influence; see discussion in Wheeler, 1991, especially Chap. 2). And having gone this far, why not go the whole hog and say your client is none other than Hitler himself, in the grips of one of his periodic polar depressions. Since his symptoms are well documented (see for example Speer, 1969), we do not have to imagine the presenting complaints: dyspepsia, insomnia, mood swings, inability to concentrate, sexual dysfunction, anxiety, depression itself (and paranoia and megalomania, we will want to add, but wait, these are surely our own diagnostic categories, quite value-loaded in themselves, and not the complaints of the client himself). All these bothersome symptoms, the client explains, are keeping him from speaking and writing and organizing effectively, and generally actualizing the clear bright figure of his life's work, which is to purify Europe, at least, of an extensive list of competing (and thus undesirable) groups—a list on which we ourselves, along with Perls and Goodman and most or all of our teachers and friends, would no doubt figure in a number of categories.[8] The question is, do you work with this client? Can you? Should you? If not, is your refusal for reasons of personal repugnance alone, or is there some theoretical basis for declining to help this particular client move from awareness to mobilization and so on through the contact cycle, with these particular figures? Or if you do work with him, is it because you believe that the work itself, through unblocked awareness, reintegrated polarities, and general organismic self-regulation, will somehow by its very nature change those figures themselves, into something less pregnant with hatred and destructiveness (that is to say, that the process will necessarily change the content—a position which, if we can defend it, will surely contain the seeds, at least, of the link we are looking for between the two domains).

What does the Gestalt model have to offer, then, to support our vivid instinctive conviction that this client's beliefs are unhealthy, dysfunctional, or wrong (or even, to return to our larger question, that those might all be the same thing)? Projection? All race prejudice, according to Goodman, is projection: the attribution to others of "traits which really belong to the prejudiced person, but which he represses from awareness" (Perls et al.,

1951, p. 252). Well, perhaps, but if this is generally true, then our client would seem to represent a special case, at the very least. Does he see his various targeted groups—Jews, communists, Christians, trade unionists, artists, sexual and other minorities, and so on—as seeking to dominate, or at least resisting domination by his movement? But these are the very qualities he would own freely, for himself and his followers. Far from projecting/ *denying* them, at least in the usual sense of this "resistance to contact," he affirms and proclaims them. Far from condemning his victims alone as "bestial" (again, Goodman's term), he would agree emphatically, with Nietzsche (and Freud, and Jung, and Goodman and Perls, and no doubt ourselves), that we have repressed the "beast within" to our own detriment, and that wholeness and health must necessarily involve the undoing of that repression, at least (which only goes to show how tricky that undoing can be, and some of the reasons for the repression in the first place). As for the desire to exterminate various ones of the competing groups altogether, this he would not even bother to ascribe to most of the potential victims at all. On the contrary, he would see the very lack of this "bestial" desire in them (not himself) as the sign of their inferiority in the competitive struggle for survival—and as the window of opportunity for himself and his program.

Autonomy, the assertion of the self-boundary, the "progression from environmental supports to self-supports" (Perls, 1973), and the accompanying rejection of confluent followership? Well, perhaps. Certainly Gestalt, we will want to argue, with its emphasis on destructuring the environment in the formation of new figure (cf. Perls's oral aggression metaphor, 1947), is inherently inhospitable, at least, to authoritarian, introjective value systems. But isn't this again to judge the client from the outside, and in the process to use and subtly impose the very diagnostic or value categories and judgments we are trying to justify? For surely the adherents of the ethical system we are trying to criticize—to say nothing of the leader—do not see themselves as controlled, confluent, or introjecting/brainwashed (indeed, they probably see *us* that way). As for other people—potential victims, for example—where is it written *in the Gestalt theoretical model* that my autonomy, my self-supports, should take any account of you and yours? That after all is, again, the question we set out asking, and once again may be tempted to beg. And what if my spontaneous dominances conflict with yours? At this point we can restate our original issue for exploration: How can a purely subjective model, which seeks to take its criteria of health only from the structural properties of the presenting figure of the moment, possibly discriminate between one figure and another, on content grounds? What can we offer from such a standpoint, theoretically speaking, other than the Nietzschean vision of life as a conflict of separate wills, followed by the pseudo-Darwinian resolution of survival of the fittest?

Or take the experiment a step further: Suppose that the new political order is already in place. Society has been more or less reorganized, and life has resumed its course, at least for those groups not targeted for the moment. However, depression, anxiety, addiction, self-destructive behavior, and sexual and other interpersonal dysfunction still occur, and now a new official state school of psychotherapy is needed. Why not Gestalt?[9] What can we find in the theory itself, articulated as we know it, that would make it incompatible with such a use—or even with such an abuse (because surely a theory of health, as much as a philosophical system, must be responsible to some degree not only for what it says explicitly, but for what it leaves out as well, and for the ease with which it can be perverted)? Organismic self-regulation? "Do not be afraid," Goodman and his coauthors admonish us, "that by dissolving conscience you will become a criminal or an impulsive psychopath. You will be surprised . . . [under] organismic self-regulation . . . how the principles that *you* ought to live by will . . . emerge . . . and will be *obviously appropriate* for living regardless of the social situation you are in" (Perls et al., 1951, p. 259). Now certainly, by "conscience" Goodman and Perls had in mind that unexamined, rigidly structured introject, more or less the Freudian superego, that exemplifies the kind of rigid ground structure we characterized above, tentatively, as an "unhealthy value system" (at least in process terms, by virtue of its impermeable boundaries, not subject to experiment). But this is just what the Nazis (and Nietzsche) meant by conscience—that received structure sometimes known as "Judeo-Christian ethics" whose destructuring and replacement by a freely embraced, opposing value system was the explicit goal of the Nazi party program (indeed, Hitler himself saw clearly that his long-range program, after the eradication of various fringe and minority groups, would hinge on a sharp reduction and eventual elimination of the power of the Church). As for the Orwellian issues of brainwashing and groupthink (the confluence/introjection discussed above), certainly we can agree that here we have a significant perversion of the spirit, at least, of the Gestalt model, with its respect for the integrity of the questing, questioning individual, grounded in body experience and suspicious of abstractions divorced from immediate felt needs. But how easily the perversion is accomplished, and how difficult it is to express the theoretical contradiction more concretely! For surely every political system, and none more than the fascistic varieties, aspires to the fully felt and freely given assent of its subjects/citizens. And they get it, in many cases at least, while we are reduced, theoretically speaking, to wringing our hands on the sidelines of the argument and assuring ourselves that their assent cannot really be real, because organismic self-regulation is not supposed to come out that way!

But the reader may protest at this point that the example is extreme in the first place, even farfetched (even offensive, a charge that Goodman particularly relished, as signifying some felt reality). Let us turn then to some more familiar problems and presentations from everyday clinical practice: What about the question of suicide? Does suicide constitute a personal (or clinical) failure, under the Gestalt model? Or is it merely a possible expression of healthy autonomous process (an ultimate right, as Camus would have it), as long as the required properties of "strong gestalt" are present and accounted for? When presented with a suicidal client, or an ambivalently suicidal client, do we fulfill our clinical responsibility by working with the client to achieve "good figure" ("brightness, clarity, unity, fascination, grace, vigor, release, etc."—Perls et al., 1951, p. 272), and then by supporting that client to realize the figure through mobilization, action, contact, and so on through the cycle, noting only to ourselves that the withdrawal following contact with this particular figure is, so far as we know, final? Or do we rather feel—theoretically, and not "just personally"—that suicide is a mistake, a case by definition of unhealthy process, even "wrong"? If so, again, is this a stance we take from inside or outside the Gestalt model? "The achievement of strong Gestalt is itself the cure" (Perls et al., 1951, p. 273). This would seem to imply on the face of it that all these questions lie outside the realm of Gestalt analysis, which is to say of process questions and issues. And yet "the figure of contact," Goodman continues, "is not a sign of, but is itself the creative integration of experience." In other words, the figure itself implicates (as we have been arguing here) the ground—unless by "figure" Goodman means something much more isolated and disconnectedly episodic than he plainly means in other contexts. "Spontaneous dominances," remember, are only an "immediate ethics" for Goodman, and are "not infallible." But then what, if anything, from within the Gestalt system, could possibly correct or enrich the "spontaneous dominance" of one figure over others, or support the choice of figure when that dominance is incomplete, as in the conflictual cases we have recognized ethical questions to be? The answer, again, must lie in ground, if it lies anywhere at all.

Of course, as we have been noting all along, it is still logically possible, at least, to assert and bring to bear value preferences, ethical criteria, from some perspective outside the Gestalt system altogether (and then either in harmony or conflict with that system, or irrelevant to it, as the case may be). With regard to suicide, many Gestalt therapists might find it ethically necessary (which is to say, figurally dominant, in order to satisfy structural demands of personal ground, where we have located the values domain) to hospitalize or otherwise restrain the suicidal (or for that matter homicidal) client. In the eloquent words, again, of Sonia March Nevis, one does this at times, but only and always with *regret*, for the violation of the autonomy of the other person. Certainly it is an enrichment of the Gestalt model to encompass and honor such complex emotional states as regret (and guilt, shame, resentment, and disappointment, and the whole panoply of such familiar and finely nuanced *interpersonal* emotional states), which may at times seem to have been treated somewhat reductively in the Goodman/Perls presentation. However, for our purposes here, the fact of this regret, in and of itself, still only begs our original question. For what is it, from a theoretical point of view, that brings us to this violation of this cherished Gestalt principle (albeit a principle, the autonomy of others, which we have been hard put to locate in the theory as articulated so far)? What other figure became dominant over that one? Or is it that the feeling of regret itself is linked to a sadness that the model itself, which one has felt compelled to depart from, has disappointed or fallen short of our needs and expectations in some way?

Or to grade the experiment down once more, in terms of the direness of the stakes (but still in the domain of serious life issues—again, we do not have any occasion to *talk* about value issues until we have already arrived at a point of seriously energized conflicting figures or desires): What of the question of divorce? Do we, as Gestalt therapists, have any theoretical bias on the question of relational commitments? And if so (or if not), how do we help a client think about such issues, and make choices informed with feeling in the direction of growth? The easy answer, of course, is to respect the autonomy of the client's choice, but work to nourish a ground of awareness, in support of that emerging figure, whatever that may be (but remember, it was exactly this easy answer that we found so troubling, in the case of the Nazi client). Well and good, but awareness of what? Of "whatever comes up"? Surely at this late date, and under the Gestalt model of all things, we are not going to advance the argument that the point of view of the participant/ observer does not affect the system! (As Lewin, and for that matter Heisenberg, insisted, to study something is to change it.) But then make your own bias a part of the client's awareness, we will say, put it all on the table. Again well and good,—but what is that bias, theoretically speaking? For what issues, or what lacunae, are we listening with our "third ear," as we follow the client's lead into "what comes up?" Do we believe, as the Perlsian dictum at the head of this chapter seems to suggest, that connections between people are something to be enjoyed when they are going well, and abandoned when they are not? Or if not for ourselves personally, do we still concede that a stance of this kind is compatible, at least, with healthy process as we understand it under the Gestalt model? Or do we rather believe that the development of a *richly articulated and fully supportive ground, one from and in which alone fully energized, vigorous, and aesthetic figure can emerge and flourish*, is dependent on the kind of intimate self-knowledge, at times desperate sharing of the self which most people, at least, can experience only by hanging in through difficult times in committed relationships (such as long-term psychotherapy, couple and family relationships, or the kind of friendships where ground itself, not just figure, is available to the other person, to influence and to share)? In other words, do we believe, with Freud (systematically) and Perls (ambivalently), that individual and society, self and other, are fundamentally opposed, and that the development of the one is in some sense at the expense of the other? Or do we rather believe, with Winnicott, and Goldstein and Lewin and Goodman (usually), that self and other are in some fundamental sense the same thing, that each is the ground for the other, and that the development of self and the development of a community of relationship are inextricably intertwined? Because surely such beliefs, one way or the other, will make an enormous difference in clinical practice; the "things that come up," clinical experience teaches us, will be quite different, out of the two different therapeutic/interpersonal grounds. And surely the Gestalt model is not completely indifferent to such fundamental questions of human process, where and how and under what conditions it takes place, flowers, and grows.

WITHDRAWAL, "DEBRIEFING," ACCOMPLISSEMENT

Human nature, according to Goodman, is that which it is human to do (Perls et al., 1951, Vol II, Chap. VI)—including, apparently, error, which in turn includes evil, or bad values. Alas, it is human to do so many things! Goodman's answer (abbreviated, but not distorted) to all the anguish of moral choices, all the agony of human history contained in those few brief phrases, is "organismic self-regulation." With this faith, he places himself squarely in the Romantic tradition of moral thought, tracing back at least to Rousseau, and with the particularly American twist found in Whitman, say, and Twain. (*Huck Finn*, after all, is the tale of a moral pilgrim struggling to reconcile received social values, or "conscience" in the Perlsian sense, with some innate, body-based, "natural" apprehension of right and wrong. Huck's heroism, finally, lies in the fact that he chooses to heed this inner voice, bidding him to honor his personal relationship with the runaway slave Jim, *even though* he cannot stand outside that received system, and believes he will go to hell for his commitment.) Goodman himself, as I have pointed out elsewhere (Wheeler, 1991) was writing in and against a ground of socially overcontrolled times—roughly from Hitler to McCarthy. Thus the Romantic faith in the moral/political corrective of the *autonomous individual* who is true to himself or herself, to his or her own spontaneous impulses (body impulses, as much as possible), to lusts and disgusts, the "natural" human, who after all could hardly do worse, morally speaking, than all the various and conflicting authority systems of these wrenching times, Church and State, communism and capitalism, fascisms of the left and right, and democracies and whole religions that stand by while the victims of all the other groups perish. And that was only the first half of the century! Thus the search for an "autonomous criterion" of "reality,"—the *gestalt*; and thus, finally, Goodman's extreme (and ultimately untenable) formulation of contact itself—the "clear bright figure freely energized from an *empty* background." The ground, as we have seen in this investigative excursion, can in no way be regarded as "empty,"—nor would the "contact" that obtained in such a case have anything to do with healthy human process as we understand it. Rather, the ground itself is a richly structured, dynamically organized "place" where all the meaningful residue of past figure, past experience is held prepotently alive, and against the structured features of which the new figure formation emerges and takes shape. Among these structural features are those metastructures, or structures organizing structures, that we understand by the term *values*. Many of these values in structured relationship, or ethical systems, may by their *content nature* work against the process values of healthy gestalt formation, figure *and ground* resolution, that we recognize as the signs and the very presence of healthy process and living—and (as Goodman says) of cure. With appreciation and respect for Goodman and Perls's healthy fear of content standards by which human beings may be evaluated or differentiated, and with a fuller awareness now of the theoretical risks of the undertaking, it is time for us to move beyond a model that was at times figure-bound, to a direct refocusing on the question we posed at the outset of this exploration, of the unarticulated link between content and process structures in the dynamic ground, under the Gestalt model.

Values are powerful prepotent organizing forces or features, located in the personal ground, urgently energized at times to the point of overriding strong countervailing needs and desires in the shaping of new figure for action. Subjectively we feel them as a push or a constraint: "Here I stand," says Luther, "*I can do no other.*" The power of the value structure is the power of the gestalt process itself: the overwhelming drive of the organism to structure experience—in this case, to structure other internal structures—in some satisfying, cohesive, and ultimately meaningful way (indeed, this is what "meaningful" means). Some such structures, we have argued, may be regarded as healthy or unhealthy, in *process* terms, like other structured ground features, according to their relative availability and boundary permeability to *experiment*, figure and ground structures testing and reorganizing each other, in an ongoing and growthful way. Beyond this, we have raised the question, and suggested various possible routes toward an answer, of whether such structures of value may not themselves be evaluated, functionally and clinically, in terms of their *content*. It lies outside the scope of this paper to follow up those suggested routes, or other routes that may be suggested, to the discovery or construction of a fuller answer to our original questions. But the questions remain, as next explorations of contact, in the ongoing experimental figure and ground that is Gestalt theory itself.

NOTES

1. The question of exactly who wrote what in *Gestalt Therapy* is unresolved, and probably unresolvable (see Davidove, 1985; also Glasgow, 1971). Goodman claimed credit for the actual writing, and others have supported that claim, but in a general way, leaving open the question of who contributed what to the ideas themselves. What is beyond question is that the *voice*, particularly in Vol. II, is Goodman's, as any reader can easily verify by making comparisons with other works of the various authors. Thus when we say here "Goodman says" or "according to Goodman," it is this voice we are referring to, without prejudice to the argument about whose thinking lies behind that voice at various points.

2. An objection may be raised here along the lines of the old behaviorist cavil about the word "altruism": namely, that since all behavior is in some sense governed by relatively desirable perceived outcome (i.e., all behavior is "selfish"), how can it be meaningful to speak of some behavior as altruistic—or here, as not governed by desired outcome? The answer is the same in both cases. Altruism refers to those behaviors, those motives, in which personal satisfaction is taken from others' gain or satisfaction. Likewise here, "values" are preferences not governed by satisfaction other than the satisfaction of the ethical or value gestalt itself.

4. Conflicting "valences," to use Lewin's terminology (1935, 1951), which applies to all evaluative choices, and not just that subset we understand under the term "values." The English word valence, which Lewin approved in translation, may have been part of his sometime impulse to join Wertheimer in his quest to bring the metaphors of psychology more in line with the metaphors of physical science. Actually, the original Lewin term, "*Aufforderungsqualitaeten*," or "demand characteristics," far better captures the subjective feeling of a pull or a pressure, in such situations of internal conflict, particularly around value questions.

5. "Do your own thing, whatever feels good to you at the moment," might seem to be an example of an ethical position that would never be associated with an internal conflict. However, this stance may be compromised or trivialized, philosophically or psychologically speaking, by the undifferentiated tautologies implied in the term "feels good." What if more than one thing "feels good" at a given moment, and neither exhibits "spontaneous dominance"? More particularly, there may be different *kinds* of feeling good, which is exactly the point under examination here. To blur such distinctions would then be to beg these questions, not to answer them.

6. And compare here Lewin's "action research" model of organizational research cum intervention for change. The best way of studying an organization, Lewin argues—which is to say, of understanding covert features of structured ground—is to try to change it, and vice versa. This of course closely parallels the Gestalt methodology of contact analysis through experiment—and for that matter Anna Freud's views on "analysis of the defenses" (Lewin, 1951; A. Freud, 1937). For discussion of the therapeutic encounter itself as a contact experiment, see Wheeler, 1991.

7. Compare here Michael Miller's provocative suggestion (1987) that a Gestalt developmental model might be constructed around the concept and function of *curiosity*. Curiosity, surely, involves that willingness to risk ground structure itself, in just the sense we are talking about here.

8. Nietzsche of course was a major philosophical source and influence for the Nazis as well. To say this is not to suggest that Nietzsche himself was a Nazi: Nietzsche would have abhorred and despised the Nazis, and the unspeakable things they did in his name. Much less is it to suggest that Perls has any affinities with the Nazis, of whom he himself was a victim. We cannot be responsible, after all, for all of our cousins, who may have taken quite different roads in reacting to the same inheritance! Nietzsche can, however, be faulted for the lack of resistance his philosophical system offered to exploitation by Chamberlain and other Nazi philosophers. By the same token, we might expect that it could prove difficult to mount a theoretical attack on Nazism from a purely Perlsian point of view—which after all is one of the things we might hope to do in this experiment.

9. Let us assume for the sake of the experiment that Goldstein's paper "The Organismic Approach" (to psychotherapy) had already been published by that time. In any case, the outline of a therapeutic model, if not a methodology is present in Lewin's and Goldstein's work of this period (Lewin, 1926; Goldstein, 1925).

11. Katzeff (1977) discriminates this seventh stage of the contact cycle, "accomplishment," in between contact and withdrawal, to emphasize the possibility of an extended climax (to use Goodman's sexual imagery), a relishing, enjoyment, or staying with the contact that may be neglected in the terms contact and withdrawal themselves.

REFERENCES

Davidove, D. (1985). The contribution of Paul Goodman. *Gestalt Journal, VIII*(1), 72–77.

Freud, A. (1937). *The ego and the mechanisms of defense*. New York: International Universities Press.

Glasgow, R. (19719. Interview with Paul Goodman. *Psychology Today*, November, 1971.

Goldstein, K. (1925). Zur Theorie der Funktion des Nervensystems (Toward a theory of the functioning of the nervous system). *Archiven fur Psychiatrische und Nerven Krankheiten*, 74.

Katzeff, M. (1977). *Comment se realiser dans la vie quotidienne et professionelle*. Brussels: Multiversite.

Koffka, K. (1935). *Principles of Gestalt psychology*. New York: Harcourt, Brace & World.

Lewin, K. (1926). Vorsatz, Wille, und Bedurfnis (Intention, will, and need). *Psychologische Forschung, 7*, 330–385.

Lewin, K. (1931). Erziehung fur Wirklichkeit (Education for reality). In K. Lewin, *A dynamic theory of personality*. New York: McGraw-Hill, 1935.

Lewin, K. (1951). *Field theory in social science*. New York: Harper & Brothers.

Marrow, A. (1969). *The practical theorist: the life and work of Kurt Lewin*. New York: Basic Books.

Miller, M. (1987). Curiosity and its vicissitudes. *Gestalt Journal, X*(1), 18–32.

Nevis, S. (1988). *Remarks at the thirty-fifth anniversary conference of the Gestalt Institute of Cleveland*. Unpublished.

Perls, F. (1947). *Ego, hunger & aggression*. London: Allen & Unwin.

Perls, F. (1969). *Gestalt therapy verbatim*. Moab, UT: Real People Press.

Perls, F. (1973). *The gestalt approach and eye-witness to therapy*. Palo Alto: Science and Behavior Books.

Perls, F., Hefferline, R., & Goodman, P. (1951). *Gestalt Therapy: Excitement and growth in the human personality*. New York: Julian Press.

Piaget, J. (1947). *Intelligence*. New York: Basic Books.

Speer, A. (1969). *Erinnerungen*. Frankfurt/M: Verlag Ullstein GmbH.

Wheeler, G. (1991). *Gestalt reconsidered*. New York: Gardner Press/Gestalt Institute of Cleveland Press.

Winnicott, D. (1986). *Holding and interpretation*. New York: Grove Press.

5

Transactional Analysis and Gestalt Therapy

ROBERT GOULDING, M.D.

I'VE BEEN ASKED TO DO A chapter in this book on TA and Gestalt. That is not so easy anymore, because I'm not really a Gestalt therapist, nor a TA therapist, nor any specific *kind* of a therapist. I'm an integrated therapist, and I use everything I know to teach, and to treat. So I'm just going to write about what I do, and how I do it, and let it come out the way I write it. Neither am I going to describe basic TA theory in this article. (Refer to Goulding and Goulding, "The Power is in the Patient", and "Changing Lives Through Redecision Therapy", for details of our theory and therapy).

I use a lot of TA principles. I think TA when I work, in terms of how the patient operates; what the patient's character is, and how I think in my belief system that he got the way he is. After all, therapy is only asking the patient to change from his belief system to my belief system. I don't care what kind of therapy we are writing about—TA, Gestalt, Psychodrama, psychoanalysis (if that really is a therapy, and I doubt it), behavior modification, desensitization, family systems theory—no matter what our belief system is, we ask the patient to change from his faulty belief system to our truer than God, absolutely perfect belief system. We may not know that that is what we are doing, but that is what we are doing. The patient believes a lot of things, about himself, about others, about the original family, and it is my job to ask him to disbelieve all those beliefs, and look at the world in a different way.

So I have to get him to believe me! That's the first step. If he doesn't believe me, trust me, think that I am right, then I am going to have a difficult time in facilitating his change. Notice that I say "facilitate his change". I believe, also, that only the patient has the ability to change. I don't have any power to "make him" change, despite all the words that Fritz and Eric wrote. He does the change, I don't change him. I just get him to trust me, to trust that what I say and do is right, and he can change himself. As a matter of fact, when people come to me from Germany, and Czechoslovakia, and Australia, and Japan, they already have begun to believe, and just that fact that they have committed themselves to the expense of coming, of flying 10,000 miles, more or less, of paying my fees for a month's training, or two weeks training, is a *big* commitment to change. So for me the writing, and the doing odd workshops in far away places, is already making some good contact. When people come here for treatment of a water phobia, they already know that I say I CURE WATER PHOBIAS, AND I DO. So they are already ready to give up their water phobias, and of course they do. Usually within three minutes. That's not magic, that's a commitment to change. (By the way, I *know* I don't *cure* people; that is a figure of speech. Everytime I get hot and write "I cure" I get a letter from someone. Please don't write to me about that loose use. The patient cures him/her self.)

OK. So what I am talking about now is the original *CONTACT*. Very important, the contact. I see someone in Germany, at the TA conference in Nordenay. She says "I want to stop being afraid of the water." I say "Oh. OK. When do you want to do it? Do you want to stop being afraid here on Nordenay, or do you want to come to California, to Mt. Madonna, and give it up next year?"

"Why not now" she says. "OK," I say, "I'll meet you in my hotel pool at 5: 00 PM tonight. Bring a cheering section, so that they can applaud you when you give it up." So she comes, and she brings a cheering section, and in five minutes, or three or ten, she is no longer afraid of the water. Magic? No, Contact. They believe me, and that's what it's all about. They believe me, after a while anyway, when I say "You are in charge. You are in charge of your behavior, your thinking, your feeling, and mostly your body. You may not believe me yet, but you are. No one else is. People don't make you feel; alcohol doesn't make you behave differently. You do it. You may have been taught by your mother that you make her feel angry, and you may have thought that she made you feel unhappy, but she did it to her, and you do it to you. So you can stop being a victim, and take charge." That is so obvious that hardly anyone believes it at first, but you do it to you, I don't. You tell yourself some kind of a story about whatever I am saying or thinking or feeling or doing, or what your spouse is doing, that leads you to think that they are doing it, but you are. (See *Changing Lives, Power,* for more about autonomy).

Contact is very important. How do you answer the phone? Do you answer it, or do you have some secretary answer it? Answer it yourself, man or ma'am. At a famous neuropsychiatric center, they were doing some research on the effectiveness of several kinds of therapies. They decided to do a random selection on the basis of what day the client called or stopped in. Thursday was group therapy day. When someone called on Thursday, they went into a TA group. They had a good TA therapist, but somehow the Thursday patients were not staying more than one or two sessions. Then they heard the secretary, who answered the phone, say "Oh, today is Thursday. All we have today is TA group therapy. Sorry!" So they had her change her first contact, by saying "Oh, aren't you lucky, today is TA day" (or Gestalt day, or whatever day it is!) No more drop outs. Contact is important. How does your office look? How does your waiting room look? Is it sterile, or is it exciting? Do you have five year old magazines, or do you have the latest reprint of your best article, in which you outline how someone cured themselves while working with you? What do you do, in your surroundings, to attract your clients, to facilitate their getting turned on even before they see you? And how do you greet them? Eric wouldn't shake hands with them, because (he writes in "What Do You Say After You Say Hello?") he doesn't know them yet. Well, how do you get to know them? The Polsters write beautifully about contact in "Gestalt Therapy Integrated." What do you say and do so that they react with "Wow, this therapist is different!?"

Contract is next. How do you set your contract? Or to put it even stronger, do you set a contract, or rather do you facilitate the client setting a contract? If not, how in the hell do you know what in the hell you are doing? If you don't have a specific contract for a specific measurable change, then you are working in the dark. My contracts, and most TA therapists' contracts, are absolutely specific. "I am going to quit smoking" is a contract. "I would like to quit smoking" or "I wonder why I smoke" or "I would like to *try* to quit smoking" are not contracts. They are experiences in frustration. "I want to stop beating my children" or "I wonder why I beat my children" are not contracts, but "I am quitting beating my children" is a contract. "I want to look at why I am so fat" is not a contract but "I am going to lose 50 pounds" is a contract. The words are important. We deal largely with words when we deal with patients, for our language is us. "We have met the enemy, and he is us."

Contact is important, and contract is important. There are thousands (perhaps hundreds) of "gestalt therapists" out there who once had a dream workshop with Fritz Perls, and call themselves Gestalt Therapists, who work absolutely in the dark, without contracts. "It is all there, in the here and now" they recite. Bullshit. They listened to what Fritz said, not observing what he *did*. If you don't get a contract, you are not doing therapy, you are doing an experience. If that. (I'm not talking about the truly great Gestaltists, of which there are legions—Simkin, the Polsters, Irma Shepherd, Joen Fagan, Howie Fink, Joe Zinker, Bob Resnick, Jan Rainwater, Lois Brien, and many many others; I'm writing about those who *call* themselves Gestalt therapists). The greatest thing that Eric Berne left to the art and science of psychotherapy, in my opinion, was the concept of the therapeutic contract.

Next, the first con. Woe to the therapist who doesn't pick up the first con. These clients, my friends, have been doing their thing for years. They are far more experienced in doing their thing than we are in stopping them from doing their thing, and if you (we) don't pick up on the first con, we have had it. Up to here. They will walk out in a few weeks, swinging our scalps on their belts. What is a con? Well, a con is what the patient says or does that states very clearly that he or she is not going to do what he says he is going to do. My favorite con, and one that I have probably quoted before in some article or book, is what one patient/therapist said when working in a peer group with a virgin therapist. "I never do what I say I am going to do, and I want to quit smoking." Wow, the poor therapist, so excited about someone quitting smoking, never heard the first part, just the second, and went headlong into a no-smoking contract, without checking out the con "I never do what I say I am going to do." She is no longer a *virgin* therapist. Other cons: "I want to work on blah blah blah." Once they have said "work on", and you buy it, you have had it. When I hear people say "I want to work on blah blah blah" I fall off my chair, roll on the ground in great pain, and say, banging my fist on the floor "Work on work on work on work on work on for ever and ever and ever." That's right. I fall off my chair. Very impressive. I get one workon each workshop. The first one. The biggest copout of all, probably, and one they will faithfully follow—they will work on, and work on, this year, the next year, and all the years forever. They are the workoners who inhabit Esalen, and the American Academy of Psychotherapists summer workshops, for members only. I call it their fecoliths.

Chronic bad feeling—the racket(s). In TA, we call the chronic bad feeling that people have a "racket.". This term comes from the belief that most bad feelings people have are the result of an attempt to get people to do something. The child, for instance, gets angry in order to get mother or father to do something for them, or give them something. Or they copy parents, who do the same thing: Mother says "You make me so angry when you spill the milk, or don't clean up your room, or stay out late, or don't wash the dishes.'' Children don't know that they don't make Mother angry; they believe this belief system, and are then stuck. So when they grow up, they maintain their bad feelings in two ways: one, by playing the same Games they have always played, and two, by going out of the here and now to another time and/or another place, in fantasy. So all I have to do to maintain my anger is to read in the paper each morning what the President has done now, go out of the here and now into yesterday or tomorrow in Washington, and I can ruin my day. To work with the chronic bad feelings, I have to teach people that they are responsible for their own bad feelings, teach them to stop playing games, and teach them to stay in the here and now, rather than going to some other place and time in fantasy.

Games: A Game in the T.A. definition is a series of transactions which end up in a stereotyped bad feeling. There is an ostensibly straight transaction which is really crooked, and which is asking for a response that is out of the awareness of the player. For instance, in the Game ''Kick Me'' as played here very often, the workshop participant asks me, while I am in the pool at night, a question about therapy. It sounds like a straight question, but the participant already knows how I hate to be asked to work in my time off. So secretly s/he is asking me to get angry, and if I do, then s/he experiences him/herself being rejected, feel angry, or sad, or whatever his/her racket is. In addition, they say something about themselves, and something about me, their existential position in the world: such as ''I never get what I want'' and ''He doesn't like me.''

So, at this time we have looked at several things that are happening between the patient and ourselves. We make good contact; we make a good therapeutic contract; we watch for the first (and subsequent) cons. We look for the chronic bad feeling, and look for the way in which people maintain this bad feeling, by Games or fantasies. We are now interested in what this bad feeling does for them—what kind of a decision did this patient make when a little child to make this feeling necessary. For instance, did this little kid decide when a little kid to kill himself some day if things got too bad? Or did he decide to never do childlike things, and take care of everybody? Or did she decide never to grow up? Whatever the child decided (and s/he decided over and over again), s/he now does things, and feels things, so as to maintain that existential position. This decision is based on the way things were back then—what people said and did, the kind of strokes people gave. For instance, if Mother says over and over again ''I wish you had never been born'' then the child may have decided he wasn't worthwhile, and that he might as well be dead. Then when he grows up he feels worthless, depressed, and may become suicidal. Thus his life plan, or script, is based upon the circumstances of his early childhood, and he plays games or has fantasies that support that depressed, worthless position. Thus one of my jobs as therapist is to tease out the circumstances, not by talking about childhood, but by facilitating the patient getting into scenes from childhood as if they were happening here and now. This is not just to get information, but to facilitate the patient having a learning, or a different, experience; to respond to the same stimulus in a different way. It is not possible to change *others* in the past, so we don't allow that fantasized ending to a scene; it *is* possible to change self by pretending to be in the past and changing the ending, to change self; to decide, even though Mother didn't want him, to stay alive and enjoy life.

So, the therapeutic work, for me, is in some way to facilitate the client getting into his free, nonadaptive Child Ego State, and make a Redecision. We look for the stuck place; the impasse, and set up the work so that the client can get out of the impasse. That's what all Gestalt therapists do, of course, if they are doing Gestalt: look for the incongruity, the ambivalence, the bipolar position, and facilitate the patient becoming congruent, resolving the ambivalence. The essential difference between a pure gestaltist and a T.A./Gestaltist is that we pay more attention to the way in which the impasse fits the patient's script, their position in life. We are interested in more than the immediate here-and-now impasse; we are interested in how that impasse is repeated over and over again in order for the patient to relive old experiences over and over again. We want a corrective experience which will not only resolve the particular impasse in the here and now, but the impasse as it relates to the life flow.

To better understand the nature of impasses, I wrote an article years ago for Voices about three kinds of impasses. The pure gestaltist, as I understand it, deals with impasses from the behavior, thinking, feeling, of the client that is ambivalent: e.g., if the client says yes, and shakes his head ''no'', there is obviously an impasse of some kind, and the gestaltist may ask the client to take both sides. The TA/gestaltist, or Redecision Therapist, would be more likely, in addition, to trace back the source of the impasse, so as to make the work more of a life change. For instance, the patient may say ''yes'' to doing something spectacular, different, perhaps a little showoffy; then we might take the ''no'' headshake to be coming from someone specifically, and not merely the ''top dog.'' We might then ask the person to be the person who didn't approve of such ''show-off'' behavior, and get into a dialogue between self and that (probable) parent that said ''don't be a show off''. Thus the dialogue takes place between the Free Child of the client, and his or her Parent Ego State. We are vitally interested, in this case, in the patient actually experiencing himself being in that Parent Ego State, so we will do much to facilitate the client's getting that experience.

In my article on Impasses, written in Voices, I explain the nature of the three kinds of impasses, which at that time I labelled first degree, second degree, and third degree. I regret having named the impasses "degrees", as this has been very confusing for many TA therapists. Berne wrote about Games as being first, second or third degree, meaning in terms of the Game's seriousness. A Third Degree Game is one in which the player ends up with physical damage or death. The impasse degrees don't mean that at all, and I am inclined to start calling them 1st, 2nd, or 3rd *types* of impasses. The first type deals with the messages that come from the patient's Parent Ego State (called P-2); these messages were very out front, very verbal, and generally had to do either with culture, or with what the parent wanted the child to do that ma or pa could be proud of—as work hard, go to college, study hard, get all A's, etc. They are then incorporations of the real words said by the real parent, and whose nature may be of "super-Ego" type, as described by Freud. The relationship between Parent Ego State and Superego is only that the superego probably was developed from many such parental messages, while the Parent Ego State is the incorporation of the parent in the client's head. (See Berne, *TA in Psychotherapy*, or Goulding and Goulding, *Changing Lives*). What the redecision therapist does is to facilitate the patient getting into that Parent Ego State, so he can experience it, and then resolve the impasse by deciding to do what he wants to do, whether the original parent, and hence the Parent Ego State, wants him to or not. There is nothing wrong with "working hard", for example, as long as the decision to work hard comes from the *present* Child as a free decision, rather than the stereo-typed adaptive response. Thus the resolution of impasses, from our stand-point, *must* come from the *Free Child*, and not be an adaption, either to old figures or to present figures, or even in a transferential response.

The second type of impasse relates to the messages coming from the Child Ego State of the original parent—the behavior, thinking, and feeling the parent demanded of the child because of the parent's own hurts, disap-pointments, and angers. (I have labored long in past articles and books to explain the injunctions and counter injunctions.) For instance, if the mother wanted a girl, having had four boys, and again had a boy, she might very easily say to the little boy in all kinds of non-veral ways "Don't be a boy, be a girl": by dressing up the baby in pink, and then dresses, letting the hair grow long, saying "you would have made such a beautiful little girl." Or father, having had four girls, and disappointed that the fifth was also a girl, may teach her to hunt, and fish, and kick footballs (not that such behavior is genetic; it is only cultural, and I am not defending it. Please don't write, I'm for ERA too.) These messages, called Injunctions, come then from mother's or father's disappointed Child Ego State, and are not at all rational to the offspring, but the parent, not knowing the possible results of such behavior, doesn't see this behavior as being irrational, doesn't even know what the little kid is doing inside his or her head in response to these messages. To get to the impasse, then, and work through it, it is necessary for the client to feel the feelings that the parent felt at the time the messages were given, and *then* respond, again from Free Child eventually. To respond from Adult is not enough. There must be a connection between the memory of the scene, the memory of the feelings in both the parent and the child, and the experiencing of that (those) feelings, which are stored in the client's Child Ego State. Yes, feelings and memories that the client at first doesn't know he remembers and feels are very available when properly cathected by the therapist. The part of the parent that is incorporated in the Child Ego State is called P-1, and is shown in drawings as being the top circle in the Child Ego State; this P-1 is called the Pig Parent by Steiner, the "Electrode" by Berne.

All of the Type 2 impasses, then, are related to the frequently nonverbal or preverbal messages, given by father and mother, and now incorporated in the client's own Child Ego State. The usual response, prior to therapy, in the adapted Child, is to listen to, and obey (or rebel against) these messages. The job, of course, is to facilitate the client deciding again to do, think or feel as he wants to, nonadaptively, whether the parents wanted him to do, think or feel or not. One of the ways of getting to this is to ask "Are you willing to do what you want to do, even if they wanted you to" in order to stop adapting rebelliously. We don't disagree in any way with the pure gestalt experience, the discovery. What we are *also* interested in, in addition, is to teach the client, by experiencing, and often by cognitive confrontation as well, that the ways in which he or she is behaving, thinking, or feeling is based on an adaptive response originally, whether the adaptive response is to obey, or disobey. Blind rebelliousness is just as adaptive as blind obedience, and the response *must* be without adaption in order to be curative. Too often the gestalt experience is a rebellious one, and not free at all.

At this point it is time to reflect on what I have written. I have referred to the 4 "c"'s of contact, contract, con, chronic bad feeling, and have skipped the fifth, chief complaint. It is not particularly relevant to this article. I have referred to the way in which people maintain their bad feelings by games and fantasy, and have referred to the early decision, the injunctions and counter injunctions, and the first two impasses. I have not yet covered the third type of impasse, which is based upon the attributes that little kids get. In these cases, the client doesn't know he got a message from anyone, doesn't believe it if you say he did, and states that he has "always been like this . . ." (angry, sad, worthless). There is no point in setting up a dialogue between top dog and under dog, or Child and Parent, because the client feels that he was born this way, and nothing can be done, that there is no one to talk to, no impasse experienced. It is important to recognize the third type of impasse, so as not to get sucked in to setting up a dialogue that the client will not resolve. Some of Jim Simkin's bear trappers are in this category.

For example, one little woman from Turkey was here. She had a driving phobia. While we were working with her, we realized that in addition to her driving phobia, she thought and experienced that she was stupid, that she had always been stupid, she was born stupid, and there was nothing she could do about it; she was especially stupid about mechanical things, like automobiles. We recognized that if we didn't first facilitate her not feeling stupid any longer, we would probably be wise in not helping her drop her driving phobia, for she was a real threat to civilization when she got behind the wheel of a car. We knew she wasn't stupid, for she had gotten her Ph.D. in psychology, and that is not easy to do if one is stupid. At least not usually. We were sure that someone had called her stupid when she was a kid, but she denied it, except to say that they "recognized" of course that she wasn't very bright, and that she got through grade school and high school and college and graduate school because she worked very hard, not because she wasn't stupid. A typical example of a type three impasse.

So, we asked her to be the stupid child, and play out that part. She did so, beautifully, with all stops pulled. Then we asked her to be the other, the "not stupid" part. She looked at us with puzzlement. "But I can't be that part; I *am* stupid". This is the usual response in Type 3 impasses. Hard to get around, especially if they are feeling stupid as the attribute. I said "pretend you are smart. You probably fooled a lot of teachers by pretending, so pretend with us." So she got in the other chair and played "smart" instead of "stupid." As she went on with the double monologue, she began to recognize that there really was a smart little girl behind that stupid front, and slowly began to switch her energy from the adaptive "stupid" part to the free "smart" part. And so she gave up her stupid position, and *then* we were willing to desensitize her, facilitate her giving up her driving phobia. The key statement was when she said "I think I am pretty smart to develop a driving phobia as long as I was being stupid; I might have killed myself!"

In the third type impasse, we always use two separate chairs from the original chair the client is sitting in. This is because we like to end up with the satisfied, finished client sitting in the chair they started out in, and we don't know how they will finish. Not all Type 3 impasses end up the way we are prejudicially predicting. So if we start out with the client sitting in her own chair, and she ends up out there in the middle of the room, what in the hell are we going to do with her? So we use two different chairs, and they can always go back to the original chair after they are through. Of course, that might be wise in all cases, but it is also a pain, to keep bringing in more chairs.

Usually, or at least often, somewhere in the double monologue, while the client is talking "I" from both sides, he will begin to say "you" and then we are probably getting into a type two impasse. For instance, in the above example, our little Turkish woman suddenly said "I wish you would stop calling me stupid". We set up a third chair and told her to be in that chair, and be whoever called her stupid. It turned out to be her three-years-older brother! Of course. So we finished the work by doing both Type two and Type three work; the Type two an I-Thou dialogue, and the Type three an I-I monologue. (the I is between the adapted and the Free Child, which are really both the same. When Free, the child is simply not adapting to either internal or external parental messages; when adaptive he or she is.)

Implementation:

So far, I have written chiefly about theory, not application. Of course, the resolution of the impasse, and subsequently the Redecision, does not take place in a vacuum. I have not dealt yet with the other "C", the copouts. By confronting almost every copout, we keep teaching the client how he fails himself, gives up his autonomy, in many ways, and most especially in his language. We teach him about tilt, try, toot, and Tonto! Tilt is the code word for saying something that indicates that he doesn't believe he is in charge of his own behavior, thinking, feeling, and body as "She made me angry" or "He made me do it" or "A thought came to me that" or "My heart's beating faster" or "My breathing is shallow." This constant confrontation, and request for a change in passive to active tense, is only language at first, but slowly the patient begins to understand that there is more than language involved as he says over and over again "I sadden myself" he begins to understand that he in fact does sadden himself, and that his wife does not "make him sad". "Try" is a copout of serious magnitude, and can be explained by a simple example: the difference between "trying to defecate" and defecating. All the difference in the world. I have a huge cowbell I ring whenever anyone says "try." There is nothing more effective than this kind of humorous behavior modification. "Toot" is for *need*. I blow a whistle when people say "need" when they mean "want", and Tonto is for using "we" when there ain't no we—as Tonto said to the Lone Ranger when the latter said, "Tonto, we are surrounded by Indians! What are we going to do?" and Tonto responded "Who we."

In the following example, taken from one of the hundreds of video tapes we have, the therapist is a quite good young man, and the client, also a therapist of course, quite experienced. She has had much training before she came here, and much therapy, but was still somewhat depressed, was lacking in basic fire and spirit, which she suppressed. Part of her history that she had discussed in prior sessions with us was that she was sexually abused by an uncle when she was a little kid, and that this scene kept "coming back", as she first put it. We had reminded her that she kept bringing it back to keep her in the same feelings of inadequacy and sadness, but her Child Feeling was one of sadness that would never "let go" because of this sexual abuse scene.

This tape starts with a good contract between the therapist and the patient. A parenthesis will indicate that I am making some comments to you, the reader, about what is happening, or am giving a description of what the patient is doing with his or her body, features, etc.

Th: OK, M., what do you want to change today?

(A good request for contract. The therapist is making some statements in this question: Statement 1: that change is possible (which many therapists don't seem to believe, and thus many patients); 2: that the patient, not the therapist, is going to do the changing, that there are no magic pills or words; 3: the change is possible today! Compare this to the AGPA Consumer's guide which goes on and on about the long time therapy takes. True, it may, but more so if you believe it takes a long time, and less so if you believe that it could happen today).

M: One of the contracts I had with Mary was coming to some kind of a resolution about getting my thesis done. I decided to get it done and figure out why I was procrastinating doing it.

Th: OK so state that in the form of a contract.

Bob; (whistles)

(I was whistling about the "why,"which I didn't believe.)

M: I want to.

Bob: I don't believe that that was Mary's contract with you, to figure out why.

M: I am to make an agreement to have it done. (she means do it, write the thesis, but therapist missed this passivity.)

Bob: I see.

Th: OK, what is it you think you need to do to reach that agreement? (We only use "need" when it is really a need, as water, oxygen, minerals, proteins, vitamins, for survival. Need is a survival word, and can be used to blackmail others into doing things. The word is "want.")

M: Mm you mean to reach the agreement for myself? Yeah. I want to make a decision to get it done, to get the thesis done, and I'm still procrastinating and when I say that I feel myself digging my heels in. As if to say I'm not going to finish that son of a bitch.

Th: OK keep digging your heels in—what does that tell you.

(She is looking sadder, and more desolate, and less energetic, as she goes on).

M: Uhm I'm not going to get it done. Those bastards aren't going to get that out of me. And as I say that, it's only me I'm fighting, I'm not fighting anybody else. I'm not fighting anybody but me. So it doesn't make sense—I don't make sense, when I do that.

(She knows about "it" and "I"—when we say "I", we take power, when we say "it", we become passive, lose power, so she is listening to herself, and beginning to become more and more aware.) (Hand in front of crotch, with feet up on the couch, legs spread apart, crotch open with one hand covering it, palm in, back of hand out).

M continues: And what I am doing is going back in my head saying what in the hell is in the battle, why do *you* keep fighting. Just do it, that's all you need to do is do it.

(Note that she says *you*, not I, which indicates that she has just switched from her Child or Adult to her Parent Ego State, repeating whatever it was that a parent or strong figure said: "Why do *you* keep fighting, just do it.")

Th: OK, there seems to be two poles, will you take one side first—take the side that says I'm not going to do it. And talk to the other part over there. Start with "I'm not going to do it."

M: This is the I won't side?

Th: Yeah.

M: Long pause, pushes him down with her other hand, waving at him, and says "I'm willing to do what you want, but what I'm now aware of is that I changed from I to you a minute ago and said (good for her, she heard herself) all *you* need to do is do it and I'm just aware of that. (Her right hand is still in front of her crotch, but she is moving her fingers up and down her left thigh.) I want to do something with that—I changed pronouns when I said "all you need to do is do it." I heard myself tell myself that, and what I am saying is I'll do what you suggested, and maybe I'll do something with that by taking the I won't side.

Th: How do you want to structure?

M: As you suggested, Jesus, I'm real aware of energy, of being angry, as I feel I won't do it. (Loud sigh) I won't finish the thesis. I won't get done with school. (Pulls hands away from crotch, but not wrist, and emphasizes with her fingers on her right thigh as she says "I won't. I won't do it." (Looks solemn, sad, tightens corners of mouth, squeezes lips together).

Th: What's happening right now?

M: I'm still back with that message, all you need to do is do it. No I need more than just to do it. (Swallows) I need (left hand comes up, makes a finger to thumb contact.) Huh, I need you to do it for me. (Grins.)

Th: Who is sitting over there.

M: (long long pause, 13 seconds) My mother. Hand (long, long pause, 13 seconds) my mother. (Hand goes in front of crotch again.) Mother won't do it, I've got to do it myself. (Scratches forehead with left hand). I gotta do it myself. Yeah, it's a battle ground. School is a battle ground (she is in a master's program, is all done but her thesis). (Now starts to pull at her hair with her left hand, which is a common very small child gesture).

Th: Are you aware what you are doing with your hand, your left hand? (He is either not aware of her right hand at all, which is unlikely, or some part of him doesn't want to point out to her that all this time she has been covering her crotch with her right hand, and my guess is that this is how he didn't bring her to the point of the impasse).

M: Yeah, I'm stroking my head, playing with my hair.

Th: What's your hand saying to the rest of your body, to your head?

M: Uh, I want to pull my hair rather than stroke it, and I won't do that, I'll stroke it instead, . . . I uh I'm what I am is angry.

Th: How do you mean?

M: This morning in that bioenergetics group, just watching those people get into all that anger, I'm really feeling stirred up.

Th: You are stirring yourself up.

(He knows about "make feels," too.)

M: Yeah, I'm stirring myself up, just feeling the charge through my body, I'm feeling charged, I'm charged. And at the same time, I won't, you can't make me, (makes a fist of her left hand).

Th: What's happening.

M: Um, I was tensing my whole body, and I was bringing up um stuff um from the past um and telling myself I wanted to stop, I'm not ready to get into this again.

Th: Do I hear you right, you want to stop.

M: Nods yes, Uhhuh, (looks sad.)

Bob: I would agree, but then what's the reason.

M: Um, I'm accessing the rape scene again, and—

Bob: When are you going to finish that?

M: (looks stricken).

Bob: I'm not asking you to do it, I'm asking you to set up a time, when you are going to put that behind you, you have been putting that off for two or three years, and then you make yourself feel bad. When are you willing to finish it?

M: (Laughs) When are you willing to finish it? (Makes fist with left hand.)

(Of course she does. She is responding to me transferentially: as Mother says "just do it," and now I say "when are you willing to do it?" and she is feeling rebellious in her Child, even though she knows I am right—the repetition with me, of course, of what the work is all about.)

M: I want to finish it.

Bob: Any idea how you are going to do it?

M: I know how I'll know when it's done, I'm telling myself "well, you've worked on it twice, in the last three years, and that should be enough, you should be done."

Bob: Thanks Mother. There she is: "All you have to do is do it."

M: Right, all I have to do is do it.

Bob: You sure withhold from that, don't you. At your own cost. The story of your life, that you withhold at your own cost.

M: Yeah.

Bob: See how that worked for you first into the rape scene.

M: Looking puzzled "Into the rape scene"?

Bob: Yeah. You were of course withholding then. But now you are still withholding, even though it's at your own cost. What you experience is that every time anyone wants anything from you, even though it's for your own good, you withhold, just as you withheld in that old, old scene.

M: Yeah, and I just contracted the whole, lower part of my body, (At this point, she is sitting with her legs wide apart, and her hand again in front of her crotch.)

Bob: Look over at the TV. (She looks, then moves her hand away from her crotch, moves it over her belly.

Bob: You invite, at the same time as you withhold. I'm not saying you are playing rapo *now*. Most of the time during this work you have held your hand down over your crotch.

M: Protecting myself.

Bob: Yeah, without even knowing where it was.

M: Yeah. No, I wasn't.

Bob: So part of your script is to withhold when people demand of you, even though it costs you. Instead of withholding when it fits for you, not when it doesn't.

M: (nods) I'd like to continue to work on that, NOW. Do I have time?

Bob: Yeah, sure. You've seven minutes (!!). (We only allow each piece of work to go on for only 20 minutes.) Get back to Jack, and will you say this to Jack?

M: Yeah, I withhold even when it costs me. Yes, I want to change that.

Bob: (To Th.) You know what the script is, Jack. (He nods).

M: I want to change that—I want to be done with the rape scene, done with the rape (nods her head).

Th: Are you willing to go back? (M nods)

(All our work is done in the present tense whenever possible. We don't tell stories about, but go back in the scene as if it were happening right now. This way we access the Child, and get together the memory of the scene and the feeling.)

Th: Describe the scene.

M: I am in the my bedroom at their house. Uh, I see my uncle come in the bedroom, and . . . he's . . . (sighs) . . . (She is sitting on the couch with her legs against her chest, her feet on the edge of the seat, her knees and calves locked closed, her head slightly thrown back). Long pause. He's pinching my body, and he's sticking . . . his fingers . . . inside my vagina. and . . . um.

Bob: Say this to him. You're sticking your fingers in me . . .

M: You're sticking your fingers in my vagina, and he's (Bob: You) and you are trying to put your penis in my mouth, and I'm wanting you to stop, and (head goes back a little further) and my aunt is in the doorway, and um . . . (she is stiffening her body, almost like a catatonic, with her left hand picked up from the couch, in the air, with the fingers rigid, clawlike.) And . . . I want to bite you . . . and I do, and you're hitting me . . . Ohhhh. and I'm telling you to stop, and I'm crying . . . (Head goes back even further on her neck) (bursts into tears, crying) I WANT MY MOTHER, I want my mother . . .

Bob: Is she in the house? (Notice *is* not *was* to keep the scene alive) Is there anybody in the house besides the two of them?

M: No, I'm all alone (crying) I want my mother. (Sobs more).

Bob: You said to him "stop it" Tell him again.

M: Stop it (Screams:) STOP IT ARNIE (Head extended now at least 90 degrees on her neck) STOP IT (Pauses, sobbing . . .)

B: What happens next?

M: (through her sobs) He's pushing my head back (as she extends it as far as it would be possible for it to go). I want my mother. (Bob: what happens next?) He goes away.

Bob: He stops, huh? (She nods her head) So you are successful in stopping him.

M: (Putting her head back in a normal position, straight) nods.

Bob: Are you successful in stopping him?

M: Yeah (nodding her head again).

Bob: Are you successful in stopping him? (I am not convinced yet that she is aware of what she has done, and repeat my question until she reacts in a comprehending way.) (M Nods) Tell him that, "I stopped you!"

M: (with more vigor) I stopped you (Say it again) I stopped you, I STOPPED YOU. (She is still sitting on the couch with her legs up on the couch, feet on the edge, held close together).

Bob: Get up and say it with some power.

M: (Stands up, holds her hands up like a boxer's victory stance, and shouts) (I stopped you Arnie (Bob: Louder) I stopped you, you son of a bitch (Waving her left hand in the air, in a fist. Surprised look on her face). I stopped him.

Bob: You did stop him. You screamed enough, and bit enough, and hollered enough, you even stopped Taj (the labrador, who is often in the seminar room). He moved away. (She laughs) You are pretty powerful, to get Taj to move. (She laughs even harder, loosening her body, rubbing her face, with a look of great glee on her face. Massages her neck. Laughs again).

M: I really did stop him, didn't I.

Bob: You did, so you are a winner, instead of a loser, not a victim after all.

M: Yeah, (grinning) I stopped him (in a childlike, amazed voice jumping up and down a little,) I stopped him, I stopped him, yeah I did stop him. (Crowd applauds, she applauds with them.)

Bob: Will you tell these people in here "I will only stop people when it is for my benefit, I won't stop them when it's not for my benefit."

M: Yeah (looking around the room) I'll stop you when it's for my benefit, not when it's not.

Bob: I'll stop *me* when its for my benefit, not when it's not.

M: (Grinning, rubbing her tummy, shoulders back, head on straight,) I'll stop me? (Questioning.)

Bob: Yeah, "I'll stop me when it's for my benefit, not when it's not."

M: (Grinning even more in understanding, rubbing her tummy, laughing now.) I'll stop me when it's for my benefit, and not when it's not. Yeah, (nodding head delightedly) (rubs her tummy, then lets her hand go down and rub her crotch).

Bob: Nice snatch you got there that you're rubbing on?

(I realize the vulgarity, and I want to continue to access Free Child, and there is nothing like vulgarity to access Free Child, especially in this patient)

M: Laughs delightedly, continuing to rub her crotch, "Yeah, nice one," Looks entirely different than she did when she was starting this work. Body loose, face relaxed excitedly. "God damn" she says, again excitedly, shaking her head as if in wonderment. "I'm done" (Just as she says this, the little timer alarm goes off, and she has finished her work in exactly 20 minutes, all the time we allow for each piece. The crowd laughs in appreciation, applauds. She says to her therapist ''Thanks for staying with me'', gets up, brushes herself off, announces once more ''I'm done'' and goes back to her chair.)

Bob: Nice work. (looking at therapist) I hope you didn't mind my coming in.

Th: Oh, not at all.

She came back in a year for another two weeks of training. She had finished her thesis, set up private practice, had straightened out her relationship with her very nice (also therapist) husband, and looked great. She reported with enthusiasm all the things she had stopped withholding, all the things she had gotten or done for herself.

And so it goes. Constant attention to details, to little things. Good therapy, in our opinion, is paying great attention to details. Bringing together the importance of the little things. For instance, the way in which she covered her crotch all the time she was working on withholding from others: a small observation, perhaps, but tremendously important in terms of the relationship between withholding from sex (in reference to her childhood scene) and withholding from putting out the work necessary to finish her Masters. Every little confrontation may be the one that loosens the flood, accesses the Free Child, gets the impasse resolved, the Redecision made. Again, the Redecision *must* be made from Free Child. When I repeated my question three times: ''Are you succesful in stopping him'' I was concerned that she was responding to me from adapted, not free child, and repeated until I knew she was now aware, exploding (as Fritz would put it) with excitement.

6

Gestalt Therapy and the Bodymind: An Overview of the Rubenfeld Synergy® Method

ILANA RUBENFELD

Singing the Body
  Healing the Soul
Moving the Mind
  Completing the Whole
    Ilana Rubenfeld

As WE APPROACH the 21st century—with ever more complex family, community, and governmental systems, along with a barrage of information such as we have never had to deal with before—it becomes clearer that people must be treated as whole human beings. As therapists and educators, we can help our clients access their whole selves.

Mastery in bodymind integration is still a scarce phenomenon in therapy, education, and health care. Many therapists do excellent work with either the body or the emotions; only a few know how to fully synthesize the two.

As late as the 1960s, verbal psychotherapeutic intervention was still considered separate from body work. Although Gestalt therapy included the body as metaphor, giving attention to posture, breathing, change of complexion, movement of eyes, and so on, the heightened use of touch, as an entry point to the whole person, was not integrated into Gestalt therapy practice until recently.

My search for this profound level of integration led me to create a new therapeutic and educational paradigm, which I call the Rubenfeld Synergy® Method. In this chapter and as part of the gestalt of this book, I will include my own story; the development of the principles, theory, and practice of my method; a Rubenfeld Synergy session verbatim; and a special way of "scoring" a slice of a session.

I want to take you on a journey with me as I tell my story, describe my relationship with Fritz and Laura Perls, the co-founders and developers of Gestalt therapy, and explain how I came to what I thought was the obvious—integrating Gestalt therapy and bodymind work. This method did not blossom overnight. It was a process of many years' duration, slowly evolving to its present form, a form that will continue to evolve for many more years.

THE BIRTH OF A COMPOSER

The roots of the Rubenfeld Synergy® Method took hold in my own life before I was even aware of body work and psychotherapy. Thirty years ago, I was a full-time orchestral and choral conductor. As a conductor, I had to develop accurate *inner listening*: the skill to anticipate the tones of the composition before the orchestra plays them.

Conductors become the bridge between the score and the musicians. Their eyes rapidly scan the musical manuscript, transforming the written symbols into live tonal vibrations. Simultaneously, the conductor "reads" the score, cues the musicians, directs the volume, projects emotions (through hands, face, and body), inspires the players, is ready to move in any direction, and *integrates* all the parts into the gestalt of the composition. I credit my conductor's training for the ability to operate on so many levels in a seemingly natural way.

I had studied at the Juilliard School of Music and with Pablo Casals, and had been an assistant conductor to Leopold Stokowski. In all my training, there was no instruction in the efficient use of the body. Conducting was stressful and I developed back and shoulder spasms. Medications gave me temporary relief, and then the pain would return. My search for a cure connected me with Judy Liebowitz, a teacher of the F. M. Alexander Technique—a method designed to teach an efficient use of the body.

As Judy greeted me I noticed that she walked with a slight limp. Despite her uneven gait, she moved with an easy grace and poise that were as balanced and harmonious as a beautifully orchestrated piece of music. When Judy and I became better acquainted, I learned that she had contracted polio as a youngster, leaving her partially paralyzed on one side. Miraculously, the hint of a limp was the only visible sign of her physical impairment, a silent testimonial to the effectiveness of her Alexander training.

I began taking lessons. During each one, Judy would make subtle adjustments in the way I was standing and moving. She touched me with a unique touch, which at that time I could describe only as *having thought in it*. I was very moved by what she did, but I had no framework to understand the process that was taking place.

Judy would say certain words softly while touching my head: "Let me have your head."

The first time I heard this I was startled and said, "Let you have what?" She calmly replied, "It's all right. Let me move your head."

I sincerely thought that I was relaxing and letting my head go. Then I would hear her say it to me again: "Let your head go forward and up." Hadn't I done just that? But as the lesson continued, I became aware that I hadn't. I only thought I had relaxed. I was surprised to learn that I was not doing what I believed I was doing. As Judy touched, me I realized that my head and neck were still taut, unmoving, and full of tension.

Although I could not grasp intellectually how or why the Alexander Technique worked, I did notice that I kept feeling better. As my back spasms decreased, I was able to perform without medication. Despite the fact that I could not understand the dynamics of this technique, I continued with my lessons.

MIND-BODY CONNECTIONS

At one lesson, while Judy gently touched, I began sobbing. After several outbursts of crying, laughing, and anger, she recommended that I see a psychotherapist. By the time I reached the therapist, the emotions released during the Alexander lesson could be analyzed only as distant memories. I had one person who touched me but did not talk, and another one who talked to me but did not touch.

I was amazed that no one had integrated the soma and psyche (I had not yet heard of the work of Wilhelm Reich). Why couldn't therapists work with both verbal and nonverbal expressions? However, I continued studying the Alexander Technique and soon became an Alexander teacher.

Finally, like F. M. Alexander, who himself restored his damaged voice, and Moshe Feldenkrais, who cured his own injured knee, I set out to heal myself—to heal the separation between my soma and psyche. This seemed like such an obvious task, but with no mentor to guide me, I soon found myself conducting explorations on my own.

In the mid-1960s I met Fritz Perls and began studying Gestalt therapy at the Esalen Institute in Big Sur, Calif. One day Fritz leaned over and said: "I hear you teach the Alexander Technique. . . . Would you give me a lesson?"

"When?" I asked, flattered.

"Tonight, I will meet you at 10: 30," he said, and quickly left the room.

I put my imaginary "Fritz" into an empty chair and began a dialogue with him.

As Ilana, I said, "What nerve, asking *me* to give you a lesson after I've paid so much money to study with you. What if you don't like it?"

Switching chairs, I became Fritz. Tilting my head to one side, shrugging my shoulders, and slowly smiling, I said, "So what!"

I returned to my chair, continued dialoguing, and concluded that I did not care whether he liked it or not.

"Get on the table," I said hastily as the real Fritz walked in. As he started to unzip his gray terry cloth jumpsuit, I shouted "No! No! Leave it on!"

"What? This technique is with clothes on?" he looked shocked. We laughed and I was delighted that our "inner clowns" met each other. Throughout the lesson, humor became very important in softening his chest and deepening his experience.

Fritz, who had a heart condition, became able to walk up the steep hill without stopping his usual three times. He was very proud of what he learned and accomplished.

That encounter was the beginning of a very special mentor relationship—marked by mutual professional respect and a warm friendship. Fritz encouraged me to experiment with the integration of Gestalt therapy and the Alexander Technique. He invited me to work with him during Gestalt therapy sessions. He would sit on one side of the client, guiding the verbal interventions, while I sat on the other, using touch and observing muscular responses to the verbal content.

Our collaboration was very exciting, and I continued to develop a method for one therapist that had previously required two. We discovered that direct contact with the whole person could be made through the simultaneous combination of touch and verbal intervention. We discussed this integration as the next step in the evolution of Gestalt therapy.

As the clients relived their stories, it was evident that emotions and memories were stored in their bodies, not just their minds. Habitual tensions could interfere with their physical, mental, and emotional flexibility. The continued release of somatic holding patterns—areas of the body that are habitually tense—established new alignment and posture. However, by adding touch we gained a more direct gateway to the limbic system, the phylogenetically older subcortical brain structures that encode emotional states. This synthesis seemed more effective than verbal intervention alone, which required the complex mediations of language (believed to originate in the cortex of the brain) with all its accompanying mental filters.

Our collaborative plans abruptly ended with Fritz's death. Now there was no one to tell me, "This is right!" or "This is wrong!" Without his support, guidance, and friendship, I continued on my own.

In 1971 Moshe Feldenkrais introduced me to his pioneering body-mind work. The intensive training in his two-tiered method of Functional Integration® and Awareness Through Movement® inspired and challenged my creativity. One of Feldenkrais's great contributions to the body-mind field was the concept that in order to produce lasting change, the nervous system itself must be reeducated. Although this is an important piece of the grand puzzle, it is not enough to reeducate the nervous system. Even after the bones and muscles have realigned themselves in gravitational harmony, the limbic system (emotional brain) may continue to send out messages for the muscles to move in their old habitual ways.

The body-mind work of F. Mathias Alexander and Moshe Feldenkrais and the Gestalt therapy of Fritz and Laura Perls became the harmonics of my practice. With these three methods as the basic "score," I took a quantum leap forward to orchestrate a new therapeutic and educational paradigm. Confident that I had the requisite theoretical base and techniques to train others, I offered the first training program in this integrative method in 1977.

EXPLORING THE BACKGROUND OF THE WORD "SYNERGY"

The word "synergy" was suggested to me by Buckminster Fuller. He felt that my unique integration had matured beyond synthesis and had become a true synergy. The original elements were now combined in new ways to produce results that were not predictable from knowing the three methods separately.

Fuller's suggestion pleased me immensely since it was in harmony with my understanding of the philosophical underpinnings of Gestalt therapy. The word "synergy," like the word "gestalt," made a statement that the whole was greater than, and different from, the sum of its parts.

ELEMENTS OF THE RUBENFELD SYNERGY®
METHOD

In this section, I will delineate the elements of the Rubenfeld Synergy® Method (hereafter referred to as RSM). This process will illuminate how Gestalt therapy and the other methods contributed to the development of RSM. We begin by highlighting the following components, and then we will explore each in greater detail:

- *Dynamic structure*: When working with clients, we must be aware of the dynamic interactions of body, mind, emotions, and spirit.
- *Responsibility for change*: Change emerges from within the client. The therapist is only a catalyst for change.
- *Awareness as the key*: The cornerstone of the healing process is the client's increased awareness, which is heightened through touch, movement, and verbal intervention.
- *Intentional touch*: what the synergist/therapist is thinking and feeling is communicated through the hands to the client. Likewise, what the client is thinking and feeling is communicated back through the hands to the synergist. For this reason, the quality of touch in RSM must be considered with as much care as is the choice of words in verbal therapy.
- *Open and listening hand*: The open and listening hand conveys an attitude of responsiveness and receptivity. The quality of touch is especially light, reflecting a nonverbal "listening" stance.
- *Intuition*: Synergists learn to access knowledge and experience stored in the somatic system. This means accessing their own intuition as well as that of their clients.
- *Self-care*: The therapist's self-care becomes crucial in every session since so much is communicated through touch. Contact/boundary issues (as defined in Gestalt therapy terms) are addressed with special consideration.
- *The table replaces the hot seat*: A special table or a mattress is used to support the client in a supine position. This position, accompanied by intentional touch, helps release fixed holding patterns in the bodymind.

Now let us investigate each of the components in greater depth.

DYNAMIC STRUCTURE

The body, mind, emotions, and spirit are all interconnected to form a dynamic system.[1] Any change introduced at any level will directly influence *all* components simultaneously, including the behavior and experience of the therapist/synergist as well as those of the client.

Intellectual Knowledge of Insights

Intellectual knowledge of insights may not be sufficient to produce lasting change. In order to integrate this change, we also need a kinesthetic experience to accompany, illuminate, and ground what we have learned. This kinesthetic awareness may be introduced by either actual or imagined experiences, each being effective for imprinting new neural pathways in the brain.

The Body Expresses the Inner World

The client's inner world and attitude toward life are continually expressed through the body and nonverbal behavior such as breathing patterns, body image, posture, habitual holding patterns, gestures, facial expressions, skin color, and tone of voice.

Emotion Affects Posture and Posture Affects Emotion

Emotions continually affect physical postures. For example, if you are feeling depressed, your body posture will express this depression, classically exemplified by slumped shoulders, caved-in chest, head and neck being down. Physical habit patterns frequently become metaphors for these emotional states.

This same posture may also induce the emotions of depression. Clients then make contact with their environment and move through life with a depressed posture.[2] The way you align yourself within your bodymind reflects how you align yourself with universal issues of life.

Psychosomatic Loops

Every memory, thought, and feeling encodes in the body. The somatic system continually organizes itself to express these thoughts and feelings into actions. When not expressed, they develop into holding patterns of tension and eventually emerge as stress-related illnesses. We can observe the first layer of these tensions through facial expressions, distorted posture, and other manifestations. However, we cannot observe deeper layers of these holding patterns without the additional use of touch as a feedback loop, a kind of live biofeedback method.

The Body Dreams

Emotions in a dream translate directly into muscle responses. In Gestalt therapy, there are ample tools for verbal intervention and physical observation. However, RSM's additional skill of specific *intentional* touch gains yet another entry point into the world of dreams. You are the dreamer as well as the dream. You are dreaming your dream with your body, mind, emotions, and spirit.

An important turning point in my own life came as the result of Gestalt dream work. One of these dreams was documented in a classic film of Fritz Perls's called *Birth of a Composer*. In that dream, I became each instrument of my orchestra—acting, singing, and moving with my whole body.

At first, the instrumental emsemble (20 flutes, 20 clarinets, 2 violins, 1 viola, a cello, a timpani, and a drum) seemed comical, unlikely, and downright ugly.

"I am an ugly sound," Fritz urged me to say.

"I am *not* an ugly sound," I responded defiantly. On the contrary, "I am a beautiful and unique sound." I became the cello's deep and mellifluous tones, touching my ancient roots—the ancestral chants of my family. With Fritz's guidance I was able to experience and *own* my own unique sound—my "essential me."

Sensory Channels as Entryways

In RSM, all sensory channels (sight, sound, touch, taste, and smell) of the human organism are acknowledged as different entryways to the *gestalt* of the client. Through these sensory channels[3] we can affect change that allows the client to become contactful, open, aware, and spontaneous, and better able to flow back and forth between thinking and feeling. The client is thus able to call upon all the resources of the authentic self, rather than remaining frozen in a single role or way of being.

RESPONSIBILITY FOR CHANG

I was delighted by Fritz's concept of responsibility
respond—to make meaningful contact with oneself and oth
I had spent several summers studying with Pablo Casals
said: ''I can rehearse this music with you by creating an atmosphere of trust
and inspiration; but it is you who are ultimately *responsible* for your own
performance.'' The existential responsibility for change rests with the client.
The synergist acts as a guest conductor; the music as well as the final
performance always belong to the client.

Change Occurs in the Present

''What are you experiencing now?'' is a classical verbal intervention. In
a psychophysical system the process of change begins in the here and now.
The client can review the past, resolve unfinished business, and integrate
these new insights with the present.

In RSM, simultaneous touch and verbal communication link somatic
experiences from the past. With the use of active imagination, this experience
is relived in real time. The nervous system responds to the memory as if it
were happening in the present. The ancient poet, Lao Tzu, has a wonderful
phrase in one of his poems: ''What is, is the was of what shall be.''

Healing From Within

Rather than ''correcting'' from the outside in, the synergist evokes the
client's innate healing ability. This healing potential already exists, waiting
to be actualized. A fundamental axiom in Gestalt theory and RSM is that
every organism has the capacity to attain an optimum healing balance within
itself and with its environment.

AWARENESS IS THE KEY

Change cannot happen without awareness. Physical and emotional habit
patterns are learned unconsciously, and as long as they remain in the background, the client has no conscious choice. Through heightening of awareness (with movement, touch, verbal intervention, and creative experimentation) they become figural. The client recognizes these habitual patterns, and

has the opportunity to explore alternate choices, develop possibilities for psychophysical change, and enhance the capacity for self-healing.

In fine-tuning somatic awareness, clients are invited to experience new movements and postures. At first, they become more aware of their gross tensions. Afterward, they learn to "listen" somatically, paying attention to subtler cues.

A client complained of severe pain in his right shoulder, which appeared much higher than the left. During the session, the right shoulder released, dropped dramatically, and was evenly aligned with the left. When I asked the client what he was experiencing, he closed his eyes and reported that the left shoulder was now much higher than the right. Then I asked him to look in the mirror, and he realized that his two shoulders were even. This postural habit pattern had distorted his experience of reality. By increasing his self-awareness and self-observation, he developed a clearer sense of his inner and outer worlds.

Confusion: Essential Element for Change

English is my third language. As a result, I am especially intrigued with the construction and meanings of words. The word "confusion" suggests many things to me. Taking this word apart, we see that "con" can mean both "with" and "opposed to," while "fusion" means "fusing" or "union." Thus, the word "confusion" can be a key concept for both pulling apart and joining—an idea that is important in all processes of change.[4]

Clients are encouraged to allow themselves feelings of confusion without negative judgment. You have to be willing to be disorganized (*con*fused), in order to get reorganized (fusion).

Spasms, tension blocks, and lack of energy indicate the existence of habitual holding patterns—old organized ways of being. When they become dysfunctional and painful, the client seeks help to change them. Confusing the patterns will transform them into another configuration: one that will move more freely. Confusion is one step along the way to reorganization, healing, and change.

INTENTIONAL TOUCH

Touch used in the somatic experience begins with the client's consent—not by forcing. The will to change emanates from within the client and moves outward toward the synergist's hands. It is the client who initiates the release of tension, and it is the synergist who responds and follows. When the client has had closure, the energy flow and muscle tone change.

Ralph Hefferline's early research showed relationships between emotional states and muscle responses. Through an educated touch we can feel these responses before they appear, through facial expressions, body language, and verbalization. Clients may appear relaxed, their voice calm, as they claim that they are no longer angry. However, when the synergist touches their shoulder and back, the muscle's rigid texture may feel like steel and clearly express the contradiction. The client may be invited to dialogue with the shoulder and give it a voice: "I feel tight and burdened" or "Get off my back!" or "I don't want to carry you anymore." This dialogue becomes the entry point of the session.

An Invitation to Experiment

In my workshops and training programs I have participants experiment with intentionality: how thoughts and feelings affect the way we experience touch. The following is a simple exercise to demonstrate this phenomenon. Take a few moments, if you will, to experiment.

Find a partner and stand facing the partner's left shoulder (from the side) . . . Ask your partner to close his or her eyes and stand quietly . . . Imagine that something is wrong with your partner's left shoulder and that you have to *do something* quickly to fix it . . . Go ahead and touch your partner with this thought . . . After a few moments, move your hands away and rest them at your sides . . . Let yourself be quiet for a few seconds . . . Now, imagine that the shoulder before you belongs to a whole person and that your intention is *not to do something* quickly to fix it. Instead, your attitude is one of not doing anything, but rather of allowing a change to emerge at its own pace . . . Go ahead and touch your partner's shoulder with that intention of *allowing* rather than *doing* . . . While you remain focused with this thought, your partner will have the time and space to release any tensions in his or her back and neck. You may feel a distinct shift in the quality and texture of your partner's shoulder . . . Now, slowly move your hands away from your partner and let them rest at your sides . . . Walk around so that you are facing your partner . . . Ask your partner to open his or her eyes slowly . . . Notice any changes that have occurred in your partner's facial expression, breathing pattern, and entire body . . . What was it like to touch your partner? What was it like for your partner to be touched with these two different intentionalities? Take as much time as you want to process what you have both learned from this exchange.

Much time is devoted to learning how intention affects touch and how touch creates a dialogue with the unconscious mind. Trainees learn that touching with intentionality builds a bridge to the neuromuscular system, which in turn gives feedback about the client's state of bodymind. There are specific techniques that I have developed to teach people how to use themselves as finely tuned instruments.

Respect for Boundaries

The client's boundaries are fully respected, no matter how they may appear. The synergist heightens the client's awareness of boundaries and thus supports the client's choice to expand, contract, or relax. This is especially crucial when working with incest and abuse survivors.

Mirroring

Often, there is a disparity between what clients think they are doing and what they are actually doing. Through astute observation, the use of touch, and constructive feedback, clients learn to build bridges between their inner and outer realities. Mirroring is achieved by miming clients' posture and actions, having them hear their own voice, placing them in front of a mirror, encouraging them to role-play, and so on.

Fertile Voids

I first heard the expression "fertile void" during a discussion with Fritz Perls, who attributed it to Wilson Van Dusen.[5] I was struck by the Zen quality of the notion that emptiness could be the womb for change. The client may be asked to "do nothing" while suspending judgment. Some of the most profound changes have emerged out of stillness and emptiness. However, the fertile void may also appear as "stuck" places or an impasse and may create anxiety for both the therapist and the client. It is important for therapists to learn how to wait and not push clients through their impasse prematurely.

Visualization

In an RSM session, clients are usually lying down and may be in a deeply relaxed state. It is quite effective to have them visualize a movement or a person rather than getting up and acting it out. The nervous system equates this visualization with the movement and the natural flow of the session is not interrupted.

OPEN AND LISTENING HANDS

Initially, open and listening hands are used to gather information that provides the synergist with an image of the client's bodymind.[6] This quality of touch "hears" whether the client's somatic observations reflect reality.

Open and listening hands are not pushy or tense. They communicate patience, caring, and a willingness to wait for the client to initiate a change. In their highest expression, they reflect unconditional respect.

Somatic movements often set the stage for verbal interventions. Without forcing, clients can express emotions and learn that they possess the power to change.

In some forms of therapy, the goal is to break down the client's armor. The synergist's approach is not to crack the armor but to *melt* it and dissolve the need for it. Just as in verbal therapy clients are not pushed to say things that do not emanate naturally from them, in RSM the synergist does not impose touch or movement that would not be meaningful. Gentle touch is used to contact the client's comfort level, giving the client time to establish trust and rapport with the synergist. Once the client lets go, the actual physical and emotional release is swift.

A young woman came to me who had been in a severe car accident that resulted in a whiplash injury to her neck. She had received numerous treatments for this injury, but she was still in pain. She complained that the treatments had brought only temporary relief. Since her physician could find nothing functionally wrong with her neck and shoulders, he recommended that she seek other ways to deal with her dilemma.

After preliminary touching, I felt a tight spasm in her upper back and neck. I asked her to describe the accident in the present tense.

"I'm driving the car and another car comes toward me. There is a man in the other car. I can see by the way he is driving that he is going to hit me—he doesn't see me." Her neck and back tightened while tears welled up in her eyes. "Look at me. Pay attention to me!" In spite of her shouting, the driver fails to pay attention to her and a head-on collision occurs.

I felt her whole body constrict as she told the story of the crash. There were areas that felt rigid and without energy, as though the life in them had drained away. I sensed that this crash contained old painful memories.

"Who else wouldn't look at you?" I asked her.

"My father!" she said sobbing. A dialogue followed on the theme of her father, his alcoholic problems, and how he ignored her. She had become stiff-necked to keep from experiencing profound pain.

I asked her to reverse roles and to play her father. She did this, alternating between being herself shouting at her father for attention, and being her father sitting passively—sometimes drunk—and ignoring her cries. After a few minutes of this interchange, her father finally noticed her. At that moment, I had my hands under her neck and my fingertips felt some softening in her muscles, yet there was still a lack of energy moving through the area. Some piece of the puzzle was still missing.

I asked her to go back to the accident. Since it was like a daydream, I told her she could rewrite that script and imagine the outcome of this event in any way she wanted. She began slowly. "I'm driving the car and I can see the other car coming toward me. There's a man in the car. He sees me. He swerves and doesn't hit me!" she shouts smiling broadly.

With my open and listening hands, I felt a profound physical release in her neck and shoulders. That area relaxed, became supple, energetic, and full of life. There could be no doubt that she had successfully rewritten her script. My hands convinced me that she had attained closure.

A year later, she wrote that the emotional and physical release had been complete and that her pain had not returned.

INTUITION

Intuition is an important element of RSM and the training process. I believe that intuitive information emerges from within us and is the culmination of our total life experience. It consists of all the knowledge and wisdom that we have inherited from our families, from our culture, and through what C. G. Jung calls the collective unconscious.

Intuition can be taught. However, some people learn to use it better than others. Two different pianists may perform the same composition with technical brilliance and yet one may leave us unmoved while the other touches us. The difference has to do with intuition. Both the synergist and the pianist express it through their touch. It becomes a metaphor of their philosophy, attitude, and life experience.

I believe that the body contains a memory and knowledge of its own. Intuitive touch develops a direct link with "cell consciousness" while inviting a learning exchange through the nervous system of both client and synergist. It is important for movement and intuitive touch to work together. I recognize this integration as a *new language*; a sophisticated way of communicating, receiving, and giving information stored within us.

I have worked with many displaced persons—those who have experienced the ravages of war as children, and had to leave their native land. I can sense the terror and anxiety in their bodies. They have memories of sudden separations, death, and escaping their homeland. These clients talk about their past traumas, but until they have worked them through on the cellular level, the terror inside continues to hide. "Healing the damaged child within" is a recurring theme in their sessions. Dialoguing with their hurt and fearful child, accompanied with intuitive touch, assists these clients to transform and integrate painful unfinished business.

SELF-CARE: THE FIRST STEP IN CLIENT CARE

Fritz Perls told me about an old friend who phoned him regularly complaining about headaches and bouts of depression. As the conversation concluded, his friend was always feeling much better, and now Fritz had the headache and felt depressed. This story humorously illustrates how self-care is vitally connected to the issue of contact/boundary.

A key question therapists often ask is: "How can I remain empathetic and take care of myself without taking on my client's anxieties, fears, and tensions?"

Sticking Your Neck Out

A psychoanalyst suffering from a stiff neck could not turn his head. He demonstrated how he sat and listened to his patients: chin jutting forward, neck sticking out, and back stooped and rounded. I invited him to exaggerate his posture. "I never knew how much I stick my neck out for my patients and get fixed into a position," he said surprised.

"You look as if you're in a postural trance," I responded.

He was silent and suddenly his eyes sparkled, "You're right, I get trancefixed!"

He learned to change this habitual posture and no longer needed to stick his neck out in order to hear his patients. He enhanced his ability to listen without becoming drained and tired.

The danger of not taking care of yourself when using touch is that you transmit your problems through your hands. Instead of releasing their tensions, you give them yours. The reverse is also true. You are particularly vulnerable, when using touch, to the somatic aches and pains of the client. Knowing how to maintain personal boundaries is essential to the therapeutic relationship.

Collaborative contact takes a great deal of energy and concentration in the best of circumstances. In order to sustain a high quality in the relationship, it is essential that the synergist pay attention to his or her posture, nourishment, breathing, centering, and physical environment. The lighting in the room, comfort of the furniture, quality of the air, sounds, colors, and smells—all have a powerful influence on the healing partnership. The care for the client grows out of knowing how to take care of yourself. The more you grapple with your own issues and continue to complete them, the less unfinished business you will project onto your clients.

THE TABLE REPLACES THE HOT SEAT

In group therapy the "staging" of a session symbolizes the relationships between therapist, client, and group. Fritz Perls clearly established his authority by sitting in front with participants facing him in a semicircle. This created defined territories, with Fritz in the position of director, commanding the attention of the "audience." When participants volunteered to work, they left their own space and entered the arena of the "hot seat," an empty chair next to the therapist. Many Gestalt therapists utilize this formal way of staging.

Laura Perls (who pioneered and co-founded the theory and practice of Gestalt therapy) and Sonia Nevis (who assisted Fritz Perls at Esalen in the 1960s and was one of my teachers) were more informal, sitting among the participants in the circle. The hot seat moved to wherever the volunteer happened to be sitting. This arrangement had variations: the volunteer might advance to the center, facing the therapist, or the therapist might move towards the volunteer.

I explored several spatial arrangements, combining those that best suited the needs of a touch/movement-centered therapy. Most RSM sessions take place on a special table or a mattress in the center of the room with participants forming a circle around the table. The synergist begins with the request for a volunteer client who leaves his or her space, proceeds to the table, and is invited to lie down. As the session continues, the client does a "piece of work," and includes the synergist/therapist in his or her territory.

At the conclusion of the session, there is a reentry phase. The client is asked to sit up slowly, get off the table, stand, walk around the room, reconnect with the group, and return to his or her space. The psychophysical sequences of lying, sitting, standing and walking are seen as important developmental stages of growing up.

As a metaconcept, the clients experience themselves as (a) establishing their place in the family and community, (b) leaving the "home" place and becoming the center of attention, (c) with the therapist's guidance, delving deeply into themselves, and (d) separating from the therapist and returning to the family and community.

The stories that emerge from clients become archetypal themes for all the participants. They witness, identify, empathize, project, and often share the anger, laughter, and tears. Usually some time is devoted to discussing the essential themes and listening to the reactions of the group members. The synergy of the group depends on the interactive quality of each individual's process.

In private sessions, the synergist and client may work with an imagined group of people—relatives, friends, and co-workers—who normally populate the client's life.

THE CONTINUING EVOLUTION OF RSM

> Once again, as so many times before the Roshi [Zen master] took the brush and seemingly without effort made a perfect circle. The student could contain himself no longer. "Master, how do you make such circles, time after time? It looks so simple when you do it." "Ah, yes," replied the Roshi, the barest hint of a smile on his lips, "fifty years of simple."
>
> Zen parable

Often clients and workshop participants remark that RSM looks so simple. In fact, it seems so because it is natural. The Rubenfeld Synergy® Method is not a radical therapeutic approach. It respects the innate and indivisible wholeness of clients. It provides an opportunity for them to explore, express, and expand through body, mind, emotions, and spirit.

RSM has been successfully taught to hundreds of people who are now certified practitioners. The application of RSM has been very successful with the following populations:

- Codependents, recovering chemical dependency abusers, and their families
- Physically abused and incest survivors

- Dysfunctional families and couples
- Displaced persons and war survivors
- People dealing with AIDS, multiple sclerosis, and cancer
- Stress-related occupations
- Mental health and health care professionals
- Corporate and business people
- Senior citizens and their communities
- Expressive artists and performers
- Teachers in all levels of education and school counselors
- Body workers of all disciplines
- Care givers—professional and family

"Body and Soul" was the title to the cover story that appeared in *Newsweek*, November 8, 1988. Apparently the scientific community is now able to confirm what has been known for centuries, that our lives are lived through every inch of ourselves, body and soul. Any change must address the entire being—every cell within the continuum of the bodymind.

RSM continues to find new applications and avenues for effective use without having to compromise or contort its basic principles or perspective. When a great piece of music is performed well, it seems simple. And if this approach at times seems simple, perhaps that is only a confirmation that it functions in harmony with nature—human nature.

NOTES

1. Albert Einstein's theory of relativity, Neils Bohr's theory of complementarity, Ilya Prigogine's ideas he called "dissipative structures," and Ludwig Von Bertanlanffy's new science of general systems theory all suggest that the parts of a system affect each other through their interactions, constantly changing the equilibrium of the entire system.

2. Posture and attitude are expressed in the same German word, *Haltung*.

3. Charlotte Selver, the founder of Sensory Awareness, influenced me greatly by her emphasis on the importance of experiencing each sense in the moment.

4. Ilya Prigogine, a Nobel Laureate, says that "falling apart is only a phase of falling together."

5. Wilson van Dusen, Ph.D., former Chief Psychologist at Mendocino State Hospital, Calif., and author of *The Natural Depth in Man*.

6. Judith Leibowitz's teaching of the "open" hand profoundly influenced the development of the touch used in RSM.

REFERENCES

Alexander, F. M. (1932). *The use of the self*. New York: E. P. Dutton. Centerline Press edition (1984), Downey, CA.

Appelbaum, S. A. (1981). *Out in inner space: A psychoanalyst explores the new therapies.* (Chapter about Ilana Rubenfeld.) Topeka: Menninger Foundation.

Barlow, W. (1973). *The Alexander Principle.* London: Victor Gollancz, Ltd.

Becker, R. O. and Selden, G. (1985). *The body electric.* New York: William Morrow and Co.

Birdwhistell, R. (1970). *Kinesics and context.* New York: Ballantine.

Brooks, C. (1974). *Sensory Awareness.* New York: Felix Morrow.

Dossey, L. (1982). *Time, space and medicine.* Boston: Shambhala.

Erickson, M. H., Rossi, E. L., and Rossi, S. (1976). *Hypnotic realities.* New York: Irvington.

Erickson, M. H. and Rossi, E. L. (1981). *Experiencing hypnosis.* New York: Irvington.

Fagan, J. and Shepherd, I. L. (1970). *Gestalt therapy now.* New York: Harper and Row.

Feiss, G. (1979). *Mind therapies, body therapies: A consumer's guide.* Millbrae, CA: Celestial Arts.

Feldenkrais, M. (1949). *Body and mature behavior.* New York: International Universities Press.

Feldenkrais, M. (1972). *Awareness through movement.* New York: Harper and Row.

Feldenkrais, M. (1981). *The elusive obvious.* Cupertino, CA: Meta Publications.

Fuller, B. (1975). *Synergetics: Explorations in the geometry of thinking.* New York: Macmillan.

Fuller, B. (1976). *And it came to pass, not to stay.* New York: Macmillan.

Gerber, R. (1988). *Vibrational medicine.* Santa Fe: Bear and Co.

Grayson, H. and Loew, C. (1978). *Changing approaches to psychotherapy.* (Chapter by I. Rubenfeld, Alexander Technique and Gestalt therapy.) New York: Spectrum Publications.

Hanna, T. (1980). *The body of life.* New York: Knopf.

Herink, R. (1979). *Psychotherapy handbook.* (Chapter by I. Rubenfeld, Gestalt Synergy.) New York: New American Library.

Johnson, D. (1983). *Body.* Boston: Beacon Press.

Jones, F. P. (1976). *Body awareness in action: A study of the Alexander Technique.* New York: Schocken Books.

Kaslof, L. (1978). *Wholistic dimensions in healing.* (Chapter by I. Rubenfeld, Alexander: The use of the self.) Garden City: Doubleday.

Kepner, J. I. (1987). *Body process.* New York: Gardner Press.

Kruger, H. (1974). *Other healers, other cures.* (Chapter about Ilana Rubenfeld.) New York: Bobbs-Merrill Co.

Kurts, R. and Prestera, H. (1980). *The body reveals.* New York: Harper and Row.

Lao Tsu (1944). *The way of life.* Translated by Witter Bynner. New York: John Day Co.

Maisel, E. (1969). *The resurrection of the body: The writings of F. Matthias Alexander.* New York: Dell.

Maturan, H. R. and Varela, F. J. (1988). *The tree of knowledge.* Boston: Shambhala.

Montague, A. (1971). *Touching*. New York: Harper and Row.

Perls, F., Hefferline, R. and Goodman, P. (1951). *Gestalt therapy*. New York: Julian Press.

Perls, F. (1969). *Gestalt therapy verbatim*. Lafayette, CA: Real People Press.

Polster, E. and Polster, M. (1973). *Gestalt therapy integrated*. New York: Brunner/Mazel.

Rosen, S. (ed.) (1982). *My voice will go with you: The teacher tales of Milton Erickson, M.D*. New York: Norton.

Rosenfeld, E. (1973). *The book of highs: 250 ways to alter consciousness without drugs*. New York: Quadrangle.

Rubenfeld, I. (1972). *Alexander Technique and innovations*. In American Dance Therapy Association, *Dance therapy: Roots and extensions*. Columbia, MD: ADTA.

Rubenfeld, I. (1973). *The Rubenfeld Synergy Method*, formerly Gestalt Synergy. Unpublished paper. Reprints available from the Rubenfeld Center, 115 Waverly Place, New York, NY 10011.

Rubenfeld, I. (Sept. 1983). *The synergy of the body, mind, and emotions. Esalen Catalog*. Reprints available from the Rubenfeld Center, 115 Waverly Place, New York, NY 10011.

Rubenfeld, I. (Spring 1984). Article about the Rubenfeld Synergy® Method. *Therapy Now*. Reprints available from the Rubenfeld Center, 115 Waverly Place, New York, NY 10011.

Rubenfeld, I. (1985). *Self-care for the professional woman: Beyond physical fitness*. In L. Knezek, M. Barrett, and S. Collins (eds.), *Woman and work: 1985 symposium*. The University of Texas at Arlington.

Rubenfeld, I. (1988, Spring/Summer). *Beginner's hands: Twenty-five years of simple: Rubenfeld Synergy—the birth of a therapy. Somatics*. Reprints available from the Rubenfeld Center, 115 Waverly Place, New York, NY 10011.

Rubenfeld, I. and Markova, D. (1982). *Variations on a theme: A look at the Rubenfeld Synergy® Method*. Unpublished paper. Reprints available from the Rubenfeld Center, 115 Waverly Place, New York, NY 10011.

Rubenfeld, I. (Autumn/Winter 1990-91). *Ushering in a Century of Integration. Somatics*. Reprints available from the Rubenfeld Center, 115 Waverly Place, New York, Ny 10011.

Rubenfeld, I. (Winter 1991). *Our Lady of Synergy. Massage Therapy Journal*. Reprints available from the Rubenfeld Center, 115 Waverly Place, New York, NY 10011.

Sweigard, L. (1974). *Human movements potential*. New York: Harper and Row.

Todd, M. E. (1968). *The thinking body*. New York: Dance Horizons.

Van Dusen, W. (1972). *The natural depth in man*. New York: Harper and Row.

Vaughan, F. (1986). *The inward arc: Healing and wholeness in psychotherapy and spirituality*. Boston: Shambhala.

Von Bertalanffy, L. (1968). *General system theory*. New York: George Braziller.

Zinker, J. (1977). *Creative process in Gestalt therapy*. New York: Brunner/Mazel.

APPENDIX A
"I don't have to hide when I'm hurt"

The Story of Sheldon: A Rubenfeld Synergy Session Verbatim

I ask for a volunteer. Sheldon, a bearded, slightly pudgy man in his mid-thirties walks up to the table, which is surrounded by a circle of workshop participants.

"I am a spiritual counselor," he announces somewhat hesitantly.

I am impressed with his face, especially his crying eyes, which contradict a curiously smiling mouth. There is a soft, nervous quality about him. In my work I have observed how spirituality can be used to camouflage or bypass difficult feelings, and my intuition is that he uses his spiritual softness to protect himself from pain.

He lies down on the table, and within seconds there are pools of sweat dripping from his hands and feet. To relieve his deep apprehension, I find ways to deflect attention from him while he adjusts himself to the table and to being in the center of the room. I busy myself by talking with a participant about her scoliosis.

I do a quick visual scan and notice that he is beginning to relax. But then I gently touch his head; it is totally rigid. I move his feet, which are wet from his perspiration. I become aware of the many places in his body that are frozen. From past experience I recognize that these places represent old psychic wounds that his body remembers.

"There are quite a few things going on in your life," I say to him.

He nods in agreement. My hands vibrate with evidence of his pain and rigidity. Speaking softly, I tell him, "So we're going to let those issues start to soften up." Somehow we must work together to soften his body so that his blocked and interdicted feelings can finally emerge.

I slip my hands underneath his left hip joint and ask him to send heightened awareness to that area, signalling it to release some of the tension. He tries but manages to send only a faint message, and I continue to keep my hands under his left hip joint. Again, I ask him to send down a message of letting go. This time his message is clear and stronger. With my hands I guide the released energy down his leg and out through his foot. I note that there is now literally a puddle of sweat around Sheldon's left foot.

I go to his right side and place my hands under his right hip joint. My hands are open and listening. They communicate patience, caring, and a willingness to wait.

"Let some of those issues start moving around." I want him to become aware that he has the power to start dissolving the armor of resistance that is blocking the flow of his life force.

Sheldon takes a deep breath and sighs. I ask him to float his knees up and place his feet on the table. I move them gently from side to side, checking to see that his hip joints are still open. I sense that he could quickly go back into his holding pattern.

Placing my hands lightly on his lower ribs, I ask him to imagine moving energy from the bottom of his spine (survival chakra), through his stomach (emotional chakra), and up to the top of his head.[1] There is a slight movement. I quickly shift to his head, slipping my right hand under his chest (heart chakra) and my left hand under his neck (throat chakra). I feel his chest becoming thicker and tighter. He senses this and begins to release some tensions in this area—a slight and subtle movement begins.

I slide my hands underneath his left shoulder, my fingertips palpating the muscles between his spine and shoulder blade. Cradling his shoulder, I feel an enormous density.

"OK. So what comes to your foreground right now?" I ask.

"I have many completions happening in my life," Sheldon replies: "a divorce, children, relationships, career, and focus in my life." As he responds, his chest gets increasingly heavy. He mentions change in his life, but there is no corresponding change in his body. There is a clear contradiction between the language of his words and the language of his body.

"Are you already divorced?" I ask searching for an entry point. Any discussion of divorce usually elicits emotional waves, especially for those who have children.

"Yes, I left my wife recently, and now I go to visit my children," he replies in a calm, upper-register voice.

"How do you feel about that?"

"I feel complete about it." Sheldon's voice is faint and without affect. My hand feels the tension increase in his back.

"Is there anything you want to say to your children?" I ask, knowing that recently divorced parents have painful issues about leaving their children.

"I love you and I'll never leave you, even though I will be traveling around a lot. I'll always be your father." As he speaks, a hint of movement begins in his chest. I am encouraged.

"No matter where I am," I add. He nods in agreement with my addition. "Do your children have anything to say to you?"

He does not respond immediately, but with my hands, I feel another energy shift in his stomach (emotional center). He spontaneously role-plays his children:

"We want to spend *more* time with you."

"How do you feel when they tell you that?" I ask.

"Wonderful," he replies, as his stomach begins to quiver.

With my right hand still underneath his chest, I feel the steel texture of his back. Following my intuition, I decide to take another tack, "What about the direction of your life? What do you want to do?"

"I want to travel, put myself out there and do healing like you do." Knots close tightly in his back muscles, telling me, "I'm not going to let anything go." Time slows down as I quietly listen to what his body is saying.

"I'm sensing some other issues in your shoulder now." Many times, I can feel an emotion before it expresses itself in sounds or words.

"My self worth," he replies.

"Your self worth," I repeat, knowing intuitively that this is an important theme in this piece of work.

"I'd like you to roll over onto your right side." He moves slowly, swinging his arms over the table.

This is literally and somatically a turning point in this session. On his back, Sheldon seemed stuck and unable to move emotionally. Perhaps he was feeling too exposed and vulnerable. On his side, he is in a "younger" position, with more options for movement. Over the years, I have noticed that specific physical positions access earlier emotional stages.

"Can you go back to an age when you felt not good enough?"

"I'm a toddler," Sheldon replies. "I just fell down the steps and I'm crying. My mother is screaming and she's asking me why I fell down."

I close my eyes and pay attention to my posture and breathing. I have my right hand under his elbow, cradling the whole arm. My left hand touches the muscles between the shoulder blade and spine. I gently pull his arm toward me and then away from me. The rhythm is uneven—stop, start, stop, start—bumpy and unsure, a kind of pantomime of someone falling downstairs.

"How do you feel, little one?"

"Scared, like I hurt *her*," he says in a high-pitched voice.

"Can you say that again? 'I'm scared.' "

He repeats, "Scared," and then adds, "I hurt myself."

"Can you say to your mother, "Don't you see, I'm hurt?"

"It's hard to say I'm hurt."

I'm rocking him gently, moving his shoulder forward and back. The shoulder is beginning to soften now. "That's right," I say. I'm totally agreeing with and supporting this little hurt body. At the same time, I am encouraging his shoulder to soften. In essence I am telling him, with my hands and my voice, "Yes, we all see that you are hurt. We hear you."

My voice shifts and I say in a sing-song way, "That's right. *I* hurt. *I* just fell down the stairs. This is *my* body. I hurt!'' As I speak in this way, Sheldon's shoulder softens dramatically. A profound change occurs.

"Pay attention to me," Sheldon says. "See how I hurt." He speaks in a child's voice with increasing energy.

"That's right," I say. "That's very important. *You're* the one who fell down, little Sheldon." I know that Sheldon is worried about his mother, although he is the one who fell down and got hurt.

In a young, tearful voice Sheldon says, "I'm bleeding. I hurt my head. I'm scared. Where's my dad?"

His breathing rate increases. His shoulder is moving easier, and tears are beginning to roll silently down his cheeks. I have been playing the role of Sheldon's ideal mother. Now his attention has turned to his father. I look around the room, checking out the group.

"Sheldon, I would like you to pick out a good daddy from this group."

Sheldon points to Alex, who leaves his chair and joins us at the center of the healing circle. Sheldon quickly reaches out to Alex, and I move around to Sheldon's back. "Ask your good daddy to tell you what you always wanted to hear."

"Will you take care of me, Daddy?" Sheldon asks.

I turn to Alex and ask him to repeat back to Sheldon what he just said. "I will *always* take care of you," he says.

I have my hand on Sheldon's back. There is a sudden release of blocked energy. Sheldon's body shakes. As he begins sobbing very deeply, I make a soft sweeping movement (about half an inch above his body) from the base of his spine to the top of his head.

"What else would you like your daddy to say to you?" I ask as I assist his sadness to release.

Between sobs, Sheldon says, "I'll always love you."

Alex, role-playing the ideal good daddy, repeats this phrase: "I'll always love you."

"What else?" I ask Sheldon.

"That's good," he replies.

I say, as if talking to a young child, "It's not your fault when you get hurt."

"Yes," Sheldon begins nodding in total agreement. He has a little smile on his face, which breaks into a laugh. His whole body laughs, loose and soft.

I turn to Alex: "He thought it was *his* fault!"

Alex and I are now Sheldon's ideal parents, full of understanding about their little boy's experience. Sheldon relaxes and sighs. I ask Alex to join me, and we kneel beside the table so that we can be at eye level with little Sheldon.

"Now, gently open your eyes," I tell him, speaking with a very soft voice. "Look at your ideal mommy and daddy."

He looks at us intently, and I continue to role-play the ideal mommy. "It's not your fault that you got hurt," I say. "The other mommy got scared and had trouble with your falling." As I speak, I place my left hand on the top of Sheldon's head (in the ancient energy system, the top of the head is the seventh chakra and represents unconditional love), while my right hand touches Alex, his positive father.

"I love you very much," Alex says.

"It's okay to be hurt. It doesn't mean you're bad," I say.

Sheldon nods energetically and tears roll down his cheeks.

'It's OK to let other people know you're hurt," I say, repeating this sentence, each time developing it and adding a bit more. I watch his reaction, visually with my eyes and tactilely with my hands. Together, we develop the theme like shaping a piece of music, and we move into complete harmony.

I turn to Alex and he says, "If you get hurt, I won't yell at you. I love you."

I ask Sheldon to roll over onto his back. I move my left hand over the front of his body, from his feet up to the top of his head, assisting his alignment of energy. I gently roll his head from side to side and it moves freely, with no resistance.

I slip my hands under his left shoulder blade, which is now very soft. The last bit of leftover tension slips away. As I knead the muscles of his left shoulder that connect to his neck, I ask Sheldon if he is ready for a surprise. I ask him to touch his shoulder.

He takes his right hand, reaches over, and touches his left shoulder. Surprised at how soft his back and shoulder feel, he remarks, "That's where I usually get a lot of knots. What a relief!"

"Which side of the table would you like to get off?"

"The left." As I assist him to sit on that side, I notice that his palms are drier.

Now I ask Alex to relinquish his role as father. He tells Sheldon, "I am no longer your ideal positive father. I am Alex." (What I use here is the modified and integrated version of the technique of negative and positive accommodator that was originated and developed by Al and Diane Pesso in their method called Psychomotor.)

Alex and Sheldon hug. Then Alex returns to his chair. For a moment, Sheldon's shoulders are relaxed and his neck has become longer than it was when we started. Then he suddenly hunches up his shoulders again. Immediately, he recognizes what he has done. He smiles and lets them go.

"You see, you don't have to live all hunched up. You can give up your membership in the Superman club," I tell him with a light-hearted tone.

"I've tried to quit the Superwoman club myself many times, but they keep mailing back my membership card."

Laughter ripples through the circle of people watching us. My joke about giving up membership in the Superman or Superwoman club has struck a common chord. A strong bond has been established between the person on the table and those in the circle. This connection is often enhanced and deepened with humor, which establishes so effectively that it is OK to be human.

I ask adult Sheldon to speak to his own inner child, and repeat the sentences he heard from his ideal mother and father: "I will love you forever and ever. I will never leave you. And if you're ever hurt, little Sheldon, I'll hold you and love you."

Gently I assist Sheldon off the table, my hands guiding him until his feet reach the floor, making certain that he establishes solid contact with the earth. Then I ask him to look around the group.

"Let's take a walk around the garden," I tell him. I take his hand and we walk around the circle. I ask him to stop and face anyone he wishes and repeat his key sentence: "I can be hurt and you'll still love me."

"And I don't have to be tough, either. I don't have to be so tough when I'm hurt," he adds.

He repeats these key sentences to several people, looking deeply into their eyes. Then I invite him to find a place to sit. He chooses the empty chair next to Alex.

I look at the faces of the participants. Several people have been crying, their faces still damp with tears. Sheldon's session has touched upon universal issues and connected with nearly every person in the room.

In each session I am moved by the universal themes that emerge, just as I am moved by the universal themes of a great piece of music. At its best, the relationship created between client and therapist elevates our spirits and breaks through barriers that otherwise seem impenetrable.

1. "Chakra," in Sanscrit, means wheels of energy that are located throughout the body, as described in ancient Eastern systems such as yoga. There are seven major chakras, which correspond to seven physical locations of the body. Each chakra, or energy center, also corresponds to a developmental phase in human experience, ranging from survival skills in the first chakra (base of spine and lower pelvis), to spiritual enlightenment and unconditional love in the seventh chakra (crown of the head). Several researchers—notably, Itzhak Benzov (*Micromotion of the Body as a Factor in the Development of the Nervous System*), Lee Sannalla (*Kundalini—Psychosis or Transcendence*), and Frances Vaughn (*The Inward Arc*)—have explored the meaning of these chakras in terms of modern psychological and medical research.

APPENDIX B
"Scoring" a Few Moments of an RSM Session

Since I have strong roots in music and experience as a conductor, I am used to reading a musical manuscript called a score. The melodic lines are linear and move horizontally from the left to the right. The harmonies are written in vertical columns and move from the top to the bottom. The conductor follows one line at a time or all the lines at the same time.

Twenty years ago, I created a score that visually demonstrated the multi-level orchestration of a session. The following diagram is divided into four columns—each representing one part of the whole interaction: somatic interventions, observations and reflections, verbal interventions, and the client's verbal and physical response. Each page of this score describes a few moments of a session. The client is lying down.

SCORE

Rubenfeld's Somatic Intervention	Rubenfeld's Observations and Reflections	Rubenfeld's Verbal Intervention	Client's Verbal and Physical Response
Slides both hands under right shoulder blade and upper back, keeping fingers flat.	Client's back feels like a sheet of steel. No energy is passing through her chest. Her breathing is very shallow. She is in a holding pattern that may be a defense against feeling her emotions. Gentleness is crucial at this juncture in order to establish trust and heighten her awareness to this area.	"I sense a lot under my fingers." Voice soft, matching the touch, a long pause.	Her eyes are closed. She opens and closes her mouth a few times without any sound.

Rubenfeld's Somatic Intervention	Rubenfeld's Observations and Reflections	Rubenfeld's Verbal Intervention	Client's Verbal and Physical Response
Hands are still under right shoulder blade and upper back.	There is a slight movement in her back.	"What is happening in your back?" Another long pause.	She moves left hand toward her mouth.
Fingertips slightly curve upward moving into this area at a different angle.	Back and chest begin to soften, more energy is passing through.	"How do you feel about the area I'm touching?"	"Should I tell you?" A few tears gather around her eyes.
Fingers flatten out again.	Right shoulder releases tensions in several waves. She decides to trust and let go. Rubenfeld watching her face and listening to her voice while hands listen to her body.		"I'm separating from my husband, John." Voice mildly choked.
Hands follow her movement until last wave of energy is complete. Hands slowly move away from her body.	The movement away from client is in the soft rhythm that has been set. Rubenfeld returns to herself for a few moments of centering and self-care.		Mouth continues to open and close without words and tears begin to run down her face.
Synergist walks around to the other side and slips hands under left shoulder blade and upper back.	The left shoulder is tight and feels out of balance compared to the right one that just released.	"How do you feel about separating from him?"	"I think it's the right thing to do." Hands move with mouth as she speaks.
Fingers curve up and gently palpate the muscles.	Exploring the theme of "unfinished" business held in her body and psyche.	"Is there anything you would like to tell John about how you are feeling?"	She begins to cry softly, then deeper sobs emerge.
Fingers flatten out. One hand remains under shoulder, while other hand moves from underneath and is placed gently on the stomach (solar plexus).	Intense feelings are quickly moving. Client needs contact in the emotional center and support in moving it through her body.	"Your feelings are okay. [pause] Imagine John here in front of you. [pause] What would you like to say to him?"	She continues to cry more loudly.

Rubenfeld's Somatic Intervention	Rubenfeld's Observations and Reflections	Rubenfeld's Verbal Intervention	Client's Verbal and Physical Response
Both hands are under left shoulder and upper back.	There is great heat pouring from her back and chest. Shoulder begins to release in several large waves.		"I'm not who you thought I was!"
Hands follow the movement of the release until it is complete.	Shoulder and back dramatically soften as tension begins to melt.		
Still facing client's left side, left hand returns to stomach, while right hand gently passes up to head and is placed on top of head.	Left hand is touching the emotional center and sensing the breathing patterns. Right hand is on the crown of the head, which symbolizes unconditional compassion in the ancient eastern energy systems. These two areas are connected and heightened through touch and strong intentionality.	"Tell John who *you* are." Giving client plenty of time.	She swallows a few times. Her left hand continues to move around as she speaks haltingly. "I'm very disorganized . . . very unstructured. I'm not able to handle things." Takes a deep breath. "I'm needy." Her voice is choking up again. "You think I'm strong. . . . I'm not as strong as I appear . . ."
Right hand moves from crown of head to under her neck. Left hand continues softly rocking her lower ribs.	Remembering the myth of Wonder Woman with bulletproof steel bracelets around her wrists. The metaphor of strength on the outside covering any weakness or neediness. Introducing humor lightens and eases her shoulder and neck areas.	Smiling. . . . "Oh! You're a member of the Wonder Woman club? I resigned several times, but I keep getting another membership card in the mail."	She laughs from a deep place and nods her head.
Hands are still in the same places.	Many women have presented themselves as so strong that they are afraid to admit that they need support.	"You want John to think you are strong?" "Can you resign from that club?"	"Yes. . . ." "Not yet." A big grin spreads across her face.

Rubenfeld's Somatic Intervention	Rubenfeld's Observations and Reflections	Rubenfeld's Verbal Intervention	Client's Verbal and Physical Response
Right hand begins to move away from top of head and touch her forehead.	In the ancient eastern energy system, the forehead is the home of the third eye, which symbolizes wisdom.	"What happens when you're not strong . . . when you feel needy?"	"I cry!" She says this amidst her laughter.
Right hand still on forehead and left fingertips on upper chest.	Her forehead is cool and much more relaxed. There is a steady stream of energy moving from her stomach through her chest and out the top of her head. Her heartbeat is steady.	"Instead of *I need*, start with *I want*. What do you *want*?"	"I want to feel peaceful inside."

As the session developed, the client went on to themes of having to be perfect with her mother and feelings of guilt concerning her children, and then back to her relationship with her husband. Touch was my guide until there was true closure—closure that both she and I could *feel* in her body.

APPENDIX C
Metastages of a Rubenfeld Synergy Session

Underlying this whole process are four metastage movements. They are awareness, experimentation, integration, and reenty into the environment. These occur separately and simultaneously on all four levels of body, mind, emotions, and spirit. As shown, this is not a linear process but a cyclical one.

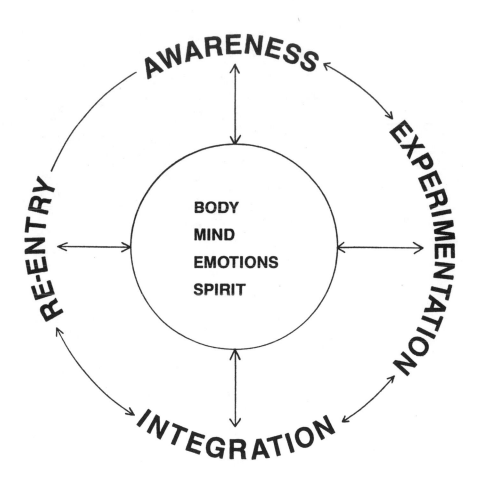

7

Psychosynthesis and the Gestalt Approach

JANETTE RAINWATER, Ph.D.

PSYCHOSYNTHESIS HAS BEEN, for me, a natural extension of Gestalt therapy. In most important respects the two are compatible, both theoretically and experientially. Both emphasize the individual personal experience of the client; both recognize that each person is unique and will require a unique therapeutic experience. Both are existentially based, holding that individuals are constantly confronted by choices and decisions and that they are responsible for the choices they make. Both stress the importance of an I-thou relationship between therapist and client.

The theories were developed contemporaneously by psychiatrists who were psychoanalysts. Frederick Perls, as most of the readers of this collection must know, lived from 1893 to 1970; his widow and the cooriginator of Gestalt therapy, Laura Perls, lived and worked in New York City until 1990. Gestalt therapy began its development while Perls was in South Africa (1935–1946) and head of its psychoanalytic institute, a fiefdom given to him by Freud and Ernest Jones. It was in this period that Perls experienced the humiliating rejection of his paper ''Oral Resistances'' by Freud and others at the 1936 psychoanalytic congress. This paper was expanded into *Ego, Hunger, and Aggression: A Revision of Freud's Theory and Method* and was published in Durban in 1942. The actual break with psychoanalysis was not made until after the Perlses had moved to New York City. Gestalt therapy was born there with the collaboration and valuable theoretical assistance of people like Paul Goodman, Ralph Hefferline, and Paul Weisz. Perls, Hefferline, and Goodman's *Gestalt Therapy* was published in 1951, and the Gestalt Institute of New York was founded in 1952 (see Shepard, 1975).

Meanwhile, back in Italy, another psychiatrist, Roberto Assagioli (1888–1974), had made a less dramatic and definitely less bitter break with psychoanalysis. Assagioli felt that Freud's formulations were too limited, that more was motivating people than their sexual libido, and that the most important elements to be discovered in the patients' unconsciouses were neither their repressed sexuality nor their repressed aggression but rather their suppressed spiritual side—including their goals, aspirations, and longings.

Assagioli's earliest opinions on the limitations of Freud's theories appeared in his 1910 doctoral dissertation, a dissertation that also introduced this new approach to the Italian psychiatric community. The dissident ideas were expanded gradually in lectures and articles, and in 1926 he founded the Istituto di Psicosintesi in Rome. The following year he published a pamphlet, *A New Way of Healing—Psychosynthesis.*

Although the first psychosynthesis institute antedates the first Gestalt institute by 24 years, the public development of psychosynthesis has been much slower and far less flashy. The Psychosynthesis Research Foundation was not incorporated in the United States until 1957; psychosynthesis centers were started in London, India, Buenos Aires, and Athens in the late 1960s. A modest and unassuming man, Assagioli did not consolidate the ideas of his many pamphlets and seminars into his first book, *Psychosynthesis*, until 1965 and only then thanks to the persistent urging of such friends as Maslow and Jung.

At first glance, his *Psychosynthesis* may seem to be an eclectic compilation of many other therapies, as he gives credit to Freud, Jung, Perls, and others and incorporates some of their methods into his set of recommended techniques. Upon closer examination, however, one can see that Assagioli had created a definitely new theory of personality and therapy while still remaining respectful of the contributions of psychoanalysis. Fundamental to his system is the self, that essence of the person that may be buried, unknown to the client who is dominated by numerous competing subpersonalities.

This brings us very quickly to one of the most essential differences between psychosynthesis and Gestalt therapy: Perls did not believe in the existence of the self, ridiculed those who did, and was infuriated when people wrote the word with an uppercase "S."

The self, however, is fundamental to an understanding of psychosynthesis. It is considered to be the essence of the personality, one's center of awareness and purpose. Eternal and unchanging, it is the belvedere point from which all the varying thoughts, emotions, and body sensations may be observed. It is a center of quiet joy that is always there, always waiting.

Many exercises in psychosynthesis are designed to help the client discover the self. One of the best known is called the disidentification exercise (which I believe to be a bit of a misnomer). The modification that I use goes as follows:

> Sit comfortably with your spine erect. Close your eyes. Take a few deep breaths while focusing on the sensations of breathing at your nostrils. Then affirm the following:
>
> I *have* a body, but *I am not* my body.
> My body may be sick or well, tired or rested, but that has nothing to do with my Self, my real "I". My body is my precious instrument of experience and of action in the outer world, but it is *only* an instrument.
> I treat it well; I seek to keep it in good health, but it is *not* my self.
> I *have* a body, but *I am not* my body.
>
> I *have* emotions, but *I am not* my emotions.
> My emotions are many, contradictory, and changing. Yet I always remain I, *my self*, whether in joy or in pain, whether calm or annoyed, whether hopeful or despairing. Since I can observe, understand, and label my emotions, and then increasingly dominate, direct, and utilize them, it is evident that they are not *myself*.
> I *have* emotions, but *I am not* my emotions.
>
> I *have* an intellect, but *I am not* my intellect.
> It is more or less developed and active.
> It is my tool for knowing both the outer world and my inner world, but *it is not myself*.
> I *have* an intellect, but *I am not* my intellect.
>
> I *am* a center of pure self-consciousness.
> I *am* a Center of Will, capable of mastering and directing my intellect, my physical body, my emotions, and all my psychological processes.
> I *am* the constant and unchanging Self. [Rainwater, 1979, p. 38, based on Assagioli, 1965, pp. 118–119]

Assagioli was fond of saying that we are dominated by any and all of those things with which we identify. As a person learns to disidentify from feelings, body, mind, thoughts, emotions, and subpersonalities, the person will know more of the experience of the "real I," the self.

This concept is apt to give Gestalt people much trouble until they distinguish between disidentifying and disowning. In no way should Assagioli's exercise and ideas be construed as permission to disown one's thoughts, feelings, or body. I have found that psychosynthesis, correctly practiced, emphasizes even more than Gestalt therapy does the necessity for being aware, for acknowledging and owning all one's "negative" features, and for taking responsibility for one's present existence. The process of disidentification carries the sense of ultimate responsibility a step farther than Gestalt theory does. (Let me put in a disclaimer here for those few psychosynthesis practitioners who are poorly grounded in Gestalt and awareness methodology and who encourage the disowning of negatives.)

One theoretical contribution of psychosynthesis that should not trouble Gestalt therapists is that of subpersonalities. Top Dog and Underdog (and Parent and Child in Eric Berne's typology) would be considered to be subpersonalities in psychosynthesis. However, the distinctly idiosyncratic qualities of each subpersonality are emphasized rather than the universal aspects.

A person would be asked to give a specific name to his Critic subpersonality, for example. (For Critic, read "Top Dog.") These names would have a very personal meaning for the individual: the Persecutor, Ms. Perfect, Pusher, Global Killer, Mr. District Attorney, and so on.

Clients are asked to dialogue with their identified Critic. They first express any resentment for the Critic's excesses, then—as Critic—explain to the self how invaluable the Critic is to the total personality and what a mess the person would be in without the Critic. Then the self acknowledges this valuable side of the Critic (the flip side of a Critic could be a Protector or an Instigator) and negotiates with the Critic about when to appear and how to behave. The self is considered to be in charge.

Every subpersonality is organized around a "want" of the total personality. Identifying the subpersonality can help a person to acknowledge and "own" the want that it represents. For instance, each major interest and aspiration in a busy and complex life has its subpersonality doing battle for the preservation and enhancement of that interest or activity. Your stereotypical middle-aged businessman has Mr. Family Man, Mr. Corporate Superman, Mr. Golfer, Mr. Lover, and perhaps the Unrequited Novelist all competing for time and energy and issuing conflicting orders to the self. It is only when clients realize that from the vantage point of the centered self they can take the helm and control these subpersonalities that some relief is found from the warring voices within their heads. I cannot emphasize enough what a powerful tool subpersonality work can be. (For a more detailed description of subpersonality work, see Ferrucci, 1982, pp. 47-70; Rainwater, 1979, pp. 26–39 and passim Vargiu, 1974).

In addition to the Critic, there are two other genera of subpersonalities considered to be resident to some degree in each of us: the Saboteur and the Victim. (I feel certain that all Gestalt therapists have helped clients work with both their Saboteurs and their Victims. Tragedy Queen is a special case of Victim.) The work seems to go more quickly and more smoothly when the subpersonalities are named, and clients are left with an intellectual handle to remind them of what is happening when Saboteur or Victim reappears.

I should emphasize here that no attempt is made to kill off a seemingly undesirable subpersonality because it represents a legitimate want of the person. The client is encouraged to negotiate and then modify the excesses of the subpersonality from the position of strength of the personal self. The aim is neither to deny nor to destroy the subpersonality, but to accept it and have it under the active control of the centered self.

You have undoubtedly observed by now the very active role that the therapist takes. This brings us to a second major theoretical difference between psychosynthesis and Gestalt therapy. In psychosynthesis there is a conscious and planned *reconstruction of the personality*. In Gestalt therapy the therapist wishes to help patients become aware of how they are right now without any value judgments about whether or how they might change. For psychosynthesis practitioners, awareness per se is not sufficient. To awareness of subpersonalities, emotions, and desires they would add awareness and further development of the quality of being at the helm of the self that makes choices and directs the personality. (In my experience, many Gestalt therapists behave similarly and still call what they do Gestalt therapy.)

A third major difference is the deliberate inclusion of the client's spiritual nature. (This is also included in actuality by many Gestalt therapists whom I know, but it was not part of Perls's system.) The ultimate purpose of psychosynthesis is to help clients release the energies of their transpersonal self. (For transpersonal self, read "soul.") Prior to this step, the secondary purpose is to help integrate or synthesize the individual around the personal self—which Assagioli called a "personal psychosynthesis" and Maslow described as "self-actualization." This secondary purpose must precede the first—which Assagioli called the "spiritual psychosynthesis." There are still a few psychosynthesis practitioners who rush in too quickly with spiritual psychosynthesis, thus helping to create "neurotic saints," to use William James's phrase. Those therapists who start with a good grounding in Gestalt therapy do not make this error!

In his egg diagram of the personality, Assagioli divided the unconscious into three parts: lower (which essentially is the Freudian unconscious), middle (fairly accessible, containing our everyday experiences), and higher. The higher unconscious, or superconscious, is considered to be the resting place of our higher intuitions and inspirations—artistic, scientific, and philosophical. It includes our highest ethical and humanitarian impulses and all those nonauthoritarian (and nonintrojected) promptings that urge us to be the best persons we can be. There are some excellent psychosynthesis exercises that help a person explore these heights (and as in Gestalt therapy, the clever and intuitive practitioner will create new ones tailored for a specific client). I would like to recommend Frank Haronian's article "The Repression of the Sublime" for an in-depth discussion of the superconscious and our need to deny it. [Haronian, 1974]

Techniques often falsely identify a therapeutic system to outsiders who do not bother to acquaint themselves with the theoretical structure behind those techniques. Such people are apt to believe that Gestalt therapy is "empty chair" work. Similarly, they may believe that psychosynthesis is guided imagery or visualizations.

Guided imagery is one of the most useful techniques in the psychosynthesis cupboard. It is a technique that is frequently overused by the beginning practitioner and misused by those who do not understand when, where, why, and how to use it. It is in many ways analogous to the experiment in Gestalt therapy. It is given to induce greater awareness in the client of a particular area or to facilitate the self's growing sense of mastery, and not done just for something to do. A guided imagery about a meadow might be a way to explore the middle unconscious. A trip through a cave or a journey to the depths of the ocean might shed some light on the lower unconscious. The well-known trip up the mountain is one of many ways to look in on the higher unconscious. (The technique of guided imagery originated with Robert Desoille, who called it the "directed daydream"; see Desoille, 1945).

Archetypes of the Wise Old Person or the Fairy Godmother may be introduced in visualizations to acquaint clients with their transpersonal or higher self. By engaging the self in the dialogue, individuals may seek guidance on important issues, ask the purpose of their life, further develop their intuition, seek understanding of love, wisdom, joy, serenity, harmony, and so on. (Care must be taken that they are not encountering one of their authoritarian subpersonalities masquerading as the transpersonal self.)

An important part of every guided imagery exercise, especially anything as esoteric as speaking with the transpersonal self, is the grounding that takes place afterward. Clients are instructed to relate the experience to their current existence and to find some practical way to put the insights or discoveries into action. The therapist can be very useful here by asking penetrating questions and exploring resistances, always guarding against suggesting any choices or outcomes. Two other ways of grounding are (a) writing down the experience or dialogue and (b) drawing it. Assagioli liked people to keep journals in which they recorded their psychological progress. He particularly recommended free drawing, as he considered it to be an even more useful tool for discovering the contents of the unconscious than dreams are.

The fourth possible difference between psychosynthesis and Gestalt therapy is Assagioli's (1973) concept of the will. Since he wrote a whole book on the subject, I feel a little foolish attempting to capture his presentation in a few paragraphs. Having said that, I feel ready to do it!

First of all, he is not talking about the Victorian concept of willpower ("I will do" such and such). Rather he means the metaforce that is a function of the self. For instance, decide that you will raise your arm. Then very deliberately raise your arm. Watch how the order is received, processed, and then performed. This calm, affirmative choice is your will. Consider where it is that your will seems to be located.

An interesting exercise for dyads is called the "sculptor." First the sculptor will form his or her cooperative partner into a statue of a person with no will. Then the sculptor will sculpt the partner into a person with much Victorian-style willpower. Finally the sculptor will mold the partner into a person who has access to psychosynthesis-style will. (After this the sculptor and partner exchange functions for another round.)

The will is developed in a series of exercises that we Gestalt people would recognize as exercises in awareness. One method is to perform your everyday, mechanical activities (brushing your teeth, washing the dishes, etc.) with intentionality, remaining conscious that it is you who is directing this action. Another method is to perform a series of useless actions, such as throwing a deck of cards on the floor and picking them up one by one.

Assagioli describes the many attributes of the developed will: promptness, decisiveness, skill, joy, courage, mastery, self-assertiveness, and strength. Historians of psychology will recognize echoes of William James here.

There is an important exercise in Assagioli (1973) for strengthening the will. With eyes closed and in a meditative position:

> 1. Picture to yourself the unfortunate consequences—past, present and future—of your inadequate will. Allow yourself to feel all the feelings. Then write them down.
> 2. Picture as vividly as possible all the advantages, joy, benefits, and satisfactions that will come to you and others as a result of your developing a more effective will. Feel the feelings. Then write them down.
> 3. Picture yourself as having a strong and effective will. You walk with a firm step; you act with decision, persistence, self-control, and focussed intention. You resist all attempts at intimidation or enticement. See yourself as you will be when you have attained inner and outer mastery. Write about this. [pp. 36-37]

My hunch is that many Gestalt therapists reading this chapter who are officially unacquainted with psychosynthesis will recognize much that is familiar and comment: "Well, I do that!" and "What's so different about that?" Bits of psychosynthesis theory, subpersonality work, and guided imagery have been absorbed into the mainstream of Gestalt therapy and other contemporary schools without acknowledgment as to their source. Assagioli would not have minded the lack of personal credit, but I do think he would have wished for some investigation of the larger picture and an understanding of the basic psychosynthesis principles.

You may be wondering how I personally have reconciled the four major differences between the two theories. Briefly:

First, as to the existence of the self: I believe in it, I have experienced it, and I find it a useful concept in working with people. I realize that Gestalt therapists who are also philosophical materialists will find the concept of the self totally unacceptable.

Second, as to the planned reconstruction of the personality: I do not take this on as a task without the knowledge and consent of clients—and typically at their instigation. Therefore, this psychosynthesis objective does not seem to me to be in conflict with Gestalt therapy principles. And I realize that some Gestalt purists could find the practice offensive.

Third, as to the attention to clients' spiritual life: Again the philosophical materialists may find a conflict here. However, I believe it is quite consonant with Gestalt principles to work with clients where they are, to "track" them, even if that tracking leads into the domain of the spiritual. I find that psychosynthesis is the best transpersonal therapy available and a very natural extension of Gestalt therapy. Currently I am working transpersonally most frequently around (a) the client's drive for purpose and meaning in life and (b) the client's awareness and fear of death.

Fourth, as to the psychosynthesis concept of will: I see no conflict, provided that you differentiate between the will and introjects. Many of the exercises are similar to Gestalt experiments or directed meditations.

I have been asked how psychosynthesis practitioners deal with resistance. This is a word that I have yet to encounter in the psychosynthesis literature or in discussions with colleagues. The term used is "objections." These objections, as in Gestalt therapy, are examined and not interpreted. For instance, the therapist might ask a client which of three choices the client will make for a suggested action: willing, not willing, or not willing for now. This is a provocative spectrum for emphasizing responsibility for choice.

In a guided imagery session the therapist will explore with the client any fears the client has about proceeding. Facilitating, not forcing, the therapist will ask what the client needs to feel sufficiently secure to continue the journey. (For instance, the client might want a torch or a rope for exploring a cave.) Later these symbols are examined for their possible meaning in the client's life.

There are three questions that are typically asked of a client in each session:

1. Who are you?
2. What are you trying to do? (Or what is your purpose?)
3. What is blocking you? (Or how are you blocking yourself?)

With the emphasis on the will the question of resistance is definitely not ignored in psychosynthesis; if anything, it is dealt with more completely than is the case in Gestalt therapy. "Contact" is another familiar term that is missing from the psychosynthesis lexicon. That is an area that psychosynthesis has sloughed over, much to its detriment. But this is part of the content for a future article in a psychosynthesis journal, "What Psychosynthesis Can Learn from Gestalt Therapy."

REFERENCES

Assagioli, R. (1973). *The act of will*. New York: Viking.

Assagioli, R. (1965). *Psychosynthesis*.

Assagioli, R. (1926). *A new way of healing—psychosynthesis*.

Desoille, R. (1945). *Le rêve éveillé en psychotherapie*. Paris: Presses Universitaires de France.

Haronian, F. The repression of the sublime. *Synthesis, 1*(1), 125–126.

Perls, F. (1942). *Ego, hunger, and aggression: A revision of Freud's theory and method*.

Perls, F., Hefferline, R., & Goodman, P. (1951). Gestalt Therapy.

Rainwater, J. (1979). *You're in charge: A guide to becoming our own therapist*. Los Angeles: Guild of Tutors.

Shepard, M. (1975). *An intimate portrait of Fritz Perls and Gestalt therapy*. New York: Dutton.

———. (1975). Subpersonalities. *Synthesis, 1*(1), 52–59.

———. (1975). In memoriam: Robert Assagioli. *Synthesis, 1*(2).

Part II

Applications

8

The Alcoholic: A Gestalt View

C. JESSE CARLOCK, Ph.D.,
KATHLEEN O'HALLERAN GLAUS, Ph.D., Psy.D.,
and CYNTHIA A. SHAW, M.S.

THE ALCOHOLIC HAS BEEN much neglected in major Gestalt writings about either theory or therapy. This is surprising and also distressing considering the prevalence of alcoholism in the population at large (approximately 10%) and its drastically higher prevalence in people seeking therapy or mental health treatment (40% in some studies; see Brown, Ridgely, Pepper, Levine, & Ryglewicz, 1989). Unless alcoholics are accurately identified and referred to specialists, these prevalance rates suggest that a significant portion of clients treated by Gestalt therapists may be alcoholic.

Despite the rather obvious need for a Gestalt model for understanding and treating alcoholism, no systematic model has yet been presented. In fact, the most extensive discussion related to the application of Gestalt theory to treatment of the alcoholic was a brief, one-page description provided by Perls, Hefferline, and Goodman (1951, p. 227). In describing the alcoholic they note: "He is a bottle-baby, a gulper, reluctant to take solid food and chew it. . . . He wants his solutions in liquid form, pre-prepared, so that he need but drink them down." On the issue of treatment, their comments were limited to the following rather general remarks: "No cure can have lasting effect or be more than a suppression unless the alcoholic ("adult" suckling) progresses to the stage of biting and chewing." That was nearly 40 years ago. Since then, much progress has been made in understanding and treating the alcoholic, and at least as much progress has been made in the development and refinement of Gestalt theory and therapy.

It is time, we think, to return to the question of how Gestalt theory can be applied in the understanding and treatment of alcoholism. In this chapter we will set forth a theoretical model and a treatment program, based on Gestalt principles, that we have found to be effective in treating the alcoholic.

A GESTALT MODEL

In our view, alcoholism represents a disorder in self-regulation. Thus, the theoretical model we have developed to understand the alcoholic is organized around Gestalt principles of self-regulation. Our therapeutic strategies flow from this model and are designed to interrupt disordered self-regulatory behavior and reestablish normal self-regulation.

Before moving into specifics of our theoretical and treatment models, we want to provide a context by presenting some fundamental principles of Gestalt self-regulation. We also want to ground readers in some of the assumptions we have had to make in limiting the scope of this chapter.

Assumptions and Boundaries

The task of summarizing the current literature pertinent to both Gestalt theory and the treatment of alcoholism in a single chapter is an enormous one. To reduce this task to manageable proportions, we have made certain assumptions about our readers and we have had to declare some issues as outside the scope of this chapter. Our assumptions and the boundaries we have set are as follows:

First, we assume that the reader is familiar with basic Gestalt terminology. Readers who are unfamiliar with Gestalt theory can consult Perls, Hefferline, and Goodman (1951); Polster and Polster (1973); Zinker (1978); and Kepner (1987) for overviews.

Second of all, we assume that the reader is familiar with the symptoms of alcoholism and is able to accurately diagnose alcoholism in a client. In this chapter we focus on the treatment, not the diagnosis, of alcoholism. For our purposes, a working definition of an alcoholic is one who meets the *DSM III-R* criteria for psychoactive substance dependence or one who self-defines as alcoholic with or without meeting these criteria. Readers who are unsure of signs and symptoms of alcoholism should consult basic sources (Bean &

Zinberg, 1981; Estes & Heinemann, 1982; Pattison & Kaufman, 1982), and those who are unfamiliar with diagnostic criteria should refer to *DSM III-R* or Seixas (1982).

Third of all, we assume that the reader has some working knowledge of the 12-step recovery program suggested by Alcoholics Anonymous (AA), and is generally familiar with AA meeting format and AA sponsorship. Maxwell (1984) and Robertson (1988) provide helpful introductions to the AA program for clinicians, and the program's basic tenets are discussed in several sources (Kurtz, 1982; Mack, 1981; *The Twelve Steps of Alcoholicss Anonymous*, 1987).

Fourth, we recognize that the alcoholic's behavior and condition impact greatly on the spouse, family, and broader levels of system; however, code-pendency issues are beyond the scope of this work. The reader can consult other sources dealing specifically with issues in the treatment of the spouse (Drews, 1980), children and adult children (Black, 1982; Woititz, 1979) and family of the alcoholic (Bepko & Krestan, 1985; Wegscheider, 1981).

Finally, issues of relapse prevention are also beyond the scope of this chapter. We believe that knowledge and skills related to relapse prevention are crucial ones for any clinician working with the alcoholic and we urge all readers to refer to Marlatt and Gordon's (1985) comprehensive treatment of relapse and relapse prevention.

From this common ground of assumptions and boundaries in terms of the scope of this chapter we proceed now to a review of the Gestalt model of self-regulation and then on to the model we have developed to describe disordered self-regulation in the alcoholic.

Self-Regulation: The Cycle of Experience

Self-regulation is essential to the health and, ultimately, to the survival of any organism. Disorders of self-regulation, if extreme or prolonged enough, lead to death. However, until something goes wrong, self-regulation is rarely thought about and generally taken for granted—that is, until something goes wrong.

That something is "wrong" with the alcoholic is often fairly obvious. The task of understanding the particular regulatory disorder that is seen in the alcoholic—what has gone awry and what to do about it—is simplified by a digression to the Gestalt model of "normal" self-regulation: the cycle of experience.

The cycle of experience describes a process whereby persons (or any organisms) interact with or make contact with their environment so that needs are met. The cycle (shown in Fig. 8-1) can be broken down into an orderly

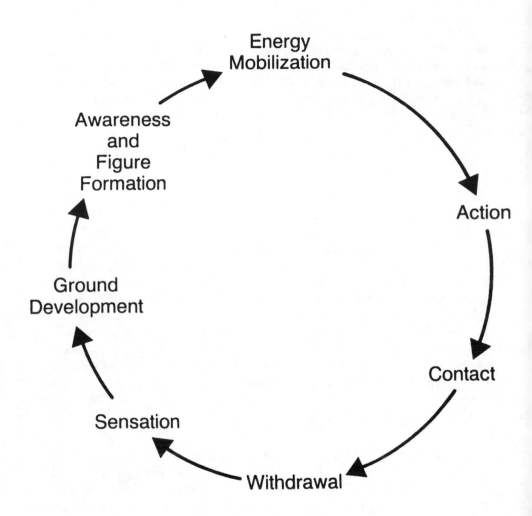

Figure 8-1.—The Gestalt cycle of experience.

sequence of behavior and experience that results in need fulfillment and self-regulation. Under optimal circumstances there is a smooth flow through the cycle. Experiences and behaviors merge and flow and their sequencing through to need-fulfilling contact in the environment usually goes unnoticed.

However, to provide a closer look at the cycle, we will break it apart as if it were composed of discrete units and consider each of the experiential and behavioral events separately in sequence.

The cycle begins in sensation/sensory input from the environment channeled in through the five senses, as well as internal sensations related to muscle tone, organ distention, and a myriad of signals related to organismic need states. These complex and undifferentiated sensory inputs are frequently termed the "raw data" of experience. They are unprocessed inputs. As these data impinge on a person they are incorporated and assimilated into ground, which is a formless reservoir composed of immediate experience (ongoing sensation), past experience, and unfinished business (Polster & Polster, 1973). Ideally, ground is fertile with present and past experience, and relatively boundless, with much of it available to be moved into awareness. It is out of this ground that an organized representation of the need state, the figure, emerges, and it is against this formless uninteresting backdrop that the sharply delineated figure stands out commanding interest, attention, and awareness. At this point, although unaware of the input and organizational processes involved, the person becomes aware of a need.

An example will illustrate the cycle process to this point. Imagine our editor, Dr. S., sitting at his desk attentively reviewing this manuscript. Unbeknownst to Dr. S. (or outside his awareness), his stomach has emptied and fine receptors in the stomach have begun to signal for more food. Their signals are joined by signals from other receptors monitoring blood sugar and the like. All these sensations are assimilated as a part of the ground of Dr. S.'s experience, although still outside his awareness. Over time, the sensations build and accumulate in ground until they are organized into a figure that stands out and commands Dr. S.'s attention. Dr. S. is now aware of his need: "I am hungry."

To explore what happens next, we leave Dr. S. for a moment to consider the rest of the cycle: The figure standing out in awareness elicits a mobilization of energy and a movement into some action directed toward contact with the self, environment, or other people. Appropriate contact is need fulfilling and satisfying, and it results in a reduction of the need state. Concurrently, there is a destruction of the figure and a drop in energy as the person withdraws from contact and assimilates the experience in preparation for the emergence of a new figure elicited by a new need state.

Returning to Dr. S., we find him still aware and focused on his hunger. In response to it, he mobilizes energy, gets up from his desk, and walks to the refrigerator. He opens the refrigerator, takes out a sandwich, and eats it. Contacting the sandwich in this way is need fulfilling. Dr. S.'s hunger abates as the sandwich is assimilated (literally, in this case), and Dr. S.'s attention is free to move to new figure. He wonders if he should take a nap. Better not Dr. S.! There is a deadline on that manuscript!

This is self-regulation. It goes on in thousands of ways daily in every one of us as we contact ourselves, the environment, and each other. It is not a fail-safe process, however. The cycle can be interrupted in several ways so that self-regulation is impeded. Interruptions to the cycle are termed resistances or defenses (we use the terms interchangeably).

Dr. S. can illustrate the principle defenses we will concern ourselves with here. Suppose, in response to hunger sensations, Dr. S. cut them off (desensitization) by focusing his attention elsewhere? Or suppose he looked over at his cat and said: "Why are you hungry? I just fed you" (projection). Or what if he got up and walked around the block instead of going to the refrigerator (deflection)? An early parental rule (introject)—"No snacking before dinner!"—could have halted the process, even without Dr. S.'s being conscious of it. Finally, Dr. S. could have used self-talk (retroflection) to talk himself out of his hungry state—reminding himself of the new diet he is on, for example. So, the natural self-regulatory cycle could have been blocked, consciously or unconsciously, in several ways that would have left Dr. S. in a continued need state.

What if, in the presence of hunger sensations, the figure of a drink—a martini—emerged and Dr. S. gulped a martini rather than a sandwich? That question brings us to the dilemma of self-regulation in the alcoholic.

Self-Regulation in the Alcoholic

Alcoholics drink in response to much of their experience of themselves, their environment, and other people. Internal sensations that normally would signal biologic need states or affective states become organized and enter awareness as a need for a drink (or alcohol). The same is true for a vast array of environmental cues and sensory experience related to social or interpersonal interaction. Alcoholism represents an extreme in disordered self-regulation.

How disordered self-regulation comes about in the alcoholic and how it is addressed in treatment will be the focus of the remainder of the chapter. At this point we want only to pause and provide you with a brief overview of the conceptual model we have developed to describe disordered self-regulation as we see it in the alcoholic.

We believe there are two levels to the regulatory disturbances shown by the alcoholic. First, alcoholics, like nonalcoholic people, develop habitual defenses and resistances that interrupt the cycle at various points and interfere with its smooth flow toward need fulfillment. We will describe these defenses as they appear in the alcoholic at various stages of recovery. However, the fact that people who are not alcoholic exhibit fundamentally the same habitual defensive styles, makes this level of regulatory disturbance fairly "normal."

The second level of regulatory disturbance is more profound and, we believe, fundamental to alcoholism.[1] The second level of disturbance is a disturbance in the cycle itself. We have shown the alcoholic cycle graphically in Figure 8-2. Although the entire cycle may be affected (as we have indicated in Fig. 8-2), the disturbances that are primary, and characteristic of the alcoholic, occur early in the cycle—in ground development, awareness, and figure formation. Distortions late in the cycle—the bypassing of contact and confluence as an end state—are secondary and represent the culmination and end result of the primary, early cycle disturbances. Thus, in the early portion of the cycle, ground is poorly developed and much is restricted from entering awareness. Consequently, awareness is restricted. The figure is fixed—to alcohol or drinking—and as we described earlier, this fixed figure emerges from ground in response to much of the alcoholic's experience (obviously, this is more true and more apparent in the more severely affected, late-stage alcoholic). Later in the cycle, action is fixed to drinking (because of the fixed figure), a response that is not contactful or truly need fulfilling (thus, pseudocontact) and that results in an end state of confluence and inadequate assimilation of experiences. Table 8-1 summarizes the primary differences between a functional cycle and what we view as the alcoholic cycle.

Overview of Treatment Strategies

Obviously, self-regulatory disturbances in the alcoholic are complex and pervasive. The fact that the alcoholic exhibits major distortions in the cycle along with defenses that disrupt the flow through the cycle explains the enormity of the task facing the therapist who undertakes treatment of the alcoholic. A treatment strategy geared to addressing all aspects of the self-regulatory dysfunctions in the alcoholic simultaneously would be overwhelming for both the client and the therapist.

To reduce overload on the therapist or the client, we organize and prioritize the work by breaking the course of alcoholism treatment into the four phases of recovery proposed by Brown (1985): the drinking phase, during which the alcoholic is actively drinking; the transition phase, wherein the alcoholic begins to achieve some sobriety; the early recovery phase, which

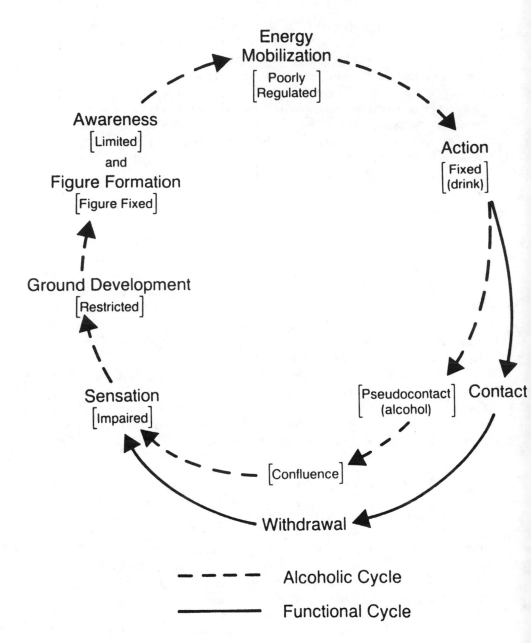

Figure 8-2.—Self-regulatory disturbances in the alcoholic.

TABLE 8-1.
Cycle of Experience:
Functional Cycle Compared with Alcoholic Cycle

	Functional Cycle	Alcoholic Cycle
Sensation	Experience (need) is richly represented in motor/ sensory/affective modalities	Experience may be altered due to prior drinking or alcoholic neuropathy
Ground development	Ground is fertile, complex Mobile, available for awareness	Ground impoverished Frozen, limited availability for awareness
Awareness and figure formation	Awareness expansive Figure flexible: appropriate to need	Awareness constricted Figure inflexible: fixed to alcohol/drinking
Energy mobilization	Modulated appropriately	May be poorly modulated/ depressed due to prior drinking
Action	Flexible, appropriate to experience (need)	Inflexible, due to fixed figure Action fixed: seeking/ consuming alcohol
Contact	Appropriate, need fulfilling	Bypassed Drinking is pseudocontact—not truly need fulfilling
Withdrawal	Figure dismantled, recedes Experience assimilated	Bypassed Confluence with alcohol Fixed figure not dismantled Experience not assimilated

spans the first year of stable sobriety; and the ongoing recovery phase, which extends indefinitely beyond the first year. It is within this framework that we will discuss our treatment strategies and interventions.

We also organize our work around some broad themes that we want to highlight. First, in the early treatment phases—drinking through early recovery—we target many of our interventions toward the early portion of the cycle and work to disrupt the fixed figure of alcohol. Initially, the alcoholic is often not capable of overriding the fixed figure of alcohol and is not able to organize and maintain an appropriate, experience-based figure. To compensate, we often direct the figure in these early phases. We relax this stance in the latter portion of early recovery and in ongoing recovery, and support (and sometimes teach) the client to work independently in attending to sensation and organizing experience and behavior so that the self-regulatory aspects of the cycle are restored. Similarly, in working with defenses, we move from a narrow focus early in treatment to a broader focus later. In the early phases we focus interventions on defenses that disrupt and distort early portions of the cycle. As recovery proceeds, any and all habitual defenses become the focus of treatment.

With these broad themes in mind, we turn now to detailed consideration of the alcoholic in each phase of recovery.

THE DRINKING PHASE

Recovery from alcoholism begins while the alcoholic is still drinking. It is in the drinking phase that the alcoholic reaches for help and achieves a toehold in a long climb toward sobriety. Understanding alcoholics and the manner in which they can be helped in all phases of recovery begins with knowledge and understanding of the thoughts, feelings, and actions of the drinking alcoholic.

Alcoholism rarely develops overnight. Usually, alcoholism develops as the quiet unfolding of an insidious process wherein a drinker consumes increasingly more alcohol over time by either drinking more on each drinking occasion, or drinking more frequently, or both. As drinking escalates, functioning deteriorates and the drinker increasingly experiences destructive consequences of the drinking in one or more major life areas. The time frame and course of alcoholism vary considerably from person to person. In some, alcoholism advances rapidly and dramatically; in others, the progression is slow. Often, the course is marked by negative repercussions of drinking that first affect those closest to the alcoholic—the parents, spouse, or children—then proceed to affect functioning in social, job, and legal arenas. More so than quantity or frequency of drinking, it is the impact of the drinking on personal functioning and the negative consequences in major life areas that define alcoholism.

It is in the drinking alcoholic that the disturbances in self-regulation stand out most clearly. Although alcoholism develops over some time frame, most people who have progressed beyond the early stages of the disease show the main features of the self-regulatory and cycle disturbances we described earlier. Foremost among these is the prominent and fixed figure of alcohol, around which most of the alcoholic's experience is organized.

Probably no alcoholic can be fully understood—certainly not the drinking alcoholic—without consideration of the process by which alcohol ascends to such prominence in organizing experience and the processes that support and maintain this prominent figure over time.

How is it that alcohol comes to dominate and organize so much of the experience and the reality of the alcoholic? This question addresses not only the process by which alcoholism develops but also the nature of etiological factors in alcoholism. Obviously, alcoholism is a complex disorder with a variable course that involves multiple etiological factors. At the very least, alcoholism involves interactions among biological, psychological, and social factors. The picture is complicated further by the fact that there are probably multiple forms of alcoholism. Without sinking into a morass of details, we would like to describe three patterns we have seen clinically that we believe may be related to the development of the fixed figure of alcohol in at least some alcoholics.

For some alcoholics, the figure of alcohol may be rooted in their own biology. These people talk of drinking alcoholically from the first drink. They may have a biologically determined, possibly genetic predisposition to develop alcoholism. Biologically, they are primed. The first drink, then, becomes a spark that ignites a fire storm. The alcoholism progresses extremely rapidly with early onset of clear-cut symptoms of physical addiction, withdrawal symptoms, and intense cravings for alcohol. Often this form of alcoholism develops in people who have an extensive family history of alcoholism. Our assumption is that in this form of alcoholism (and in any alcoholism that has progressed to point of physical addiction), the figure of alcohol emerges, at least to some extent, in response to biologically based cues signalling a very real "need" for a drink.

> Jack considers himself an alcoholic from the first drink—an event he remembers with amazing clarity. From the first drink, Jack drank compulsively and always to the point of drunkenness. At the age of 35, he has suffered most major symptoms of alcoholism and is in an advanced stage of liver disease.

The figure of alcohol or drinking can also have its origin in early learnings, and through associative learning or modeling, this figure can come to predominate in the organization of experience. Children and adults reared in alcoholic homes (ACOAs), for example, have had extensive opportunity to see alcohol or drinking closely associated with all manner of tension or mood states. For some of these ACOAs this close association results in confusion. Their own experience of strong feelings becomes organized around competing figures, one representing immediate experience and the other the associated figure of alcohol or drinking.

> Jamie was confused, "I don't know what I feel—maybe I'm mad—I think I need a drink. I don't know."

For some ACOAs the associations between feelings and alcohol are so strong that feelings and drinking seem to be almost the same thing.

> Nancy, a 20-year-old recovering alcoholic and ACOA, told us, "I used to sit and watch my parents drink and I couldn't wait until I got old enough to drink so I could have feelings too."

Most people reared in our society develop some association between drinking and pleasure or the reduction of need states. This is a drinking society. ACOAs represent an extreme in that they may have developed a very strong association early on between alcohol and the reduction of needs. Such being the case, the ACOAs who drink run a considerable risk of strengthening alcohol's role in the organization of their experience.

Finally, the figure of alcohol can come to predominate through a process that begins when a person who is clear and fully aware of an experience or need state does not move into appropriate and satisfying contact, but takes a drink instead.

> Jessica was worried about her heavy daily drinking and self-referred for a diagnostic interview. With two alcoholic parents and a sister who was an alcoholic, Jessica was concerned about the pattern she had fallen into of handling the stresses of school and the single parenting of young children by drinking. An educated insightful woman, Jessica could *see* the destructive turn her drinking was taking. She could enumerate many things she could do besides drinking to reduce her stress and anxiety. "I know all the right things to do," she exclaimed, "but, I just go on drinking instead. It's easier."

The good news about deflecting into drinking to handle stress or other dysphoria is that it works. With little effort, tension is reduced, and reduced fairly rapidly at that. That is the bad news, too—at least in the long run. Over time, this pattern of managing experience or needs reinforces the primacy of the figure of alcohol. Alcohol becomes "magic"—larger than life. It mellows experience, reduces tension, and quiets and sedates needs. Continued use of this bottled magic leads to a generalization of the pattern so that more and more experience is dealt with through drinking. At the same time the cycle process is short-circuited such that experience and needs become more and more directly and immediately organized around the figure of alcohol.

These three patterns suggest ways that alcohol may come to dominate the drinker's experience. Clearly, they do not exhaust the possibilities and, as we have shown, mixed patterns often occur.

What about the processes that support and maintain alcohol as the dominant figure over time? To understand these we examine denial and other defenses and explore the belief system that filters the alcoholic's experience.

Of all the defenses in the alcoholic's repertoire, denial is perhaps the most pervasive, and, at times, the most frustrating for the clinician to encounter. Very simply, denial is a process whereby alcohol-related adversities are systematically excluded from the alcoholic's awareness. In its starkest forms, denial resembles a systematic, circumscribed psychosis that renders alcoholics oblivious to the reality of their drinking. In Gestalt terms, denial appears to be a disorder of awareness or figure formation, at least at first glance. However, since awareness is dependent on the nature and composition of the ground available, it is likely that denial is a symptom of inadequate or insufficient ground supporting the awareness function. Jean Berggren suggests that denial represents an impairment in the development or maintenance of ground over time. Specifically, she sees the alcoholic as unable to assimilate experience in a way that makes it a part of ground (Berggren, personal communication, July, 1988). In her view, the alcoholic suffers impoverished ground, which, in turn, undermines awareness and distorts figure formation. A second possibility is that ground is essentially intact but the alcoholic mobilizes intrapsychic boundaries to actively exclude some ground from entering awareness. If this is the case, experience that is denied at one time could enter awareness at another time when denial is less solidly entrenched. If, on the other hand, denial results from experiences not assimilated, a more "permanent" loss of experience could be expected. In fact, our experience in treating alcoholics indicates that both mechanisms are involved in denial. In treatment, as defenses soften some experiences are recovered; others are not.

Denial develops as drinking becomes more of an obsession to the alcoholic and as the negative consequences of drinking become more numerous and extreme. As denial develops, awareness shrinks to a narrow band.

> Dr. T. was a college professor referred by her department chair for a diagnostic interview. In making the referral, the department chair stated that Dr. T. had been observed to be under the influence of alcohol, on several occasions, at college and that recently she had been arriving drunk to her 9: 00 a.m. class. Her teaching and academic proficiency had been sliding downward precipitously for the past 3 years. When Dr. T. arrived for the interview she was obviously under the influence of alcohol. She denied that alcohol was a problem in her life or career and denied drinking prior to her morning classes. She stated that she had had a few drinks prior to our interview only to calm her nerves. In her view, her primary problems stemmed from stress and a problem with her lower back. She was not interested in pursuing the idea that she might have an alcohol problem and terminated therapy to seek help from a chiropractor.

Denial is shored up and supported by an intricate belief system that comprises a significant portion of the ground of the alcoholic's experience.

The beliefs that sustain denial, as well as alcohol as the organizing figure, often are linked to cultural values and to stereotypes regarding characteristics of "the alcoholic." Often, these beliefs are learned or introjected without close examination or critique. They do become, however, potent influences on both the experiences assimilated into ground and the experiences that are made available for movement from ground into awareness. This belief system serves as a "filter." Understanding it is crucial to both understanding and treating the alcoholic.

Our culture instills a strong belief in and strongly positive values around self-control. Like most of us, the alcoholic generally holds the belief that "I should be able to control myself" or, more specifically, "I should be able to control my drinking (everybody else can)." Similarly, the alcoholic has absorbed the cultural values that being in control is good, normal, and acceptable, whereas being out of control is bad, abnormal, and possibly immoral. These beliefs and values militate against alcoholics' acknowledging that they are unable to control the drinking. Also, these beliefs and values serve to screen out experience that would indicate that drinking is out of control or leading to adverse consequences in important areas of personal functioning. The net result is that, as a prominent figure, alcohol is preserved rather than challenged. Worse yet, rather than being led toward a realization of loss of control and an admission of powerlessness over alcohol, alcoholics are led into an extended series of encounters with alcohol in an attempt to prove they have control. Over time, this process escalates with increasingly disastrous consequences for them. On some occasions they are able to exert control (all alcoholics report at least some drinking episodes during which they are able to control their drinking). But, in the main, the alcoholic loses in the "battle with the bottle" (see Bateson, 1971).

> John was incensed that his employer would refer him for a diagnostic interview. He held a high-level managerial position in a large company and prided himself on being "on top" of everything at work and in his life generally. To him, the employer's suggestion that he might have a problem with alcohol was a personal insult and a criticism of his ability to take charge. Despite the fact that he had just received his third DWI and his wife was threatening to leave because of his drinking, John requested a treatment plan that would allow him to "prove" to his employer and wife that he could control his drinking.

Alcoholics who, like John, are out of control and yet obsessed with proving they are in control often manage the dilemma by developing a highly polarized self. One side is highly controlled, compulsive, and constrained, whereas the other side is poorly controlled or uncontrolled—a Dr. Jekyll/Mr. Hyde polarity. With drinking, the disowned, uncontrolled side emerges and there is loss of control of not only drinking but also feelings, thoughts, and urges that can result in disaster for the drinker and those around the drinker. Once unleashed, this uncontrolled side may impel the drinker into sexual abuse or promiscuity, physical assault, or the acting out of other proscribed or illegal behaviors.

Like most of us, the alcoholic has internalized some stereotype of the characteristics and qualities of "the alcoholic." Regardless of the accuracy or details of this stereotype, it often constitutes another part of the belief system that serves to maintain alcohol as the predominant organizing figure. This is so because drinking alcoholics almost never "look like" their own stereotype of the alcoholic (nearly every drinking alcoholic can point to someone whose drinking is more destructive—someone who is a *real* alcoholic). Frequently, alcoholics defend their drinking to themselves and others by noting how different they are from this stereotypic alcoholic. "I can't be alcoholic, an alcoholic can't hold down a job . . . always drinks in the morning . . . always lives on skid row," and so on. To complicate matters further, most of us, the alcoholic included, have introjected the notion that the alcoholic in some way is bad, no good, or immoral. Again, these stereotypes and values block acceptance of the condition of alcoholism and support denial of information to the contrary.

> Bill was in great distress and acknowledged multiple alcohol-related negative consequences in his life. When, toward the end of the diagnostic interview I told him I believed he was suffering from alcoholism, he was shocked. "That's impossible," he exclaimed, "I never missed a day of work because of drinking in my life. My next door neighbor misses work every Monday . . . and nobody's calling him an alcoholic."

> Jeanette was a young aerobics instructor with a relatively brief, but markedly disastrous history of alcohol use. When I diagnosed her as an alcoholic, she objected, "Call me mentally ill, call me crazy, but don't say I'm one of 'them'."

As the alcoholism escalates and the consequences of loss of control of drinking become more serious, other beliefs come into play—for example, that one should be a good person or good husband or good mother—and these further block awareness of contradictory information. Over time, to the extent that negative consequences of drinking do enter awareness, new alcohol-related beliefs may form, such as, "I am no good" or "bad person" or a "lousy mother," which contribute to the shame, low self-esteem, and depression frequently seen in the later stage alcoholic.

> Kelley was originally referred for treatment of depression. She ruminated constantly over the idea that she was a "rotten person" and particularly that she was a "terrible mother." An extended assessment revealed that Kelley had

introjected these notions based on angry, critical, and punitive statements directed toward her by an irate husband and mother who were fed up with her disheveled state and irresponsible and neglectful behavior during her frequent drinking binges.

Not only are there many beliefs that serve to support denial, but they in turn are supported by rationalizations, another defense that is pervasive in alcoholics. Thus, the belief "I should be a good, responsible person" is supported by the rationalization "I wouldn't drink so much [be a bad, irresponsible person] if only he were a better husband" . . . or "she were a better wife" . . . or "they paid me more at work" . . . or "I weren't so depressed."

Drinking alcoholics often judge themselves very harshly and may habitually retroflect with critical and punitive self-talk. This defensive style frequently emerges as failures occur in the denial process and the alcoholic becomes aware, sometimes only fleetingly, of inappropriate or embarrassing actions performed under the influence of alcohol. Such glimpses of the toll taken by drinking might lead some people to question the drinking itself. The alcoholic, however, lashes the self with punitive self-blaming statements. For many alcoholics negative self-statements fuel the fires of depression, anxiety, and low self-esteem and undermine the energy required to evaluate or look objectively at the consequences of the drinking.

> Jim began the diagnostic interview with, "I'm a jerk." He followed this with vivid descriptions of several incidences in which he had experienced disasters due to neglected and mismanaged responsibilities at work, and situations in which he had greatly embarrassed himself by acting in a foolish and inappropriate manner in social situations. A perfectionist at heart, Jim responded to all situations with self-condemnation and censure and a litany of critical and blaming self-statements. So harsh and vociferous was he in his attack on himself that Jim was blind to the fact that his heavy use of alcohol was a central theme in all the circumstances and escapades that brought him shame and embarrassment.

Alcoholics are often harsh with others, too. Overwhelmed with shame and self-blame, they defend by lashing out and projecting blame, criticism, and anger onto those around them. The alcoholic who would be overwhelmed by consciously thinking "I am a bad, selfish, self-centered person" disowns any awareness of this part of the self and projects it onto others. Thus, the spouse, children, employer are seen as bad, self-centered, cruel, and so on. Once this defense is in place, the alcoholic then conveniently maneuvers into the role of victim. In the role of victim, unaware of the projections, the alcoholic is in the position to rationalize further, "I wouldn't drink so much if my wife weren't so self-centered, cruel,'' and so on. The victim role also supports retroflections of self-pity, "poor me," and "nobody loves me."

> Jerry was a persecuted man who came to his diagnostic interview to complain about his wife and employer who badgered him constantly about his heavy drinking. In Jerry's view the wife and employer were self-centered, always put their own needs first, and exhibited an unrelenting focus on alcohol. When confronted, he denied that any of these attributes described him and, in a paranoid-like fashion, focused outward on the conspiracy against him that the wife and employer were mobilizing. He truly saw himself as the victim of an unsympathetic and uncaring world.

As the disease progresses, the alcoholic increasingly faces an outside world that is out of control, hostile, and frightening. The internal world of the alcoholic is equally chaotic, confused, and hostile. Trapped, the alcoholic must dampen down, muffle, and, if possible, completely shut out sensation from within and stimulation from the outer world. The alcoholic desensitizes to escape and to preserve some semblance of order internally. The intrapsychic boundaries limiting awareness become more rigid, awareness narrows even further, and feelings become more constricted. Drinking and the sedating effects of alcohol deaden and dull sensation and numb alcoholics to their experience of themselves, other people, and their world.

> Angela appeared nearly dead as she sat, slumped, through the diagnostic interview. In a monotone she recounted a chaotic childhood and an adulthood marked by heavy continuous drinking and alcohol-related assault, abuse, and trauma. When asked if she used alcohol to manage her feelings, Angela raised lifeless eyes and said, "I don't know. I don't think I have feelings anymore."

To the extent that alcoholics are dependent on alcohol, they may be heavily dependent on other people—spouse, children, or friends. These interpersonal relationships are often highly confluent. That is, the relationships are characterized by a lack of differentiation from the "other," a lack of assertion, and a passive "going along with" the actions, wants, or needs of the other. Passivity and the avoidance of conflict or energized contact are the hallmark of these relationships. In some alcoholics the confluence appears to be supported by feelings of low self-esteem, shame, or depression. For others, avoidance of contact or conflict with the other seems motivated by an unconscious wish to keep a low profile interpersonally so the drinking is not noticed, discussed, or confronted. Interpersonal confluence of this sort is more prevalent in the female than in the male alcoholic, probably for cultural reasons and because of factors related to women's socialization.

> Juli described herself as the "invisible person." She acquiesced to the wants and demands of a domineering husband and acceded to the needs of friends and

relatives. She was paralyzed by even the hint of conflict, disapproval, or dissent on the part of others. Her goal in life was to "make others happy." Juli numbed herself to her own wants and needs by drinking large quantities of alcohol throughout the day. Although the alcohol freed her, in a sense, to focus on and merge with others, her drinking seriously undermined her self-esteem. When asked about her own happiness Juli sighed, "I don't deserve to be happy. I'm only a drunk."

Therapist Tasks

Clearly, the alcoholic in the drinking phase presents with more issues and concerns than can be addressed at once. The challenge facing the therapist is to keep a clear focus on the drinking and to reduce or cut through issues by deferring many to be worked on in later stages of recovery. The ultimate goal is to stop the drinking as soon as possible. This requires a direct assault on early portions of the cycle where the alcoholic is "stuck" with the fixed figure of drinking. In the drinking phase, we concentrate mainly on disrupting or displacing this fixed figure either directly, by directing the figure ourselves; or indirectly, by freeing up ground, reducing denial, and altering the alcoholic's belief system. Usually, we do all these things more or less simultaneously.

In directing the figure we attempt to dislodge the fixed figure of drinking and to replace it, even if only temporarily, with a new figure. "I am an alcoholic—I cannot control my drinking." It is around this new identity as an alcoholic, a person who cannot drink, that we want to begin to organize, or reorganize, the client's experience.

Often, much of the experience that would support the new figure "I am an alcoholic" is denied by drinking clients. Thus, a second major task is to heighten clients' awareness of the quantity, frequency, and pattern of drinking and to support clients in connecting their distress, dysfunction, and life crises to the drinking. To achieve this we rely on information from a complete history of clients' drinking and life circumstances or from direct observation of clients' functioning over a period of time. Since clients are not always the best source of information, because of denial and other defenses, we also frequently obtain information from the spouse, significant other, children, or even employer. Regardless of the source, the information is used to reduce denial, to heighten awareness of alcohol-related consequences, and to support the new identity as an alcoholic.

We intervene with clients' belief systems in several ways. First, we elicit clients' stereotypes of the alcoholic by asking for their personal definition of an alcoholic. Using this as a starting point, we instruct clients in the vast variety of alcoholic people and symptoms of the disease, striving always to modify their stereotype so that it fits more closely with the clinical "picture" they present.

We send any clients who are interested in stopping drinking to open AA meetings as soon as possible, whether or not they are able to stay sober. Attendance at AA meetings further reduces stereotypes of what an alcoholic is like. Moreover, by listening to recovering alcoholics recount their drinking experiences, clients often examine their own drinking history and experiences in a more open manner. Open examination of drinking and its consequences undermines denial and supports the new identity as an alcoholic. Finally, contact with recovering alcoholics and the AA program often raises the client's expectations and hope that recovery is possible and that a life without alcohol can be full and rewarding.

We frame alcoholism as a disease to intervene with beliefs and values that cast the alcoholic as bad, immoral, and sinful. This alleviates much of the self-blame, self-criticism, and negative thinking that intensify low self-esteem, depression, and anxiety in the client. Also, the notion that clients are experiencing symptoms of a disease assists further in reducing their denial.

The client's movement through the drinking phase toward recovery is dependent on the therapist's ability to hold the focus on the drinking and to present and adhere to a treatment goal of sobriety and acceptance of an identity as an alcoholic. Obviously clients' denial, their other defenses, and general confusion will be stumbling blocks to the attainment of this goal. There are at least two other pitfalls. First, clients often present in therapy because they want to "cut down" or "control" their drinking. To the naive therapist a request like this elicits visions of elaborate behavioral plans—timing and scheduling of drinks, and so on. For the experienced therapist, a request like this ought to set off red flags and alarms. People who ask for professional help in controlling their drinking are probably already very much out of control. The problem with instituting flashy behavioral plans to help drinkers control their drinking is that this kind of intervention is almost always "more of the same" and not enough. Not only do plans for controlled drinking fail to address the core self-regulatory disturbances, they perpetuate drinking alcoholics' futile search for a way to drink normally.

The second major pitfall is illustrated by the client who presents with psychological problems such as depression or anxiety, or with marital problems, along with a drinking problem. Which is primary? Certainly there are many clients who could be diagnosed as alcoholic and also as having a psychological or psychiatric disorder. Our experience with these dual-diagnosis clients is that the drinking must stop before other psychopathology can be evaluated and before any psychotropic medication can be employed.

These pitfalls aside, work in the drinking phase continues until the client has mobilized at least tentative interest in sobriety. Then, the client has moved into the transition phase.

TRANSITION PHASE

During the transition phase the alcoholic begins to turn toward abstinence. The defense mechanisms of denial and rationalization have been weakened. What emerges is the beginning of a desire to stop drinking, an at least tentative willingness to consider an identity as an alcoholic, and the beginning realization of loss of control of drinking. Movement into the transition phase thus represents a major turning point in the journey toward recovery from alcoholism.

> Tom was a 37-year-old alcoholic who requested individual psychotherapy at the suggestion of an alcoholism counselor after Tom had repeatedly relapsed during an outpatient alcoholism program. Tom indicated during the first session that he had been through two 30-day inpatient alcoholism treatment programs within the last 5 years. Tom reported that the longest period of continuous sobriety had been 45 days. Tom expressed a strong desire to stop drinking, identified himself as "alcoholic" but would continue to attempt to "control" his drinking during the first 2 months of psychotherapy.

In their AA leads, alcoholics refer to this turning point as "hitting bottom." Recovering alcoholics will often report specific incidents or experiences so powerful that they temporarily overrode defenses and led them to begin to acknowledge their loss of control of alcohol.

> One client, Bob, self-referred for treatment after a near head-on collision with a carload of teenagers while he was intoxicated. By the end of the first diagnostic interview, it was evident that this incident had occurred long after Bob had experienced legal, financial, and family problems as a result of his drinking.
>
> Another client, Alice, an administrative assistant, trembled as she reported in her first diagnostic interview that she believed her drinking was negatively impacting her ability to perform at work. Alice, quietly, with head hung down, remarked, "I think I am an alcoholic, and my job is all I have left."

Both clients reported previous failed attempts to control their drinking. In retrospect, both were able to identify some point at which they crossed an imaginary self-defined line in their drinking when they were willing to admit they were "out of control."

During the first several months of the transition phase, the basic beliefs "I am not alcoholic" and "I can control my drinking" may continue to be a central identity issue for the client. The therapist will need to support the acceptance of the new beliefs "I am alcoholic" and "I cannot control my drinking" by continuing to heighten the client's awareness of the consequences of drinking-related behavior and drinking episodes wherein loss of control is a central theme.

This shifting from "control" to "loss of control" creates an internal struggle that is a common polarity for the alcoholic in the transition phase. As with other polarities, one pole is acceptable and the other is walled off by powerful introjects. As we noted earlier, the alcoholic has likely adopted the belief that being in control is good, normal, and acceptable (Top Dog), while being out of control is bad, weak, and unacceptable (Underdog). If the alcoholic continues to struggle against acceptance of the disease with efforts to control drinking, the Underdog will always win in the end.

Within our sessions, we design experiments to externalize this internal conflict around control. We instruct the client to dialogue from both positions, emphasizing the exaggeration of nonverbal behaviors of both parts. The dramatization of the conflict can heighten the client's awareness of the intensity of the internal struggle of control against loss of control. However, with most clients in the transition phase, the conflict and internal struggle will continue for several months. The figure that often emerges first is a desire to stop drinking.

> As Bob continued his outpatient therapy after his near accident, he began attending AA as part of his treatment. For the first several months Bob did not accept that he was alcoholic but rather reported that he thought the program was good for the "rest of those people" and that he just needed "to stop drinking."

With the alcoholic who was sexually or physically abused in childhood, the intense need to be in control results from a history wherein a parent out of control was the abuser. The client's strong belief in the importance of being in control is an attempt to disidentify with the abusive parent. We have found that in-depth work on these issues is best addressed in the ongoing recovery phase.

As in the drinking phase, the early months of the transition phase continue to be a time of further reducing stereotypes of what an alcoholic is like and expanding the ground available for awareness concerning the alcoholic's drinking history and experience.

> As treatment progressed, Bob who initially had sat scowling in AA meetings to keep others away, fondly remarked about the feeling of warmth and caring he was experiencing in his contact with AA members.

> In the same session, Bob broadly smiled as he reported that in last night's AA meeting, someone else told *his* story.
>
> This identification process with others in AA began to lower Bob's resistance to accepting his new identity of "alcoholic."

Some alcoholics may resist the move toward abstinence; often they have not experienced enough losses related to their drinking behavior. In addition, they may have periods of being able "to control" their drinking. We often need to help the client explore the meaning of "loss of control," which, simply stated, is alcoholics' inability to be assured of successfully controlling their drinking whenever they reach for an alcoholic beverage. When we work with a resistant client we actively redirect the client's awareness to drinking episodes that evidence loss of control and its resulting negative consequences.

One client, Tom, continued to successfully control his drinking during the first several weeks of treatment. In a session after the holidays, Tom was visibly shaken as he told me how he had lost control of his drinking at the office Christmas party, blacking out after three drinks. The following day, he had discovered through friends that he had made sexual advances to his boss's wife.

> In this session I then focused Tom on various other times in his adult life when his failure to control his drinking had resulted in serious consequences. I focused Tom on the negative impact of his drinking upon his marriage, which ended in divorce. We examined how past financial and employment difficulties were directly related to his failure to "control" his drinking.
>
> Working with Tom to explore how over enough time, one drink leads to episodes of loss of control of his drinking, helped him to shift his understanding of the meaning of "loss of control."

Another common tactic for the resistant alcoholic is an attempt to deflect to what is perceived as an underlying issue that causes a drinking episode. The alcoholic may seek to divert the focus to depression, anxiety, or stress level at work in an effort to maintain a nonalcoholic identity and to continue drinking. It is important not to collude with the client in these diversions but rather to redirect awareness to the continued negative consequences of the client's drinking behavior.

When clients have self-referred for other issues like depression and marital difficulties or when they have been referred by an outside source, projections may surface toward any therapist who confronts drinking behavior. These projections can sometimes be forceful and hostile. When confronted with these intense projections, we do not become reactive or engage in further escalation of a conflictual nature. Instead, we attempt to engage with the client by moving beneath the projection to contact the disowned parts of the self.

> Steve, a management analyst, was referred by his supervisor for a diagnostic interview as a result of his absenteeism and tardiness. When I started to question Steve about his alcohol use, he became angry and in a loud, abusive tone of voice accused me of working with management to get him terminated from his job. Speaking in a soft, gentle tone of voice, I reassured Steve that I only wanted to help. I discussed the issue of confidentiality and my role as a therapist. Steve began to visibly calm down during the interview when I suggested that he talk to other employees about my trustworthiness. Several weeks later, Steve called for an appointment. At that meeting, Steve was able to discuss his excessive use of alcohol and his negative feelings about himself due to his declining job performance.

Another type of projection that results in alcoholics' appearing somewhat paranoid is the projection of fear and distrust onto the world. Clients may report feeling that others are laughing at or talking about them.

> One client, J.J., was visibly upset as she entered my office for her session. J.J. reported that while in the waiting room she had seen a counselor from the treatment center where she had recently been a patient. When I asked her what she had imagined, J.J. indicated that she believed the counselor was at my office to get her recommitted—not once had J.J. considered that the counselor might also be a client.

The central issues in the transition phase, if abstinence is to be maintained, are acceptance and admission of powerlessness over alcohol. In a society that highly values willpower and self-control, the admission by the alcoholic of powerlessness over alcohol often creates an internal struggle due to the belief "I should always be in control" and the increasing awareness of being out of control of drinking.

Therapist Tasks

We continue the process of working to break down denial and confront rationalizations. As in the drinking phase, we accomplish this by directing and expanding the client's awareness to alcohol-related losses. Often we must be active in directing the figure.

We actively work to support the new belief system "I am alcoholic" and "I cannot control my drinking" in solidifying the new identity.

> After 3 months of abstinence and attendance at AA (only because she wanted to stop drinking temporarily), Betty began her therapy session by asking me if I thought she was an alcoholic. I quietly began to list the behavioral indicators of alcoholism for her, at which point Betty with tears in her eyes quietly whispered "I guess I am an alcoholic."

Betty, like many alcoholics, experienced high levels of self-hatred and shame related to transgressions while drinking. In response to Betty's self-recriminations, our treatment strategy was to begin immediately to contain and focus Betty's negative affect by separating her drinking self from her nondrinking self. Over time, Betty was supported in distinguishing between behaviors such as the neglect of her children that arose from her drinking self and the caring for and nurturing of her children that emerged from her loving and sensitive nondrinking self. With both time and support, Betty became more affirming of herself and replaced the self-hatred and shame with self-forgiveness for drinking-related behavior that was inconsistent with her basic values.

As Betty's treatment illustrates, the transition phase is often too soon for us to intervene actively to heighten sensation and awareness of feeling. Heightening sensation at this point in recovery may prove too anxiety producing for newly abstinent alcoholics and could result in a return to their drinking to manage the uncomfortable sensations or feelings. Instead, we often need to support conscious use of defenses such as desensitization and deflection to appropriate action when newly recovering patients experience uncomfortable sensations, feelings, or thoughts that in the past have moved them to drink.

Directing clients to the action stage of the cycle may represent the bulk of our work during the transition phase. First, we direct the figure to sobriety, then help clients identify appropriate actions to take in maintaining abstinence. Often these are actions such as attendance at AA meetings, calling a sponsor, and the avoidance of people, places, or things that in the past have been triggers for drinking. To facilitate the execution of action plans, both we and the clients are aware of and focus on old behavior and thought patterns that support drinking behavior. Lack of awareness of these patterns poses a risk as it, in turn, supports alcoholics' drinking and reduces the likelihood of maintaining abstinence.

Finally, during early abstinence we often provide alcoholics with a picture of what a life without drinking can be like and the hope that sobriety is possible.

> During our first interview, Mary reported that she had been through three inpatient alcoholism treatment centers and each time she had relapsed within a week after her discharge. In a monotone voice and with no eye contact, Mary revealed feeling hopeless and ashamed. Mary had never identified herself as alcoholic because of a strong negative stereotype of an alcoholic. I began by affirming her worth and telling Mary that she was a valuable, loving human being with a disease from which recovery was indeed possible. Mary softly replied, "Maybe this time."

EARLY RECOVERY

The early recovery phase is characterized by a deepening of the processes begun in the transition phase. The alcoholic begins to solidify a new belief system and shift in identity. The shift in identity is characterized by an acceptance of the beliefs "I am alcoholic" and "I cannot control my drinking."

With disruption of the fixed figure of alcohol and even the temporary removal of this central figure from their life, alcoholics often experience a sense of dependency and vulnerability that will heighten the need for external support. It is especially at this juncture in recovery that the 12 Steps of AA begin to provide alcoholics with the spiritual roadmap for continuing sobriety. Alcoholics in early recovery will find much needed external support as they begin to work the first three steps of the AA program.

Step 1. We admitted we were powerless over alcohol—that our lives had become unmanageable.

Step 2. Came to believe that a Power greater than ourselves could restore us to sanity.

Step 3. Made a decision to turn our will and our lives over to the care of God as we understood Him.

By working these three steps, the alcoholic begins to experience the paradoxical nature of change in that by embracing what is, one finds the way out—accepting one's powerlessness over alcohol is the beginning of regaining control in life; surrendering one's will and life to a higher power (thereby admitting dependency) increases one's sense of autonomy.

In the face of the increased vulnerability in early recovery, old beliefs may surface, such as "I shouldn't need anyone" and "I should be able to handle my own problems." As this struggle arises within the newly recovering alcoholic, it is more helpful to bypass the underlying introjected material and direct and mobilize the client to the appropriate actions alcoholics can take to reduce their sense of vulnerability, such as calling sponsors or attending more AA meetings.

With many alcoholics, their ability to socialize with others was dependent upon their use of alcohol. The alcohol also served to cover their underlying inadequacies and fears of other people. Supporting involvement with AA serves as an intermediary step that the newly recovering alcoholic can take without directly dealing with deeper issues of inadequacy and fear, which can be more effectively worked in ongoing recovery.

In early recovery, the alcoholic may also experience a grief reaction to both loss of alcohol and other losses associated with drinking behavior. As a result of their grief, alcoholics may experience sadness, anger, depression, guilt, and shame. The degree of intensity of this grief reaction is often related to unconscious beliefs around rigid standards of right and wrong. We heighten the alcoholic's awareness of these beliefs. Sometimes it is against these beliefs that the alcoholic has rebelled while drinking, and these beliefs often form the basis of what can be characterized as the black-and-white thinking of many alcoholics. Beliefs such as "I should always be perfect," "I should never hurt anyone," and "I should never get angry" often reflect a rigid system that has been internalized without challenge by the alcoholic. We consistently support the alcoholic in questioning these "always and never" statements of belief.

Along with these beliefs will be cognitive retroflections in the forms of self-statements of shame, self-loathing, and self-hatred. At this phase in recovery, if it appears to be too anxiety provoking to work on core beliefs and self-statements, we opt to contain and set aside this material and to redirect the figure to appropriate action necessary for the maintenance of sobriety, deferring additional grief work to the ongoing recovery phase.

Sometimes we teach the client to identify and block critical self-talk and to consciously substitute affirmations or nurturing self-talk as a means of beginning the process of self-forgiveness.

> After 6 months of recovery, one client, June, began to experience severe depression as a result of her guilt and shame at having lost the custody of her children while actively drinking. First, I bounded out this behavior from her nondrinking self. Next, I taught June to substitute loving, gentle self-talk such as "I am a loving, sensitive woman" in place of her critical, self-recriminatory verbalizations. Reframing her behavior in terms of her disease also served to reduce June's guilt and shame.

In early recovery, other compulsive behaviors often emerge, such as compulsive overeating, addictive relationships, bulimia, compulsive spending, and workaholism. These compulsive behaviors surface to relieve the alcoholic's anxiety and depression. These compulsions can result in additional difficulties for the newly recovering person or lead to exhaustion, either of which may lower resistance to the impulse to drink.

Finally, by using the cycle of experience within each session, we begin to teach the alcoholic the importance of identifying pertinent and manageable pieces to complete within a session while leaving time at the end for assimilation and withdrawal. By simply focusing clients on their breathing in conjunction with a brief guided imagery, we heighten their self-awareness and emphasize the value of slowing down in the moment.

Therapist Tasks

In early recovery, we still take an active role in directing the figure and supporting clients by directing them into action that is need fulfilling and consistent with abstinence. Alcoholics are vulnerable during this period and may required additional emotional support and direct guidance in specific action to take to remain sober. The figure of alcohol is likely to be elicited, at least periodically, and will be experienced by clients as an urge or craving for alcohol and drinking. As mentioned earlier, any therapist who works with alcoholics in this phase will need a rich and thorough understanding of the AA program. No therapist can adequately direct clients into appropriate action that will help maintain abstinence without some working knowledge of AA.

To facilitate appropriate actions when the impulse to drink arises, we work with clients to bring to the foreground those internal and external cues that in the past have supported their drinking and that now pose a risk for relapse. By heightening alcoholics' awareness of sensations, behaviors, and thought patterns that provide a stimulus for a return to drinking, we reduce the likelihood of a relapse. For example, if in the past, the alcoholic drank to numb anxiety, fear, depression, or rage, we focus on teaching the client desensitization through a deflection to positive action when these feelings begin to surface and become uncomfortable. The concept of turning it over to a higher power is also useful when dealing with uncomfortable internal sensations.

We monitor self-care and self-nurturing behaviors continuously. Lack of sleep, excessive caffeine use, poor nutrition, and high stress levels must be examined and reframed as warning signals for relapse. Thought patterns that often support the drinking behavior are obsessive thoughts, future projections, and hopelessness at one's ability to change. Again, we heighten the client's awareness in the here and now to short-circuit obsessive thinking and future projections and support deflection to appropriate action.

In early recovery, we keep things simple. Often, newly recovering alcoholics undergo physiological changes as they continue to detoxify. They often describe their first 6 months of abstinence as if slowly they feel the "fog lifting." As projections into the future often heighten the client's sense of anxiety, we keep the focus on the here and now, living one day at a time, not drinking, and going to meetings.

Finally, with those clients who experience intrusive thoughts or emotions from past experiences of abuse, incest, or rape and with those who used alcohol to desensitize painful memories, we try to contain and set aside this material suggesting a time in the future where this issue can be thoroughly

TABLE 8-2.
Therapist Tasks in Ongoing Recovery

Early	Middle	Late
Focus on sensation-awareness Emphasize resensitization Strengthen basic contact functions Identify habitual defenses	Improve contact functions Break up characteristic defense patterns	
Begin exploring family of origin as ground for present strengths and deficits Form early themes	Continue family of origin exploration through depth work on resistance Develop and begin to work themes/grief work	Conduct family of origin sessions with family members present
	Identify disowned parts Greater differentiation of self-concept Deeper contact with core self Increase self-acceptance/self-nurturance	Deeper contact with higher self/spiritual self
		Develop career and leisure interests

dealt with in ongoing recovery. At this point in recovery, material must be dismantled into pieces that are manageable for the client.

ONGOING RECOVERY

——Since ongoing recovery encompasses a protracted period, from 1 year until as much change as was desired has been completed, we have divided this period into early, middle, and late ongoing recovery. Because of the complexity of this phase, we describe only the basic goals of each stage (see Table 8-2).

The motivation to pursue psychotherapy in this phase comes from a variety of sources. Clients typically present with relationship problems, sexual difficulties, depression, low self-esteem, uncontrolled rage, feelings of isolation/alienation, and flooding of painful memories as the numbing effects of the alcoholism lift.

In ongoing recovery, we loosen up and make more judgment calls about choice of figure. At this stage, the client's thought processes and physical experience have stabilized and may more easily be trusted, dramatically reducing the need for us to direct the figure. In making clinical decisions regarding the directions to take with particular clients, we keep several factors in mind in assessing the client: extent and quality of attachment to the AA program, assessment of the client's overall functioning, degree of trauma, and developmental lags and gaps.

As in all other phases, we make sure that supports are in place. The client should be well attached to AA and working with a sponsor with whom there is a solid relationship. Some clients will want to change or add a sponsor in later ongoing recovery when a less directive and more flexible person may be needed. Frequently, clients in this phase will be sponsoring numerous new members in AA and may not have a sponsor in place themselves with whom they actively confide. With men and women, exploration of the nature of the client–sponsor relationship can avert potential problems. Superficially the alcoholic may seem to be working a good program: attending several meetings a week, using the same sponsor for several years, chairing meetings, and sponsoring many new members. Upon deeper exploration, we sometimes find that the client rarely meets with the sponsor, does not disclose important concerns to the sponsor, is not actively working the 12 steps, and seldom presents problems in AA discussion meetings. Even in ongoing recovery, we make the client aware of such program holes and see that these are repaired before engaging in significant uncovering work, particularly when there are relapses or slips in the client's history or when there are symptoms that point to possible physical, emotional, or sexual abuse issues. A loosening of the tie to AA and its program tools is a red flag for relapse.

Assessment of the client's overall functioning also aids us in planning the content and the pace of the work. If the client is employed and performing at an acceptable level, involved in a stable marriage or committed relationship, and connected with encouraging friends and family, then a firm foundation is in place to support work in therapy. At times, deep excavation work is called for; at other times we elect to bury, divert, or reframe material that threatens to overwhelm the client. At all times, we modulate work in accordance with the internal and external resources available to the client. Since alcohol is no longer available for coping, more primitive defenses often surface (e.g., dissociation). Underlying or concurrent psychopathology may also become more evident (e.g., depression). The client may appear worse, regressed, or more primitive.

A third major area of assessment concerns clinical decisions regarding how much awareness the client can bear. Through careful ongoing assessment of client resources and functioning, we evaluate how much awareness the client can tolerate at a given moment.

Many alcoholics, in their drinking days, violated deeply ingrained personal values. Often, by the time they reach therapy, their lives are in shambles. Many have been divorced by spouses, have been fired from jobs, and have lost custody of children. Some have been abusive toward children, co-workers, or friends, and others have engaged in prostitution or other illegal activities, or participated in a multitude of other destructive acts. We continually gauge the degree to which the alcoholic can face such damage and carefully titrate the awareness process. Otherwise, guilt and shame may be overwhelming.

> Jerry was a 50-year-old divorced, recovering alcoholic. He had five adult children, none of whom would have anything to do with him as a result of his verbal and physical abuse during their childhood and adolescence. The extent of his abusive behavior was impossible to assess early on since Jerry apparently was frequently in blackouts. Jerry had himself been abused as a child by his alcoholic father. I spent considerable effort dealing with his early abuse before beginning to address Jerry's abuse of his own children. Later in therapy, one by one, Jerry's male children agreed to meet with him in therapy sessions to deal with their feelings about him. Some trust was slowly built over time and Jerry was able to establish a fragile relationship with each of his three sons. His two daughters never would agree to come in. There is some chance he may have been sexually abusive with them since Jerry had also been a victim of sexual abuse and he displayed other characteristics of perpetrators. He had no memory of having behaved sexually inappropriately with his daughters and resisted exploring this further.

In response to the often overwhelming feelings that arise as clients get more in touch with feelings, some therapists panic and are tempted to medicate the client. We advise therapists to address their own anxiety in other ways, and if at all possible, to weather this period of chaos. Therapists may also first want to heighten the client's contact with personal resources and strengths. In addition, we encourage the client to use the therapist–client attachment as a source of support, as well as the tools of AA.

Clients are likely to experience anxiety both in response to the emergence of such primitive defenses and in response to the therapist's interventions aimed at accentuating awareness of and interrupting habitual defenses. We frame these defenses as protections that once served clients well in managing intense feelings that were not acceptable or safe to express. We find that clients are more receptive to such interventions if the purpose of our close attention is made clear. So that clients will not experience our interventions as invasive, they must be clearly educated that awareness of sensation will result in accurate labeling of feelings and subsequent awareness of wants and needs and more complete working through of unfinished material from the past.

Finally, we assess the developmental level at which the client is arrested. Depending on the age of onset of alcoholism, certain developmental tasks may need to be acquired that were not mastered in a sober state at the appropriate age. Once alcohol has been removed, tasks such as sober dating, social, and sexual behavior must be learned or relearned.

> Bill is a 30-year-old recovering alcoholic with 2 years' sobriety. He has never been married and lives with his mother and two sisters. Bill has never dated or been sexual in a sober state. He reports being very anxious in social situations and feels insecure and awkward in approaching women for even casual conversation. In his drinking days, he'd bolster himself with a few beers before initiating contact with women and act out a role he'd developed that he described as acting like "a real hot shot." Stripped of his role and his anesthetic, Bill resembled a 15-year-old.

As Bill exemplifies, developmental lags must often be ameliorated once sobriety has been achieved. In his case, Bill has never been emancipated; and while unhappy living with his family, he is fearful of the responsibilities of living on his own. But much must be accomplished before Bill will be able to negotiate that transition successfully. His negative self-view required modification and reorganization. In a sense, a psychological differentiation must take place before he will be able to physically stand on his own. Much of his self-view is based on the messages and modeling of his alcoholic, abusive father and subsequent frequent rejection by his peers and teachers. Bill must develop a more accurate view of his abilities, strengths, and talents as well as learn basic social skills as part of his remedial program. At 30, Bill is lucky, however, for it is not uncommon to see similar developmental delays in recovering persons who are 40 or even 50 years old. Clients may experience much dismay at encountering such anachronistic parts. Self-flagellation may compound recovery unless clients can come to accept where they are developmentally.

Early Ongoing Recovery

Although we acknowledge that the therapeutic process is a creative dance between client and therapist, much of the work in this phase involves the first quarter of the cycle of needs satisfaction, with a focus on sensation and awareness, and we have found that a more structured approach to the therapy process is generally effective at this stage. During this phase, the client must be trained much more thoroughly in techniques of focused awareness. Once abstinence is maintained, the client is ready to develop greater interoceptive awareness. We artificially direct interventions toward the awareness phase of the cycle, helping the client to deepen intrapsychic contact. The importance of this part of the cycle cannot be overestimated since excitement begins with sensation and awareness. For most alcoholics, sensation has been severely deadened through both the numbing effects of alcohol and the client's defenses. In fact, numbing has often progressed to such an extent that we have wondered if life could ever be restored. Clear, lively figures are formed out of the ground of a wide band of sensation and awareness. Awareness of sensations can help the person to fulfill needs more adequately, to complete the working-through process more fully by accessing feelings and bodily accompaniments to verbalizations, and to recover old unfinished experiences (Polster & Polster, 1973). Another important function of this work on sensation and awareness is to build a stronger internal barometer. Therefore, our early moves are directed toward the goal of expanding sensation awareness. Initially, clients may be self-conscious in response to interventions, but as they are able to connect more fully with their feelings, they soon experience in a deeper way the payoff of this approach. For example:

> Lyn was rattling on about a new man she was dating and her questions about how to handle the disclosure of her alcoholism. He had taken her out several times and seemed puzzled about her refusal to drink alcoholic beverages and was pressing her about her nondrinking behavior. I interrupted Lyn, directed her to slow down her verbal monologue, and attend to her breathing and feelings. After resisting several of my attempts to focus her inward, Lyn finally closed her eyes, took a couple of deep breaths, and in a small quivering voice spoke of her fear of losing this man for whom she had quickly developed an attachment. When I directed Lyn's attention to her quivering voice, tears began to well up in her eyes as she described the loss of another budding relationship when the man discovered she was a recovering alcoholic. I then directed her awareness to her rapid blinking as she tried to push back the tears. In a soft voice, I added, "It's OK to be sad, let the tears come, breathe . . ." Slowly, Lyn allowed a few tears to come before she held her breath once again and changed the subject.

At this stage we have found that simply directing clients' awareness to their verbal or attentional distractions and muscular constrictions may be enough since the resurrection of such feelings often triggers anxiety and retreat onto other topics or into a deadened state of awareness. Our first goal is to support the client in taking ownership of these protective maneuvers. Sensations are still unfamiliar and are often at odds with early restrictive messages. These messages may be named at this time, but work on dislodging introjects typically comes later. In addition, we focus the client's awareness on any nonverbal evidence of feelings in an effort to encourage fuller expression. To facilitate this work we use homework assignments such as event-feeling-sensation logs and body maps that help clients locate different sensations and reinforce the body focus (Carlock & Frey, 1989).

We consistently find that alcoholic clients require considerable support to focus on sensations around an emerging figure (for example, sadness) in order to allow excitement to grow and expand into feelings that can then be expressed.

> One client, Jim, was beginning to uncover his grief over abandonment by his alcoholic father when he was 6 years old. Typically, when he would approach an event that generated feelings of sadness, Jim would suddenly slam shut his internal door and retreat to his secret place inside. This was an old protection that Jim developed in his family where his mother's anger at his father permitted no other feelings to be expressed. In addition to sorting out the messages that supported his repressed sadness—such as "I'm bad if I feel sad about losing my father," "Being sad about my father means I'm disloyal to my mother," and "Sadness is weak and unmanly"—I invited Jim over time to prolong his focus on sensations around the figure of his grief.
>
> Jim was asked to focus on his softening eyes, flushing face, and quivering lip and chin to promote awareness of an expression of sadness. Jim was also asked to notice what he did muscularly to keep "under control" his feelings of loneliness, sadness, anger, and longing for contact with his dad.

In sensation work we unrelentingly direct attention to internal sensation, gestures, body movements, posture, breathing, changes in skin color, skin tone, tension or softening around the mouth and eyes, and any gross or subtle physical manifestation. Clients can be trained to report sensations; we often also report internal sensations to model the skill and use as data for the interaction. Wherever possible, we help the client to destructure labels back to sensation, thereby expanding the experience of an emotion. For example:

Client: I'm anxious.
Therapist: What in your body lets you know that you are anxious?
Client: My throat is tight; my breathing is shallow; I feel a fluttering all over.

Initially, many alcoholics will answer "Nothing" or "I don't know" to such a question; therefore, early on, we share our observations based on visual, vocal, or tactile data and direct the client's attention inside (for example, "What do you notice in your chest? Your throat? Your breathing?"). This early client training is critical. Expect to encounter resistance since, as stated before, early sensations are not likely to be pleasant and the client is apt to hit well-ensconced introjects that restrict awareness.

An important aspect of support during sensation work involves teaching clients to dip in and dip out of feelings so as to modulate experience and avoid being overwhelmed by feelings of rage, sadness, fear, or joy (Keleman, 1975). We find it helpful to teach clients to go up to the point where they can bear the feeling of being sad, fearful, glad, or excited without feeling overcome by the feeling. We teach clients elective muscular retroflection at points when they experience signs of being swept away by the feeling. This is accomplished by directing them to employ slight muscular contractions in order to inhibit excitement so that they can bear staying with the feeling without being overwhelmed by it. Clients may also be taught elective distraction (looking at birds out the window, petting the family dog, reading a happy children's book) and, gradually, to tolerate more intense feelings. Over time, clients can come to expand their experience to a whole spectrum of feelings. For example, they may be taught to control feelings of sadness while at work or in public, yet allow themselves to completely let go into uninhibited sobbing in private. Ultimately, the client will be able to choose varying degrees of expression fitting the context—from hysterical (sobbing) to controlled and rigid (tightened throat and chest).

Often psychotherapy with the recovering alcoholic is enhanced by involvement of the client in ongoing body work (for example: massage, Trager, Lomi, or other forms). Such hands on body work can assist in the resensitization process. Dance therapy, movement therapies, or movement experiments can also facilitate the development of body awareness. Even classes in social dance, modern dance, or movement experiences as well as an active exercise/sports program can increase body awareness.

We also use the existential encounter between ourselves and our clients as a vehicle for restoring sensation and feelings. That relationship, when free of rules that overly limit self-expression, is perhaps one of the most intimate and powerful relationships in which the client is engaged. As such, the relationship holds within it the key to long-ago locked internal doors. A loving encounter can provide an experience of intimacy with the self.

> Larry, a recovering alcoholic with 3 years' sobriety, entered therapy following a suicide attempt. He grew up in a family with an alcoholic, abusive father who was thrown out of the house when Larry was 7 and a mother diagnosed as paranoid schizophrenic. After his father left, his mother took on numerous boarders to help meet expenses over the years. Many of these boarders were emotionally abusive to Larry.
>
> Larry presented as a lifeless character, numb to feelings, isolated, and alienated. Little impact was made with attempts to identify early introjects or work with retroflections alone as I tried to unearth the lost child within. What

did begin to soften his protective shell and draw him out were repeated self-disclosures on my part about how I felt in the moment-to-moment encounter with Larry—angry, sad, closed out, lonely, loving. As I allowed my feelings to be known and to *show*, Larry crept closer and closer. Moments of loving affirmation and contact provided Larry with the safety he needed in order to allow beginning stirrings of long-lost feelings and, ultimately, the hope that life could be different.

Through this approach and with the technical power of Gestalt methodology, Larry was gradually guided to fuller contact with himself and others.

Another purpose that this focus on sensation and awareness serves is to help the recovering person (particularly women) build a stronger internal barometer. As a result of continued invalidation of their emotional and perceptual experience, many alcoholics grew to mistrust their perceptions and feelings. When reporting their feelings and perceptions as children, they often heard responses such as: "Everything is fine." "There's nothing to be upset about." "Oh, you shouldn't feel that way." In other homes, the child's feelings were simply not heard or acknowledged.

> A depressed recovering alcoholic woman was explaining to her father how bad she felt. Her father responded by preaching evangelistic platitudes in an attempt to minimize or eradicate her feelings. He had his own frame and could not bear his daughter's pain even when his lack of contact was pointed out. A major task of therapy became undoing such damage.

For most recovering alcoholics, as with other clients, the task of reawakening the deadened sensorium extends throughout the therapy process. We see it as even more crucial with alcoholic clients who have compounded the usual numbing through their alcohol use, and for some it is a creative way to survive growing up in a dysfunctional, often abusive family system.

Middle Ongoing Recovery

Once contact functions (looking, listening, touching, talking, movement, smelling, and tasting) have been strengthened, body awareness has been improved, and blocked or withheld feelings have begun to be experienced and expressed, the recovering person has attained a degree of self-support that provides the base for learning how to self-nurture and let go of or revise faulty beliefs about oneself and about how one must behave (roles and rules). Greater differentiation and integration of personality parts can also be accomplished now. Work in this phase typically involves depth work on the family of origin.

Familiar themes should be formed by this point, evident through process observations as well as the content of the prior work. Clients typically report problems such as: periodic depressions; being overwhelmed by emotions; not knowing what they feel and "not knowing what to do with the feelings"; relationship breakups; feeling disconnected; Temporomandibular Joint disorder; butterflies in the stomach; headaches; panic attacks; difficulty disengaging from negative relationships; shame over prior promiscuity, prostitution, or abuse; inability to set limits; fear of getting close to others; nightmares with violent and sexual themes; feeling anger all the time; grief over prior losses; insecurity about physical attractiveness as well as overall worthiness (Black, 1982; Woititz, 1979; Carlock & Shaw, 1988; Frey & Carlock, 1989). Common resistance patterns characteristic of the client are apparent, particularly projection, introjection, and retroflection.

One of our main thrusts in this period involves helping the client mobilize and sustain energy toward the completion of self-enhancing actions in order to meet needs. Deeper work with retroflections often leads to the identification of central polarities since retroflections frequently consist of both the urge toward expression and the forces inhibiting action. Typically, a complex of introjects blocks the urge to express and this conflict between the parts of the self must be resolved in order to undo the retroflection (Kepner, 1987). The first layer of introjects the client is likely to encounter will be around avoided feelings such as anger, fear, helplessness, and sadness. Resolution first necessitates the honoring of both sides of the conflict. In the case of Lyn, described earlier, the inhibition of her urge to cry was based on repeated incidents where she was shamed by her mother when she cried ("What are you, a crybaby? You're nothing but a little baby") or threatened ("Shut up or I'll give you something to cry about!"). Full exploration of such messages with subsequent revision of learnings can proceed in this phase. Rules around expressive functions may be learned through verbal or nonverbal messages, through modeling, or as a result of traumatic incidents where early decisions were made. When these messages are fully established, the expressive boundaries gradually may be stretched through the client's experimentation and reinforcement and modeling by the therapist.

The more creative we are in expanding the contact functions, the more likely is the client to experiment with foreign and forbidden expressive behavior. We use artwork, puppetry, sculpting, and other less verbal interventions. As energy is freed up through such expressive release, the alcoholic may mislabel the excitement as dangerous and become frightened or overwhelmed by it. Reframing this energy as excitement and supporting the client in increasing tolerance of this energy is helpful.

Throughout early ongoing recovery, when uncovering and opening are under way, various internal conflicts can be identified. These conflicts can be worked as polarities (e.g., need to control, desire to let go; longing for closeness, fear of abandonment/rejection; desire for the safety of dependence, urges toward freedom and independence).

A task of middle ongoing recovery involves moves toward greater familiarity with internal polarities in an effort to move toward a gradual integration of personality parts. Once projected parts are claimed and the intention of each part is appreciated, internal conflicts subside and greater serenity can be achieved.

A polarity we commonly see among recovering alcoholics is the conflict between "agentic" (tough-minded, logical, strong) and "communal" (sensitive, gentle, emotional) parts of the self. Typically, one pole is considered acceptable and the other is walled off by powerful introjects. The shadow part, underdeveloped, erupts now and then, creating considerable anxiety. (In the past, when the client was drinking and under sedation of the alcohol, this shadow part may have emerged more readily and with less distress for the client.) For example:

> Sid held the belief: "Men are tough, strong, confident," but inside he often felt gentle, sensitive, and scared. In order to fulfill his role as a man, he was forced to disown, suppress his natural feelings and present a facade that fit the stereotype. In order to hide his "soft" feelings he was continually angry. However, since his soft side continued to send Sid powerful signals, in order to compensate for such unsettling feelings, Sid frequently acted out the polarity in exaggeratedly aggressive, macholike behavior, creating problems both at work and in his marriage.

Women often have difficulty accepting the sexual, sensuous, angry, or aggressive sides of their personality.

> Marsha had been sober 3 years when she entered therapy. She reported feeling anxious about being in the middle between her sponsor and another friend, trying to please both and avoid hurting anyone. She also reported excessive guilt over how she treated her mother and blamed herself for problems she was experiencing with her boyfriend. She believed if she were more giving, more attractive, more something, men would treat her better and her relationship with her mother would improve. When she tried setting boundaries with others, she felt bad about herself, thinking this was selfish.
>
> Marsha did not permit herself to be angry or resentful or to protest any behaviors in others. She took total responsibility for any problems in relationships and had lots of difficulty being firm with others and acknowledging, honoring, and expressing her feelings and wants.

Reevaluating introjects around such themes is an important goal. We attempt to provide a safe environment in which the client can experiment and reevaluate limiting introjects and expand expressive boundaries. The 12-step program involves learning to accept one's shadow parts and reducing guilt through the acceptance of "what is," a basic tenet of the Gestalt theory of change as well.

The rigidity and black-and-white thinking of alcoholics causes them to be excessively harsh with themselves and/or with others. Although there are some recovering men who use intropunitive or self-blame defenses and some women who blame others, we see more men tending toward blaming others and women tending toward blaming themselves. Self-hatred is, nevertheless, at the core for both.

Very often men enter treatment reporting excessive unmodulated anger, seething with rage, blaming others, and becoming, at times, explosive. Frequently, at the core of these anger and rage reactions is a projective process, and often the rage is a cover for hurt, pain, and sadness.

> David presented with a rage problem, feeling he was losing control at work. He had experienced multiple angry and explosive encounters with a supervisor at work who he perceived was picking on him. In exploring who had picked on him in the past, he identified his father, who was physically abusive and excessively critical of him as a child.

The process of defusing David's rage reactions was threefold. First, he had to accept that he had projected the image of his abusive father onto his supervisor. Then, David had to own his rage toward his own father, and finally he had to own and experience the deep-seated feelings of pain and sadness he submerged as a child.

On the other hand, anger may be turned inward rather than outward. A pattern we see commonly in women is to internalize anger and rage by turning back on themselves with angry, critical, or at times rageful self-talk. At times, this maladaptive handling of anger is also combined with a projective process. Rarely is this pattern identified by the client as a rage problem.

> A 34-year-old recovering woman, Jenny, a former prostitute, reports feeling guilty and "dirty" when her daughter stares at her. Her daughter was recently reunited with Jenny after many years of separation. Rather than consider that her daughter's staring may indicate her "worshipping" Jenny or being fascinated with her new-found mother, Jenny believes her daughter is judging her because of her prior sexual behavior.

Jenny projected onto her daughter negative feelings she held toward herself as a result of her incestuous relationship with her father and her subsequent involvement as a prostitute. In response to the judgments she perceived as coming from her daughter, Jenny turned on herself in a retroflective manner and unleashed hostile and punishing self-statements.

For those who tend toward self-blame, we have found the following process to be helpful in working through unintegrated material and in learning self-nurturing behavior (Oaklander, 1986):

1. Ask the client to be specific about the hated parts (example: sensitivity, pushiness, selfishness).

2. Have the client exaggerate or personify the hated parts. The therapist might ask the client to select a famous person to characterize each part. Ask the client to identify what is considered to be the ideal polar opposite for each of the hated parts.

3. Encourage the client to express aggression outwardly toward each of the hated parts (this reverses the retroflection). Inquire who in the family of origin displayed this hated part. Explore feelings related to this family member, revising rules, reframing, and restructuring in the process.

4. Direct the client to identify or create an accepting, nurturing part. Can this nurturing part identify any contexts in which the hated part, or some aspect of it, could be positive?

5. With the client, devise a list of specific self-nurturing activities and assign these to the client.

6. Have the client identify a real or imaginary loving figure. Ask this loving figure to speak to each hated part or the young child within who absorbed distorted beliefs about himself or herself.

7. Direct the client to own this loving figure and the nurturing accepting words expressed. Ask the client to direct these words to the inner child.

8. Encourage the client to purposefully create a nurturing environment accepting of these once hated parts. Direct the client to engage in nurturing activities when needed.

9. Set up activities that permit positive expression of these hated qualities (or derivatives of these qualities) in appropriate contexts.

Additionally, hated parts can often be connected to specific incidents in childhood when clients received negative messages about themselves. When relived, feelings generated by these incidents can be experienced and expressed and clients can be encouraged to update their decisions regarding these rules or messages.

In addition to the internalization of particular attributes, in some instances core beliefs have been swallowed that negate the entire self, not just one aspect of the person—for example, "I am worthless" or "I am defective." Such beliefs are often formed out of early abuse, neglect, rejection, or abandonment. In such cases the web of introjects supporting this distorted belief about the self must be thoroughly evaluated. Parental projections and family role prescriptions must be identified and transgenerational legacies clarified to make room for the formation of new beliefs about the self.

For those recovering people who experienced significant trauma during their development, the healing process is more involved. Of course, the earlier the trauma, the greater the degree and frequency, the longer the duration, and the more that power and force were involved, the more damaging is the impact. The effects can be wide-ranging and can significantly complicate attempts by the recovering alcoholic to rebuild relationships affected by the alcoholism.

> Jenny reports feeling ashamed of her reactions to her daughter, Tina. She "gets cold" when her daughter reaches out to touch her. Jenny stopped touching Tina when she was 3 or 4 years old. In a session with her 16-year-old daughter, I suggested that Jenny imagine herself touching Tina. In response to this image, the client reported intense feelings of discomfort, rage, stomach turning, and pain in her genitals. She connected this with rage and anger toward her father. Moving the daughter aside, I processed Jenny's feelings. Later, I helped the daughter to see that her mother's negative feelings are related to someone else and not to her.

Incest during adolescence was beginning to surface for Jenny. The unfolding and working through of this abuse along with other early trauma and deprivation took several years. When clients have worked through and reduced the intensity of their feelings related to the family of origin (feelings of abandonment, loss, rage, and fear), they may be coached to relate to family members in a new way. Once the client is able to grieve what was not there, identify patterns that require change, begin to see parents as ordinary human beings, and claim the resources available in the family, specific plans can be made to develop a different relationship. Frequently, distanced or cut-off family members are brought closer, and further healing of family relationships takes place. In other instances healthier boundaries are established, especially in cases where family members are still actively chemically dependent or untreated for some other significant problem.

Middle ongoing recovery can be an awkward time for recovering people. As stated before, those whose heavy drinking began early in life (puberty, adolescence, or early adulthood) often fail to complete necessary developmental tasks. Development is often forestalled at the onset of heavy drinking. Normal developmental tasks not mastered in a sober state will have to be negotiated in sobriety. In addition to the relationship tasks described previously, other identity issues often come to the foreground as the recovering person begins to resume work on tasks forestalled by the onset of alcoholism. It is common for confusion to arise around sexual identity and for social competencies to be questioned. Those who have lost spouses, children, or even careers through their drinking behavior may experience an even more dramatic identity crisis and begin to question who they are besides a mother, father, wife, husband, business owner. Individuals at this stage may also begin to question their career choice and identify gaps in leisure activities.

We think it is critical to assess the developmental level of clients and to provide the safety and encouragement needed for the client to renegotiate tasks and to process feelings of embarrassment and shame that frequently arise as a result of gaps in mastery. It is hard to be 50 and feel like 16. We have found group therapy to be very useful in providing a safe environment where individuals can experiment with new behaviors. The acceptance that the alcoholic can receive in a group can help ameliorate the negative self-view and reinforce positive attributes.

The tendency of recovering alcoholics to focus on negatives is something we are aware of in all phases of treatment. Nevis (personal communication, 1986) emphasizes that since many people are fixed on negatives what easily becomes the focus are faults. We find this to be especially true for the alcoholic. Step 4 of the AA program, which requires recovering people to complete a moral inventory, can reinforce this tendency.

Step 4. Made a searching and fearless moral inventory of ourselves.

Many of our clients focus solely on their character defects and must be specifically directed and supported to include positive traits. Emphasizing positives helps begin to unknit their negative organization and helps them to begin to be easier with themselves. By underlining strengths and resources, our clients can more readily call upon them in times of stress.

Skills of "letting go" and forgiveness are also essential in order to bear increased awareness. Letting go allows any figure to go back into the ground, according to Nevis (personal communication, 1986). Such skills include learning to have faith, "turning it over" to a higher power, and learning to grieve. Reinhold Niebuhr's serenity prayer can be a source of comfort in this process: "God grant me the serenity to accept the things I cannot change, the courage to change the things I can; and the wisdom to know the difference." Since the letting-go process often involves loss and grieving, we design rituals that can help the recovering person to grieve. We also support the letting-go process as it is addressed in AA. Step 5, which involves admitting to another person the exact nature of our wrongs, provides healing in that it requires contact with a person who listens without judgment to the recovering person.

Step 5. Admitted to God, to ourselves, and to another human being the exact nature of our wrongs.

In being heard, there is a joining and letting go (Nevis, personal communications, 1986). As therapists, we also serve as "witness" and help move clients to their contact boundary. Step 8 invites clients to make amends for their wrongs.

Step 8. Made a list of all persons we had harmed and became willing to make amends to them all.
Step 9. Made direct amends to such people whenever possible, except when to do so would injure them or others.

We facilitate this cleansing experience by helping clients make decisions about when and how such amends might best be carried out. We use two-chair work with absent or deceased family members or friends; therapy meetings with parents, children, colleagues, or friends; letters; and other healing rituals to facilitate the grief process.

Late Ongoing Recovery

We attend to a number of different tasks during this phase of recovery. The work largely falls within the contact and withdrawal phases of the cycle of experience. We focus clients to begin to assimilate prior changes more fully; to learn to enjoy rather than suffer through life; and to come to terms with themselves, their current family, and family of origin in a new way. We find that goals for the future begin to emerge as the alcoholic begins to hope and dream again. Values may need to be updated, and oftentimes we support clients in reevaluating their relationship to AA in this phase. In addition, we may focus on deepening the client's spiritual life at this time.

One major task is to support the clients to assimilate changes as fully as possible. We find that this is a time of integrating new parts, becoming comfortable with new ways of being in the world and with people. As the alcoholic begins to flower, test wings, and experiment, we direct the energy toward new experiences and discoveries. Many clients begin to recapture their childhood or aborted adolescence and we support them to be excited by and accepting of these fresh perspectives.

We actively encourage clients to attend to and follow budding interests in education, careers, sports, and hobbies. We work to revise introjects limiting joy, pleasure, and excitement as they surface and become prominent. Many of our clients grew up in families where they were shamed for playful childlike excitement. As a result, we work through unfinished memories and the revising of restrictive rules in order to make room for new decisions and new feelings to emerge and self-expansion to continue. As a part of this work, our clients often begin venturing beyond the safe nest AA has provided. Predictably, anxieties and insecurities arise and require management since AA has been their nurturing refuge during this recooperative period.

One of our major goals in this period is to continue to work on helping clients to redefine themselves by asking: "Who am I? What are my values? What do I like? What do I want?" By providing both internal and external support, we transform this normal anxiety into energy and excitement. We freely stimulate clients in creating new dreams and plans for themselves and in acting more spontaneously on their wishes. As they arise, we continue to work on issues around sexuality and intimacy, and conflicts about needs for dependency versus these for control and autonomy, though the work at this point is more a question of refinement. As always, if we notice that client anxiety peaks precipitously, we shift to cognitive/behavioral methods, especially if urges to drink arise. Typically, sobriety is solid by this time, however, and the dangers of relapse are minimal.

Much of our work in the late phase of ongoing recovery involves addressing issues common to those who grew up in dysfunctional families. Thus, common themes that emerge at this point involve (O'Gorman & Oliver-Diaz, 1985):

- Further work on boundaries
- Spiritual development
- Focus on self-other acceptance
- Abandonment/enmeshment issues in intimate relationships
- Balance of work and play
- Parenting behavior
- Direct work with client and family of origin or current family

We have found that, at this late stage of treatment, meetings between the adult alcoholic and the family of origin often can be enormously beneficial (Framo, 1982). In such meetings, we support clients to address issues about family relationships that have concerned them through the years. Key events may be talked about, roles and alliances surfaced, and childhood perceptions clarified. These sessions provide our clients with a chance to know their parents as real people and to initiate peerage with parental figures. Major shifts in the recovering alcoholic's perceptions of family members commonly result, and family strengths and resources can be reinforced. Although these sessions can be painful, family members generally find the experience extremely beneficial.

We also focus on current family relationships (spouse and children). Often, issues of power and control must be resolved and new role behavior must be developed so that greater levels of closeness can be achieved. Our clients often require practice in recognizing their dependency needs, asking for what they want ("humbling themselves"), and taking responsibility (Bepko & Krestan, 1985). In addition, they often have minimal parenting skills, having themselves been raised in chaotic and sometimes abusive families (O'Gorman & Oliver-Diaz, 1987). Not only do they lack adequate parenting skills, but some of our clients also lack the desire to parent, often feeling resentful about the deficits in nurturing and support in their own childhood. Since modification of the core characteristics is a lifetime process, issues of control, black-and-white thinking, confusion about feeling states, as well as other core difficulties can continue to complicate efforts to improve all relationships. Self-help groups such as Adult Children of Alcoholics (ACOA) and other codependency 12-step groups are helpful as a supplement to AA in working through such issues.

We also supplement the work on core issues by encouraging our clients to take a daily personal inventory and to take responsibility for feelings and behavior (the good, the bad, and the ugly) while also moving into action to resolve issues. This supports the client in introspection, constructive assessment of feelings and actions, and rapid resolution of internal or interpersonal difficulties. This work is also fostered by work on the 10th step:

> Step 10. Continued to take personal inventory and when we were wrong promptly admitted it.

Following step 10 helps keep recovering people honest with themselves and others. Continued efforts to help recovering individuals concentrate on self/ other acceptance, avoiding self-righteousness and judgment, will add balance and serenity. Taking responsibility rather than externalizing problems, yet, at the same time, accepting, forgiving, and loving oneself, is the ultimate goal. Hardly any of us reach total enlightenment but the AA program does provide a path for transcending much of life's suffering.

It is in this late stage of recovery that we become even more aware of the support to therapy provided by AA. The AA program and other related recovery groups set in motion a series of changes that continue through a lifetime. The AA program supports our work in that it provides a new way to live life—a formula to end suffering and to renew the spirit. Although our clients may eventually grow away from the program, the program rarely leaves them. One of the major gifts of the AA program is that it sets members on a course of connecting or reconnecting with their spirituality. In late ongoing recovery, our clients frequently make an even deeper commitment to spiritual development. We support them in maintaining and enhancing their spirituality through regular spiritual practices: relaxation, affirmations, breathing techniques, dream work, guided imagery, spiritual readings, as well as various forms of meditation and prayer (Whitfield, 1985). The AA program supports this work explicitly as shown in the 11th step:

> Step 11. Sought through prayer and meditation to improve our conscious contact with God *as we understood him*, praying only for knowledge of His will for us and the power to carry that out.

In this phase recovering clients are often ready to create a new relationship to AA. Dependency needs have largely been resolved and individuals have room to evaluate beliefs learned through AA, which though vital to their survival in the past, may now be revised to fit the client's current needs. Just as with adolescents leaving their family, some recovering alcoholics need help separating from AA, establishing additional goals, and experimenting with new interests.

Most recovering people require some kind of ongoing connection with AA, but the strength of this tie generally lessens as individuals develop greater security in themselves and their newly formed lifestyle. Some individuals may experience guilt as they begin breaking confluence with AA and differentiating intrapsychically and interpersonally.

However, if therapists assist recovering people in thoroughly reviewing gains made through the program and encourage clients to express gratitude to all those who have guided them through their recovery, more adequate assimilation can occur, paving the way to a more complete resolution. Continued service in the form of sponsorship can also help give the recovering person an active avenue for expression.

> Step 12. Having had a spiritual awakening as a result of these steps, we tried to carry this message to other alcoholics and to practice these principles in all of our affairs.

CONCLUSION

Alcoholism is a complex disorder and the task of moving with the client from drinking to ongoing recovery is a long, and at times, an arduous one. In this chapter we set out to provide the therapist with a map of the recovery process as we see it and at least a glimpse of the richness and flexibility provided by a Gestalt approach to the treatment of alcoholism. It is our hope that we have provided not only a foundation and sense of groundedness in the specific applications of basic Gestalt techniques and principles but also a sense of freedom to create, explore, and experiment with Gestalt method as a way of joining with and leading the alcoholic into recovery.

ACKNOWLEDGMENT

We extend our thanks and gratitude to Jean R. Berggren, M.D., who provided us with much support and guidance in the development of portions of the theoretical model we present in this chapter.

NOTE

1. Although the second level of regulatory disturbance is fundamental to alcoholism, we believe this model can also be applied in understanding self-regulatory disturbances as they are manifest in many other syndromes of addictive or compulsive behavior, including drug addiction, eating disorders, compulsive gambling, workaholism, and so on.

REFERENCES

American Psychiatric Association. (1987). *Diagnostic and statistical manual of mental disorders* (3rd ed., revised). Washington, DC: Author.

Bateson, G. (1971). The cybernetics of "self": A theory of alcoholism. *Psychiatry, 34*(1), 1–18.

Bean, M., & Zinberg, N. (1981). *Dynamic approaches to the understanding and treatment of alcoholism*. New York: Free Press.

Beattie, M. (1987). *Codependent no more*. New York: Harper and Row.

Bepko, C., & Krestan, J. A. (1985). *The responsibility trap: A blueprint for treating the alcoholic family*. New York: Free Press.

Black, C. (1982). *It will never happen to me*. Denver: M.A.C. Publishers.

Bradshaw, J. (1988). *Healing the shame that binds you*. Pompano Beach, FL: Health Communications, Inc.

Brown, S. (1985). *Treating the alcoholic: A developmental model of recovery*. New York: Wiley.

Brown, V., Ridgely, M., Pepper, B., Levine, I., & Ryglewicz, H. (1989). The dual crisis: Mental illness and substance abuse: Present and future directions. *American Psychologist, 44*, 565–569.

Carlock, C. J., & Shaw, C. A. (1988). *Self-esteem for adult children of alcoholics* (Cassette recording). Muncie, IN: Accelerated Development, Inc.

Drews, T. R. (1980). *Getting them sober* (vol. 1). *A guide for those who live with an alcoholic*. South Plainfield, NJ: Bridge Publications.

Estes, N. J., & Heinemann, M. E. (Eds.). (1982). *Alcoholism: Development, consequences and interventions*. St. Louis: Mosby.

Framo, J. L. (1982). Family of origin as a therapeutic resource for adults in marital and family therapy: You can and should go home again. *Family Process, 15*, 193–210.

Frey, D., & Carlock, C. J. (1989). *Enhancing Self Esteem*. Muncie, IN: Accelerated Development.

Johnson, V. E. (1973). *I'll quit tomorrow*. New York: Harper and Row.

Keleman, J. (1975). *Your body speaks its mind*. New York: Simon & Schuster.

Kepner, J. I. (1987). *Body process: A gestalt approach working with the body in psychotherapy*. New York: Gardner Press.

Kurtz, E. (1982). Why A.A. works: The intellectual significance of Alcoholics Anonymous. *Journal of Studies on Alcohol, 43*, 38–80.

Mack, J. E. (1981). Alcoholism, A.A., and the governance of the self. In M. H. Bean & N. E. Zinberg (Eds.), *Dynamic approaches to the understanding and treatment of alcoholism* (pp. 128–162). New York: Free Press.

Marlatt, G. A., & Gordon, J. R. (Eds.). (1985). *Relapse prevention: Maintenance strategies in the treatment of addictive behaviors*. New York: Guilford.

Maxwell, M. (1984). *The AA experience*. New York: McGraw-Hill.

Oaklander, V. (Speaker). (1986). *Helping children and adolescents become self-nurturing* (cassette recording). Long Beach, CA: Maxsound Educational Tape Division.

O'Gorman, P., & Oliver-Diaz, P. (1987). *Breaking the cycle of addiction*. Pompano Beach, FL: Health Communications, Inc.

Pattison, E., & Kaufman, E. (1982). *Encyclopedic handbook of alcoholism*. New York: Gardner Press.

Perls, F., Hefferline, R., & Goodman, P. (1951). *Gestalt therapy*. New York: Julian Press.

Polster, E., & Polster, M. (1973). *Gestalt therapy integrated*. New York: Brunner/Mazel.

Robertson, N. (1988). *Getting better: Inside Alcoholics Anonymous*. New York: William Morrow.

Seixas, F. (1982). Criteria for the diagnosis of alcoholism. In N. J. Estes & M. E. Heinemann (Eds.), *Alcoholism: Development, consequences, and interventions* (pp. 49–67). St. Louis: Mosby.

The twelve steps of alcoholics anonymous. (1987). New York: Harper/Hazeldon.

Vaillant, G. E. (1981). Dangers of psychotherapy in the treatment of alcoholism. In M. H. Bean & N. E. Zinberg (Eds.), *Dynamic approaches to the understanding and treatment of alcoholism* (pp. 36–54). New York: Free Press.

Wegscheider, S. (1981). *Another chance: Hope and help for the alcoholic family*. Palo Alto, CA: Science and Behavior Books.

Whitfield, C. (1985). *Alcoholism, attachments and spirituality*. East Rutherford, NJ: Thomas W. Perrin, Inc.

Woititz, J. (1979). *Adult children of alcoholics*. Pompano Beach: Health Communications, Inc.

Zinker, J. (1978). *Creative process in gestalt therapy*. New York: Random House.

9

Gestalt Work with Psychotics

CYNTHIA OUDEJANS HARRIS, M.D.

"**P**SYCHOTICS" MAY BE DEFINED as individuals who are sufficiently impaired by their psychological state to require—at some point—hospitalization and medication for their mental illness. Hospitalization and medication are needed because such persons are either dangerous or profoundly upsetting to themselves or to others. They may have attempted to kill or harm themselves; they may have suffered from inner voices which made them so distraught that they were unable to sleep for many days before help was finally sought; they may have been for days or weeks under the spell of inner dreams and urges to create and invent so compelling that they found it unnecessary to sleep at all and became annoying, upsetting, or alarming to their families and friends; they may have threatened to harm others or may actually have done so; they may have been adjudged to be "criminally insane" and been referred by a court to the hospital; they may have found themselves simply unable to get out of bed or to function at all at work or at their college or university. These and many other faces of disturbance may be seen by those living with, or seeking to help, the severely disturbed. For those about them they can be scary, strange, frightening, and sometimes physically dangerous.

Inservice training in a state hospital or in a hospital serving schizophrenics and other severely disturbed and psychotic individuals is an immensely valuable part of the training of any person expecting to work with emotionally disturbed people. There is no substitute for having had day-to-day experience with psychotic persons over a substantial period of time. One's observational skills sharpen and one learns to develop early hunches about causality and diagnosis which later on will be tested by empirical means.

In whatever setting, even in "real life," it is valuable to have some awareness of what kind of person one is encountering. I will never forget the handsome young man whom the police brought late one night to the hospital door. (In those days involuntary commitment was legally possible.) I was just 5 weeks into my psychiatric residency and was the psychiatrist on duty. I interviewed the young man and found him sound. I was angry that the police had had the temerity to bring him in. I wanted to call the chief of the hospital and ask permission to refuse to admit him, but my co-worker, an experienced nurse, reminded me that he could as well be sent home the following day. He was not sent home. It turned out he had been *born* in a mental hospital and I worked devotedly with him for several months; I recall, among other things, working hard to get a trumpet for him to play. Despite my efforts, he was ultimately transferred to a more permanent facility. He suffered from schizophrenia. If I had met him a year further into my training, I would have had at the very least a healthy suspicion regarding his condition and possibly even the right diagnosis.

Students and young professionals are most likely to encounter psychotic individuals in state hospitals, where the majority of therapists receive their inservice training. Many of the psychotics are schizophrenics. Schizophrenic persons are disproportionately represented in our poorer classes and also consume a disproportionate amount of the available psychiatric services. For these reasons roughly half the patients in our state hospitals at any given time are schizophrenic individuals, although only 20% to 30% of the mentally ill *are* schizophrenic.

This chapter will consider Gestalt work with schizophrenic persons primarily. Although different parts of the Gestalt discipline may be emphasized with different psychiatric conditions—depending on the symptomatic phenomenology of the patient—the basic posture of the Gestalt therapist remains the same irrespective of the patient's diagnosis. All the ways of thinking and acting described below can be useful in dealing with the severely disturbed of any diagnostic label.

Nor will I discuss here Gestalt family therapy and Gestalt group therapy, although these modalities are often preferable to individual therapy in working with psychotics. Gestalt principles remain precisely the same in family or group work but are recast to subserve the interpersonal relationships between family members or group members rather than the more intrapersonal functions emphasized in individual therapy.

As with any serious psychotherapy, Gestalt therapy cannot be learned from a book. The best training may be one's own therapy, or, as a second choice, an extended experience-based training course coupled with extended supervision by a Gestalt therapist.

OVERVIEW

I will begin with a brief discussion of the context of care of the mentally ill and of the motivation needed to deal meaningfully with our psychotic population. Then I will briefly describe the many needs of the severely disturbed and the services they require, after which I will discuss the pharmacologic treatment of the mentally ill and how medication and psychotherapy are complementary. Finally, I will discuss in some detail the role of Gestalt theory and methodology when confronting the psychotic process and dealing with it psychotherapeutically. I will close with a summary.

The Context of Care for the Mentally Ill

Dostoyevski said: "The degree of civilization in a society can be judged by entering its prisons." He might have added, "and its mental hospitals."

The acutely disturbed need care that is expensive. At the minimum they require 24-hour attendance, some semblance of medical attention, and adequate food and shelter. Moreover, their needs tend to be long-term: They usually require some hospitalization, followed by long outpatient day treatment. They are often rehospitalized at intervals. They are frequently poor. For all these reasons governmental care has been the rule for the majority of the severely disturbed. There are some notable and important exceptions, such as the Menninger Foundation, the MacLean Hospital, and Chestnut Lodge, among other private institutions, which have pioneered in ways of treating and caring for the severely mentally ill.

Since governmental care, chiefly state hospital care, has been and is the rule, politics and economics play central roles in creating our impressions when we enter "mental hospitals." It therefore behooves anyone working in such a hospital or being trained in one to cultivate an awareness of the particular political and economic pressures operating in her/his hospital. Only by doing so can one adequately assess the level of care offered one's patients.

Motivation for Work with Psychotic Persons

Great devotion is required to work with psychotic people in their most common environment, the state hospital or its outpatient department, in anything approaching the long term. The roots of such devotion can come only from strong ethical or religious convictions. Such conviction is no longer as easily nourished as it used to be, but the individuals who are so motivated will become badly needed and highly valued professionals. Indeed, the earliest form of real care for the mentally ill in the United States was called "moral treatment." Benjamin Rush, a signer of the Declaration of Independence, was the founder of moral treatment. He is called "the father of American psychiatry," and his likeness appears on the seal of the American Psychiatric Association. In 1810, Rush described his own motivation:

> There is a great pleasure in combatting with success a violent bodily disease, but what is this pleasure compared with that of restoring a fellow creature from the anguish and folly of madness and of reviving in him the knowledge of himself, his family, his friends, and his God! But where this cannot be done, how delightful the consideration of suspending by our humanity their mental and bodily misery! [p. 284]

At present, no school of psychology incorporates ethical or religious convictions as theoretically important for the practitioner. Nor does any deal with the "pleasure" and "delight' cited by Rush. "Convictions" are regarded as "private" matters. "Important" matters are theories of personality, an understanding of dynamics, skill in appropriate intervention, a knowledge of medications.

Going along with, creating, and being created by the spirits of the times, psychology and psychiatry have so far avoided the most serious areas of human concern. Therefore, awareness of such issues should not be sought within the psychology/psychiatry curriculum. The driving force behind sound, responsible, caring work must come from other sources.

Meanwhile psychological and psychiatric theory must be learned thoroughly. Patients and clients, if they are to be served well, will call upon every shred of knowledge and skill possessed by the practitioner.

In sum, the source of our drive to help and care for the severely disturbed is not fueled by a knowledge of psychiatry or psychology. Our drive and our therapeutic energy come from deep roots within ourselves, perhaps from our past, perhaps from our family's past. Our ability to help, by contrast, comes from what we have learned and know. At the same time, we can help because we know how to put aside everything that we know in order to attend to the patient or patients before us. Our healing force lies in our attending to the patient, not in our attending to our knowledge. In Gestalt terms, as the patient becomes foreground, our knowledge remains available to us but becomes background.

Further, our ability to function well within the hospitals where the bulk of our severely disturbed either live or are cared for on an outpatient basis—if they are cared for at all—depends in some measure on our knowledge of the particular political and economic constraints within which our own individual work space exists.

THE NEEDS OF OUR PSYCHOTIC POPULATION

For optimal care, psychotic people require the services of many disciplines in the acute as well as in the rehabilitative phase of their care. For example, if they seek help or if help is sought for them during a period of acute illness, they will, in all probability, need medication and hospitalization until their florid psychotic activity has cleared—until the hallucinations, delusions, hyperactivity, inability to sleep, and so on have substantially lessened. During their hospitalization they will also need medical care, both for diagnostic purposes—that is, to rule out any physiological basis for the psychosis—as well as to rule out or to care for any accompanying medical illness. I will not forget the therapist whose patient refused to get out of bed to see him and who, thinking it was up to the patient to decide to come to his office, left him there. Fortunately, an examining physician came by and discovered the patient could not move because of acute appendicitis.

During their hospitalization, such patients need skilled psychiatric nursing care and good milieu therapy, and will certainly benefit, particularly following the acute episode, from group therapy, occupational therapy, and family therapy. All of this care will probably—although this is no longer necessarily the case—take place under the oversight of a psychiatrist, who may or may not also be the physician who deals with the patient's medical problems and who may or may not be the patient's individual psychotherapist.

The Role of Psychotherapy During the Acute Phase

Let us assume that the patient has now been hospitalized, is having his basic needs for food, shelter, and clothing taken care of for the moment by the cooks and nurses and janitors of the hospital; is having his moment-to-moment psychological needs cared for by the psychiatric nurses and aides on the floor; is receiving antipsychotic medication from his physician/psychiatrist; is having the needs of other family members cared for by a psychiatric social worker who at the same time is investigating the patient's job- or school-related problems; is being helped by the occupational therapist to get something done or made during the long, often boring days of hospitalization. All these services are being moved into place to assist the patient in his recovery from the acute episode. First, medication usually helps the patient biochemically and helps the patient's sleeping, eating, and thinking. Then psychotherapy plus medication helps emotionally, as the confusion and inner chaos begin to clear. And finally, psychotherapy, group therapy, family therapy, and social work provide necessary help, as recovery and learning and growth lead to the ability to return to family or work or school.

During the time of the acute psychosis, it is probably wasteful of professional resources for the therapist to attempt more than brief, if frequent, visits to the patient to assure her of the therapist's presence, concern, and availability and to provide perhaps some sense of continuity, of being listened to, and hopefully of being fully cared for in the period of terror and distress. These initial interactions, further, help the therapist to gain early impressions of the patient's problems and potential strengths: Even in this emergency situation strengths of character and mind, such as stubbornness and intelligence, may be discerned which can, later on, provide important ground in the therapist's mind, against which the figure of the psychotherapeutic intervention can be fashioned.

The therapist on the multidisciplinary team caring for the patient—particularly if he or she is also the head of such a team—must stay closely in touch with the other members of the team from the other clinical disciplines. The coprofessionals may observe things about the patient that the therapist has not had opportunity to see, or the other team members may need the therapist's insights to guide their own interactions with the patient.

Almost invariably, when hospitalization has been required during the acute phase, the patient will benefit from psychotropic medication. Therefore we will now turn our attention briefly to the pharmacologic aspects of treatment.

The Role of Medication in Psychosis

Background Considerations   Currently, we stand firmly on the threshold of new and important discoveries about the molecular biology and the microscopic and submicroscopic neuroanatomy of emotion. Studies in the monkey have demonstrated that learning produces structural and functional changes in specific nerve cells (Pardes, 1986). Kandel and his co-workers, working with *Aplysia californica*, a mollusc, have demonstrated that learning is accompanied by changes in the effectiveness of neural connections. Kandel remarks that this fact leads to "a new way of viewing the relationship between social and biological processes in the generation of behavior" (p. 1207). He goes on to note that at present psychiatry, psychology, and medicine tend to differentiate between "organic" disease and "functional" disease, but that the work of his group makes this distinction unwarranted. Since the classification in the third edition of the *Diagnostic and Statistical Manual of Mental Disorders* is based on this distinction, it is clear that our whole way of conceptualizing mental illnesses is on the threshold of major change.

Because of the new discoveries one can—even at this early stage—assume that clearly definable changes take place within the nervous system both as concomitants of mental illness and subsequently as results of medication, psychotherapy, and other effective treatment modalities. As we learn more about the basic cellular-neurochemical-neuroanatomic systems within our skulls which subserve our emotions, our ability to medicate more specifically for particular psychic ills, and thus to influence specific neural circuits, will increase. The old boundaries between "mind" and "brain" and "body" are beginning to blur. An awareness of these developments and an openness to the ones that will come is important for individuals who work with persons taking psychotropic medication.

Therapeutic Considerations   When working with patients taking psychotropic medications, we need to develop our own orientation in three essential regards. First—and against the very minimal background offered above—we need to develop our own clear belief system, our own philosophy of the mind–body dichotomy or, as some will prefer, the holistic interaction. Second, for the most pragmatic of reasons, all persons working with psychotic individuals need to have at least rudimentary knowledge about the medications patients are taking: effects, side effects, duration of effects, and so on. And third, each of us needs to develop, especially if working psychotherapeutically with these patients, our own individual way of dealing with our patients' feelings about taking psychotropic medications.

First, to develop our own individual philosophy, however tentative, we need at the start to honor the body–mind, brain–mind dichotomy: For the last 350 years it has been central to the way people in the Western world have conceived of their reality. This way of thinking has proved immensely powerful for thinking about *things*. The wonders produced by medical science over the last 150 years are evidence of its validity. Without this way of thinking you or your mother might not have survived your birth; you might have died of diphtheria, measles, polio; you might have gone crazy, ultimately, from tertiary syphilis. Thus, the ability to search logically for reasons until "causes" are found should remain a cherished capability for each of us personally, as well as for the natural scientist among us. However, nowadays the subject–object paradigm has lost credibility as the sole way of addressing reality. Holism is "in" and will doubtless remain so. We need it in our search for a vision of man to guide us in the new world that is just beginning. For those in the field of mental health, the new ways of thinking are at work before our very eyes. But what should we do, how should we think, once we have honored the body–mind, brain–mind dichotomy? The hardest thing to do is not to require an immediate answer and to be willing to stay with the present dilemma until it lifts. For some this ambiguous posture is so difficult that they turn to magic and mysticism as rafts that may keep them theoretically afloat. Those who can bear not to know right away—those who can keep an open mind and a flexible brain and who can bear to live on and wait out this hiatus, those who realize that both the language of logic and the language of feeling are at present valid and in conjunction in a way they never have been before, those who are willing to try to speak both of these languages—those are the persons, I believe, who may begin to glimpse the outlines of the new visions we so sorely hope for.

Second, non-medical professionals seeking to work responsibly with people using psychotropic medication need to know a fair amount about these compounds. They need to know where the most recent edition of the *Physicians Desk Reference* can be located and they will refer to it often and become familiar with the more commonly used compounds. Armed with such knowledge, they may be the first people to notice that a particular patient seems overmedicated. Or they may be the people who first suspect the rare side effect.

Third, anyone responsible for severely disturbed people needs a well-thought-out approach to dealing with such patients regarding their medication. The approach needs to be useful and acceptable to the patient as well as meaningful and appropriate for the practitioner. I like to use a metaphor and say something like: "Just as you need a cast when you break your leg so your body can work at healing itself, so you need this medication to support your mind during the time you're healing yourself; the medicine will help you to pay the greatest possible attention to your own healing process." That approach has worked well for me. But such interventions always work best when the practitioner or therapist invents or discovers the singular words that feel really right to him or her, sometimes different words for each patient.

Medication is most effective for, and most frequently prescribed for, the symptoms of acute psychosis: hallucinations and delusions. The use of psychotropic medication tends to make psychotherapy possible sooner and useful sooner. To date we have only a small understanding of the mechanisms of action of these drugs.

We do, however, now know several things about the interactions between medication and psychotherapy. We know that (a) in the acute phase, inhospital individual psychotherapy produces no statistically significant positive effects, whereas medication alone, without any other treatment, leads to considerable improvement; (b) in the rehabilitative (usually outpatient) phase of treatment, the evidence shows that psychological intervention, particularly group or family therapy, together with medication, yields significantly better results than do drugs alone; indeed, psychotherapy has been shown to be *ineffective* unless combined with drugs (Davis, 1985); and (c) failure to receive psychotropic medication during the acute episode *probably* does harm that persists over a 3- to 5-year period (Davis, 1985).

What do these observations mean from the theoretical point of view? How do the drugs act and how does psychotherapy act? As yet we do not have the answers to either of these (important) questions.

The theory that fits best at this moment in time, and that accounts best for all the research findings, is that drugs affect the brain in one way, namely, in reducing hallucinations, delusions, and the thought disorder characteristic of schizophrenia, whereas psychological intervention improves intrapsychic and interpersonal functioning. According to John M. Davis, Director of Research at the Illinois State Psychiatric Institute:

> If the *psychologically* focused theories were true, . . . in the long run psychotherapy should produce an etiological cure and schizophrenia as measured by specific symptoms would disappear. If schizophrenia were a truly *biological* disorder, the drug treatment would benefit the symptomatic variables and the psychological treatments would have no effect on any variables. According to the dual-mechanism theory, the drugs should produce a good effect on symptoms, and the psychological treatment should improve the intrapsychic conflict and social functioning. The latter is what is empirically observed. [Davis, 1985, p. 1506].

Dosage must be carefully monitored as the patient moves out of the acute episode. Because of the long-term side effects—most notably tardive dyskinesia, the sometimes irreversible gait disturbance—the usual effort is to get the patient off drugs as soon as possible or, if that is not possible, to make the maintenance dose as low as possible, perhaps including "drug holidays." Furthermore, a patient taking more medication than necessary is less able to make maximum use of psychotherapy. Therefore, optimally the dosage should be monitored frequently by the prescribing person in close consultation with the therapist and the nursing staff. Clearly, anything which blurs the patient's sense of self and of at least minimal self-responsibility—be it delusions, hallucinations, or medications—is deleterious to the healing process.

The Context of Psychotherapy with Psychotics

One way to think of the severely disturbed/psychotic individual is to think of him or her as temporarily unable to take, or even to try to learn to take, the degree of responsibility for self to which others of us, less circumscribed, may aspire. This view, however, is not adequate to the situation in which we find ourselves in the mid-1980s: It is now obvious that some people simply are unable, whether constitutionally or otherwise, even to begin to take basic responsibility for themselves. At this time they fill our parks and streets in summer and cover the gratings over our subways and basements in winter. There are some movements in the direction of help for them. Still, it is clear that our distaste and unbelief run high when we are confronted by their condition.

Chlorpromazine (Thorazine), still the most widely used of psychotropic medications in the care of schizophrenia, was first synthesized in France in 1950. It was tried on psychotic patients shortly afterward, and its remarkable effects were reported in the literature in 1952 (Swazey, 1974). Chlorpromazine did its job of alleviating the most troublesome psychotic symptoms so well that we began to look with horror at our human warehouses—the immense state hospitals housing thousands of patients each. The patients looked so well to us in the hospitals that we decided to discharge them and save the money. Only now are we learning very gradually how to house, care for, medicate, and monitor our street people at moderate cost (Street People, N.Y. Times, Nov 11, 1986). In the late 1960s, we had hoped that pills and minimal outpatient follow-up would suffice. They did not.

At this time about 70% of patients hospitalized for an attack of acute schizophrenia will be asymptomatic within 3 months, and 85% will be out of the hospital within a year. About 60% of those patients will be socially recovered 5 years later and will have been employed for more than half of that time. About 30% will be handicapped and show some psychopathology but will still be living in the community most of the time. Only about 10% will require continuous hospitalization (Lehamnn & Cancro, 1985).

In a time of tight purse strings, the questions of *which* patients in public psychiatric facilities should be afforded psychotherapy will often be asked. Therefore, it will become increasingly important to predict which patients will benefit from psychotherapy. My own experience has been, however, that we can never know with real certainty how a patient will respond to psychotherapeutic intervention until we try and try hard. And Charles G.

Schulz (1985) of the Johns Hopkins University School of Medicine recently stated that despite present knowledge it is still impossible to predict who will benefit from psychotherapy without a prolonged trial. He further noted that some of the most difficult management problems turn out to give the best response to therapy. Perhaps this is because a patient can sometimes take the stubbornness and power involved in combatting care givers and turn it to combat his/her illness. So, until our predictive capacities and our knowledge of which psychotherapeutic modes best benefit which groups of patients improve, we must bear our ignorance in mind and make the best guesses we can.

Furthermore, the interventions of devoted first-year social work interns have been noted to be, on occasion, more effective with severely disturbed patients than has been the work of their seasoned supervisors. Intuitively, it does make sense that some severely disturbed individuals will respond to the freshness and élan of particular young students.

Our confusions about how to care for the mentally ill result from our ignorance regarding the causes and nature of the illnesses. It is to be hoped that this ignorance will gradually lift. In the meantime we must use the guidelines offered by the knowledge we do possess and by our pragmatic experiences.

Empirically, psychotherapy is now recognized to be one of the essential elements of care for the severely disturbed. The best results over the long term are achieved by a combination of drugs, psychotherapy, and psychosocial training and intervention (Liberman, 1985). Although it is believed that the use of these modern interventions has shortened the length of hospital stays and has drastically reduced the most disruptive and destructive aspects of the psychoses, these measures have failed significantly to increase the actual number of full, permanent recoveries (Lehmann & Cancro, 1985). We should not minimize the immense value of shortened hospital stays, coupled with less pain for patients and their families. Nevertheless, our failure to make better progress against the schizophrenias bears witness to the complexity and stubbornness of these disorders.

Psychotherapy with Psychotic People

Perhaps more than therapy with neurotic individuals, psychotherapy with psychotic individuals requires a long-term commitment on the part of the therapist, and the establishment of a solid, honest, and ultimately trusting relationship between therapist and patient. The meaning of the therapeutic relationship to the patient has recently been eloquently stated by a young schizophrenic.

A year and a half ago my therapist asked me if psychotherapy had helped me. I was a bit stunned but answered almost automatically, "Yes, of course it's helped me." . . . But that was not the end of the issue. I began to wonder if therapy was really helping me and how.

My therapist's question was prompted by the controversy about whether schizophrenic patients could truly benefit from talk therapy or were best helped by drug therapy. I was somewhat angered by the thought that some schizophrenic patients were being treated only with pills and a monthly rendezvous to pick up a prescription. Perhaps the most dramatic symptoms such as delusions and hallucinations may respond to such treatment, but there is so much more involved in the life of a schizophrenic patient than just these manifestations. . . .

Psychotherapy, in combination with drug therapy, supportive emotional day treatment, and a weekly group therapy session, has worked for me. Most of my program supports psychotherapy, which I consider the center of my treatment and which has been the one thing to remain constant through hospitalization and program changes. . . . I have seen lights in the sky, heard choruses of people inside me—taunting, tormenting me, pinning me against the wall, driving me into insanity. The drama is endless, and the agony and the terror are even more so. . . .

For so long I wondered why my therapist insisted on talking about my relationship with him. He was not my problem. . . . His persistence in talking about "us" made me curious and later made me feel, despite a twinge of guilt, that maybe it would be nice to talk about "us." The guilt came from the fact that there *was* an "us." For so long it had been "me" and "them." It took a long time, but finally I saw why it was important to explore my relationship with my therapist—it was the first real relationship I had ever had: that is, the first I felt safe enough to invest myself in. I rationalized that it was all right because I would learn from this relationship how to relate to other people and maybe one day leave behind the isolation of my own world. ["Recovering Patient," 1986, pp. 68–70][1]

This statement beautifully underscores the validity of psychotherapy with severely disturbed persons and underscores the centrality of the relationship between therapist and patient to the therapeutic process. Within this context, what is the meaning, contribution, role of the Gestalt discipline in working with a psychotic individual?

GESTALT THERAPY WITH PSYCHOTIC PEOPLE

Recently, the author of a long-term follow-up study of schizophrenic patients, concluded that "in some instances exploratory psychotherapy may even aggravate schizophrenic illness by exposing patients to memories and insights that they are ill-equipped to handle emotionally" (in Fishe, 1986, p. 275). When in experienced and attentive hands, Gestalt therapy, with its emphasis on the centrality of immediate experience in the here and now and its inherently noninvasive quality, avoids this particular pitfall. Phenomenologically speaking, schizophrenia consists of the loss of self-awareness and the loss of the ability to make contact. The Gestalt methodology affords opportunities to teach patients the self-awareness which they may never have truly developed and which is unquestionably impaired. It also affords opportunities for the therapist to design experiences which will heighten the patient's ability to "make contact" and thus foster interpersonal competence. In these ways Gestalt methodology is a psychotherapy uniquely fitted to deal with the schizophrenias.

Schizophrenic delusions and hallucinations may be conceived as effective ways of suppressing self-awareness and of preventing contact with others. Delusions and hallucinations are often the symptoms that bring the patient to the hospital and that are seen in the opening phases of institutional treatment. The disease itself may have smouldered for some time prior to hospitalization or it may have struck with suddenness. The panic and terror underlying these experiences tend to be overwhelming.

In virtually all cases insight is absent. This makes good existential sense: The patient's essential need is to avoid awareness (an integral piece of insight) of self and thus to avoid contact with others and instead to create his or her private inner world.

As the more florid symptoms of the psychotic process recede with medication, the patient becomes less terrified and more able to function within a protected environment. The psychotic process becomes more restricted. There are fewer hallucinations and delusions. On the inner front, the psychosis tends to be limited in its expression to dreams, fantasy life, and projections; on the outer front, fear of intimacy, low self-esteem, and vulnerability remain. Insight becomes somewhat more available. The patient grows more willing and able to be aware of present experience and gradually becomes more able to take ownership of that experience. The patient's language changes gradually from "My arm hit him" to "I hit him." Ultimately the patient may become able to experience the "normal" sequence of awareness, contact, and withdrawal in the Gestalt cycle of experience. This sequence of events and experiences, moving from terror, hallucinations, and delusions, through dreams, irreality, and misjudgment of the outer world, to the reowning and mastery of inner experience and outer choice, takes many months, even years, and sometimes it never occurs at all. Even in the best of cases there are many reversals, many regressions, periods of return to former states of the psychosis which may have felt safer.

As noted earlier in this chapter, most patients reach a certain level of recovery and remain at that level; some few patients do make a full recovery. In each of these phases Gestalt methodology has much to offer.

The Paradoxical Theory of Change

A major contribution of Gestalt theory is the paradoxical theory of change. This theory appears paradoxical only because we tend to think of the sequence of change as follows: First we want to change, then we decide to change, meanwhile we intend to change, then we do change, and finally we make changes. Fritz Perls's belief was that our wish to change splits us into our Top Dog, who wants to change, and our Underdog, who must do the changing. In the ensuing struggle the Underdog generally wins and refuses to change. The Gestalt therapist, therefore, seeks to let what *is* be—and fully be—possessing the faith that change is thereby given opportunity to occur, unconsciously and without willing it. The more fully and completely we can experience what we are doing or being in this moment, the more likely it is that change may come in the next moment. Thus "staying with the present experience" is the methodology of the paradoxical theory of change.

This methodology is appropriate at virtually any stage of the psychotic process. With an acutely psychotic person, it can have the beauty of acknowledging the personhood of the patient and the patient's experience without lending support to the psychotic process itself.

Consider the following exchange, for example. Nancy is 22 years old, has had two prior hospitalizations for acute psychotic episodes, and has recently reentered the hospital. Medication has controlled her most terrifying symptoms. Among other psychotic symptoms, Nancy reports that "people put ideas in my head."

Therapist: How do they do that?
Nancy: Well, I feel influenced.
T: Let's try something. Would you put an idea in my head?
N: (giggles)
T: I'm really serious even if it sounded silly. Let's do an experiment and check on how ideas go from one head to another. . . .
N: (hesitantly) You should go to church more. . . . (Nancy has already told the therapist about her *own* ambivalence about attending church.)
T: I hear you but I don't think that fits for me. . . . I'm going to give that one back to you to use for yourself if you like. Shall I try one?
N: Yes.
T: You should rest more.
N: What for? I'm not tired.
T: I don't feel as though I'm influencing you. How is it for you? [Claire Stratford, unpublished article, 1974]

Here the therapist acknowledges Nancy's experience and thereby validates Nancy but without validating or supporting Nancy's psychotic experience.

The therapist further evokes interpersonal activity from the patient: "Would you put an idea in my head?" And when the patient finds that funny and giggles, the therapist again invites the patient—"I'm serious even if it sounded silly"—and the patient is then able to try to put an idea in the therapist's head. The therapist then watched, I am certain, to be sure this attempt did not provoke too much anxiety for Nancy, who had recently been extremely confused. The supportive aspects of this interchange include the therapist's clear delineation of interpersonal boundaries: "I don't feel as though I'm influencing you." This statement is at once supportive and modeling: The therapist models by reporting her own sense of what is happening—"I don't feel as though . . ."—and qualifying the validity of her own feeling by checking with Nancy about *her* experience. The therapist has thus created a small situation in which she can model self-awareness and other awareness and invite the patient to do likewise. This example also demonstrates the therapist's use of her own creativity. It is important that the therapist have as much fun as is possible in the therapy. Fun lightens what is basically a serious situation and, at the same time, kindles the mind and spirit of the therapist.

In the art of staying with what is, it is of course essential to be *aware* of what is. Hence the centrality of awareness.

Awareness and Contact

In the Gestalt model of human health, the ability to tune in at will to what is happening within oneself and to name it with clarity at any given moment is regarded as a foundation stone of one's psychological health. A second such stone is the ability to distinguish between one's own self and other persons. By knowing this boundary, one can make contact with another person or persons and later withdraw from such contact.

In the psychotic process, these basic human functions of being aware of what is going on within one's self (awareness) and of knowing where one's own person ends and the other begins (one's boundaries) and the arts of being with and relating to other people (contact) are in fundamental disarray. Therefore a schizophrenic person, either in the acute phase of the illness or in decompensated chronicity, is unable to mobilize energy to set about getting needs and wants satisfied. Because of its concentration on the basic functions of awareness and contact, the Gestalt discipline quite directly offers tools to help psychotic patients learn to regain full (or fuller) use of these functions.

Further, the discipline offers the therapist a repertoire of ways to design interactions and relearning experiences for the patient.

Work with psychotic persons requires immense simplicity and clarity and minute attention to how the patient is reacting to what is going on. Body language may be the only language the patient is at first able to speak, so emphatic attentiveness to that language is of special importance. A firm base of trust must precede any other sort of work. Psychotic patients require a great deal of affirmation, support, comfort, and reassurance before being ready to explore their feelings. Because of the obduracy of the psychotic state, big changes cannot be expected soon and the therapist needs to learn to be content with very small steps taken over and over and over again.

"Glue" and "Solvent"

In our slang "coming unglued" is an expression for going crazy. We also talk of "getting stuck," meaning, at a more neurotic level, being unable to take the next appropriate move in a task, such as finishing a dissertation. If we are unglued, we need to get glued back together. If we are stuck, we need a solvent to get us unstuck.

As neurotics we tend to need relatively more psychic solvent and relatively less psychic glue; as psychotics we need a lot of psychic glue to glue us back together before we can risk a tiny bit of psychic solvent. The affirming/glueing posture is comforting, reassuring, understanding, supportive. The questioning/solvent posture is by contrast curious, exploratory, challenging.

Therefore, it is helpful to know which kinds of interventions are psychic solvents and which are psychic glues. In the past, Gestalt therapy has been better known for its more dramatic solvent work than for its supportive glueing qualities, although competent therapists have always used good measures of both, whether working with neurotics or with psychotics.

Of course our very lives are filled with glueing experiences and solvent experiences. Growth and development are not possible unless old, former, no longer valid behaviors and ways of thinking can be dissolved to make place for newer, improved ones. In the words of Paul: "When I was a child, I spake as a child, I understood as a child, I thought as a child: but when I became a man, I put away childish things" (I Corinthians 13: 11). It is perhaps no accident that these words of Paul are part of his eloquent passage about the nature of love, since we cannot muster the courage to face much change without the glue of love and support, and perhaps even of faith.

The Gestalt therapist Sonia Nevis (1980) has named the force which makes personal intimacy or communal life ever and again possible "gluon."

From the existential, phenomenological point of view, the schizophrenic has not found enough gluon to be able to function in the world and so has instead created a private world. Gluon, which may be an ongoing exchange of affirmation and support, of being and of letting be, is essential in making our world a safe place to live in, a safe place to be ourselves in.

The recovering schizophrenic quoted above wrote: "I had drawn so far inside myself and so far away from the world, I had to be shown not only that the world was safe but also that I belonged to it, that I was in fact a person." ("Recovering Patient," 1986, p. 70.)

Awareness and Boundaries

Our awareness of ourselves is what lets us know that we *are* ourselves; awareness helps us to define our own edges, helps us get a sense of being a self, a me, a person. Our awareness of ourselves also lets us know what is *not* ourselves, what is "other." For the mentally ill, both the awareness of self and the distinction between self and "other" are dulled, if available at all. Because the patient has trouble realizing her own existence and hence has trouble distinguishing between herself and the "other," she cannot "relate" to another person.

Psychotherapeutic work with a severely disturbed person thus involves, at first, calming and reassuring the patient in order to help her gain the courage and hope necessary to begin to try to heal herself. For the therapist this means providing a lot of "glue." Later, the patient needs to learn to be more and more self-aware. And finally, she needs to learn to be more clearly aware of others and to use her knowledge of self and other to make contact with others and then to withdraw from such contact in comfortable sequences.

These three processes—comforting/reassuring, teaching awareness, teaching contact and withdrawal—do not, of course, occur in sequence. The therapist's artistry is revealed as the therapist uses the patient's own experience and statements and movements to help create the meaningful experiences designed for that particular patient at that particular moment of his or her therapy.

Comforting and Reassuring What are the guidelines for comforting and reassuring the psychotic individual? Awareness cannot be explored until anxiety has calmed, until the patient has gained confidence that he will not be drawn irretrievably into another person's sphere of influence, until his racing, chaotic consciousness can slow, and until he trusts the therapist to be present and to help ward off the terror of feeling nonexistent, of drowning in nothingness. The therapist must stay in touch with the anxiety level of the patient and take the responsibility of being the guide, protector, and caretaker.

Contact with our "internal comforts" is reassuring. Internal comforts may be such things as awareness that one's values are appreciated by another person or awareness that one's comments have been acknowledged and validated: It is comforting to hear that one is "right." The patient will gradually teach the therapist which comforts are most helpful to him and the attentive therapist will adjust interventions to fit the particular patient's style. An acutely psychotic person who is feeling suspicious may even find just being looked at unsettling. When this is the case, Stratford suggests the following.

> The therapist can make contact less threatening by sitting with the patient, slightly turned from him and making only brief, unintrusive, gentle eye contact. If the therapist contacts the patient in this manner and initiates even less contact than the patient can assimilate, the patient may begin to feel safe and seek more contact with the therapist through whichever mode is most comfortable for him. [Stratford & Brallier, 1979].

Often work can begin by experimenting with which physical distance between patient and therapist allows the patient to feel most comfortable and/or to perceive the separateness between themselves and the therapist. Such experimenting proceeds with many repetitions and continuous checking: "Can you see me now? I can see you—all of you—from head to feet. Is that comfortable for you? Should I be farther away?" The therapist needs to provide data rather than interpretation so that the patient can discover for himself that being seen can be all right, that being seen and heard can even enable him to feel noticed and validated. Very gradually, patients may come to experience—regardless of the thoughts or wishes of others—their right to have their own, real, very personal reactions and hence to experience their own inherent right to exist.

Teaching Awareness   The therapist needs also to help the patient learn to be more fully aware. This can begin with very simple body awareness. "Are you comfortable sitting like that? Don't move or change it—I just wondered if you were comfortable." Learning to be aware of such simple things again supports the patient's sense of reality and lessens the inherent anxiety. A goal with psychotic individuals is to help them permit themselves to become more aware of their wholeness and more confident of their bodily integrity. One way to encourage this development is for the therapist to mention (without too much emphasis) that he or she noticed small movements the patient has made. "I noticed you put your head on your hand just now."

This sort of statement helps the patient become more fully in touch with his or her existence and way of being in the world.

When the patient has discovered that awareness of sensations and movements can help him to be noticed and validated, his awareness of emotions and of thoughts is more easily accessible. The therapist must repeatedly give data on whether or not his or her awareness squares with that of the patient because this data is very important to the patient in the process of getting clear about where he or she ends and the therapist—the other person—begins.

"Staying with the process" is *not* a valid way of working with a psychotic individual. Indeed, it is the very chaos of that inner process which has led the patient to his present situation. The therapist must remain a reliable guide and protector and should not permit the patient to flounder—as a therapist might well do when dealing with a confused neurotic—but rather must carefully guide the patient to successful closure.

Sometimes, particularly during the acute phase of the illness, the patient may be having hallucinations and may want to talk about them. If it "feels right" to the therapist—and she is not just "curious"—she may want to express her honest interest in the voices that have been or are so troubling to her patient. The hallucinatory experience, however, should not be given undue attention; it should be handled briefly and casually. The patient's ability to be aware of reality is so impaired that the therapist's interventions almost always need to be supportive of the patient's reality testing and reality awareness. Recently flooded by inner experience, the patient has lost some contact with external reality. Attention to hallucinations is attention to a function that is purely intrapersonal—a function to which the therapist has no direct access and which therefore cannot be checked out. Thus the therapist's close attention to hallucinations does not help the patient in stepping away from the psychotic process and back into "life."

Similarly, the therapist needs to de-emphasize the ruminations of psychotics as they feverishly try to make sense out of their thoughts. Like hallucinations, ruminations serve to distance the person from the immediate awareness of his surroundings. Again, it behooves the therapist to help the patient come into more direct contact with his immediate environment: "Can you still *see* me while you're saying all that? I feel left out—as if you're not talking to *me*."

Contact and Withdrawal   How can a therapist teach contact and withdrawal and the contact/withdrawal rhythm? During the comforting and reassuring of the patient and when teaching awareness, the therapist has shown the patient, in a number of ways, that the patient is in fact a separate human being. The therapist has modeled the distinctions between the therapist's experience and the patient's experience innumerable times. It is hoped that the patient has begun to learn to distinguish between his or her own experience and that of others, and to appreciate the validity of both. The foundations of the ability to relate are slowly being laid. In Gestalt terms, the patient is learning something about how to be aware of self and something about how to be aware of the other person. With this kind of data available, relating to/interacting with another person may become less frightening.

Some Special Gestalt Techniques in Work with Psychotic Persons

Some of the ways of working in Gestalt therapy deserve special attention in work with psychotics. We will briefly attend to the areas of self-disclosure, two-chair work (polarities), and work with dreams.

Self-Disclosure   In reporting on his own experience to the patient, the therapist needs to be sparse and clear and generally to limit his self-reporting to the immediate transactions with the patient. For instance, statements such as "When you change the subject and look away I feel more remote from you and a little lonesome" may strengthen the patient's willingness to be aware of what she is doing and how it is affecting someone else. But statements about the therapist's life outside the session—indeed, even the therapist's life wisdom—are of little value when dealing with psychotic individuals. The psychotic patient usually lacks the ability to take a general principle and apply it to her or his own condition in the here and now. A more direct mode of statement is more useful to such patients. Basically, the therapist working with a psychotic needs to be calmer than he might have to be when working with a neurotic. A psychotic person is easily derailed if confronted with an excited therapist.

Polarities   Working with polarities requires special attention to clarity about what is being done. In the well-known two-chair technique, for example, the patient emphasizes two separate aspects of her personality, an inner polarity. Since the psychotic person has difficulty being clear about inner as well as outer-boundaries, such an exercise can be confusing to the patient unless the therapist repeatedly underlines that the patient is acting out two separate sides of her own personality but is not two separate people. Otherwise the patient may become confused about who she is—a most undesirable development. Unless used with care, work with polarities can serve to dissolve what tentative integrity the psychotic individual may have, rather than to support and reinforce it. Brallier and Hoffman (1971) underline this in their article on polarity work with a psychotic patient.

Dreams   Some of the same cautions apply to work with dreams. If—as is most often the case—the dream has been a bad one, the patient can be asked to tell the dream again and to recount in some detail the comforting, good-feeling parts of the dream. Or one can invite the patient to retell the dream and to stop when he feels discomfort. Then, the patient can be invited to create an ending he would like the dream to have. These are "gluing" interventions. They also enable the patient to experience some degree of mastery over his or her own inner life, and this can be very supportive of the healing process (Stratford & Brallier, 1979). A basic principle common to all these interventions is that they give patients the opportunity to learn from their own experience. For patients this can be highly self-validating.

In Gestalt work with psychotic individuals the therapist has two main functions: (a) to support and encourage the patient, and (b) to invent exercises, experiments, and work for the patient to do. Of course, these exercises and experiments must be graded in difficulty so that each one enables the patient to take the next single small step forward. They must be difficult enough, but not too difficult. If done well, such work provides the patient with experiences which help her to affirm once again her own wholeness and selfhood.

SUMMARY

The treatment of psychotic individuals requires many disciplines and services to provide optimal care and treatment. From research results we now know that a combination of medication and psychotherapy, in a context of supportive services, leads to the optimal results that professionals together with their patients are able to achieve at the present time (Davis, 1985).

Because of its realistic, here-and-now posture, Gestalt therapy is well suited for working with the severely disturbed, both immediately following a flagrant episode and in the rehabilitative months and years which follow. The Gestalt discipline is also uniquely useful, as Claire Stratford shows in this volume, in creating a therapeutic milieu for the severely disturbed.

In this chapter I have also pointed out that the moral and ethical values upon which care for the psychotically disturbed is optimally based, cannot, at present, be derived from any psychotherapeutic school. Rather these values come from our religious beliefs and ethical convictions. These beliefs and convictions find their way, through our governments, to the hospitals and other places where our society provides services for the mentally ill.

When discouraged in our work with schizophrenic patients, we may gain hope from the words of the young schizophrenic quoted so often in this chapter who wrote:

THE GREATEST GIFT

The question of whether the fragile ego of the schizophrenic patient can withstand the rigors of intensive therapy seems to me an unfortunate hindrance to the willingness of psychiatrists to attempt psychotherapy with schizophrenic individuals. A fragile ego left alone remains fragile. It seems there must be some balance that can be achieved so that schizophrenic patients can receive the benefits of psychotherapy with therapists who are sensitive to their special needs and can help their egos emerge, little by little. Medication or superficial support alone is not a substitute for the feeling that one is understood by another human being. For me, the greatest gift came the day I realized that my therapist really had stood by me for years and that he would continue to stand by me and to help me achieve what I wanted to achieve. With that realization my viability as a person began to grow. I do not profess to be cured—I still feel the pain, fear, and frustration of my illness. I know I have a long road ahead of me, but I can honestly say that I am no longer without hope. ["Can we talk," 1986, p. 70]

NOTES

In this chapter I have chosen to name the sexes of patients and therapists, to say "he" and "she" when referring to individuals in each category and varying between these two ways of reference. In doing this I have avoided saying "they" and "them" and instead have particularized and individualized "her" and "him"; in a similar vein I have referred to "psychotic individuals" rather than "psychotics" when I needed to refer to patients' present condition. I hope this choice is not offensive to our readers. Gestalt therapy at its best always stresses the individuality and personhood of its clients, patients and practitioners. I have sought to do so in this chapter.

REFERENCES

(Anonymous) Recovering Patient. Can we talk? The schizophrenic patient in psychotherapy (1986). *American Journal of Psychiatry*, Vol. 143(1), 68–70.

Editor's Note to "Can We Talk?" The Schizophrenic Patient in Psychotherapy states: "The reader may be assured that the author's psychiatrist (with whom the author allowed us to consult) is fully in accord with its publication. The diagnosis, moreover, has been firmly established by the clinician investigators of a major national study of schizophrenia in which the author participated as a subject. At our suggestion, the paper is published without the author's name in the interest of maintaining confidentiality.''

Brallier, L. W., & Hoffman, B. S. (1971). Assisting a psychotic patient with the integration process. *Psychotherapy: Theory Research and Practice*, Vol. 8(4), 304–306.

Davis, J. M. (1985). Antipsychotic drugs. In H. I. Kaplan & B. J. Sadock (Eds.), *Comprehensive textbok of psychiatry/IV*, Baltimore/London: Williams & Wilkins.

Fishe, E. A. (1986, June-July) [Review of Stone, M. H. (1986). Exploratory psychotherapy in schizophrenia spectrum patients, *Bulletin Menninger Clinic* 50, 287–306] *Digest of Neurology and Psychiatry*, p. 275. Hartford, Institute of Living.

Lehmann, H. E., & Cancro, R. (1985). Schizophrenia: Clinical features. In H. I. Kaplan & B. J. Sadock (Eds.), *Comprehensive Textbook of Psychiatry/IV* (p. 712). Baltimore/London: Williams & Wilkins.

Nevis, S. (1980). *Center for the Study of Intimate Systems News*, I, 3. Cleveland, Gestalt Institute of Cleveland.

Pardes, H. (1986). Neuroscience and psychiatry: Marriage or coexistence? *American Journal of Psychiatry*, 143, (10), 1205–1212.

Rush, B. (1810). Letter of the managers of the Pennsylvania Hospital. In C. E. Goshen (Ed.), *Documentary history of Psychiatry*. New York: Philosophical Library, 1967.

Schulz, C. G. (1985). Schizophrenia: Individual psychotherapy. In H. I. Kaplan & B. J. Sadock (Eds.), *Comprehensive textbook of psychiatry/IV* (p. 746). Baltimore/London: Williams & Wilkins.

10

Gestalt Therapy with Children: Working With Anger and Introjects

VIOLET OAKLANDER, Ph.D.

T HERE ARE TWO IMPORTANT issues that come up over and over again in my work with children: negative introjects and the expression of anger. They are hopelessly intertwined, but for the sake of discussion I will approach them as though they were separate.

I observe the development of the healthy infant as my therapy model. I watch as she makes full use of all her senses—first for survival (sucking, being touched), then to learn more about her world (seeing, hearing, tasting, touching). I see her exercise and use her body zestfully to acquire control and mastery. I notice that she expresses her feelings congruently. Her intellect develops rapidly, and she discovers language as an important tool for expression of feelings, needs, wants, thoughts, ideas. The healthy, uninterrupted development and expression of a child's organism—senses, body, emotions, and intellect—is the underlying basis for the child's sense of self; a strong sense of self leads to good contact with her physical and social environment.

A tiny infant is utterly dependent upon the adults in her life for all her needs. As she grows, she becomes more and more skilled at meeting some of her own needs. She can make them known and she can begin to have

awareness that besides needs, she has a lot of wants (and does not wants.)
Who she is as a person in this world becomes more and more defined. Her
boundary begins to take shape.

Concurrently the growing child acquires belief systems about herself and
about how to be in the world that will affect her for the rest of her life. How
parents meet the child's needs and wants or react to her expression of them
and how they react to her undaunted development of her senses, body,
emotional expression, and intellect profoundly affect her belief system about
herself. During this time many negative introjects are taken in because she
has not yet learned the art of spitting out, or rejecting, that which is toxic
for herself. As yet she cannot discriminate between that which is true about
herself and that which is not true about herself. She takes in for her own that
which comes from those she trusts or longs to trust, from those upon whom
her very life depends.

Piaget (1962) describes the egocentricity of the child. According to his
construct, only after the age of about 7 or 8 is a child able to take another
person's point of view without losing his own, and he acquires this ability
gradually. In view of this developmental phenomenon, one can understand
the vulnerability of the younger child's boundary and his susceptibility to
faulty beliefs about himself. In other words, he believes everything he hears
about himself—covert as well as overt—to be true and takes everything
personally. If his parents argue, he assumes their conflict to be his own fault.
If he is ill, he must be bad. As if this were not enough, children tend to
reinforce the negative more often than the positive. For example, if a 2-year-
old child believes that he is a clumsy clod because his father yells at him
harshly for breaking something, he reinforces this belief thereafter with
other awkward, ungainly acts. It is as though it takes a thousand "success"
experiences to make up for one severe parental appraisal.

Because the child has a powerful thrust for life and growth, he will do
anything he can to get through the task of growing up. This life force is
positive in that it often opposes his negative belief system regarding his self,
yet it may get him into trouble with his parents, teachers, and society in
general. The organism in its healthful surge for growth seems to make its
own determination about how to function in the world. Let me explain.

The child thrives upon acceptance, approval, love. At an early age when
he is still fairly congruent, he may express an angry feeling toward his
mother, for which he may meet disapproval, rejection, and what feels to be
a loss of love. He begins to learn that the expression of angry feelings is
fraught with danger to himself and that he must do whatever he can to
avoid further injury. Since anger is all but unavoidable, he must make some
determination about what to do when he feels it. He usually decides to push

the feeling down, to keep it in. "I go into my room until it goes away," said one 8-year-old boy to me. The unexpressed emotion lies within the child like a rock, interfering with healthful growth.

The organism, however, relentlessly seeks to achieve homeostasis. If an emotion lies below the surface, it must be expressed in some way for some sense of satisfaction to be achieved so that the organism can deal with its next need, and so on in its everlasting cycle of growth. The organism appears to choose some kind of expression of the emotion with or without the cooperation of the child's awareness.

The sequence goes typically like this: The infant cries to get his needs met. The parents think he is wet and check his diaper. The infant cries louder since he really wants to be held. Finally, one of his parents picks him up and he stops crying. It is hit or miss with crying as his only means of communication. In a few months his cries begin to take on meanings of their own, giving his parents better clues for meeting his needs. Also his facial and bodily expressions begin to show more awareness of his own needs. Although the young child soon begins to learn to use language as an important tool for clear communication, he does not yet have a good repertoire of words to express what he needs to say. Whereas saying "I want a drink" is easy, emotional expression is fairly abstract. So he may say, "I hate you!" to his mother where an older child would say, "It bugs me when you talk on the phone instead of listening to me." Mother reacts in shock, disapproval, or perhaps sadness that her own child hates her. She may even yell, "Don't you ever talk that way to me!" The child is confused at the many reactions he hears, sees, senses. Even the most enlightened mother may flinch at his hateful remark. Although he has done the best he could to reflect his inner feeling, to make his statement, he feels disapproved of, rejected, and worse, invalidated. In a subsequent exchange he may try again to express his emotions. To his older brother who has just pinched him he says, "I'm going to kill you!"—the only way he knows how to say with some power, "Don't do that to me!" His father rushes in, imagining he is raising a murderer. "Don't you *ever* say that again!" he says with anger far more vehement than the child's own. At some point such as this the child decides that for his own survival, he had better find some other way to deal with his feelings.

From this point on, the process gets more complicated. Initially, the child may feel terribly guilty for having even a mild feeling of anger. As he gets older the guilt may build to intense feelings of resentment or he may feel so bad, shameful, and invalidated that his feelings of selfhood shrink like wilted flowers. But because the individual life force is so strong, he looks for ways to survive the dilemma, ways that may be painful or even self-destructive.

The organism pushes on in its constant attempt to achieve homeostasis. It will release or take care of the energy of anger in some way. One child may retroflect anger. She sometimes literally does to herself what she would like to do to others. She may gouge herself, pull swatches of hair out. She may choke herself into an asthma attack, burn her stomach lining until she gets an ulcer, or constrict her muscles into headaches, stomachaches, and so forth.

Another child deflects the anger. He does not under any circumstances express the authentic feeling. In fact after a time he has forgotten what the feeling was. Nevertheless, the energy remains and must be expressed. He chooses to punch out and hit. He feels good when he does this, but only for a moment. Since the moment of good feeling disappears rapidly, he tries again and again to retrieve it through continual acts of deflection.

Still another child's body expresses the feeling through bed-wetting or through one of her few means of control: withholding bowel movement. (The most common form of encopresis that I have seen is exhibited by the child who withholds bowel movements with determination until the body, in its need to rid itself of toxicity, expels the feces at inappropriate times.)

Some children project their wrath onto others, imagining that everyone else is angry at them or that others, rather than themselves, are the angry ones. To deflect or dispel the anger energy, some set fires, and others go into hyperactive routines. Some are so fearful of the power of their internal anger that they pull in to try to hold themselves together—they become withdrawn, silent, sullen, cold.

Anger is the most difficult emotion for a child to express. The child can find a way to express to some extent other emotions such as fear, sadness, and joy, since these appear to be more easily tolerated by parents and our culture. But expression of even these emotions may be thwarted, particularly if it is carried to an extreme. The child, afraid of monsters (sometimes a projection of the child's own anger), is able to indicate this fear in some way. The child's parents, however, typically do not validate this fear, instead vigorously reassure the child that there is no monster under the bed. More powerful fears such as of abandonment, rejection, and loss of love are left unexpressed because they are so profound that the child cannot find words to signify them.

Some tears of children are accepted in our culture, even boys' tears on occasion. But many parents are generally disapproving of more than token crying. As a result, most grief is usually left unfinished. Grief over most losses—a parent or grandparent, a home or city, a pet, friends, a favorite toy—is usually stifled. In some cases parents consider a child's loss (such as that of a toy) trivial or invalid; in other cases, they think they need to protect their children from harsh realities by getting their mind off the subject of grief.

We all encourage happiness. We view childhood as a time to be happy-go-lucky, and we smile patronizingly over the antics of a child, antics that seem to express happiness. Should the child, however, continue the expression of joy too long or too loudly or too excessively, the child again reaps frowns. Recently in Switzerland I watched as a little girl, about 2½ years old, got off her chair at the hotel restaurant to run around with abandon and joy. She laughed delightedly at being free from the chair and swung her arms up high as she ran up and down the aisle between tables. Her parents, thoughtful of the rest of the diners, swept her up, sat her down with a thud in her chair, and admonished her severely. Since a child of her age cannot possibly have the skill to understand the needs of others (in this instance, the diners), she undoubtedly took in a message—however formulated—that there is something terribly wrong with feeling happy and, further, that she herself is a bad girl for feeling happy. Since sometimes she probably perceives that others enjoy her smiling and laughing, she now must deal with the confusion that results from receiving mixed messages.

Anger seems to have the most insidious effects in our society, perhaps because it is the least tolerated emotion. Most of the symptoms that children evidence that eventually result in therapy directly relate to the suppression of anger.

Anger, I think, is the most misunderstood of all emotions. It has the image of a fiery, uncontrollable monster that will rip and ravage if let loose. In very early childhood, what is thought of as anger actually is the essence of taking care of oneself, getting one's needs met, making one's statement, establishing one's position in the world. So if the child is making attempts to take care of herself, she is perceived as angry. If she says, "No! Don't do that to me!" or "I don't want that!" with the energy and vehemence of a small child who is trying to mobilize some strength and power for herself, she is observed as angry. (Often the child attempting to express some power appears angry.) Further, since she experiences not being heard, she must shout these declarations, and then she is certainly perceived as angry. If she learns that she must inhibit her statements as well as all the small angers she experiences, an energy potential will build that is much greater than each specific incident and might feel monstrous indeed. Children often fear the buildup of anger they feel inside themselves.

To add to the confusion, children get double messages about anger. They learn that it is not acceptable for them to be angry, yet they experience the wrath of anger from adults either very directly or in the indirect form of icy disapproval.

The suppression of emotions, particularly that of anger, intrinsically relates to the taking in of negative introjects. A child's emotions form her very core, her very being. When her feelings are not validated, she is not validated. When her feelings are scorned, explained away, ridiculed, responded to harshly, she feels deeply rejected. Though she and her body may find some way to express the feeling in an oblique quest for health, the child nevertheless harbors the feeling that she is bad. She does not consciously choose these—they just well up. In dismay she feels unentitled to have them; she feels unentitled to be, to exist, if she has them, particularly since these feelings as well as she herself cause her parents so much concern, disapproval, and anger toward her. Further, the behaviors she engages in to take care of herself bring even more wrath upon her. She cannot win. She knows deep down that something is very wrong with herself.

As the child begins to absorb these negative messages about herself, she tends to feel an actual loss of self. She begins to interrupt and constrict her own growth even as she is growing. She shuts down her senses, contracts her muscles, withholds expression, shuts off her mind. Her sense of self may become so diffuse that she must engage in a variety of defensive behaviors to maintain some semblance of being alive. Some children become confluent: They must hear from others who they are, or even literally hold onto others at all times to feel a sense of self. Others try to please as much as possible to gain some acceptance and good feeling. Others become cautious, timid, or obsessive as a way to maintain some sense of power and control in a world where they feel weak and helpless. Some children steal for the thrill of momentary accomplishment, for the flush of excitement that masquerades as a feeling of self. Some avoid telling the truth about anything since the truth is sometimes too painful to cope with. Some children lash out at others or have violent temper tantrums, not only as a way to dispel anger energy or to dissipate the frustration of never being listened to, but as a way to feel some power and selfhood.

The very behaviors that bring children into therapy are those that they use to gain some feeling of self, to achieve some sense of power in a world where they feel so powerless, to express who they are and what they feel. They employ these behaviors, inappropriate as they may be, to grow up, to survive, to fill up their voids, to contact their environment, to meet their needs. These behaviors actually evince the organism's crusade for equilibrium. They often become children's way of being in the world—their patterns, their process. They not only form an assumption about who they are on the basis of the reaction of their parents and the society to their very personhood, but they determine how they must be in the world to survive and grow up. This way of being, without therapeutic intervention, may haunt them throughout their adult lives.

When a child is brought into therapy, I know that I must assist this child in her quest for strength and self-support. I need to find a way to help her remember, regain, renew, and strengthen that which she once had as a tiny baby but which now seems lost. As her senses awake; as she begins to know her body again; as she recognizes, accepts, and expresses her buried feelings; as she learns to use her intellect to make choices, to verbalize her wants and needs and thoughts and ideas, and to find ways to get her needs met; and as she learns who she is and accepts who she is in her differentness from you and me, she will then find herself once again upon her rightful path of growth. I need to help her learn that her survival behaviors are nonproductive and that there are new choices of behaviors that will produce more satisfying results for her. I need to help her understand the faulty messages about herself that she has taken as her own and how she might manage and cope with these messages throughout her life.

Before I go into further discussion of introjects, I would like to present a few examples of small pieces of work to illustrate the actual therapeutic process related directly to the expression of anger.

I recognize four phases in working with children's anger:

1. Talking with them about anger; what it is, what makes them angry, how they express it, how it relates to the body
2. Helping them learn to *acknowledge* and *accept* their angry feelings, then to *choose* ways to express them; experimenting with practical methods of expression, since directness is not always practical in the child's world
3. Helping children move toward the actual feeling of anger they may be holding and making it possible for them to give emotional expression to this anger as we work together
4. Giving children the experience of being orally direct with their angry feelings: saying what they need to say to the person they need to say it to; giving them experience with taking care of themselves: asserting themselves when need be

Many children are so out of touch with their feelings that we need to do a great deal of talking about feelings. They are particularly not acquainted with all the subtleties and nuances of feelings, and the more experiences they have with these various forms and descriptions of feelings, the better they are able to communicate them. Anger, for example, can range from mild irritation and annoyance to downright rage, wrath, and fury. Besides just talking we may do the following:

1. Draw pictures of all kinds of angry feelings, sometimes using just colors, lines, and shapes
2. Use a drum beat to express various forms of anger

3. Use music to illustrate kinds of angry feelings

4. Use creative dramatics to show anger—an excellent way to involve the body

5. Tell stories and read books with angry themes

6. Play games with cards that say, "What bugs you?" or "What makes you furious?" and similar things

7. Make lists of things that make us angry

I asked a group of children to tell me all the words they used or thought of when they were angry. I wrote them on a large chalkboard as they yelled them out. After we had a long list, we looked at them and found that some were attacking, striking-out words, while others were inside feeling words. We talked about this and then discussed our own individual ways of handling anger, inside or outside. I asked them to close their eyes while I led them in a relaxation exercise. I asked: "What kinds of things make you angry?" "What do you do?" "Do you go inside or outside?" They all drew pictures of what it feels like inside their bodies to be angry and what they do when they are angry. Each child's anger process was clearly depicted. One 11-year-old boy drew a maze with stick figure pictures of his friends in the upper right-hand corner and a picture of himself in the bottom left. He wrote "Which way to go" next to the picture of himself, and "Lonesomeness" at the top of the picture. He said that when he was angry, he just did not know how to be with his friends and he felt separate and lonely. When children begin to see how they deal with their anger, we can then move on to helping them find more satisfying ways.

Children need many suggestions for ways of getting rid of angry feelings in ways that will not be destructive for them. As I remarked before, adults do not allow children to be angry; yet the anger must be expressed. But before children can even begin to engage in healthful expression, we must go through several essential steps. First, I help children to become aware of the anger, to recognize the anger. This is the first step in children's feeling strong and whole instead of fearfully running from and avoiding angry feelings or discharging them in indirect ways that might harm themselves or alienate others. Second, I help children learn that anger is a normal, natural feeling that we all feel, that anger is merely anger—an emotion that is neither good nor bad. Third, I encourage children to accept their own feelings of anger. They can then make a conscious choice about whether to express the anger directly or to express it privately in some other way. Finally, we experiment with many outlets: punching a pillow, tearing newspaper, wadding paper, kicking a pillow or a can, running around the block, hitting a bed with a tennis racket, yelling in the shower or into a pillow, writing about the anger, drawing the anger, squeezing or pounding clay.

Kevin, a 6-year-old, retroflected his anger by literally tearing at himself and destroying things he owned. He would not admit to ever being angry. Many sessions were spent in special activities to help him strengthen sensory and body perception. One day as we played with clay I asked him about the other children at school. His body tightened, as did his voice, as he mentioned the name of one boy. I very gently asked if the boy sometimes made him mad. Kevin nodded and told me how the boy teased him. I asked what he did when he felt angry at him. He hung his head and said, "I don't know." I placed a pillow in front of us, saying, "Let's pretend that boy is sitting on this pillow. What would you like to say to him?"

Kevin: I don't know.
Violet: Well, I know what I'd like to say to him. I DON'T LIKE IT WHEN YOU TEASE MY FRIEND KEVIN! THAT MAKES ME MAD!
  K: (giggles)
  V: Can you tell him you're mad?
  K: (shakes his head)
  V: (punching pillow) I'd like to punch you for teasing Kevin!
  K: (laughs out loud)
  V: You try it.
  K: (tentatively punches the pillow)
  V: Let's do it together.

We both begin to punch the pillow, Kevin laughing and giggling all the while. Soon we were both talking to our imaginary adversary on the pillow. I told Kevin he could punch a pillow or his bed whenever he felt mad at someone. His foster mother (the fourth in his young life) reported that he did this every day after school for a long while, and that he had stopped scratching at himself.

The story of Kevin's life actually is quite complex. Kevin had experienced a hard life in only 6 years. Physical abuse and abandonment had left him deeply disturbed. In many ways he showed signs of not wanting to live, of feeling unentitled to exist. The survival part of him felt deep rage, a rage that terrified him. I felt that in our work I could provide him with some needed tools for dealing with feelings that frightened him, as the smallest anger did. As we directed his aggression outward, he began to develop a stronger sense of himself. At each succeeding session he worked on his process of dealing with anger in his present life. He expressed little bits of angers in many ways: through puppets, through clay, through story telling, through sand tray scenes. At the same time that he was expressing his angers, he was also feeling validated by me in having such feelings. He began to feel a stronger sense of self with every statement about himself that he made. Soon he was able to act out with doll figures his physical abuse and scenes of abandonment. Many other feelings related to these episodes emerged, always in increments. Finally Kevin felt strong enough to deal effectively with his bad feelings of self.

Expression in small doses is the essence of child therapy. Children come to therapy with resistance as their only ally, their only means of protecting themselves. As they begin to trust me and as they begin to feel more of their own support, they may choose to allow themselves to open, to risk, to be a little vulnerable. We meet resistance over and over during therapy. A child opens a bit, then closes. Each occurrence of a child's closing is a sign of progress, for it is the child's way of saying, "This is enough for me right now! The rest will come later." And the rest does come later, a little bit at a time.

Billy, aged 9, had been deflecting his anger. He was referred to me by the public school for rebellious behavior—hitting, kicking, fighting. Because of his father's Navy career, Billy's family had moved many times during those 9 years. From the very first session with the parents it was clear that the whole family was in trouble: Billy's mother was visibly depressed; his father denied the existence of any problem. A younger sister, not present at this first session, was later disclosed to be suffering from eczema, asthma, and chronic bed-wetting. Because Billy aroused the most attention, he was the one brought in for help. The parents refused any parent or family therapy and just wanted me to "fix" Billy.

I am not averse to working with a child even though it is clear that the whole family needs "fixing." Billy has already formed a belief system about himself and a process of living that was self-debilitating. If his family was willing to bring him for therapy, I was willing to help him gain as much self-support as possible. At our first session Billy huddled in the corner of the couch as his parents rattled off a list of complaints about him.

It is important for me to have the child present during this first session to hear everything that is said. It is my time to begin to make some contact with the child and to let him know that although I am listening to the parents, I am just as aware and respectful of his point of view. It is also an opportunity for me to begin to change his feeling that he was brought, perhaps dragged, into therapy, to a stance of choice and responsibility for coming.

As the parents talked I often made eye contact with Billy, asking him if he agreed with what they were saying. He shrugged and said, "I don't know." I smiled at him, and we all continued. I spent 5 minutes alone with Billy at the end of the session, telling him a little bit about how I work with children, and showing him my office, and he agreed that he would be willing to come back.

At our next session the rebellious child came in quietly, no words to say, body constricted, face pinched. Because he had seemed particularly interested in the paints during the first session, I asked Billy to paint a picture—anything he wanted to—and he reluctantly agreed.

Billy: What should I paint?

Violet: Anything you want to.

B: I know, I'll paint something we're studying in school.

V: Do you mind if I watch?

B: It's OK. (He painted with great absorption as I sat and watched.)

B: This is a volcano.

V: Tell me about it.

B: This is not an active volcano, it's a dormant volcano. This is the hot lava (red lines inside a brown volcano with thick walls) that hasn't erupted yet. And this is the smoke coming out of the volcano. It has to let off a little steam.

V: Billy, I would like you to tell me about your volcano again, and this time I'd like you to imagine that the volcano has a voice. It can talk, but you will be the voice, like a puppet's voice. So tell me about your volcano again. Start with, "I am a volcano."

B: OK. I'm a volcano. I have hot lava inside of me. I'm a dormant volcano. I haven't erupted yet. But I will. I have gray smoke coming out of me.

V: Billy, stand up and imagine you are the volcano. (Billy stands up.) If you really were a volcano, if your body were the volcano, where would the hot lava be?

B: (very thoughtful—finally placing his hand on his abdomen) Right here.

V: Billy, what would that hot lava be for you, a boy instead of a volcano?

B: (after some moments of thought, eyes very bright) ANGER!

I then asked Billy to paint me a picture of what he thought his anger looked like, just using shapes, colors, and lines. He painted a large, thick, red circle with colors inside. I wrote on his painting as he dictated: "This is Billy's anger inside his stomach. It's yellow, red, and gray, and orange. Smoke is coming out." We then listed some of the things that made him angry: "My sister messing my room. When I get in fights. When I fall down off my bike. When I broke my lock."

At this point Billy realized how much he had revealed of himself, and he would talk no further about his anger. He had opened as much as he was willing to for this session, and he then enveloped himself in his protective wall. We finished the session with a game of checkers.

At the session that had just ended, Billy was not ready to give expression to his anger except through painting. Furthermore, he would admit to only very surface angers. At each subsequent session Billy was willing to own more and more of his angry feelings, working with clay, the sand tray, drawings. As he expressed some angry feelings, other feelings would emerge: grief over the loss of friends each time he moved, fear of making new friends because he knew they would move again, feelings of despair and loneliness, and feelings of helplessness regarding his depressed mother.

In one session Billy made a circle of animals in the sand tray. A lion came on the scene and attacked the surprised animals.

V: Which animal are you?
B: I'm the lion.
V: What about the lion reminds you of you?
B: I don't know.
V: Do you ever feel like attacking?
B: Yeah!
V: Who would you attack?
B: Well, there are kids who bother me at school.
V: What do you do when you get angry at your Dad?
B: I don't get angry at him! He'd whip me!
V: How about your Mom?
B: Sometimes she yells at me and I get mad. But she tells my Dad.

Then we talked a little about being angry and the need to express it.

In later sessions Billy's expression of anger through symbolic means accelerated. His owning of the anger was minimal, but there. Once Billy made two teams of men in the sand.

B: Here are two armies.
V: What happens?
B: They have a war.
V: Make it happen.
B: OK.

Billy proceeded to enact his war. At the end one side was left with a sole survivor who sadly buried his comrades (his own words) while the other side celebrated its victory.

V: Which one are you?
B: (after some thought) Him (the captain of the winning team).

V: What does it feel like to win the battle?

B: Good!

V: What do you imagine he feels like? (pointing to the sole survivor of losing team)

B: (voice soft) He feels bad. He's all alone.

V: (gently) Do you ever feel like him, Billy?

B: (very soft—mumbling) Yeah, all the time.

We discuss this awhile, until Billy shrugs and again puts on his suit of protective armor.

I had worked with Billy for only 4 months when his family again moved, this time to Okinawa. During the 4 months Billy became calmer, more contented with himself. His disruptive school behavior stopped. As he gained an understanding of his own fears and angers, he began to understand some of his mother's depression. He literally became something of his mother's therapist (a very common happening). The parents gave very little credit to Billy's therapy for his changes. "He must have been going through a stage," they said. Billy knew better. A letter I received from him said: "I wasn't afraid to move this time because of all the things we talked about. I remember everything. I'm making friends too. I guess I'll have friends all over the world this way. Maybe I'll see you again. Love, Billy."

Sometimes, as their children's angry feelings are unleashed, parents express the fear that I am teaching their children how to be angry, violent people. I tell them the following true story as an example of the importance of moving through a feeling.

Soon after my 1978 book *Windows to Our Children* was published, I was interviewed by Channel 2 News in Los Angeles regarding my work. They wanted to film me in an actual working session with a child. John, aged 10, and his parents agreed to the filming. Here is a condensation of the experience.

Violet: How has your week been, John?

John: Terrible.

V: How come?

J: No one will play with me at school because I'm no good at sports. I don't have anyone to play with at home either.

V: Would you draw a picture of how that feels, just using lines, colors, and shapes?

J: (drew lines of gray and blue across the paper) This is how it feels at school. Bad.

V: And at home?

J: (He then drew a similar one for home.) I feel bad there too.

V: What's it like for you to feel bad at school, bad at home, bad all the time?

J: Bad. (And he drew another picture with flat, dull colors. We spread the pictures out and looked at them.)

V: When you look at these pictures and see how you feel all the time, what do you think of?

J: I think that I'm mad that it's like that for me.

V: Could you draw a picture of that mad?

John began to draw somewhat lethargically, then became more and more engrossed. He drew dark black and red swirls, a gun with bullets shooting out of it, a knife with blood dripping from it, some boxing gloves. The television cameras caught it all.

V: Could you tell me about it?

J: (shouting) I feel so mad I'd like to stab someone. I feel so mad I'd like to punch someone hard. (As John talked he made thick black marks all over the paper.)

V: (As I was wondering what to do next, in panic of all this power on public display, I noticed that John suddenly took a deep breath.) How do you feel now?

J: Good! I liked doing that!

V: Could you draw how you feel now? (John drew a very beautiful picture of pinks and yellows and rainbows and sun.)

J: (smiling, relaxed) I feel really nice, not like I felt before. Why did just drawing these pictures make me feel good?

It is not unusual for children to ask such questions. John had been angry at his plight, but had retroflected the anger and as a result felt bad, hurt. (Hurt feelings are clues to retroflected anger.) He was lethargic, flat, devoid of energy. When his angry feelings were released, he felt good instead of bad. We could then begin to deal with the issue of making friends.

As previously mentioned, there is a close connection between the suppression of feelings and the formation of negative introjects. As children begin to acknowledge, accept, respect, and express their own feelings, they begin to feel a much stronger sense of themselves and of their entitlement. It is then that we can begin to look at some of their faulty beliefs of self. All infants express feelings, regardless of the cultural milieu. The inhibition of feelings is a learned experience. Some children learn to inhibit feelings, most commonly anger, at such a young age that they have no skills with which to express them, no memory of ever feeling them, no words with which to describe them. These children have concluded very early that they are shameful beings.

Children who are disturbed have an impaired sense of self, which in turn interferes with good contact with others. Deep down they feel that something is missing, they are different in some way, they are lonely, something is wrong. They blame themselves—though they may outwardly and defensively blame others—and imagine that they are bad, have done something wrong, are not good looking or smart enough.

Even favorable introjects can be harmful, for even they are not assimilated into children's being as their very own. Often there is a disbelieving aspect of the child that says, "That's not really true. I'm not that good." And here again a fragmentation rather than an integration occurs. Only when children more fully experience themselves can favorable introjects become their own. The adolescent or adult who has never experienced the integration of favorable introjects often says, "I feel like a phony."

My task in working with children becomes one of making it possible for them to remember, regain, renew, and strengthen that which they had as a tiny baby. I need to provide many experiences to awaken children's senses, to give them back the joyful, zestful use of their body, and to connect them with their feelings. I need to help them use their intellect in conjunction with language to make declarations of who they are (and who they are not), what they need, what they want, what they like and dislike, what they think about, what their ideas are.

As the child begins to develop a stronger sense of self within our therapeutic relationship, we can then take on the task of confronting negative introjects. It is very difficult for a child to say openly, "I am bad," "I am a rotten person," "I don't like myself." Usually children are busily defending the vestige of self they feel.

We work with introjects in several phases:

1. Recognizing their existence
2. Using very specific examples—rather than saying, "I hate myself," specifying parts of the self that one hates
3. Elaborating on and personifying those hateful parts
4. If the child is old enough, understanding where the original message came from
5. Isolating the polar opposites of each of the negatives—the nurturing, accepting, likable parts
6. Learning to be self-accepting and self-nurturing

In my work I use many creative, expressive, and projective techniques, such as guided fantasy, graphic art forms, collage, clay, story telling, puppetry, the sand tray, creative dramatics, sensory activities, body movement, music, the camera. These techniques are important ways for helping children to express what is kept hidden and locked and to experience and strengthen lost parts of themselves. They are particularly invaluable for isolating and dealing with negative introjects.

A 9-year-old girl tells me a story about a "girl with messy hair" from a scribble picture. When she finishes I ask, "Does that story fit for you in your life in any way?" She answers, "Well, I don't like my hair."

Violet: Show me how your hair looks to you. (She draws a large face with very messy hair.) Now show me how you wish your hair looked. (She draws a face with beautiful long blonde hair.) Talk to your messy hair. What would you like to say to it?

Child: I hate you! Why can't you be like her? (pointing to blonde hair)

In this session we exaggerate and elaborate on her feelings. She feels validated and accepted. If I should say, "Oh, I think you have lovely hair," I would only discount her feeling. So even though I may think this, I do not offer my opinion at this time. Sometimes even in a session like this, the source of the introject comes through.

V: Does anyone else like your hair?

C: No. Well, my mother sometimes.

V: Does anyone agree with you, about not liking it?

C: Yes, my father.

V: How do you know?

C: He says says, (anger in her voice) "Go brush your hair!" and things like that. And he loves my sister's hair. (begins to cry)

It is obvious that a deeper rejection has been symbolized by discussing hair. We begin with what she will discuss. The issue of rejection will emerge again. If I should ask more specific questions about rejection at this point, she would almost certainly shrug and say, "I don't know," to signal her resistance to dealing right then with such a weighty subject.

Even very young children have a very well developed critical self. They often do a better job of criticizing themselves than their parents do. This judgmental stance is extremely detrimental to healthful growth. The child may say "I should do better," knowing that the enactment of this wish is beyond his or her power and comprehension. Thus the very will to "be better'' or ''do better' may enhance the child's despair. Further, each trauma, large or small, takes its toll on the child in terms of unexpressed feelings, ''unfinished business,'' and most particularly the blaming of the self.

The negative beliefs that children develop about themselves can never be changed by an outside agent, in my opinion. Self-acceptance of all of one's parts, even the most hateful, is a vital component of unimpaired, sound development. Such self-acceptance comes about through the growth and development of children's own loving, nurturing part of themselves, which must come together with the ''bad'' self to accept, understand, comfort, and love it. As children accept and experience all aspects of themselves without judgment, they grow and expand joyfully. As we dig out those darker aspects, illuminate them, and bring them into contact with the nurturing self, children experience integration.

I read a story about demons to 10-year-old Andrew. We talked about demons as representing parts of ourselves that we do not like, that get in our way.

Violet: Close your eyes for a minute and think about the parts of you that you don't like. Pick one of those parts and draw a picture of it when you're ready. Give it a name.

Andrew: (drew a cartoonlike figure with large legs and arms and with bandages, bruises, cuts, and dark spots all over it) This is the part of me I hate. I'm always falling down, bumping into things, getting hurt.

V: Be that part and tell me about yourself.

A: I'm Mr. Klutz. I'm always bumping into things. I'm always getting hurt. I have cuts and bruises all over me.

V: (I had a dialogue with Mr. Klutz and he told me about each cut and bruise and where it came from.) Andrew, what would you like to say to Mr. Klutz?

A: I hate you! I wish you'd go away. You get in my way. You embarrass me. You make me feel bad. (Andrew made faces and noises at Mr. Klutz.)

In previous sessions we had dealt with Andrew's very athletic dad's high expectations of him, so we already had a sense of where this feeling of klutziness came from. Andrew had already expressed sadness and anger regarding his father's rejections and demands. His bad feeling of self remained, however.

V: How do you wish you could be?

A: (described a lithe, athletic, beautiful fantasy person)

V: Andrew, imagine you have a fairy godmother and just as you, Mr. Klutz, have cut yourself or bumped into something, or fallen off your bike, she appears on the scene. What might she say to you?

A: Oh, I don't know. (I wait) Let's see. Maybe she'd say, "Don't feel bad. I like you. How do you ever expect to learn anything new if you don't feel klutzy at first?"

V: Would your fairy godmother criticize you?

A: I guess not. She'd say, "I like that you take risks" (his own words). "I like that you try things. Don't worry that you hurt yourself. That shows you do new things and I like you for that."

V: Now your fairy godmother disappears and you are here with Mr. Klutz. Could *you* say the same things to Mr. Klutz?

A: (repeats what he said before)

V: How did that feel to say those things?

A: Yeah! It felt good. I *do* try new things! (deep breath—often a sign of a completed gestalt—big smile)

We talked a bit about what happened in this work. I'm sure there's more to be done.

Twelve-year-old Ellen tore her hair out and wore hats to cover up the bald spots. She was a lovely child who despised herself. She was born ill and for the first 7 years of her life cried almost continuously, until she started to get better. At one session, both parents were present:

Violet: Ellen, see this doll? Let's imagine it's you as a baby and she's sick and she's crying. How do you think she feels?

Ellen: Terrible!

V: (to Mom and Dad) What would you like to say to her?

M: (beginning to cry) Don't cry baby, I wish you wouldn't cry. I wish you wouldn't be sick. I'm so worried about you.

Dad: We're trying to find out what's wrong with you. We love you.

V: Ellen, imagine you're the baby, and you could talk, even though you really can't. What would you say?

E: Whaaa!!!!! Help me! Help me! I'm sick! I'm sick!

V: What do you think the baby thinks about herself? You probably can't remember.

E: I don't know.

I explain to Ellen and her parents that when a child is sick and in pain, as she was, she blames herself, feels that she is a bad girl. Further, her parents are desperate, beside themselves, feel awful when they hear her cry; and the baby, sensing this, blames herself for this too.

E: Yeah! I remember feeling bad when I was about four, like I was a bad girl.

V: Right! And you probably started feeling that way even as a tiny infant! If you could go back in a time machine and talk to her, what would you say to her?

E: Can I pick her up?

V: Sure!

E: (cuddling baby) Baby, it's not your fault. You're a wonderful baby. You're cute. I love you. There, there. (She rocks the baby.)

M: (to me) We kept telling her that.

V: It was hard for her to believe you. Now she has to tell it to herself. (Ellen really gets into it, repeating over and over that the baby is good, etc.) Every time you feel bad inside, Ellen, remember that it's your baby self feeling that way. She needs you to hold her and love her.

E: Yeah!

This work was the beginning of Ellen's learning to be more accepting, more caring of herself.

Another time we talked about all the nice things Ellen could do to make herself feel better sometimes. I gave her an assignment to try out each one of those things until the next session. Then one day her mother called in a panic to tell me that Ellen had had a bad experience at school and was inconsolable. I asked to speak to her. Ellen was crying hysterically. I spoke to her firmly.

"What could you do right now to make the little girl who feels hurt inside of you feel better?" Through her tears, she mumbled, "Music." "OK!" I said.

Ellen reported later that she played some of her favorite records and felt much better. There was no way that Ellen's mother or father could make up to Ellen for what happened to her when she was little. Only Ellen could do it now.

There seems to be a definite sequence in helping children learn to be self-accepting and self-nurturing. Once children have had numerous experiences in reacquainting themselves with their senses, their body, their emotions, their intellect—in other words, once they have experienced their *self* in many ways—they begin to have enough self-support, enough strength of self, to examine with some objectivity their more hateful parts, as well as other faulty messages of self and how to be in the world. The power and vitality they may then feel also serve to help them contact that nurturing self. The goal is to assist children, with full awareness, to make that nurturing self truly their own, to know that it really is a part of them. The sequence goes something like this:

1. The child can imagine that a fairy godmother, or some other loving figure like the all-loving ideal good mother archetype, is speaking to the child's hateful part or to the younger child or baby part that originally believed, swallowed whole, the flawed idea of self.

2. The child speaks to the hateful part or little child part.

3. The child speaks to himself or herself.

As children go through this process, it is important that I check with them as we go along whether what they say feels right and true. Often children can speak as a fairy godmother but cannot yet own this "good mother" part for themselves. And sometimes I must at first take the speaking part of children's fairy godmother before they can begin to try it out for themselves.

I first experienced this kind of work with Dr. Jack Rosenberg (a therapist in Venice, Calif., and author of the book *Body, Self & Soul*). It was he who first gave me the fairy godmother idea, and I have used this powerful tool with many of my adult and adolescent clients. Here is a vignette showing how I used it with a 7-year-old girl.

Angie and I were sitting on the floor with several puppets before us.

Violet: Angie, choose a puppet that most reminds you of how you feel right now. (She chooses a sad-looking green dog. I pick up another puppet and, as the puppet, begin to talk to her dog.) Hi!

Angie: Hi!

V: What's going on with you today?

A: Oh, nothing.

V: I wonder what about you made Angie pick you.

A: Because I look sad.

V: What are you sad about?

A: Oh, school.

V: Do you have trouble with school?

A: Yeah, reading.

V: You feel bad about that?

A: Yeah.

V: (to Angie herself) What would you say to your dog about that?

A: You're so dumb!

V: (to dog) What do you have to say to that?

A: (as dog) Well, I try! (and as Angie) But you're dumb!

V: (to Angie) I guess you feel dumb when you have trouble with reading.

A: (mumbles) Yes.

V: Your dog says she tries. I guess you try and still can't get it and then a part inside of you calls you dumb.

A: (nods head and makes a face)

V: What's that face about?

A: I think I'm dumb.

V: Angie, pick another puppet here that might be nice to your dog who tries and then feels dumb, maybe the fairy godmother puppet, or any other that would be nice. (Angie picks the fairy godmother puppet.) What does she say?

A: (as fairy godmother to dog) You try hard. I know you do. And you're not dumb because you can do other things. You're good in math! You couldn't be dumb and be good in math!

V: (to fairy godmother) Could you tell the dog that you love her even when she's dumb?

A: (as fairy godmother) I love you even when you're dumb.

V: How did it feel to say that?

A: Well, I don't think she's dumb! I think she'll get good at reading. She needs some extra help.

V: Angie, you say that to your dog. (She does and then hugs the dog.)

Angie had been suffering from reading anxiety. At the next session she said to me: "My tutor came yesterday and I didn't want to do anything. Then in my mind I was hugging my dog part who feels dumb, and I did good!"

In my work with children, I know that some day they grow to be adults and take with them all their earlier inhibitions, interruptions, and faulty introjects. In my work with adults I know that they bring with them those same childhood patterns, traumas, and introjects. So when I work with children, I find myself at the beginning of a continuum.

REFERENCES

La Chapelle, R. (1975). *Demons.* Pure Diamond Press.

Oaklander, V. (1978). *Windows to our children: A Gestalt therapy approach to children and adolescents.* Highland, New York: The Gestalt Journal, 1988.

Perls, F. S. (1969). *Ego, hunger and aggression.* New York: Vintage Books.

Piaget, J. (1962). *Play, dreams and imitation in childhood.* New York: W. W. Norton.

Polster, E., & Polster, M. (1973). *Gestalt therapy integrated: Contours of theory and practice.* New York: Brunner/Mazel.

Rosenberg, Jack Lee, and others: *Body, Self, and Soul: Sustaining Integration.* Atlanta, Georgia: Humanics Limited, 1985.

11

Gestalt Approach to Couple Therapy

JOSEPH C. ZINKER, Ph.D.*

I. INTRODUCTION

A COUPLE IS COMPOSED of two people who make a serious commitment to each other over time, and who share important life tasks together: work, friendship, children, making a home, playing, loving, educating. Couples come to therapists with a history, the background of their separate relationships and with assumptions about love, marriage, family, child rearing, and sexuality. There is very little that is "standard" about couples. They can be roommates, close friends engaged in creative projects, or a man and a woman trying to build a life together.

My work with couples takes place in the context of their unique history, their comparative maturity, their apperceptive mass. Some couples are still playing house and are not yet psychologically married (not having disengaged from their respective families and unable to create a strong bond with each other), other couples have a long and heavily invested relationship which is undergoing change and needs assistance.

In this chapter, I want to examine psychotherapy with couples in the context of the development of love, the themes of fusion, differentiation and notions about complementarity and middle ground. I will also address myself to the couple as a system, a "third entity," and to the question of values held by Gestalt therapists working with couples.[1]

II. GESTALT VIEW OF COUPLES

A. Love as Fusion

The original dream, the first dream, is of union with mother. It is a powerful dream/wish, probably the most fundamental—one which cannot be reduced into more basic components. It is the wish to be one with another. The union within oneself originates with the union with another.

Fusion is a very compelling, ecstatic experience. It is the first principle. "Falling in love" is a form of psychological alchemy, creating the golden ring out of opposing forces. It is the creation of a new self through fusion.

In the beginning of life this fusion is not "love" in the usual sense. This "need," this image, is a kind of undifferentiated longing—before the words are there—before one can utter "I love you" or "I long for something"—it is a physiological sensation without awareness. At that time—the time of physiological sensations—when the need for union is not met in some way, the infant, the child, is forever damaged.

It is only later that this enormous longing acquires words. These words are different in different cultures. Erich Fromm points out that some individuals, when they can't experience human union, turn to alcohol, drugs or gambling to experience it.[2] Different societies have developed different ways of meeting this unmet need. Therefore, love has different meanings at different times of one's life, at different stages of one's development. During adolescence people learn to make the words "I love you" signify this primordial feeling. At this point in an individual's development it is fueled by hormones. Later the sexual dimension is added to and complicates his/her existence. The words "I love you" are physiologically arresting, compelling, dizzying and upsetting. At the cognitive level it has, still, very general meaning:

> I want you.
> I can't live without you.
> I am empty without you.
> You are my sunshine.
> You are beautiful.

Without you I am nothing.
You are the better part of me.

There is some recognition that somehow, without the other, one is not whole, one is not fully oneself. There is no recognition of the other as a whole, especially-designed being. Mostly, there is a reading into what the other is—the fantasy overpowers one's sense of curiosity about the actual other.

It is only much, much later in life when this profoundly basic need is partially met, and when the person becomes a person in his/her own right, that the "I love you" begins to mean:

I want to know you.
I want to make myself known to you.
I want to give you what you want.
(not the projection of what I want).
I want to sit and talk with you.
I want to learn about your ideas.
values and feelings.
I want to share with you—only when.
you care to hear—my ideas and feelings. One adult with another.

Union is like alchemy in putting things together and creating new form. In alchemy our ancestors put opposing metals together and tried to make "gold." This, in a sense, is what I think the golden ring of engagement or marriage is about.

There also is alchemy in the biology of heterosexuality. The male and female are different, and it is the mystery inherent in the difference of the other that is so compelling.

B. Need for Differentiation

But fusion in itself fails. If the fetus stays in the womb, it dies. If a young person stays at home with mother, s/he dies spiritually as well as in other ways.

What must follow is separation. And separation involves differentiation.

Differentiation means that as the couple begins to move away from fusion, they must develop their own selves. This is, in Jung's terms, "individuation." In Gestalt terms, this is boundary formation.

In Gestalt Theory, we say that the only way you can have adequate contact is to have adequate boundaries. You know you can't have contact with mush. You can't have conflict with mush either. You must evolve from a psychologically homogenized blob into a differentiated bound organism with your own ideas, feelings, preferences, and buoyancies.

Then, when you get together out of your boundedness and your specialness, you have fire. Fire not only consumes, it illuminates.

1. Rhythm of Fusion and Separation

I conceive that what happens in a two-person system is a rhythm of fusion and separation. We touch each other at different places in our lives and in our rhythms of daily life. We also touch each other with different intensities. Sometimes we touch each other with ecstatic or rageful intensity, but most of the time we touch with just a nice bit of magnetism.

After this touching, we move away from one another. And then we come together again—it is this process of getting together and moving away that is the dynamic juice of being in a relationship.

The theme of fusion and of separation is a lifelong experience. It appears in the couples' life in different forms and at different times.

When couples first fall in love, they experience fusion. They are inseparable. They sit and stare into each other's eyes. They profess love for each other for ever and ever. They "can't live without each other." Later, as they proceed with the tasks of life, and as they grow more familiar with each other's ways, there is a slow and subtle process of separation. During this period, there is a greater recognition of differences and a return to the task of self-actualization. Fusion and differentiation occur at the same time as the individuals move toward and away from one another—in play, vacationing, making love, working together and rearing children.

Fusion is more difficult when children are born. It may be sublimated into the system which includes children and the family as a whole.

Separation is again experienced when children grow up and leave. Once again the couple is alone, hopefully as more mature and separate adults who choose to become deeply intimate with each other. Later, illness and death confront the couple with separation and with the fantasy of fusion with some eternal power beyond themselves in an experience of transcendence.

One is brought into the world only to give oneself away again and again.

2. Gaining an Awareness of Self

At the earliest level of development, the therapist works with the couple's ability to make contact without "falling into each other."

Each person must learn to differentiate his/her internal experience from the appearance, awareness and experiences of the other. So, we might ask each person to say sentences like: "I feel . . ." and "You look like . . .". Introjection, projection, and confluence are favorite resistances to contact at this level: "I feel like you look hungry", or "I feel tense and you look tense", or "You look angry with me."

Each person needs to gain an awareness of self as a separate entity different from awareness of the other. The therapist supports individual boundaries: "I feel tired and you look very alert right now." It is difficult to achieve differentiation with another when one is not aware of one's own internal differentiation: "One part of me feels tired and another part says I should finish writing this paper." The Gestalt therapist may wish to intersperse individual sessions with couple sessions to allow each partner an opportunity to work on awareness, differentiation and boundedness.

So at this early stage (longing for fusion), the couple learns how to respond to their own internal process and how, at the same time, to see and hear the other. On the surface, this would appear to be a simple task but, in actuality, it is quite difficult for many couples. The pursuit may require much time, effort and discipline. The diadic system is such as tempter for one's own projections!

Before the couple can experience the "we", the contact between them, they need to articulate the:

"I sense . . ."
"I feel . . ."
"I want . . ."
"I don't want . . ."

Each says these things in turn and not reactively to the other. It is much later when internal vision becomes illuminated, that each can truly care about, and even validate the experience of the other.

3. Validating Differences

The need for asserting the "I" as between mother and child follows fusion. After the falling-in-love experience, each stands separately and is once again confronted by the self—its internal needs, conflicts and special talents. Each partner tailors his/her mode of functioning in the relationship, the partnership, to make it work.

Here, confluence-contact is replaced by conflict-contact. One cannot have differentiation without conflict. But many couples have been conditioned by

Hollywood to feel that conflict means "we are no longer in love" or that "we are not really suited to each other" because they may never have witnessed resolution of conflicts—followed by expression of caring—in their own families of origin, the couple may be scared, fearing failure of the relationship. At this point, the Gestalt therapist needs to teach the couple how to fight cleanly and how to resolve or integrate differences in a way which enhances both and does not cause loss of esteem for either.

The therapist validates the experience of each and encourages both to respect the other's way of seeing a situation. Having supported both partners, s/he moves on to support the "we" in encouraging them to find a creative integration of their divergencies.

In my book, *Creative Process In Gestalt Therapy*, I have offered one model of such work—a model which requires one to hear the other, to own projections, and to move toward a compromise without losing face.[3]

The heat of the resolved conflict leaves the couple drawn to each other with renewed interest and even passion. Differentiation is followed by fusion. And so this rhythm goes on.

Some differences are not reconcilable and must be accepted as unreconcilable. One can love and respect one's partner and learn to accept the existential reality that not all problems are solvable. Just as Hollywood sold us a myth about love as fusion, the personal growth movement sold us the myth that all interpersonal problems are resolvable. This ethic forces some couples to fanatically negotiate and re-negotiate all differences until both are exhausted, experiencing shame, failure and disappointment in the relationship.

Differences are essential in a mature relationship. Differences keep the relationship alive.

C. COMPLEMENTARITY AND MIDDLE GROUND

1. Finding one's "better half"

Complementarity is the functional aspect of differentiation. It is how differentiation is lived out.

From a developmental point of view, one partner chooses another to complement the parts of oneself which are not in awareness, are not accepted, or are aesthetically repugnant. The qualities are seen in the other in a romanticized form. Two half-people come together to make one whole being to more effectively cope with the world.

The extrovert chooses the introvert as a symbolic gesture to one's inner world. The introvert chooses the extrovert so s/he can come closer to people, objects and events in the environment. The feeler moves toward the thinker, the concrete one moves toward the theorizer, and so on.

The complementary function is accepted and appreciated in the other as long as it is not experienced in oneself. Later, when that disowned quality begins to move to the surface in oneself, the partner's complementary behavior may be experienced with annoyance, anger, irritation and embarrassment. What was romanticized is now seen in its utmost crudity—the sociable one is seen as a "loudmouth," the introspective one is seen as "depressed."

2. Experimenting with Disowned Polarities

At this point, the Gestalt therapist can help each partner to experiment with each one's disowned polarity. When the introverted partner moves into the extroverted realm, the behavior of the other loses its "caricaturish" quality. Moreover, the one who was formerly "responsible" for dealing with the world is now able to recede into quiet self-introspection without worrying that external reality is not being dealt with adequately by the couple.

Some complementary modes—both characterological and stylistic—will remain as stable characteristics in a particular partner, no matter how much individual growth takes place. It is here that true (non-neurotic, non-projected) complementarity can work to lend variety and excitement to the couple's life.

The more fully each partner develops individually, the more one's own polarities are filled out and stretched, the more one can appreciate the "crazy" or idiosyncratic behavior of the other.

3. Appreciating the Ordinary

Life takes place in the middle, not at the extremes. Mostly, life is ordinary. It is only when we take the time to stop, look and reflect that the extraordinary aspects of life emerge. So it is with the life of couples. There are chores, work, the paying of bills, the errands, the phone calls, the morning showers, the meals, resting in one another's arms at the end of a long day.

Where complementarity stresses differences, middle ground acknowledges similarities. Whereas complementarity raises the voltage, the excitement of the couple's life, the middle ground provides a place to rest, a place where energy is even, rather than peaked—where energy levels are synchronized. Whereas complementarity stimulates conflict, the middle ground is the repository of quiet confluence.

4. Balancing Complementarity and the Middle Ground

The couple's survival and growth are determined by a balance between complementarity and confluence. The figure of differences is only meaningful against a background of agreements, understandings, compromises and ordinary pleasures. The figure of confluence is viable only against a ground of color, difference, lively discussion, arguments and emotional explosions.

One could say that the survival index of a couple is some ratio between confluence and conflict, or between middle ground and complementarity.

When a couple comes into the office fighting, the Gestalt therapist must recognize that they didn't bother introducing him/her to their middle ground. To balance the work, as well as the couple's perception of themselves, the therapist may wish to explore their middle ground:

How did you meet? (A magical question!)
What did you like about each other?
What are your common beliefs?
What do you enjoy together when things are all right?

Answers to these questions remind the couple of their common ground, of their loyalty, devotion, friendship and hard work—or the therapist may readily discover that this couple's middle ground is not ground at all, but a sheet of thin ice. The therapist may find, in fact, they didn't use their best judgment in moving toward each other. Each may have denied feelings in himself/herself and lied to the other or that there is impoverished friendship. Finally the therapist may discover that loyalty and devotion are strangely unused feelings for this couple.

The therapist can judge in the here and now how much conflict this particular system can tolerate without breaking up. S/he may need to confront the couple with these questions—to ask them if they are willing to start building a basic ground of trust between them in order to sustain the kind of conflict they are engaged in.

5. One Couple's Middle Ground

I have wedged into Bill and Jean's middle ground, between their complementary modes (see table).

Bill and Jean are both Orthodox Jews. That is a very powerful factor. Jean left Bill once and went back to her mother and father. Her parents said

TABLE 11-1

BILL'S COMPLEMENTARY MODES	THE COUPLE'S MIDDLE GROUND	JEAN'S COMPLEMENTARY MODES
Concrete	Jewish Orthodoxy	Abstract
Thinking oriented	Family life includes extended family	Feeling-oriented
Logical	More focus on family than self	Intuitive
Extraverted	Marriage is for life	Introverted
Adventuresome	Emphasis on hard work	Reactive
Rebellious	Old-fashioned values of devotion, loyalty, sacrifice, stability, generosity	Naturally suspicious of new ideas
Need for power and control	Involvement in community	Need for being heard/appreciated (passive reactive use of influence)
Projects	Conservatism	Introjects
Needs to be served	Love, care of their children	Needs to serve
Obvious	Importance of sexual contact and play	Mysterious

to her, "Go home. You have a child. You think you are going to leave him? You have to work it out. You are married and you will stay married."

As a result, Jean went home. The couple saw a therapist at Jewish Family Service, but they were not doing better. They went to someone else, and somebody else after that, and they still hung in there.

The point I want to make is that their orthodoxy is their middle ground. It keeps them together. Around sexuality they believe in purity, looking out for one another and paying attention to one another. Family life is important and it includes extended family. On Passover, if one has a poor brother in Chicago who cannot afford to come to the Seder, one pays the brother's airfare and makes sure he is at the Seder with the rest of the family. So, in part, this couple sticks together by maintaining family ties. Jean is the child of concentration camp parents. By a miracle, both parents survived. She cannot even conceive of the family not being together on a holiday. There is almost more of a focus on the family—they have two children—than on the individual selves.

Part of their middle is "marriage is for life." There is an emphasis on hard work as a value and they have other (what I call) old-fashioned values.

Bill, a consultant, travels all over the world. One time when I saw him alone I asked, ''Do you ever . . . get tempted by women?'' He turned pale and said, ''When you're married, you don't fool around.''

Other middle ground values for Jean and Bill are devotion, loyalty, sacrifice, stability, generosity and involvement in the community. In their case, involvement in the community means involvement in a synagogue.

As I began analyzing Jean and Bill and other such couples, I realized that each of them has a specific middle range which keeps them together. To stay together as a system, there seem to be two kinds of ingredients: there is division of labor, or complementarity, and a thick middle system with a kind of balance that takes care of ordinary daily experience. It is quite exciting to study this. I'm selfish—I want to understand how my wife and I had survived in a couple for 28 years.

III. GESTALT PROCESS IN COUPLE THERAPY

A. Recognizing the Third Entity

Our greatest weakness as Gestalt therapists is our training in attending to the individual and his/her behavior in the therapeutic encounter. Even when we attend to the encounter quality of the therapeutic relationship, we tend to shy away from an analysis of this diad in its own right. We re-focus on the one who, after all, needs our help. And so, when we are faced by the couple, it is very difficult to abandon our tendency to see each person separately without factoring in the context of the other. It is, in fact, an extraordinary shift from the Gestalt of the one to the Gestalt of this new, two-headed organism.

The couple is a system, a Gestalt. It has a changing internal space within: the interaction between two people. The Gestalt therapist focuses on the space where they meet and not on their internal space. This system has a special boundary, different from the individual boundaries within it.

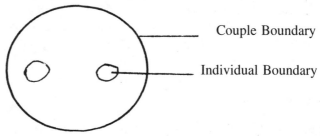

The boundary of the couple defines how they relate to the world around them. Some couple systems, for example, have very thin, overly permeable boundaries, allowing everyone to intrude into and disrupt their lives. On the other side are the couples who are too thickly bounded, living secret lives, isolated from others, not asking much of the world and not giving much to the world.

In order to see this system, this third and larger entity, the therapist must move away from the system enough to see both of them at once in her/his visual field, to watch their physical swaying and tilting—one in relation to the other—to listen to the orchestration of voices as they bounce off each other in anger or in tenderness, to attend to how much energy they create together—how much awareness together, how much movement together, how much contact together. The therapist's interventions are addressed, for the most part, to this third entity:

> "You two are so cautious, I see you tippy-toeing on eggs around each other."
> "When you start arguing logically, both of you close up shop."
> "When you, Leonard, begin to talk about your work, you, Jenny, begin to stoop over and look down."
> "You two remind me of a quiet lake before a storm."
> "You are like a hippo mostly submerged in water with a little bird sitting on top of its mountainous back."

The balanced intervention stresses interactional characteristics. The metaphor does that also, but leaves room for other mysterious possibilities which the couple can explore. The metaphor is the most powerful tool of reminding the couple that they are one organism; that they individually contribute to the shape and functioning of this organism; that each cannot take whole responsibility for its survival or failure. (The notion of seeing a single spouse to solve a problem of marriage is not tenable with this model.)

B. The Empty Chair as Third Entity

The therapist cannot be a direct advocate for the system. S/he must evolve a creative method for advocacy within the couple. When couples are in crisis, polarization between them causes focus on individual needs, complaints and attacks on the other. There are monotonously repetitive attacks, counterattacks, rationalizations, justifications, and otherwise fruitless efforts to preserve one's own esteem in relation to the other.

The therapist finds himself muttering, "Who the hell is looking out for the house? If I do it, if I keep saying, 'Your marriage needs this and that,' then I am taking them off the hook around taking ownership of that entity."

In my work with couples, I teach both of them to use the empty chair as a place from which each can take a turn to speak on behalf of the relationship as an actual and separate entity. This method forces the couple to think in system terms, rather than in individual ego-protection terms.

The couple is instructed that when they get into an impasse, one is to move to the empty chair and speak for the third entity. If Charlie speaks from the empty chair, he must first address himself to the individual Charlie (the chair he just left) before speaking to Roberta. This prevents Charlie from using the third entity chair as a parent figure to give Roberta a sermon. He must give himself hell for his half of the couple's failures before turning to Roberta and telling her where she neglects the relationship.

The couple practices seeing how each contributes to the situation by speaking from the empty chair as a third entity. They become, in a sense, their own process observers and their own therapists.

Freed from the encumbrance of advocacy for or against the relationship, the Gestalt therapist can be more creative in the use of process observations, metaphors and the reporting of his/her own internal experience in the couple's presence. The therapist can share experiences, tell stories and use paradox to mobilize the system to see its own ongoing process with greater clarity.

C. Values

Implicit in this philosophy of Gestalt-systems treatment are values which are rarely articulated by the therapist—as if therapists are valueless. In fact, we do have values, not so much related to what a couple should do in a given situation, but rather how we can best relate to them as partners. Here is a sampling of these process-oriented Gestalt therapists' values:

Respect the couple's system as is.
Work in the present.
Stay outside the couple's system (don't take sides or be trapped by the system's conceptualization of itself).
Look for the contribution of each in any couple's action.
Underline mutuality and complementarity of relationship: "You protect your wife in a way that inhibits her, and you elicit unnecessary protection from your husband with great skill."
Do not refer to intrapsychic conflicts and individual motives.
Support the couple sub-system when it is in danger of intrusion from other systems (kids, parents—boundaries too loose). Also, help loosen boundaries when the couple is in danger of isolation.
Discourage looking at the "why" causes and effects and encourage the "what" and "how."
If possible, focus on process and not content in your interventions.

Teach each to be an advocate for their relationship (to be the "watchdog" of the third entity).
Show appreciation for the things that the couple does well.
Show compassion for their pain, struggle, stuckness.
Share your own internal experience of being in their presence.
Support a healthy rhythm between contact and withdrawal (teach each to respect the boundaries of the other).

What do these process values imply to the couple? By practicing these process beliefs, what beliefs do we, the therapists, suggest to the couple? Here are some possibilities:

Look out for #3 (the third entity).
Appreciate each other's differences and use differences to enrich your own experience.
Respect the other's boundary (particular needs, privacy).
Don't try to change the other; change yourself; change how you relate.
Value fighting "clean"—stay with process and learn to tolerate frustration.
Appreciate your confluence (agreement, quiet times, doing the ordinary).
Develop the capacity for living with problems.
Be "mindful" of the other and act on your mindfulness.
Be gracious and compassionate (for example, learn to say "no" kindly).
Make demands and learn to accept "no."
As long as #3 is not threatened, support the other's need to satisfy growth needs out in the world.
Cultivate your sense of humor and sense of the philosophical—and don't forget to play.
When in trouble, protect your system from those who threaten its integrity and turn to those (i.e., therapist) who will help to change it safely (triangulation).

D. Cycle of Experience in Couple Therapy

We have discussed the development of a couple and the framework upon which couple therapy lies, now we turn to the specific model we use in couple work. The model for this process is based on The Gestalt Experience Cycle, described in detail in *Creative Process in Gestalt Therapy*. In this case, however, the cycle should be seen as an *interactive* event rather than an intrapsychic one, so the process of couple therapy moves more or less from sensation to awareness to energy and action, to contact, and finally to resolution, closure and withdrawal. This process works both at the level of an individual session as well as a way of examining the ongoing process of the entire therapeutic experience.

1. Sensation

In this early stage, couples tend to look at each other, often intensely, but not to see or hear each other. Each is rehearsing his/her own "tape," his/her own rebuttal. They are simply too busy making internal lists to actually use their senses externally. The therapist asks the couple to sit opposite each other so that they look at one another rather than at the therapist. The therapist encourages expression of what each partner sees in the other. This form slows down the process of rehearsed confrontation and forces the couple to settle down into the existential experience of being in this room together, sharing a dilemma together. (Sitting so that they *face* the therapist deflects the couple from observing their own ongoing process and reinforces an adversary system in which the therapist is expected to judge one of the partners.)

In this phase the therapist begins to encourage both partners to observe not only what the other is saying or feeling but also how their process is unfolding. S/he reinforces statements like "we seem to be sitting miles apart" or "both of us are holding our breath." The Gestalt therapy model for couples and families is clearly a process model. Clear observation of its own process teaches the couple most of what they need to learn about the malfunctions in their system (as well as what they do well together).

2. Awareness

Clear, strong sensations lead to clear, strong awareness between partners. Often partners feel things inside whch are not expressed verbally: it is one thing to have an internal hunch, and it is another to say it directly to another. This is a bigger jump than most people realize. Sharing experiences with each other takes extra effort. Mutual awareness also requires taking time to listen to and process what the other is actually saying before responding. The Gestalt therapist makes sure that there is emphasis given to what is said by one of the partners by asking the other partner to repeat what was said before responding.

To care about another's experience requires a sense of curiosity about it, to ask the other what it was like to feel that way or to give more details, i.e., "You've been so quiet today—I wonder if you're worried about something you didn't share with me." The therapist reinforces this active process of being curious about the other. To want to know "what it's like for you" is one way of loving that person.

The couple is encouraged to express clearly what they want from each other and what they experience individually. It is impossible to satisfy the partner's need or to understand his/her feelings when these feelings and desires are not expressed. Even people who love each other can't read each other's minds.

The most common resistances at this level of process are introjection and projection. Sonia Nevis[4] points out that these resistances should be seen at a systems level rather than intrapsychically: "Introjection can be seen in a system when there is a force-feeder (one who expects the "food" of his/her opinions or information to be swallowed as given), and when there is a swallower (one who does not chew what is given and spit out what is not wanted), and when others who are present do not interfere. Projection also requires two people: one who gives little information and deflects and discourages questions, and another person who is willing to guess and fill in the gaps . . ." The therapist's task is to point out these resistances to contact and each partner's role in making that miscommunication happen.

It is in this stage of work that the couple learns to negotiate mutually agreed upon ideas, goals, perceptions and awarenesses of what is going askew between them. The therapist reinforces their process of creating cognitive clarity and not getting stuck in repeated cycles of mutual blaming.

Therapist interventions are strong, simply-stated and always grounded in the process of the ongoing session. Interventions are sparce (sparceness delivers punch) and are generally addressed to the couple as a system.

3. Energy and Action

Having arrived at clear, mutually agreed upon ideas about their dilemma, the couple begins to experience energy to do something about their mutual needs. Mostly, they want to do something later, at home, not in the therapeutic situation. The Gestalt therapist will often translate their ideas and transform their energy into an event, perhaps an experiment which will give the couple a sense of "having done it," of having acted upon what needed to be expressed in the lively moment. (The therapist may also invite the couple to carry out other experiments in the safety and privacy of their own home. Unfortunately, many couples resist by not carrying out these experiments.) At the culmination of a successful experiment, the couple can congratulate each other for "breaking through" something which, until that moment, felt like an awful stuckness, a morass of unpleasantness.

In this stage of the session (or therapy) the Gestalt therapist makes sure that the energy exchange is not uneven in the system, that one partner doesn't overwhelm the other (with the other allowing him/herself to be overwhelmed). Confluence occurs when one "gives into" the other's pushing for the "sake of peace," or to avoid the painful process of pushing right back and making sure one's ideas are taken into account. The therapist also watches for the most common resistance to mutual contact in this phase: retroflection. The couple, fearing smoke and fire, colludes to turn energy inside themselves rather than expressing it toward each other. The therapist will notice signs of physical discomfort and will teach the couple how to express their energy (often anger) in a safe, unthreatening way in the therapy room. Couples who retroflect tend to draw tight boudaries around their (individual) selves or around themselves as a total system: "We can do this alone . . . we don't need other people's help," they say. They turn out to be isolated couples, distanced from the support of their community. The therapist may encourage such a couple to ask for help from friends whom they respect and trust (or to at least share their feelings with other couples).

4. Contact

Active use of energy and experimentation makes the couple feel closer and good about one another. Even good expression of anger can lead to a strong sense of contact. There is sharing about what happened, what seemed to be difficult and how each partner contributed to the creative resolution. The therapist makes sure that the couple doesn't jump into premature self-congratulation (confluence), avoiding the chewing on something that both consider "unpleasant" or "shameful" to express. Having ascertained that genuine contact is taking place, the therapist reinforces the couple's success and their ability to talk about it: "We didn't call each other names this time" or "It was nice not to get stuck in our sulking."

5. Resolution, closure and withdrawal

Some couples can't let go of processing their experience. Here, the therapist keeps the couple from mulling over again and again how it went wrong or what was done differently. There is encouragement to move on. In addition, the therapist emphasizes the unique complementary style in which each partner contributed to the process of the work. At this stage individual boundaries are encouraged.

As the withdrawal stage approaches, the therapist teaches the couple that silence in this context is a form of groundedness. There is both a sense of mutual peace and a slow building of energy for future use. In the culmination of the cycle, the therapist also emphasizes the importance of each partner's independence and self-support.

IV. CONCLUSION

The above process is true (ideally) of each session, as well as of the therapeutic process on a grander scale. Over a period of months, couples tend to get stuck in awareness when therapy starts. There is a tendency to talk about, rather than doing something active in the session. When the couple is filled with their thinking and clarifying, the therapist coaxes them to more actively explore their process in the therapy situation. Thus, middle sessions are imbued with energy and experimentation. Ending sessions are characterized by good, healthy contact; resolutions come more quickly because there is more clarity about what is happening, each partner taking responsibility for his/her own experience. Intellectual clarity leads the couple to a sense of their own competence, as well as to confidence in creating their own problem-solving experiments. In the very last sessions, the couple begins to withdraw from the therapist, to wean themselves from the therapeutic situation. They feel more sure of their own skills and a greater sense of independence from the therapist. The therapist's task at this juncture is to give the couple permission to ''go home'' with his/her blessing.

What does the therapist hope to accomplish with his/her process interventions? If not to save the marriage, is it to help the couple part? No, not really. We assume that in their deepest wisdom the partners must know what is best for them. For myself, I hope to teach the couple:

*How to rise above themselves to see what their process looks like—to observe themselves.
*How to start, develop and complete difficult situations.
*How to make good contact and be aware of contact disruptions.
*How to withdraw and rest, rather than clinging to unfinished bits and pieces of circumstances.
*How to support each other without losing themselves.
*How to turn to others for nourishment and, also, to give it.
*How to enhance the continuing growth of each without losing the precious commodity of intimacy.

These are some of my thoughts on Gestalt work with couples. The most important learnings have been to not get hooked by individual arguments, but to see the couple as a system struggling for resolution. When I find myself becoming biased toward one partner, I invite another therapist to co-lead the couple sessions with me. Generally, the spouse I dislike turns out to have some behavior which I cannot tolerate in myself.

The couple is very rewarding to work with because they generate much energy and don't seem to drain the therapist. This is especially so if the therapist manages to maintain his/her own boundary and does not merge with the system.

NOTES

1. These formulations have been heavily influenced by my colleagues at The Gestalt Institute of Cleveland. I am particularly indebted to Ed and Sonia Nevis and Wesley Jackson.

2. Fromm, Erich. *The Art of Loving*. NY: Harper & Brothers, 1956.

3. Zinker, Joseph. *Creative Process in Gestalt Therapy*, NY: Brunner/Mazel, Inc., 1977.

4. Nevis, Sonia and Zinker, Joseph. *The Gestalt Theory of Couple and Family Interactions*, Cleveland, Ohio. Gestalt Institute of Cleveland, 1981.

REFERENCES

Keirsey, David and Bates, Marilyn. *Please Understand Me*, Del Mar, CA: Promethean Books, Inc., 1978.

Jung, C. G. *Four Archetypes. Princeton, NJ: Princeton University Press, 1959.*

Jung, C. B. *Psychological Types*, Princeton, NJ: Princeton University Press, 1971.

Jung, C. G. *Symbols of Transformation*. Princeton, NJ: Princeton University Press, 1956.

Mayeroff, Milton. *On Caring*. NY: Perennial Library, Harper and Row, 1972.

Perls, Frederick, Hefferline, Ralph, and Goodman, Paul. *Gestalt Therapy*, NY: The Julian Press, Inc., 1951.

Polster, Erving and Polster, Miriam. *Gestalt Therapy Integrated*, NY: Brunner/ Mazel, Inc. 1973.

Zinker, Joseph. "Phenomenology of the Loving Encounter," in Stephenson, F. Douglas (ed.) *Gestalt Therapy Primer*. Springfield, Ill: Charles C. Thomas, 1975.

Zinker, Joseph. "Complementarity & The Middle Ground: Two Forces For Couples Binding," Cleveland, Ohio. The Gestalt Institute of Cleveland, 1980.

12

An Overview of the Theory and Practice of Gestalt Group Process

MARY ANN HUCKABAY, Ph.D.

WIDESPREAD USE OF GROUP psychotherapy began during World War II as an expedient application of individual psychotherapy aimed at reducing the length and cost of therapy while increasing its availability to the growing numbers of people who needed treatment. Over the last 40 years, the burgeoning field of small-group theory and practice has come fully into its own as diverse streams of theorists and practitioners have explored the unique possibilities as well as the problems and dilemmas inherent in the use of small groups for individual learning and change. There are applications to populations not dreamt of at the end of World War II: to organizational and administrative settings, to educational and spiritual endeavors, to professional training programs (law, medicine, psychology), to political forums dealing with the explosive issues of profound human differences, to individuals seeking growth rather than cure.

By now it is no news that groups are better suited to accomplishing some "people-changing" objectives than is individual work. Groups provide their members with a community of peers, whose experience and understanding echo the vicissitudes and wisdom of one's own life. Groups provide a safe harbor for exploring essential life issues, and one's mere presence in a group confronts one with life's perennial choices: when to join and when to withdraw, when to fight and when to flee, and when and how to love (Glidewell, 1970). The multiplicity of relationships and points of view allows for consensual validation and reality testing—both antidotes to what Sullivan calls the "parataxic distortions" of human interaction. Jourard makes the case that mental health requires self-disclosure and that it is in groups that people can best pratice and bear witness to the human need to "come out" as who they truly are. And Gestalt groups uniquely provide more latitude for experimentation and liveliness in the present, thus marshalling the group's resources for increased creativity in the service of human development.

Our purpose here is to locate within the broad spectrum of group work a particular contribution made by one branch of the Gestalt tradition. Our aim is to describe the kind of group work that is taught and practiced at the Gestalt Institute of Cleveland (GIC).[1] This approach to groups, referred to as "Gestalt group process" (Kepner, 1980), is a set of intervention strategies that are based on a synthesis of theoretical contributions from three different but interrelated fields: general systems theory, group dynamics literature, and classical Gestalt theory. While most Gestalt practitioners draw on a variety of theory bases for group work, it has been the GIC that has most explicitly attended to an integration of these three fields in developing and disseminating its group intervention theory and practice.

We will look first at these three fields separately, presenting those elements of each theoretical framework that have contributed most significantly to our understanding of the behavior of small groups. The premise of this chapter is that together these three frameworks provide the why, the what, and the how of effective work with small groups. General systems theory lends the why, the explanatory undergirdings to the work; the group dynamics field provides the what, the focal elements to be observed and monitored; and classical Gestalt psychology contributes the how of the work, a way to focus awareness on what is occurring in groups.

In the following section, we explore a set of intervention strategies and choices premised on these theoretical assumptions. We assume that the reader is familiar with three fundamental concepts of Gestalt therapy: the theory of resistances (Perls, 1969, *Ego, Hunger and Aggression*); the concept of experiment (Polster & Polster, 1973, *Gestalt Therapy Integrated*); and the organismic self-regulation process of sensation, awareness, mobilization of energy, contact, withdrawal, and assimilation (Perls, Hefferline, & Goodman, 1951, *Gestalt Therapy*).

THEORETICAL CONTRIBUTIONS TO GESTALT GROUP PROCESS

General Systems Theory

General systems theory offers all three theoretical strands their common base: that organisms can be fully understood only when they are viewed as being embedded in a field, a context, an environment, and that the relationship between the organism and its environment is of utmost importance, theoretically and behaviorally. This theoretical assumption is the foundation of general systems theory, which is the conceptual umbrella under which both Gestalt psychology and group dynamics can be subsumed.

HISTORICAL CONTEXT The original impetus for general systems theory came from von Bertalanffy, a theoretical biologist writing in 1950. He was joined, in that same decade, by Boulding, an economist; J. G. Miller, a psychiatrist and psychologist; Ashby, a bacteriologist; Rapoport, a mathematician; and a host of others, all of whom were interested in discovering isomorphisms and analogies between biological and chemomechanical systems (Berrien, 1968).

General systems theory arose as a response to the limitations of Newtonian and Copernican science, with its emphasis on causal linearity, properties of closed systems, and the mechanistic penchant for the analytical reduction of phenomena into the smallest discernible subparts. During the 20th century, advances in physics, the behavioral sciences, the information sciences and mythology and religion have drawn attention to the inability of the prevailing scientific models to explain the complexity of living, open systems in active interaction with their environments.

General systems theory is the overarching schema for integrating our understanding of enormously diverse phenomena, ranging from the inorganic through biological systems to symbolic and epistemological levels of systems. What is a system? A system is a bounded collection of mutually influencing, interactive parts (subsystems) arranged for the attainment of some purpose. The subparts are therefore highly interdependent, and are organized to meet specific ends, that is, to perform specific system functions. For example, reproduction provides for species survival and evolution, religion exists to explain a culture's relationship to the unknown, and groups and families exist to "grow" their members. Von Bertalanffy, stressing this interdependent nature of a system, has defined system simply as "a set of units with relationships among them" (Miller, 1965, p. 200).

Despite the fact that systems always display a single or common purpose, with subparts that are characterized by functional unity and a high degree of internal interdependence, it is also true that all systems, that is, all wholes, are embedded in even larger wholes. Systems are like Chinese boxes, each one nested in the text. These Chinese boxes are separated from one another by information and matter–energy boundaries that create differential energy states on either side of the boundary. For example, a theme that is explored inside the context of a group seldom carries precisely the same valence when discussed by a group member with his or her lover later that evening. Similarly, the human body's temperature is roughly 98.6° F while the surrounding temperature of the room may be 65° F. Despite the fact that it is possible to view and work with discrete, if nested systems, it is nonetheless true that ultimately, system definition is an arbitrary perceptual and conceptual bounding process. It is also true that in order to understand the actual parameters of a system, it is necessary to know something of the nature of the system on either side of the one under study; that is, to fully understand the system you are working with, you must go up and down at least one level of system (Feibleman & Friend, 1945). For example, to understand a group you need to know something about the organizational or community context of that group, and you need to know something about the nature of the subgroups that are operating in the group.

Five systems concepts are particularly important for explaining what happens in small groups: holism, open and closed systems, entropy and negative entropy, homeostasis, and equifinality.

HOLISM   Like the field theories of Gestalt and group dynamics that are subsumed within it, general systems theory is premised on the assumption that the whole is greater than the sum of its parts. That is, it is not possible to derive the nature of the whole, the complexion of the beast, by any amount of intimate knowledge of its subparts alone. The metaphor most often used to explain the nature of holism is that of the three blind people each attempting to describe the elephant that they are all touching. The one touching the tusk claims that the elephant is smooth and hard. The one whose hands are on the elephant's tail says it is round and long, like a snake or a garden hose. The one touching its flank says it is baggy, bumpy, and hairy.

Because of the high degree of interdependence of all subsystems, a change in one has an effect on the whole and on all other subsystems. And membership in a system will both constrain and enhance the condition of the subpart; it never leaves the subpart unaffected. I am reminded of Nancy, a group member, who remained chronically ambivalent for about 4 months about staying in her group. She eventually did a major piece of work on what her ambivalence meant for her, and she began a series of graded experiments on "showing up for her life" on the one hand, and disengaging more actively on the other. She decided to commit to the group for the following 6 months. Two sessions after her decision, there was a pivotal discussion involving the whole group about what the group had and had not given them. The most lively and widely shared figure centered around how the group would need to function differently for everyone to engage more deeply. The connection between Nancy's individual work and the subsequent work at the group level was unmistakable: an individual's resolution of any particular theme (e.g., commitment or engagement) creates a fertile void in which that same issue can reverberate in other subsystems or the group system as a whole.

If a system is performing optimally, it is sometimes the case that its subsystems are not. That is, the independent performance of subsystems is frequently constrained by the nature of the relationship between those subparts that is required for optimal full-system functioning. For example, a basketball team's effectiveness rests not on the stellar individual performance of its players, but on the teamwork produced by those players. Similarly, a symphony by necessity constrains the virtuosity of an individual musician, and a viable marriage may require compromises on the part of one or both spouses.

What is particularly important about the principle of holism for understanding what goes on in small groups? First, it implies that it is not possible to understand the complexion of the group by knowing what is going on with each of its members. It suggests that group members' behavior will be constrained by the group environment of which they are a part. It also suggests that when attention is paid to developing the group as a system, the needs of individual members must of necessity be subordinated to that task.

OPEN AND CLOSED SYSTEMS The characteristics of openness versus closedness pertain to a system's relationship to its environment. Closed systems are those inert or inorganic systems that exist without any kind of exchange of matter-energy or information with an environment external to themselves. A hermetically sealed tube is an example of a closed system. Most systems, and certainly all living systems, display some degree of openness because of their need to import and export matter-energy and information to and from their environment. No system is completely open or closed, and in human social systems, these constructs form two fictional endpoints of a continuum that describes the degree of system permeability. The degree to which a system is open or closed depends upon the nature of the organism's internal and external boundaries: The more closed the system is to its subparts or its environment, the less it imports and exports information or matter-energy across its boundaries. The more open a system is, the less "filtering" or screening the system does.

This concept of permeable boundaries is very important with respect to group phenomena. The contact boundaries between each individual and the group as a whole, between one individual and another, or between subgroups are extremely dynamic and are one of the main foci of the group's as well as the leader's attention and intervention. The condition of these subsystem boundaries will determine the system's ability for internal self-regulation, which in turn is related to the next property of systems to be discussed—entropy and negentropy.

ENTROPY AND NEGENTROPY All open systems have a tendency to wind down over time, to lose energy to their environment, to become progressively less organized. A pan of hot water becomes cool when removed from its heat source. The human body and its organs and functions begin to deteriorate and fail as we grow old. Entropy, also referred to as the second law of thermodynamics, is the systems theory vernacular for death. Curiously, living systems simultaneously display negentropy (negative entropy), or a force for life, for the maintenance of the system within certain parameters by the assimilation of matter-energy and information. Group members' willingness and ability to share what they are presently aware of is an example of negentropy in that information becomes food for thought, grist for the group mill, a data base from which a lively figure and subsequent action can arise. Conversely, group norms that disallow the expression of anger or vulnerability, for example, mean that information about those feelings that exist in the group is not available to be worked with and assimilated, leading to progressive malnutrition of the group system.

The concept of self-regulation, to be discussed next, is essentially the organism's tendency to achieve a steady state by maintaining negentropy in a changing field.

HOMEOSTASIS OR SELF-REGULATION Living systems also display the tendency to maintain a steady state. Our bodies work to maintain body temperature at 98.6° F. Family systems develop implicit rules and agreements to maintain known and accepted definitions of their individual members, the task of the system, and prescribed boundaries between subparts. Cultural belief systems and socialization exist to regulate and control who has access to what kinds of people, places, and things, including information, thereby maintaining that culture's status quo.

Groups, like families, regulate themselves according to certain parameters by assigning roles to members, and by implicitly creating powerful unspoken norms that govern what behavior is permissible in the group setting and what is not.

However, as was discussed above with the concept of negentropy, living systems also go beyond the principle of homeostasis, in that they exhibit needs not only for stability and regularity but for growth, elaboration, and progressive differentiation. Paradoxically, in open systems, the very concept of homeostasis requires constant adaptation to a changing set of environmental circumstances.

EQUIFINALITY: THERE ARE MANY PATHS TO ROME Living systems display purposeful, teleological, or goal-oriented behavior. A cat will stalk the neighborhood for beetles and mice, an orangutan will find its way to a suspended banana, and humans will go in search of a loved one or a better paying job. If one route to the desired goal or outcome is not available, we select another. The concept of equifinality means that there are multiple routes to the same end.

In a group setting, the following example may clarify the principle of equifinality: A large subset of the group has expressed the desire for more closeness between members of the group. The group then launches a series of acts, interventions, and experiments over the course of the next two sessions, all of which have an impact on the sense of closeness and intimacy in the group. Discussion ensues in the third session on what interactions had what effects on the group. Some actions had been more successful than others. Some had been more deliberate and aware than others. In a situation as complex as a group, it is not possible to determine a single best solution or response to the wish for more closeness. The perfect solution does not exist. Rather, the group's ability to take care of its members' wish for more cohesion depends upon the requisite variety, that is, the breadth of the behavioral and affective repertoire that exists within the group for responding to the need as well as the group's ability to improvise with imagination and inventiveness.

The Field of Group Dynamics

HISTORICAL CONTEXT It was during World War II that Kurt Lewin, who had been trained in the field theory of Gestalt psychology in Germany, first used the term "group dynamics" in reference to the emerging view that small groups, as social entities in their own right, had characteristic and predictable properties, purposes, and processes. Lewin had already founded the Research Center for Group Dynamics at Massachusetts Institute of Technology, when, in June of 1946, he and a set of colleagues agreed to hold a series of discussion groups on dealing with intergroup tensions for the Connecticut Interracial Commission. The commission had been created to implement the new Connecticut Fair Employment Practice Act. Their aim was to bring together a wide range of community leaders—teachers, businesspeople, labor leaders—to explore how to deal more effectively with interracial tensions, so that the community leaders, in turn, could help other people change their racial attitudes. The principal training method was discussion of live "back home" problem situations and role-playing to explore alternative solutions.

Although Lewin's main task was an applied one, he (with his usual insistence on the marriage of action and research) had brought with him a set of nonparticipant research observers who recorded the behavioral interactions and dynamics that occurred in each discussion group. Lewin, the group leaders, and the research team would gather each evening to discuss the emerging research data. When participants learned of these postmortems, some asked to attend. With reluctance and uncertainty about what the effect would be on the participants of hearing direct observations of their behavior, the staff ultimately agreed to their attendance.

> Actually, the open discussion of their own behavior and its observed consequences had an electric effect both on the participants and the training leaders. The conversations inexorably widened to include participants . . . (as) members reinforced or qualified the data furnished by the observer.
>
> Group members, when confronted more or less objectively with data concerning their own behavior and its effects . . . might achieve highly meaningful learnings about themselves, about the responses of others to them, and about group behavior and group development in general. [Bradford, Gibb, & Benne, 1964, p. 82–83].

Thus was born, with the aid of serendipity, the first T-group (originally called "basic skill training group" and later shortened simply to "T-group") with its powerful methodology for human development that has evolved into a major stream of group theory and pratice over the last 40 years.

KEY ELEMENTS OF GROUP DYNAMICS THEORY Five key elements of group dynamics theory will be presented: goals, norms, roles, stages of group development, and levels of system.

Goals and Outcomes of Small Groups Out of this laboratory education tradition come a set of goals articulated most clearly by Warren Bennis (1965) as (a) expanded consciousness and recognition of choice; (b) a spirit of inquiry; (c) authenticity in interpersonal relations; (d) a collaborative conception of the authority relationship; (e) conflict resolution through rational means. (Bennis, in Schein and Bennis, 1965, p. 30–31)

Elsewhere, group dynamics theorists have emphasized the cybernetic perspective of the developmental goals of small groups by stressing factors strikingly similar to the goals of Gestalt groups. For example, Mills (1967) speaks of a group's capacity for adaptation (increasing the range, diversity, and effectiveness of its channels of information intake and its contacts beyond current boundaries) and integration (differentiating into subparts while maintaining collective unity).

Norms   Norms are the powerful spoken and unspoken rules that govern human interaction in any given situation, including but certainly not limited to group settings. They will vary from context to context, and they determine what is and is not acceptable behavior for each context. Norms determine things such as how much openness or disclosure a group will tolerate, how conflict will be managed, how the authority relationship between members and the leader will be arranged, and how much novelty and difference will be invited or allowed into the group. The most powerful norm of all is the norm that determines whether it is permitted for group members to examine explicitly the norms that are currently operating in the group. Because they are the principal means of system self-regulation and are such powerful determinants of the health of the overall group system, norms must be subjected to periodic scrutiny by everyone. Frequently, norms that once served a useful purpose become obsolete or dysfunctional as the group develops over time. Left with unexamined norms, the group and its members are held captive to a set of injunctions that govern their behavior in ways that may obstruct or impede their purpose.

Roles   The role a group member assumes is that set of behaviors that characterizes a member's participation in a group over time. Groups evolve and distribute a variety of roles among their members in order to fulfill group functions such as focusing a group on its goal, setting standards for group performance, assuring that all members are heard from, expressing a contrasting point of view to that held by a majority of the group, or propelling the group forward in its development. A set of roles in a group is like a cast of characters in a play—their breadth and richness define and constrain the range of human possibilities available to the group. Sometimes roles are contingent upon the stage of the group's development, and those that were salient and functional at one point in time may be unnecessary or anachronistic later on.

As is the case with norms, it is important to attend to member roles because when roles are made explicit they can be more easily changed or choicefully and consciously assigned.

Stages of Group Development   So much has been written about stages of group development that only an abbreviated summary is possible or appropriate here. We include a discussion of stages because stage theory can give us a sense of what is and is not possible, even probable, at various points in the life of a group. Further, an understanding of stages provides one with the capacity to differentiate what is to be expected, what is usual and ordinary, from that which is anomalous and bizarre. And finally, knowledge of the leader behaviors required for each stage can provide a schema for organizing an intervention strategy that supports or is in conjunction with one's own personal/professional development as a group leader.

Theories of group development, like those of individual development, are epigenetic in nature. That is, the issues that characterize one stage must be addressed somehow before the group can attend fully to the tasks and issues and concerns of the next stage. These issues and concerns pertain to members' inner emotional states, members' relationship to the leader, their relationship to the task of the group, and the like. Thus, because a group's capacity for intimacy is contingent upon the development of several antecedent conditions, it is not realistic, for example, to expect that a group will achieve high levels of intimacy or interdependence during the early phases of its existence, just as it is not probable that an infant will walk before it crawls. Developmental stages evolve like spirals that repeat themselves sequentially but at ever-deepening levels. Thus, once a group has achieved an initial degree of interdependence, it will cycle back to the issue of identity and inclusion, but with much more complexity and depth. At each later stage, the residues of earlier stages can be detected. It is not that certain issues arise only at particular points in a group's history. All of the basic human issues that arise when people relate to one another are always present in a group. Rather, we are saying that at particular times, certain issues take on an emotional charge and a salience that those same issues did not previously have.

A condensed summary of several authors' presentations of group stages is given in Figure 12-1.[2] They are presented here in some detail because stage theory is central to the intervention strategies presented in latter part of the chapter.

Group Composition by Level   Because the group dynamics field arose out of the context of social psychology and human interaction rather than individual psychology, the primary focus or unit of analysis has been social units of two or more. This focus has allowed for a careful tracking of dyadic, subgroup, and group level functions and processes, and has brought a

FIGURE 12-1.
Stages of Group Development

Stage 1: Inclusion, Identity, Dependence

Stage 1 is characterized by the following:
A concern with one's identity in the group:
Who will, can, must I be here? Who else is
similar to me? What of myself will I have to
relinquish in order to belong here? How safe
am I?
Boundary and definitional issues: What
tasks/people will be in this group and what
and who will not? What is out-of-bounds
here?

Stage 2: Influence, Autonomy, Counter-Dependence

Stage 2 is characterized by the following:
A concern with authority and status. Who
has clout in this group and why? Issues are
attended to more because of who says them
than what gets said.

The group's relationship to its leader,
counterdependent challenging of
assumptions and offering of alternative
actions.
The formation of cliques and subgroups
competing for control and status. Conflict
and nonconfluence.

Stage 3: Intimacy, Affection

Stage 3 is concerned with:
A heightened awareness about the issue of
interpersonal distance between members. A
value on increased warmth and cohesion,
purchased at the price of some conformity
and groupthink.

Stage 4: Interdependence

Many groups never enter this stage; they
may be time bound or end before they have
developed this far. Membership in a group is
seldom stable over time and as people come
and go, the group's complexion and
character are altered. But when a group
reaches this point, the following descriptors
are apt:
A time of peak group performance, due to
highly developed integration and
differentiation. Tolerance and support for a
lot of collaboration and intimacy. Conflict is
accepted as are the publicly acknowledged
differences between members.
The group has built in enough requisite
variety to respond with improvisation and
ingenuity to a very broad set of conditons.

sophistication to our understanding of how all these levels impact on one another.

For present purposes, four levels of system are identified:

● *Intrapersonal level.* We are defining the intrapersonal level as dynamics and properties that pertain within the boundaries of the self-system—for example, focusing on where and how a person experiences awareness of being afraid.

● *Interpersonal level.* By interpersonal level, we mean dynamics that occur between two individuals or between an individual and a subgroup or the full group—for example, two people revealing that they are each afraid of the other, or a lone man in a group describing to all of the women present what it is like to be the only man.

- *Dyadic or subgroup level.* The dyadic or subgroup level refers to dynamics and properties that pertain to the dyad or subgroup as a system in its own right—for example, a subgroup of young, politically active women examining how their shared political values support and impede the personal risks each is willing to take in the group.
- *Group level.* The group level refers to dynamics and properties that pertain to the group as a whole—for example, one group in a graduate program has come to be known as "the cranky, complaining group" despite the fact that no single individual's behavior in that group warrants such a reputation.

Classical Gestalt Theory

HISTORICAL CONTEXT   Fritz Perls was first and foremost an individual therapist, for whom groups were above all a collection of individuals to be worked with one at a time. His groups began as an expedient way to demonstrate his theory and practice to larger numbers of clinicians. For Perls, it was almost serendipity that personal learning occurred for all who witnessed a piece of individual work, and he never seized the opportunity to use the group itself to potentiate individual change (Kepner, 1980).

GESTALT THEORY RELEVANT TO SMALL-GROUP PHENOMENA Although Perls did not make it, the theoretical translation from individual to group level phenomena was easily made. Four theoretical assumptions are particularly relevant to group work: organismic self-regulation, contact, awareness, and an emphasis on the here and now.

Organismic Self-Regulation Gestalt therapy was influenced by the work of the early Gestalt psychologists Koffka, Kohler, and Wertheimer, who discovered that human perception was governed by an innate human need for organization and integrity; that is, people want to make whole or complete patterns out of incomplete or partial stimuli. It was this process of forming whole figures from a less specified ground and assigning a different meaning to the whole than to the accumulation of discrete parts that was described by the early Gestaltists as the whole being more than the sum of its parts. They found that attention or awareness remains with a figure (a gestalt) until it has arrived at as "good a form" as is possible under the circumstances.

What began as a discovery about perceptual responses to visual stimuli led to theories developed and later applied by Lewin and Goldstein to motivation and to total organismic functioning. A set of criteria for healthy human functioning therefore became a person's generic capacity for allowing a recognizable need to emerge (organismic gestalten), mobilizing oneself and one's environment to satisfy that need; replacing that completed need (gestalt destruction) with the next most pressing need, and so on, ad infinitum. Goldstein referred to this process, so vital to psychological as well as physical survival, as organismic self-regulation. When this process is interrupted, when people remain "stuck" with unsatisfied needs or unfinished business, they cannot proceed robustly to genuinely new experiences in life.

For example, early in her therapy, a depressed adult client speaks of her loneliness and isolation. She entered therapy with no clear expectations for her therapy nor has she ever asked the therapist for anything. It soon becomes apparent that, as a child, this woman had systematically learned to rely solely upon herself because of her narcissistic and alcoholic mother's self-absorption and physical and emotional unavailability. This client's ability to solicit from her environment the contact and succor she needed had been interrupted and underdeveloped. The first chapter of therapy therefore is to destructure her overdeveloped capacity for retroflection by exploring the points at which she interrupts herself in getting from her environment what she cannot provide for herself. Does she, for example, experience the sensation? How does she recognize her need? How does she mobilize the energy regarding her felt need?

Similarly, a young couple who have been together two years are exploring the possibility of living together. Each time they consider this possibility they end up fighting and withdrawing from each other and the decision they face. The therapist works with them to explore how they interrupt their excitement and their desire to "move into closer contact," paying special heed to the wisdom of their shared resistance to contact.

Groups exhibit their own tendency toward self-regulation and wholeness in a variety of ways. And this tendency operates well beyond the control or influence of any individual group member, including the leader. For example, an intimate encounter between two group members may be interrupted because of the more pressing need to sharpen the full group's diffuse boundary by attending to the inclusion of a member who has been silent and withdrawn for two sessions. Or consider the situation in which a group seems unable to focus on a member's need to explore his faltering marriage because of feelings evoked but not addressed by a previous piece of work. Groups, like individuals, cannot proceed to new experiences as long as unfinished business stands in the way. Put differently, groups will move into present experiencing toting along and glancing backward toward that which is unfinished as though it were a piece of obscure and cumbersome baggage.

Contact and the Contact Boundary The locus and function of and the "organ" for all this self-regulation activity is the contact boundary between the organism and its environment. As described by Perls, Hefferline, and Goodman (in Polster & Polster, 1973):

> The contact boundary is not so much a part of the organism as it is essentially the organ of a particular relation of the organism and the environment. [p. 102]

> Fundamentally, an organism lives in its environment by maintaining its differences and more importantly by assimilating the environment to its differences; and it is at the boundary that dangers are rejected, obstacles are overcome and the assimilable is selected and appropriated. Now that which is selected and assimilated is always novel; the organism persists by assimilating the novel; by change and growth. For instance, food, as Aristotle used to say, is what is 'unlike' that can become 'like' and in the process of assimilation the organism is in turn changed. Primarily, contact is the awareness of, and behavior toward, the assimilable novelties; and the rejection of the unassimilable novelty. What is pervasive, always the same, or indifferent, is not an object of contact. [p. 100]

The contact boundaries available for individual work include the assimilable differences within the individual, and between the individual and the therapist. In interactive groups, the contact boundaries function in an identical manner, but are multiplied tenfold. Boundaries within each member (e.g., between a woman and her stage fright); between members (e.g., between a man who sees the least appealing attributes of his mother in a female group member who has studiously avoided him because of what she experiences as a familiar and dangerous attraction to "men who abuse me"); between different subgroups (e.g., between those in the group who support and identify with the leader and those who feel constrained by the leader's centrality); between the individual and the subgroup (e.g., between a silent and inactive member and a vociferous, energetic threesome in the group); and so forth. Because growth can and will occur in so many places in groups, it is all the more important to have a set of intervention approaches that capture the "big, buzzing confusion" of group life and its attendant possibilities (James, 1890, p. 224).

Awareness Before contact is possible, however, the organism must become aware of and be able to recognize what it needs and does not have. At an early workshop, Perls said that there are only three things to pay attention to: what you are aware of, what you want, and what you are going to do about it. Thus, awareness is the bedrock, the raw data for the self-regulation process. Perls saw awareness, or focused attention on what is actually happening, as so central to Gestalt therapy that he originally called his approach "concentration therapy."

The awareness function for the individual organism and that for the group organism are identical although they "look" and "feel" different to the observer, and like an individual, a group's awareness of itself and all its members allows for a more complex and richly textured ground, a larger apperceptive mass from which a lively figure can emerge.

The Importance of the Here and Now "To me," Perls said, "nothing exists except the now. Now = experience = awareness = reality. The past is no more and the future not yet. Only the now exists" (in Fagan and Shepherd, 1971, p. 14). It is because of such statements that Gestalt is mistakenly thought of as an ahistorical therapy. Perls's concentration on processes occurring in the present does not mean that he placed little value on people's history. Rather, he believed that all that was unfinished from the past would manifest itself in the here and now.

Similarly, the group does not need to attend to a member's past in search of unfinished business, since the characteristic ways one organizes or interrupts one's experience will manifest themselves in the here and now of the group. In the context of the present and evoked by it, history becomes an enlarged ground from which even more here and now interaction can spring.

Theoretical Links Between General Systems, Group Dynamics, and Gestalt Theories

It is easy to see that there are areas of considerable theoretical similarity between these three sets of theories. Both Gestalt theory and general systems theory attach central importance to system self-regulation, or homeostasis, and the group dynamics field offers norms and roles as the principal means by which this self-regulation occurs.

Gestalt and group dynamics theories draw from general systems theory the notion of "system openness," and share the assumption that system functioning is optimized by boundaries that are intact and definable, yet pliable and semipermeable. In the context of systems theory, a semipermeable boundary allows for the process of negentropy or the importation and exportation of matter-energy and information. In the context of Gestalt theory, the development of the contact boundary allows for the injection of that which is assimilable, and the rejection of that which is unassimilable. In the context of group dynamics, semipermeable boundaries allow for a greater "data base" for expanded choice and consensual validation.

The Gestalt tradition and the group dynamics field both emphasize a here-and-now focus. For the Gestalt therapist, history is alive and present in the current situation, and for the group dynamics trainer, the current situation is the only one that can allow the vital process of consensual validation and reality testing since here-and-now events constitute the only shared data base available to a group.

Gestalt theory's attention to closure—that is, the organismic need for completed gestalts—is somewhat akin to the group dynamicist's attention to the sequential and epigenetic nature of stages of group development. In both traditions, some tasks and needs must be completed or resolved before the group can proceed to its next set of priorities.

There is a theoretical relationship between the general systems concept of equifinality (that living systems will find multiple routes to the same end, there being no single best route) and Gestalt therapy as the first nonadjustment therapy. Prior to Gestalt therapy, the aim of all therapies was to assist the patient in adjusting to an externally defined standard of health. But Gestalt's emphasis on organismic self-regulation contributed a radical definition of health in the sense that it viewed organismic well-being as the creative reciprocal adjustment between the organism and its environment. Through contact, both are changed (Perls et al., 1951, vol. 2).

This concludes our discussion of the theoretical contributions of each of the three fields. Next we will present a set of intervention strategies premised in the marriage of these theories.

APPROACHES TO GESTALT GROUP PROCESS INTERVENTIONS

In this section the preceding theoretical contributions form the ground for a discussion of four specific approaches to group process interventions. These are (a) the goals of Gestalt group process work, (b) stage-related interventions, (c) level-related interventions, and (d) regulatory system interventions.

Goals

The goal of the Gestalt group process approach is to work toward expanding the group's (and its members') ability to mobilize itself to get what it needs from within and without and to develop its capacity for social responsibility—that is, "response-ability" to and among its members. This is accomplished by (a) increasing the group's awareness of itself and all its members, (b) increasing the total area of choicefulness available to the group and its members, and (c) increasing the group's capacity for contact with its environment and its subparts by developing all essential boundaries with integrity, permeability, and flexibility. In order to accomplish these goals, group leaders must consider stage, level, and regulatory system–related interventions. The remainder of this section is given over to a discussion of these three classes of interventions.

Stage-Related Interventions

Some interventions are uniquely suited to particular stages of a group's development. Figure 12-2 identifies leader goals and activities that are stage related.

Level-Related Interventions

Use of the analytical construct of levels can lend coherence to leader experience and intervention choices. Work must occur on all levels of the system to maximize growth at any single level. Group phenomena are occurring at all levels of the system simultaneously, and a leader's choice to intervene at one level precludes, for that moment, the option to intervene at a different level—a different choice that often would have been equally appropriate. Equifinality operates here as in all social system phenomena: There are many paths to the same end, and groups move toward increasing awareness, choicefulness, and contact, in short, toward system self-regulation, via a bewildering array of behavioral innovations at various levels.

Consider the following two examples of interventions that might be made at different levels of system, based on the same behavioral observation.

EXAMPLE 1. A participant in a weekend workshp with four hours left, states that his mind is elsewhere and that he does not feel very "hooked into the group with so little time left." At the individual/intrapsychic level, the therapist might ask, "How does it feel to be here and not be here at the same time?" At the interpersonal level, the therapist might ask others in the group, "How is it to hear that John is packing his bags?" At the group level, the therapist might remark, "You may be speaking for the group, John, which may be currently struggling with the choice between, on the one hand, "How should we use the four hours we have left?" and, on the other, "What's the use? In four hours, I'll never see these folks again."

EXAMPLE 2. A tear appears on a woman's cheek. The therapist might ask her, "What are you doing to block yourself?" or "Is there someone

FIGURE 12-2
Stage-Related Interventions

	Leader's Goals	Leader's Activities
STAGE 1 Identity and Dependency	1) To set up relationships with and between members quickly 2) To get data generated about the following member concerns: a) Myself and my identity in the group b) How others here will relate to me c) The process and goals of the group	1) Contracting and setting boundaries 2) Encouraging interpersonal contact of members with each other 3) Giving information about the methods to be used 4) Legitimizing work at all levels of system
STAGE 2 Influence and Counter- dependence	1) To increase member differentiation and divergence 2) To increase member role flexibility	1) Heightening awareness of the norms that are operating in the group 2) Encouraging challenge and open expression of difference and dissatisfaction 3) Differentiating roles from persons
STAGE 3 Intimacy and Inter- dependence	1) To support the occurrence of real contact within and between members 2) To enable the group members to monitor and maintain their own functioning as a system	1) Maintaining a consultant role and staying out of the way 2) Helping the group arrive at some closure 3) Acknowledging the unfinished business

From "Gestalt Group Process" by E. Kepner, 1980. In B. Feder and R. Ronall (Eds.), *Beyond the Hot Seat: Gestalt Approaches to Group*. New York: Brunner Mazel. Copyright 1980. Adapted by permission.

here you want to make a statement to right now?" or "I'm wondering if this group is a safe place to cry?"

A leader's ability to shuttle between levels of the system provides the group with more mastery over its own process by increasing its awareness and its response repertoire and choices. Shuttling or creating a balance among intervention levels also energizes the system for work. Sometimes individual or dyadic work becomes clear or assimilable only when it is translated to the group level. I recall an energized discussion between two men in a group about their experience in Vietnam. What in the moment appeared to be an engaging if anomalous and isolated exchange between two members subsequently emerged as a significant group theme about courage and risk taking in our group. The exploration and deeper articulation of this theme at the group level provided both men with a greater degree of integration than they had previously had, and lent the group a greater degree of trust and cohesion.

And finally, shuttling between levels supports the steady development of the group. Because groups are integrated social systems with properties of holism, development at any one level supports the development of other levels. Conversely, the lack of development at any one level impedes the growth of other levels. For example, a women's group was foundering and unstable until the fact that there was a subgroup of heterosexual women and a subgroup of lesbian women had been openly identified and explored by the whole group. An intervention with the group as a whole will always affect the individuals in it, and similarly, an intervention with an individual will always change the complexion of the full group.

Figure 12-3 presents goals and examples of leader interventions at the various levels of the group. A host of factors go into a leader's choice about the level of the intervention.[3]

PERSONAL EXPERIENCE, SKILLS, AND VALUES OF THE THERA-PIST In part, the intervention choice is a perceptual one—we tend to stage interventions based on the figure that is uppermost to us in the moment, on that which has most grabbed our attention as a result of our own personal history and training. Those who come to group work from a long history of doing individual psychotherapy are more likely to see opportunities for intrapsychic interventions. Those therapists who come to group settings from organizational, educational, and administrative backgrounds may be more keen on larger system interventions (subgroup and full group).

The notion that values are attached to an intervention choice deserves further discussion. Mention has been made elsewhere of a significant values shift from Perls's emphasis on each person for himself or herself to a greater appreciation for the social responsibility humans have for one another (Kepner, 1980). Earlier, Perls was quoted as saying there are but three conditions for self-regulation: attending to what you are aware of, what you want, and what you are going to do about it. Compare that to the following set of conditions from GIC training materials in 1980:

> First, you need to know that you exist. Then you need to know what you are feeling. Third, you must make known what you feel. Fourth, to know what you need that you don't have. Fifth, to ask for what you need. And last, to develop responsibility toward others.

FIGURE 12-3
Levels of Interventions: Goals and Examples

LEVELS OF INTERVENTION	*GOALS OF INTERVENTION*	*EXAMPLES OF INTERVENTION*
INTRAPERSONAL LEVEL Dynamics and properties that exist within the boundaries of the self system.	To bring the self system into better contact with its internal or external environment by enhancing the individual's sensation, awareness, energy flow, contact, and withdrawal capabilities.	1) An individual explores a split in himself by enacting the body posture of each side or having a dialogue between the two estranged sides. 2) An individual focuses on her relationship to her colitis by speaking, first as herself to her illness, and then as her intestinal tract, or as the food passing through. 3) An individual speaks to each group member about what he imagines they think of him on a particular theme, not as an interpersonal event, but as a way of accessing disowned and projected aspects of self.
INTERPERSONAL LEVEL Dynamics that occur between individuals or between an individual and a subgroup or the full group.	To make clear the boundary (limits, rereceptivities, vulnerability, barriers) that exists between an individual and another and the exchange that takes place of influence, affection, information, nurturance, and stimulation. To heighten contact, usually through differentiation.	1) Two people who have been in an accusatory exchange are asked to make only I-statements to each other for the next 5 minutes. 2) Two group members who have become friends outside the group are arguing over the amount of time they spend together. One woman is eager to spend more time together, and the other is firm in protecting the small amount of time she has to herself. They are invited to tell each other how the value so important to the other actually benefits and enriches their friendship, e.g., "Jennie, tell Alice what you gain by her insistence on alone times, and Alice, tell Jennie what you gain from her insistence of more time together."
DYADIC OR SUBGROUP LEVEL Dynamics and properties that pertain to the dyad or subgroup as a system in its own right.	To develop and heighten a consciousness of the two-person system or the subgroup system having a	1) The therapist makes the following observations: "The reference has been made to the 'lunch bunch'; those of you

Figure 12-3 (continued)

LEVELS OF INTERVENTION	GOALS OF INTERVENTION	EXAMPLES OF INTERVENTION
	life of its own, larger than that of its individual member, usually through defining joint or shared characteristics.	who eat together every Thursday. How does that subgroup impact the rest of you?" 2) To two men in the group, the therapist says, "What I notice is that the two of you rely on each other almost exclusively, seldom reaching out to others here. Do you have some shared belief about doing that?" 3) "Sharon and John, I've noticed that the two of you share a concern that we not open the group to new members right now. I also see you both reminding us to start and end on time. I'm wondering what it's like for the two of you to be the 'keepers of our gates' in these ways?"
GROUP LEVEL The group level refers to those dynamics and properties that pertain to the group as a whole.	To develop and heighten a consciousness of the group having a life of its own, with its own characteristics, which are more than the sum of its parts.	1) The group is avoiding talking about the inclusion-exclusion issue and two subgroups are forming. The therapist says, "I notice that the price of admission seems to be to do a piece of personal work. Those persons who have not yet done a major piece of work are not saying much and are not being spoken to directly. Bob, Cindy, Carol, and Greg, on the other hand, all talk a lot to each other. Does one have to do a piece of personal work here in order to be in the 'in-group'?" 3) There is consistent and humorous reference to one member's tendency to be "prickly" and argumentative. The therapist might say, "What does John's combative stance do for this group? It seems to draw a lot of our energy and attention."

Adapted from "Levels of Interventions,"
Second Year Post-Graduate Training
Program lecture materials, Gestalt Institute of Cleveland, 1984.

This espoused value of a "wider ecology," of nurturing the social and physical field or environment within which we are embedded, has major implications for the practice of group psychotherapy. It means that work at the dyadic, subgroup, and group levels of the system must be viewed as ends in themselves, and it begins to close the gap between the goals and purposes of T-groups and therapy groups.

ASSESSMENT OF WHERE THERE IS AVAILABLE ENERGY FOR WORK Clues to working at the intrapsychic level include movement or agitation by an individual, interruptions with words or gestures, noticeable affect, or a member's long silence. At the interpersonal level, an intervention may be called for when two members appear stuck in circular or dead-end interaction, where the distance for interaction seems inappropriate, or where both people are projecting. A group level intervention may be appropriate when there is either very high or very low energy in the group, when member roles are too rigid, or when the group is divided over a particular issue (Fredericson, training materials, Santa Barbara Gestalt Training Center, Calif.).

IDENTIFICATION OF THE LEVELS IN NEED OF FURTHER DEVELOPMENT Because system levels are interdependent, work must occur on all levels of the system to maximize growth at any single level. Conversely, inattention to the development of one level of the system will limit the growth potential of other levels. For example, the comfort level of the most sexually anxious member will impact the group's ability to deal with the issue of sexual attraction.

STAGES OF THE GROUP'S DEVELOPMENT Some interventions at specific levels of the system are stage dependent. This is perhaps most true when a group is in the first stage of development. People come to a therapy group to do work that will provide them with significant personal gains as individuals, and although that work may require interpersonal interaction, the participant attaches most importance to the intrapsychic consequences of the interaction with others. So people come eager to begin working immediately—usually before members have come to know one another and before the idiosyncratic complexion of the group system with its attendant norms, roles, and milieu has emerged. When a group member makes a bid to do an important piece of individual work early on, the leader is faced with a choice: If the work is allowed to proceed with an intrapsychic focus, group members are not able to support that work with sufficient concentration because they are absorbed in their own joining process, and the group is not adequately bounded or defined yet as a cybernetic system to be able to contain, assimilate, and use the important information being presented. The result of the group's inability to respond adequately may be the sense that this is not a safe arena in which to work.

Instead, the leader may opt to reframe the issue as an interpersonal or group level issue on the basis of the assumption that every issue raised in a group in its most generic form resides in more than a single individual. In the interest of discovering the areas of similarity among members and developing a shared data base (tasks that support the creation of a group's boundary), the leader may ask who else feels the same way or identifies with that member. Reframing this as an interpersonal option invites inevitable dependency on the leader as social engineer to provide a level of activity and influence not expected of other members and may initially frustrate the initiating member's wish for a fuller piece of intrapsychic work. But the interpersonal or group levels of system are the only levels that can sustain any significant amount of activity and attention at this point in a group's development.

Another stage at which interventions at particular levels are indicated is the stormy second stage of influence and counterdependence. During this phase, there is more mileage to be gained in interpersonal and group level intervention. Encouraging interpersonal contact between members and between members and the leader in a way that heightens differences and conflict supports the steady development of the group. Group level interventions that point out emerging norms and group maintenance roles (gatekeeper, harmonizer, tough battler, etc.) allow the group both to appreciate what it has created in support of its own self-regulation processes and to destructure that role-bound residue that is no longer useful.

Yet another stage at which one level of intervention is preferable to another is at the end of a group. Here, members need to begin the process of disengagement and assimilation of what has been learned and what the group has meant to them. In light of this task—a highly individual one—it is not useful to invite further work at the interpersonal level of system or to invite the introduction of any new material at all, for that matter. Group level observations and interpersonal contact may well be necessary—but they should be made in the service of closure at the intrapsychic level.

TYPE AND POPULATION OF THE GROUP For an inpatient group of schizophrenics whose ability to separate inner from outer experience is severely limited, interventions at larger levels of the system are likely to exacerbate their identity diffusion. On the other hand, a training group composed of therapists whose professional practices are made up solely of individual patients may be in greatest need of development at the subgroup and full group levels.

THE TYPE OF RESISTANCE THAT IS MANIFESTED In work with a confluent couple or a confluent group that resists differentiation, it may be more useful to support each person's boundaries via intrapsychic work than to emphasize the already well-developed sense of the "we" of the couple or the group. Similarly, when projection and retroflection are occurring (externalizing unwanted aspects of oneself and internalizing those impulses to act on one's environment by acting them out toward oneself), opportunities should be created for interpersonal contact that can support the destructuring of those resistances.

THE LEVEL AT WHICH THE GROUP MAY BE STUCK When a group is stuck, it can usually be unfrozen by shifting the group's awareness to a level other than that at which the group seems stuck. For example, it is frequently the case that deeper intrapsychic work seems appropriate, given the issues members have presented, and yet there seems to be little energy available in anyone for taking the plunge. As a leader, I must ask myself whether there is unfinished business at the interpersonal level, or whether some developmental task needs attention at the group level. A member of one group I led seemed unable to marshal the energy to proceed to a rather pressing piece of work on her incestuous relationship with her father until the group had dealt with a budding romance between two group members that had not been openly spoken about in the group. In another instance, a long-simmering conflict between two separate factions or subgroups emerged out into the open only when a member whose participation had been minimal and whose attendance had been erratic was finally perceived to have joined the group. My assumption here was that until the system level boundary, that is, the boundary around the group itself, had been made whole and complete, energy was bound up with this subterranean inclusion issue that would otherwise have been available for working the subgroup conflict issue.

Regulatory System Interventions

Group mechanisms such as norms and role assignments comprise the "wiring" of a group's self-regulatory system. As previously mentioned in the group dynamics theory section, norms must be examined periodically to allow for maximum awareness and choice. For example, the very norms of politeness, consideration, and tentativeness that provide initial safety are the same norms that people experience as stifling and frustrating as a group presses toward conflict and member differentiation.

Similarly, group roles that initially served a purpose can become rigid, stereotypic, or the exclusive domain of a single group member. This occurs even though those roles emerged in large part as a response to the needs of the group rather than the manifestation of individual preferences.

> A group, like an individual, requires that certain functions be performed to enable it to go through the cycle of experience of awareness, energy, contact and withdrawal or completion. Depending on how people behave in the early stages of a group, one person is more likely to carry or be identified with one of these functions. For example, the person who initially provides the energy to get things moving in a group gets "assigned" to this role, and the other members, and perhaps the leader, rely on or provoke this person to energize them. Some people carry the awareness function because they are particularly good observers and reporters of their own experience, or of what they see, hear or sense going on in others. Some people who are outgoing and caring, tend to carry the contact or caretaker function; those who are assertive or more sponta-neous provide the impulsivity and creativity in the group. All of these functions are positive ones and help the group to accomplish its work. However, when these functions are identified with one person rather than being seen as a function which everyone has the capability of expressing, everyone's behavior is more stereotyped. Once roles become somewhat fixed, group members are likely to resist the attempts of any one person who deviates from the assigned position, since a change in any one person in a system affects the functioning of everyone else in the system. [Kepner, 1980, p. 20]

As is the case with norms, a leader needs to invite the group to examine the patterns, functions, and limitations of its role assignments.

This concludes our discussion of the four key approaches to Gestalt group process interventions: goals, stages, levels, and regulatory system-related interventions.

CONCLUSION

This chapter has attempted two tasks: first, to spell out the theoretical contributions to our understanding about Gestalt group process made by three different but interrelated fields, general systems, group dynamics, and Gestalt theory; and second, to present a set of intervention strategies and considera-tions in doing Gestalt group process work.

ACKNOWLEDGMENTS

I am indebted to the following people for helpful comments and suggestions on earlier drafts of this chapter: Jesse Carlock, Isabel Fredericson, Joseph Handlon, Sybil Perlmutter, Susan Straley, and Jean Westcott.

NOTES

1. Many of the ideas presented here are the result of a collaborative effort of a number of GIC's professional staff members over the last 20 years: Frances Baker, John Carter, Isabel Fredericson, Leonard Hirsch, Elaine Kepner, Carolyn Lukensmeyer, Ed Nevis, Claire Stratford, the late Richard Wallen, and Joseph Zinker.

2. I am indebted to the late Don Keller, Department of Organizational Behavior, Case Western Reserve University, for this summary of Bennis-Shepherd, Slater, Tuckman, Schutz, Srivastva, and Obert.

3. Drawn from lecture materials, second year Post-graduate Training Program, GIC, 1984.

REFERENCES

Aronson, E. (1972). *The social animal*. San Francisco: W. H. Freeman.

Beisser, A. (1971). The paradoxical theory of change. In J. Fagan & I. Shepherd (Eds.), *Gestalt therapy now*. New York: Harper Colophon Books.

Bennis, W. G., Berlew, D. E., Schein, E. H., Steele, F. I. (1973). *Interpersonal dynamics: Essays and readings on human interaction*. Homewood, IL: Dorsey. Third Edition.

Berggren, J. (1982). *Contact boundaries in Gestalt therapy*. Working Paper, Gestalt Institute of Cleveland.

Berrien, F. K. (1968). *General and social systems*. New Brunswick, NJ: Rutgers University Press.

Bion, W. R. (1959). *Experiences in groups*. New York: Basic Books.

Bradford, L. P., Gibb, J. R., Benne, K. D. (1964). *T group theory and laboratory method*. New York: John Wiley.

Buckley, W. (1967). *Sociology and modern systems theory*. Englewood Cliffs, NJ: Prentice-Hall.

Cartwright, D. & Zander, A. (1968). *Group dynamics research and theory* (3rd ed.). New York: Harper and Row.

Cohn, R. C. (1971). Therapy in groups: Psychoanalytic, experiential, and Gestalt. In J. Fagan & I. Shepherd (Eds.), *Gestalt therapy now*. New York: Harper Colophon Books.

Feibleman and Friend, 1945, "The Structure and Function of Organization," *The Philosophical Review*, 54: 19–44.

Glidewell, J. C. (1970). *Choice points*. Cambridge, MA: MIT Press.

Hare, P. A. (1977). Theories of group development and categories for interaction analysis. In R. T. Golembiewski & A. Blumberg (Eds.), *Sensitivity training and the laboratory approach* (3rd ed.). Itasca, IL: F. E. Peacock Publishers.

Harrison, R. (1977). Defenses and the need to know. In R. T. Golembiewski & A. Blumberg (Eds., *Sensitivity training and the laboratory approach* (3rd ed.). Itasca, IL: F. E. Peacock Publishers.

James, William, *The Principles of Psychology: Volume I*, New York: Henry Holt & Co., 1890.

Jourard, S. (1973). "Healthy Personality and Self-Disclosure," in Bennis, Berlew, Schein, and Steele, *Interpersonal Dynamics*, 3rd edition, Homewood, Illinois: Dorsey Press.

Keller, D. (1980). A summary of theories of small group development. Unpublished manuscript, Case Western Reserve University, Cleveland, Ohio.

Kepner, E. (1980). Gestalt group process. In B. Feder & R. Ronall (Eds.), *Beyond the hot seat: Gestalt approaches to group*. New York: Brunner Mazel.

Kingsbury, S. (1972). Dilemmas for the trainer. In W. G. Dyer, *Modern theory and group training*. New York: Van Nosstrand Reinhold.

Kolb, D., Rubin, I., McIntyre, J. (1984). Group dynamics. In *Organizational psychology: An experiential approach*. Englewood Cliffs, NJ: Prentice-Hall. Fourth ed.

Leupnitz, D. A., & Tulkin, S. (1980). The cybernetic epistemology of Gestalt therapy. *Psychotherapy: Theory, Research and Practice, 17*(2).

Lieberman, M. A. (1977). Up the right mountain, down the wrong path: Theory development for people-changing groups. In R. T. Golembiewski & A. Blumberg (Eds.), *Sensitivity training and the laboratory approach* (3rd ed.). Hasca, IL: F. E. Peacock Publishers.

Marmor, J. (1983). Systems thinking in psychiatry. *American Journal of Psychiatry 140*(7).

Miller, J. G. (1965). Living systems: Basic concepts. *Behavioral Science, 10*(3), 193–411.

Mills, T. M. (1967). *The sociology of small groups*. Englewood Cliffs, NJ: Prentice-Hall.

Nevis, E. C. (1987). *Organizational consulting: Gestalt approach*. New York: The Gestalt Institute of Cleveland Press.

Perls, F. S. (1969). *Ego, Hunger and Aggression*. New York: Random House.

Perls, F. S. (1971). Four Lectures. In J. Fagan & I. Shephard (Eds.), *Gestalt therapy now*. New York: Harper Colophon Books.

Perls, F. S., Hefferline, R., & Goodman, P. (1951). *Gestalt theory*. New York: Dell Publishing Co.

Peters, D. R., & Joslyn, L. M. (1977). Transference phenomena in laboratory training groups. In R. T. Golembiewski & A. Blumberg (Eds.), *Sensitivity training and the laboratory approach* (3rd ed.). Itasca, IL: F. E. Peacock Publishers.

Polster, E., & Polster, M. (1973). *Gestalt therapy integrated*. New York: Random House.

Schein, E. H., & Bennis, W. G. (1965). *Personal and organizational change through group methods: The laboratory approach.* New York: Wiley.

Shepherd, I. L. (1971). Limitations and cautions in the Gestalt approach. In J. Fagan & I. Shepherd (Eds.), *Gestalt therapy now.* New York: Harper Colophon Books.

Sullivan, Harry S. (1968). *The Interpersonal Theory of Psychiatry.* New York: W. W. Norton & Co., Inc.

Von Bertalanffy, L. (1967). General systems theory and psychiatry an overview. Presented at the 123rd annual meeting of the American Psychiatric Association, Detroit, Michigan, May 8–12, 1967.

Wallen, R. (1971). Gestalt therapy and gestalt psychology. In J. Fagan & I. Shepherd (Eds.), *Gestalt therapy now.* New York: Harper Colophon Books.

Wheelis, A. (1973). *How people change.*

Yalom, I. D. (1970). *The theory and practice of group psychotherapy.* New York: Basic Books.

Zinker, J. (1980). The developmental process of a gestalt therapy group. In B. Feder & R. Ronall (Eds.), *Beyond the hot seat: Gestalt approaches to group.* New York: Brunner/Mazel.

13

Gestalt Thinking and the Therapeutic Milieu

CLAIRE DENNERY STRATFORD, M.S.W.

GESTALT THERAPY WAS ORIGINALLY developed as a modality for individual process. Although the focus on individuals remains the primary level of application today, a literature is developing having to do with applications to groups, couples, families, and organizations. Just as the most basic principles of Gestalt theory can be used as a basis for interventions and facilitation with groups, couples, families, and organizations, these same principles are applicable to the development of interactive environments for learning and healing. This is a specialized focus on a complex larger system that aims at impacting the interface of environmental system and individual development. Such a therapeutic environment can support the improvement of impaired functioning and the enhancement of natural growth and development of individuals. In this chapter, it is my intention to discuss some Gestalt principles as they apply to the social psychological climates of living settings, to the organizing and administrative aspects of such programs, and to the system as a totality, as well as to the interpersonal interactive transactions that take place in such settings.

In his development of a novel therapy, Fritz Perls made use of his training in psychoanalysis and his reactions to that training. In interaction with field theory, perception theory, and existential philosophy, the prevailing intellectual crosscurrents of his own milieu, he developed a root system of thought capable of stimulating fresh possibilities for psychotherapy (Smith, 1976).

The highly synergistic interaction of Fritz and Laura Perls, Paul Goodman, Isadore From, and others strengthened this root system into the development of a sturdy plant. These roots have fed a present Gestalt methodology that gives attentiveness to the organism in its environment; to past and present internal and interpersonal dynamics; and to the importance of context, meaning, and quality of experience.

In the arena of psychotherapy, however, most attention is still focused on the individual, couple, or family as figure, and the broader processes of the living environment remain ground. By turning attention to the environment as figure, it is possible to develop a consciousness of the variety of existing processes in any milieu. With such consciousness, choices can be made that help to provide support and opportunities for growth-promoting challenge to clients and helpers alike in the healing environment. It is also possible to be more conscious of the subtle noxious forces at work in many treatment settings that may undercut the main work of the system.

These awarenesses and choices are potentially available in a wide range of learning/treatment environments such as hospital programs for psychiatric patients, group-living settings, day treatment programs, sheltered workshops, and many kinds of educational programs. There is also a growing interest in the applications of Gestalt concepts to a variety of larger system settings in business and industry (Merry & Brown, 1987; Nevis, 1987). This chapter derives primarily from experience within psychiatric settings, where I have had an opportunity to develop programs based on Gestalt notions about experiential process.

There is a long history of therapeutic milieus and considerable literature in the mental health field that addresses the concept. Maxwell Jones pioneered and documented the results of therapeutic community in England in the 1950s, and others continued to explore that treatment method in a variety of ways in the following three decades (Jones, 1953, 1968). Traditionally, therapeutic milieus have concentrated on the following four concepts: establishment of positive expectations, involvement of community members in their own fate, development of group cohesiveness, and an accentuated group pressure and support for healthy behaviors. Additionally, a cornerstone of the therapeutic milieu has been the daily or weekly community meeting, where gains and lapses are brought to the attention of the community and decisions regarding privileges and status are made at the community level (Kraft, 1966). Any or all of the just-mentioned hallmarks of therapeutic milieus may be integrated into an environment that builds on Gestalt concepts. A Gestalt theory base provides some additional and different useful factors, which will be discussed in the remainder of this chapter.

UNDERLYING GESTALT-BASED PRINCIPLES AND ATTITUDES

The four basic perspectives listed below can be used as the framework for thinking about the therapeutic milieu from a Gestalt theory base. In their applications and implications, they form a procedural and interactional climate very different from that of many treatment environments based on more traditional psychiatric or educational thinking.

1. Attention to influencing the environment as well as to influencing the individual within the environment
2. Regard for the environment as a new and different level of system from the individual or interpersonal level of functioning
3. An attitude that looks for and emphasizes strengths and health
4. Inclusion of the administrative process in attention to consistency of the processes that support health and development

The first essential principle is that the design of the therapeutic milieu requires the practitioner to pay as much attention to influencing the environment as to influencing clients. It is almost impossible to overemphasize this orientation. The goal is to produce an environment that offers its inhabitants the maximum possibility of coherent interchange, stimulation, and nourishment, a culture within which individual growth and development can take place. Attention is placed on the vitality, growth, and development of the milieu at the same time that the goal of the particular program may be the vitality, growth, and development of the individuals within that milieu.

There are some important differences between working with individuals and designing a milieu. Gestalt theory has always attended to the individual in terms of internal and interpersonal processes and assumes that personal vitality requires an interchange at the self boundary. The general emphasis has been to support individuals to heighten awareness of their responsibility for the self. Therapy, then, has involved drawing attention experientially to self-defeating patterns, developing a larger range of behavioral options, and encouraging the person to seek a more gratifying way of life. It is expected that unresolved prior experience is carried into the present in the form of obsolete responses to current experience. This historical material and the encrustations of habit that have layered the original experience are impacted in the present by energized contact with current experience and can be shifted to new and better ways of interaction with the self and the surrounding world.

In the development of a therapeutic milieu, the patterns of interaction that the environment as culture offers, suggests, or demands become the figure. Thus the emphasis is still on organism in environment and the inter-change across a boundary. However, the object of intervention becomes the environment. In the case of therapeutic environments aimed at healing, it is necessary to build an interactive process through this attention to the milieu that will support the repair of impaired internal processes of its inhabitants. Many people who enter a treatment program have not developed strong internal self-regulatory processes. It is unrealistic to expect that they can shift self-defeating patterns at the same time that the environment may offer inconsistent messages and nonreciprocal processes, a situation that is com-mon in many "therapeutic milieus." A responsibility resides in the environ-ment to provide a healing culture.

As an example of a nonhealing culture, a community meeting may offer several messages to its members that contradict each other, such as: "You have the right and ability to decide" and "We (the staff) will interdict when we don't agree." "This is a positive incentive system" and "You can count on being publicly shamed if you do something wrong." "Privacy is a value" and "There is no place to hide." Such a contradictory process may stimulate an increase in the already dysfunctional patterns of self-protection of the clients in the system.

An example of a consistent and healing message is the expectation that personal self-care and dress can support self-esteem, accompanied by avail-ability of suitable clothing, assistance in selection, attentiveness and appreci-ation, good modeling, nonacceptance of pajamas as daytime wear, staff who wear street clothes, absence of white coats, learning opportunities in the skills that support attractive appearance, opportunity for individuality, and so on as well as a consciousness of the dysfunctionality of shame as a method of stimulating self-esteem. In the matter of dress, if the emphasis is on simply getting a patient to wear attractive clothing, staff may be tempted to make fun of inappropriate dress. If the emphasis is on the development of skills of selection, sense of appearance, and pride in appearance, the environmental suggestions and supports will take on a different tone. Clearly, the emphasis of leadership in such a program will be a key factor, and the modes of transmission of the emphasis will also play a role in the fabric of the milieu.

To recapitulate the first principle, in order to create a therapeutic milieu, one must pay as much attention to influencing the kinds of things mentioned in the examples above as to influencing specific individuals in the setting.

The second essential principle is that a milieu is a system level set of processes. By raising to awareness the characteristics of a milieu, prac-titioners are able to develop the particular processes that will be most helpful to a particular population of clients who will use that culture. Some specifics of this will be addressed later. However, at the outset it is important to acknowledge that what is most difficult for practitioners to achieve is the ability to think of process at a larger system level. People who move from the practice of individual therapy to family therapy must make a shift in consciousness in order to be able to perceive and conceptualize at the level of family systems. It is a similar leap of cognition to move to apprehend an inpatient program, a halfway house, or a classroom as a total system in operation that encompasses all levels, including administrative processes and staff–patient or teacher–student interactions.

As an example, if a program is aimed at treating people who characteristically behave in a dependent way and passively accept the opinions of others (in Gestalt terms are chronic introjectors), we obviously expect that involvement in decision making on their own behalf and support for their expression of opinions will lead to greater self-differentiation and to a more active stance. In addition, in the interests of consistency and coherence, the system patterns of developing goals and action plans for the program itself have an impact on all who are involved in the program. Encouragement on the part of the administration of the program for independence within the staff will have an effect on the degree to which patients or clients within the program experience tolerance for self-determination. The expectation of independent acts must be embedded across many layers of the system. The covert messages within an environment are always louder than the overt ones. Without focus on the subtleties of the milieu and a capacity to think at a total system level, the best intended programs run the risk of undercutting the expressed goals. Perls (1973) often said that one should pay attention to the obvious. Unfortunately, the obvious is often unseen when the emphasis is on the behavior or "pathology" of the patient and the ground of pathology within the environment is undernoticed.

The third principle that is basic to a Gestalt framework for therapeutic milieus is that the environment must respond to health as well as to pathology or dysfunction. A Gestalt perspective sees dysfunctional behavior as anachronistic fixed patterns of perception and behavior that result in inability to make contact with current contexts. This dilemma is remediable by development of "safe emergencies," which provide an opportunity for a fresh response. In traditional individual therapy, this calls for the therapist to produce a microenvironment in which safe emergencies can occur. A comparison of the patient's dysfuntion to an ideal process remains available in the consciousness of the therapist, and the therapist pays particular attention to the areas of strength and health in the patient that can support fresh behavioral alternatives. This attitude, which attends as closely to that which is working well as to that which is causing trouble, is indispensable to the design of a healthy environment. It is not possible for a person to develop a healthy sense of self in a setting where the positive aspects of personhood are experienced as invisible. There should be nothing in the processes of a setting designed for healing or learning that will cause persons to feel any more incompetent, ill, helpless, or out of control than they already felt at the time of entry. Acknowledgment of a person's strengths at the time of entry into a therapeutic milieu is a strong step in this direction.

An environment in which staff can perceive only pathology or are trained to note and respond to pathology and respond neutrally to health is, by definition, untherapeutic. However, in most clinical training of mental health professionals of all disciplines, we systematically teach people to recognize and respond to abnormality and pathology. We teach them to be more interested in what is not going well than in what is going well.

For instance, our clinical records are a relatively unbalanced account of the failings and shortcomings of patients. Rarely is there a substantive description of the healthy aspects of the patient. The actuality of this repository of uncomplimentary information is in and of itself a noxious reality. We are naive to think that the existence of such a record does not have many subtle effects on the attitudes of staff and on the subject of the report. An example of larger system process awareness in relation to perception of strengths is attention to written material and an active policy that supports a balanced account. A potential for supporting awareness of strengths and existing skills is to build such awareness into any transmission of information system, thus making it more figural to staff and inevitably reflecting that consciousness back to clients.

In keeping with the second-mentioned principle of relating to system level sets of processes, the degree to which the strengths of the program as well as its problems are acknowledged and addressed in a balanced way will have an effect on the degree to which individuals also will maintain a consciousness of individual strengths.

The fourth basic principle and cornerstone of any program is that the processes of the system must be internally consistent and coherent. That is, particular attention must be paid to the existence of double messages and systemic "isometric exercises." Such an isometric exercise is the situation where the staff works very hard to encourage some skill, self-definition, or particular attitudinal stance in clients and, at the same time, some process or procedure within the program has the effect of undoing that same goal. In many instances, there is no consciousness or acknowledgment that this is the case on the part of the staff of a program, which compounds stress on the client. This type of system ambiguity is common, and the most usual response of staff is to sense that the situation exists, but feel powerless to modify it. The staff do not address it and thus contribute an element of passivity and denial to the larger system. Often, the newest staff members are best able to articulate the contradictions, yet lack the positional power to address them. A healthy milieu makes it easier for this articulation to be heard and values the freshest perspectives. Many programs exhort clients to take responsibility for their own behavior while, at the same time, the setting does not take responsibility for its "behavior." Thus the client often experiences both being surrounded by an environment that does not take responsibility for its own behavior and at the same time being asked to take responsibility while hemmed in by many regulations and prohibitions. The client experiences a double message, and the staff have engaged in the futility of putting energy into two mutually exclusive or contradictory processes. Such double messages are not altogether avoidable in any system. Some are less toxic than others. Erving Goffman's writings about total institutions speak to the worst examples of negativity of environment (Goffman, 1961, 1963). Yet, many treatment programs abound with small and avoidable examples of inconsistencies and undermining of goals. The prerequisite for guarding against this inconsistency is the ability to think at a system level and to see the isomorphism of processes at various levels, both positive and negative.

Gestalt theory is based in perception and meaning. System level awareness is dependent on sufficient consciousness on the part of enough individuals to provide an embeddedness in the culture of a particular kind of perception or knowledge. In the case of the therapeutic milieu, the total system's ability for self-awareness and perception of the relationship of its internal processes to its reason for existence is crucial. If there is no one present in the system who can think in terms of the metaprocesses that exist, there is a situation of ill health in the system that is analogous to a situation where an individual is unaware of self-defeating patterns. This, of course, is the work of Gestalt organizational consultants (Nevis, 1987). In the field of business and industry, such self-defeating processes lead to lowered worker morale and energy invested in work, and productivity decreases. In the field of human services, where the product is the well-being of people, the absence of awareness becomes even more crucial.

It is always useful to look at the total picture of system dynamics and individual participation. This need not produce a conflicting polarization. That is, factors in the environment may induce certain experience and accompanying behavior in clients. This does not relieve clients of the responsibility for undesirable behaviors. At the same time, clients' responsibility for altering their behavior in the world does not relieve the treatment team, which includes both clients and staff, of the responsibility for using the situation to identify and begin to teach the missing skill. Likewise, the personal responsibility of clients for their own behavior does not relieve the staff of the responsibility for evaluating how a factor in the milieu supports or hinders the larger purposes of the program and other efforts to teach the needed skills.

As an example, in psychiatric hospitals there are often patients who display "inappropriate" sexual behavior. However, there may also exist a belief system that the staff is not aware of, that staff are sexual creatures and patients are asexual. This assignment of asexuality to patients may be the result of anxiety on the part of staff because there are no opportunities for healthy development of adult sexuality for patients within the hospital. Thus, expressions of sexual feelings on the part of patients automatically become "inappropriate." Should a staff member wear attractive clothng that stimulates a patient to behave "inappropriately," one could define the issue as a behavior problem on the part of the patient, as an issue of interpersonal insensitivity on the part of the staff member, or as an environmental issue that requires attention to more explicit awareness of the need for supports to staff and patients to develop avenues for healthy sexuality for patients.

DESIGNING AND IMPLEMENTING A THERAPEUTIC MILIEU

A milieu treatment program seeks to be attentive to and take advantage of the ongoing processes of life in whatever form presented to facilitate healing. This supposes that whatever the pattern of behavior, discomfort of feeling, or problem of relatedness that causes difficulties in everyday life, it will become evident within the milieu and will be an active force in relation to those involved in living with the client, that is, other clients and staff. This is good; it allows for better study of the problem. The environment will invariably provide a wide range of skilled and unskilled people along many behavioral and experiential dimensions, and the skills available can be used in constructive ways. Unfinished business from the past is available in present patterns. offering an opportunity to work experientially in the present. All of the just-stated suppositions apply to the two-person system of client and therapist in individual Gestalt therapy and to the social/psychological system of a treatment milieu. Gestalt methodology focuses on the minutiae of experience, building on the basic building blocks of experience. These building blocks are sensation, awareness, figure formation, energy mobilization, action toward desired ends, and contact with that which is fresh, resulting in need satisfaction and assimilation of the previous experience. Movement through this series of processes in a smooth way is the prototype of healthy process. This scheme of process prototype has been designated in the litera-ture as the "cycle of experience" (Zinker, 1977).

People who are unable to move easily through these processes develop difficulties in living that can respond to remedial interventions. Habitual interruptions, or resistances to a smooth process flow, are designated in Gestalt terminology as desensitization, introjection, projection, deflection, confluence, and retroflection. Psychoanalytic terminology would call them defense mechanisms. All of these "resistance" processes are potentially both advantageous and disadvantageous—for example, desensitization to physical and/or emotional pain can be useful or disastrous depending on the context. As a total way of life desensitization is extremely dysfunctional. If any of these interruptions/resistances are totally missing, the person (or system) is impaired. If a resistance is overused habitually out of awareness, life prob-lems are likely to ensue. Although Perls directed his attention to neurotic functioning as the overdependence on specific responses that no longer work (Perls, Hefferline, & Goodman, 1951), one can also define more severe disturbances as the absence of certain basic skills that are necessary to the modulation of healthy processes (Stratford & Brallier, 1979).

When the resistance of desensitization is used as an example, it can be seen that inability to screen out some stimuli through desensitization results in flooding and poor capacity to focus. Thus, some people are in difficulty because of oversensitivity and inability to desensitize. Other people are in trouble because they are insensitive to important internal and external signals. A therapeutic milieu should have the potential to support some people to resensitize to stimuli (e.g., their own or others' sadness or anger) and also be able to teach others some desensitization skills (e.g., to real or imagined criticisms). One of the most basic healing experiences for all of us is to be recognized and seen as individuals. The staff of a therapeutic milieu, in their ability to sort our individual patterns of dysfunction and to respond differentially to individuals, provide a field within which various skill devel-opment tasks can be achieved. Thus, programs that are too rigidified in their procedures mirror the problems of patients who are too rigidified. Programs that are incessantly and rapidly shifting lack integrity. The process of strug-gling with the complexities of flexibility and constancy is mirrored in the searches for personal health and system health.

Therapists occupy themselves with the patterns of a particular person. In designing a therapeutic milieu, it is more useful to think in terms of providing opportunities to practice a variety of more generally needed missing skills/resistances within an environment, preferably built into daily routines.

What does skill development mean? What are the skills of living that allow for some resiliency in meeting the stresses that are a part of normal times and a reserve for extraordinary stress? The following list should suggest many more skills that can be built into the teaching repertoire of a milieu setting.

- How to spend time alone
- How to start a conversation with another person
- How to argue, fight, protect oneself emotionally
- How to be direct, how to be indirect
- How to hold one's tongue
- How to choose battlegrounds more carefully, be more strategic
- How to apologize, how to not apologize
- How to ask for what one needs
- How to accept from others
- How to shut out others when one needs time alone
- How to slow down, how to speed up
- How to locate energy resources
- How to know what one feels and to name it
- How to be less vulnerable to influence
- How to feel entitled to be alive

All of the above involve a number of processes. For instance, saying "I'm sorry" involves more than just saying the words. It involves letting go of a bitterness or anger, or not tying apologizing to total identity, or looking at the relationship as a whole. There are several layers to the teaching of a particular skill in a milieu. Apologizing might involve a particular incident with a particular other person. It might involve witnessing other apologies. It might include discussion with a number of people prior to the experience of trying to apologize sincerely. It will certainly involve being witnessed and responded to by at least one other person. It will be influenced by the atmosphere of allowing people to be wrong and not holding grudges that exist more generally.

As another example, many people who enter a psychiatric setting struggle with a lifelong sense of disenfranchisement, of not really being entitled to exist with any equality. This is often lumped into the general category of poor self-esteem. For many it stems from a pernicious and more basic lack of validation in early childhood and results in endemic depression. Institutional settings have a difficult task in responding to this kind of difficulty inasmuch as size alone leads to depersonalization and lack of individualization. However, if the "skill" that is being taught is a sense of entitlement, the setting needs to be planned so as to have small enough living units and consistency of staffing such that clients can experience being seen, noticed, and responded to persuasively. There needs to be an expectation that clients can make requests and demands of others as well as respond to requests and demands of staff. There needs to be psychological space for the extension of each client's self into the environment.

The important basic skills of really seeing, hearing, feeling; of using sensory awareness; of knowing one's own physiology and respecting physical needs and messages from various body parts; of balancing expenditures of energy; and of thinking ahead, making guesses, checking hunches, and reality testing must be built into staff training. A willingness on the part of staff to study their own processes supports their ability to understand the many steps along the way to change. By working with their own process, they become better able to understand clients and also to understand the supportive power of the total milieu. The literature about experiments with this aspect of staff development and training emphasizes the necessity of strong support of such self-awareness from the top down (Jacobs & Spradlin, 1974).

All service delivery programs are under pressure to increase efficiency and to become cost-effective. Because of the pressures of funding, there frequently is little value placed on staff self-learning and little appreciation of the payoff in end results. Yet no program can produce changes as effectively as one where the consistency of effort is embedded in all layers.

When the work is from a Gestalt base, change in behavior alone is not the goal. Behavioral change is one aspect of organismic self-regulation, along with movement toward better quality of experience and more mutually satisfying interchange with others. Therefore, emphasis is not simply on attempting to eliminate a behavior. Rather than concentrating on attempting to get clients to give up a pattern of behavior with which they have survived so far, an environment based in Gestalt principles supports the development of a broader repertoire that will give the person an opportunity to feel more effective and not so dependent on the previous patterns. In a particularly poignant definition, Ernest Becker (1969) has described a symptom as "a merger of poverty and ingenuity" (p. 14). The work of a truly therapeutic environment is to take advantage of the natural ingenuity of people when offered more resources to stimulate this ingenuity. A therapeutic environment must teach missing resistances and defenses as well as other skills, thus offering the option of greater flexibility in the face of stress. One might define health as flexibility rather than a fixed state of being. We are always faced with shifting environmental stressors and only a flexible repertoire of responses allows us to keep our balance in a changing world.

Most of our training as psychotherapists is in the service of learning how to teach things one on one. In a therapeutic milieu, one looks additionally for ways in which the processes of the environment itself can be used to provide opportunities. For instance, getting up, eating breakfast, and entering into the day's activities are always present in any daily schedule. If the intention is to use these activities to promote fresh behavioral learnings, breakfast may become the opportunity for making choice, the opportunity for attention to taste and pleasure, the occasion for conversations with new people, and the time for telling dreams. If the mentality of the program is the efficient feeding of a number of people, breakfast is seen as a time when the client group does not interact with staff, when a routine is being followed, and when a totally different environment is produced, which may foster obedience and quiet. If after dinner time is seen as a time to support people to learn a kind of slowing down that supports their own sleep pattern, the isometrics of excitement followed by sleeping medication will be avoided. Part of the design of therapeutic environment must be attention to the way in which individual choice is supported. At the same time, some care must be paid to choosing system level activities that will build comfortable and successful experiences for individuals when they have a history of limited options for choice and impaired capacity to regulate.

PLANNING THE PEOPLE PART OF THE ENVIRONMENT

People are a major aspect of any environment. When we think of designing a healing environment, the qualities needed in staff become less attached to professional training and discipline and more attached to the total balance of other qualities. For instance, in the hiring for a program, one criteria might be the ability to be direct with clients in an effort to avoid double messages. Another criteria might be the ability to take the initiative in interactions with others while not having to take control. Another criteria might be the ability to have fun. In work with populations that are characteristically unskilled in experiencing pleasure or joy, the contagion of having fun can be a major tool. It is unusual for an administration to look at the mix of personal competence skills and stylistic traits as a basic part of a staffing plan. More usual is an emphasis on numbers, disciplines, and coverages more related to the demands of custom, funding, and regulatory bodies than to the internal well-being of the system. Heightening awareness of these dimensions can lead to a staffing that will strike a balance of responsiveness to critical internal and external programmatic needs. In the staffing of programs aimed at healing, it is wise to include a large age and life-style range so that all clients can find someone who seems to be like them on the staff. Otherwise, clients who typically feel different and stigmatized for their difference will again feel either alone or only like those who are on their side of the us and them of clients and staff. And, again, when this is the case, the efforts of staff to form human connections with clients will involve counterbalancing a subtle and always-present system dynamic.

The inclusion of varied styles of people creates a need within a program to manage tensions that arise from differences. This models in the environment what many people struggle with internally in relation to conflicting internal wants and ambivalences. Many dimensions of choices will always exist in determining staffing goals. In making the necessary choices to emphasize some dimensions and ignore others, the system will again be attending to the metalevels of context and meaning and, by this attention, will sharpen the skills present to attend to system level phenomena. The important point is that it is necessary to think about the milieu as needing particular people resources to deal with particular treatment goals. Knowing that it may be important to avoid double messages, to be able to support varying balances of activity and passivity between staff and clients, and to provide some contagion of humor with a population that tends towards anhedonia is in itself a sign of a healthy environment.

Often, it is thought that good-hearted people who like others and who are generally caretaking make a good staff. Treatment programs can be overstaffed with people with maternal sentiments or with those who are overly "professional" in the sense of distancing. John Enright (1976) speaks to the need for paraprofessionals "because so many professionals become 'para-people' " (p. 66). A genuinely therapeutic environment requires genuine personal contact. While some clients are in need of reparenting, usually a larger number are stuck in an inability to maintain other than one-up or one-down relationships. The ability to develop and maintain genuine peer relationships is often missing. Additionally, it is important that clients feel respected for their opinions and for their own inner wisdom, which is always there regardless of the problems. An environment filled with professionals who operate as experts who always know better than the client what is wrong and what is needed to fix it is counterproductive.

In keeping with the Gestalt notion of all work taking place at the contact boundary of internal or external experience, a treatment setting has to pay attention to the capacity of the staff to provide clear and vigorous opportunity for contact with others and to their ability to model contact with self. Milieu treatment programs are notorious for contributing to the phenomenon known as burnout in staff. This is usually attributed to the steady contact with severe prblems and difficult clients. However, much of the time the experience of such weariness is the result of contending with the lack of teamwork or the systemic contradictions. Contact in the Gestalt sense of clear and direct interaction with another is generally stimulating and enlivening. It is the repeated experience of having to hold in or retroflect or the steady experience of managing mixed signals that has a more debilitating effect.

The importance of having a staff that can respect the inner wisdom of even the most disturbed client cannot be overstated. This expectation of self-determination is a hallmark of Gestalt therapy. Even with client populations where faith cannot be placed in a self-regulating inner process, self-image is best supported by maintaining as much self-determination as possible, with structures available to set limits as needed. This requires staff who are flexible in their thinking and can shift plans to match need. Too often, programs get bogged down in fixed gestalts about how things have to be, and end up losing treatment opportunities. It means running a program with ''loose knees.'' Such a program is alive and lively.

EXPERIMENTATION

The use of experiment is a hallmark of the Gestalt method. Opportunities to shift ways of making meaning and patterns of behaviors come through safe emergencies that allow experimentation with the novel. Gestalt methodology seeks experiments that offer opportunities to practice needed skills. When we think about a milieu as a whole, it becomes clear that to the degree to which the program itself can remain open to experiment, a kind of metamodeling can take place that allows clients to also expect that something different can hold promise. Even a client who comes into a program for a short period of time picks up something of this air of hopeful expectation. If staff are steadily involved in trying new possibilities and seeing what they have learned from the experience, clients too will feel themselves immersed in an experiential marinade that supports their own loosening of fixed expectations. Conversely, in an environment that has become inflexible, no matter how useful the arrangement seems at the moment, there is a quiet message that there is only one way.

A simple way to exemplify how easy it is to maintain a set toward experimentation is to take a look at some of the many dilemmas that beset any program, those aspects of a program where there are advantages and disadvantages to whatever solution is proposed. Often the scheduling of meetings falls into this category. If the leadership can maintain an attitudinal set that encourages periodic shifts in scheduling with opportunities for evaluating the upside and the downside of each experiment, it sends a message that there is no best or right way, only various possibilities, each of which contains some learnings about the makeup of the larger system. It also encourages the staff to continue to seek a balanced use of resources. A fresh combination or arrangement of resources often shifts the load. When the administration and staff of a program feel burned out and despairing of being able to do anything different because of inadequate resources, a not uncommon situation, the efforts of staff to inspire hope and energy in the client group in relation to their personal difficulties is going to be an uphill climb. The administrative level of a program staff has a particular contribution to make to the establishment of an air of openness about new possibilities. Frequently, programs become fettered by policies and procedures that support a need for control and accountability, and staff find over time that a program that began with excitement and success has become increasingly less effective as it has become more established and thoroughly predictable.

DESIGNING FOR SPECIFIC CLIENT GROUPS

Therapeutic environments need to take into account the range of problems that will be dealt with and to seek to develop a process diagnosis of the major learning tasks that will be important to that problem area. For instance, in an inpatient short-term psychiatric program where a common problem group are people having acute psychotic episodes, establishment of ego boundaries is a commonly needed skill. Difficulties often take the form of the inability to differentiate between data and interpretation, and the inability to locate opinion, ideas, feelings within the boundary of the person who originates them. Frequent problems are the introjection of messages from others without any personal processing and the projection onto others of messages, feelings, and opinions that reside within the self. For this purpose, a helpful environment will contain people who are able to differentiate between data and interpretation and who value this differentiation. Staff have to learn to be meticulous in their devotion to such differentiation. I have seen anxiety levels drop in miraculous ways, and medication doses drop accordingly, simply by the staff's observing this rule. (Studies published by Paul and Lentz, 1977, document shifts in medication needs related to milieu and behavior modification methods.)

Some examples follow. ''I know you are tired, you need to go to bed now,'' results in some subtle confusions about how the patient's possible tiredness is being conveyed and a message that others know what is best. He would be better to say: "We are getting ready to turn the dayroom lights down now. Are you at all tired?" Or "I see your eyes looking a little droopy. Are you tired or does your medication feel too sedating?" Sometimes the real message is that the staff member is feeling tired and wishes that it was time for all of the patients to be in bed. If so, it would be better for a staff person to say, "I am awfully tired this evening." That is a capacity to be direct. Willingness of staff to be clear about what sensations exist in themselves and not confuse them with projections onto patients will support patients both to feel safe (decreased anxiety) and to establish their own ego boundaries. Telling people how they feel and making assumptions about their internal state based on insufficient information increase people's feelings of disempowerment, add to their confusion about their own feelings, and decrease their sense of their own boundedness. Maternalistic approaches often err in this direction and inadvertently undercut the treatment goals. (This is not to imply that kindness and concern are not powerful healers or that cold attention to process is healing.)

The difference between simple attention to interpersonal process and a system level consciousness is the degree to which, in this case, the value placed on differentiating data and interpretation is *embedded in the setting*. This embeddedness will be reflected in periodic evaluation of this factor in general, of integration of this factor into the staff training procedures, and also of the degree to which such differentiation also takes place at all levels of staff–staff communications.

In most programs that respond to clients who are not able to function well in the everyday world and are in need to a live-in setting, the major issues are boundary establishment and influence testing. In my own experience of leading at least one group therapy session a day over a 5-year period with hospitalized patients, regardless of the content of these groups, the process was invariably focused on identity or boundary issues and influence issues. Although these are the major problem areas for most people who enter milieu settings, most people who enter these settings also have some degree of competence at the same time that they are weak in these areas. A helpful setting has both to recognize the competence and respond to it and also to offer strengthening opportunities and good modeling.

One experience that stands out in my memory was a day program where deinstitutionalized patients were encouraged through a variety of means to form more positive self-images. At the same time, it was noticed that staff often walked through the halls averting their eyes so as to avoid conversations with patients or gravitated into clusters of staff to chat together. There was little awareness of the behaviors and no consciousness of the contradictory forces or the negative impact of such simple nonverbal messages. Had one of the patients the courage to ask if a staff person was avoiding him or her, I think that the staff person would honestly have denied the avoidance, thus contributing to an actively crazy-making experience in the classic double bind genre (Bateson, Jackson, Haley, & Weakland, p. 252). Several options could exist for making the situation healthier. One would be to provide staff with the opportunity to discuss what makes entering the public spaces uncomfortable and to address those discomforts more directly so that the patient group would not be systematically subjected to a disqualifying experience in the particular area of self-image that the program sought to ameliorate. A program that can notice and attend to this kind of problem offers the staff support to face all interactions with contact that speaks to the integrity of all people in it.

Supporting a concept of therapeutic milieu does not imply an underestimation of the usefulness of individual therapy. However, most of our skills of living and patterns of dysfunctional behaviors are gathered by us early in life by a kind of osmosis, a soaking up of the varied experiences in which we are immersed. We learn many things by example and by existing in a common experience with others, by existing in a reality supported by the weight of numbers. For the kind of disturbances of living that move people into milieu treatment settings, the combined impact of group, individual, and environmental forces are more likely to result in changes than an hour a week or an hour a day in individual therapy or assignment to a milieu that undercuts the basic goals.

When a person does enter a milieu program, the existing expectations, those of the setting and of the client, will often clash. Articulating the differences is an opportunity for boundary clarification. Again, if there is a rule against the articulation of differences at other levels of the system, such as between staff members and between frontline staff and supervisory staff, or between middle management staff and leadership, it will be hard to use the highlighting of differences in the clinical aspects of the program. It is a mark of health in a treatment program if differences can be acknowledged. When a healthy set of processes are in place in the program, the staff can keep these processes going so that people entering the program can get on board. Expectation that people will be able to get on board is an important part of the milieu. That expectations have impact in themselves is a well-documented phenomenon. On an inpatient unit with which I worked, patients and staff cooked breakfast together on Sunday mornings. There was a maxim that hallucinations were no excuse not to scramble the eggs. The program picked up on the simple everyday living acts to support people to try new things, to support people to feel a part of a "normal" life, engendering a positive circle of effects. Feeling good about a simple experience can lower anxiety, diminishing some of the pressure to hallucinate.

In a similar experience, in which we took a group of people who had a long history of hospitalization on a camping trip, a milieu in which most folks pay attention to the most basic aspects of everyday life, our mutual need to face crises as they arose was emphasized. Pleasure in the completion of simple tasks, and the opportunity to see one another in a less stylized or role-bound situation, allowed everyone to shift definitions of self and others.

This does not suggest that medication is not useful for lowering the confusions and concentration difficulties of thought disorders, but suggests that the combination of attention to internal and external processes concomitantly leads to a particularly powerful combination of forces for healing. Just as psychotropic medication can affect internal experience, attention to the external reality stress factors can affect the need for medication interventions.

A powerful lesson from the earlier mentioned inpatient program was that when the environment was sane and flexible, attentive and responsive to strengths and problems in some equal way, dysfunctional behaviors, even patterns of many years' duration, were positively affected.

ADMINISTRATIVE PROCESSES

The administrative processes are as important as the more explicit treatment processes in setting a healing environment. Ideally, the power hierarchy should be clear, and responsibilities should be clear and accompanied by sufficient empowerment to carry them out. Keeping in mind a Gestalt model of healthy functioning, one considers all members of the living environment as important sensors. Decision and action steps are most likely to lead to successful outcomes when they incorporate some distillation of the information that resides in various parts of the system and when the process of moving into action allows for enough awareness and energy to gather across enough people to support that action. This system level movement through a cycle of experience is a process that individuals in treatment in the setting are learning to use in their personal lives.

In a healing environment, if an aide, social worker, or nurse cannot feel well listened to by a psychologist or physician, it is unlikely that a patient will feel that way either. In an educational setting, if a teacher's aide cannot feel well listened to by a teacher or a teacher cannot feel well listened to by the principal, it is unlikely that the environment supports the voice of the child either. This is not to say that crucial decisions must be made by the least experienced or that hierarchy should not exist. The point is that hierarchical power can be set aside in the service of hearing expressions of personal influence. To be heard and responded to is to experience one's influence. When hierarchy results in one-way communication from the top down, the client, who most often occupies the lowest rung on the ladder, will experience the resulting systemic pressure of that directional flow in subtle and not-so-subtle forms of disqualification or invalidation of expression of self. In general, clients are engaged in forming more coherent lives and empowering themselves to negotiate the stresses of everyday life and to maneuver through interpersonal experiences in more effective ways. That always involves efforts to influence others and acceptance or rejection of influence by others. The way in which the system itself allows all members to be heard and acknowledged will infect all layers.

Leadership has a vital opportunity to establish a sane and respectful mode of operation or a negative process. When negative administrative processes are in force, staff must choose to interrupt the larger processes to establish a different process between themselves and those who occupy a lower position in the hierarchy. For instance, if the mode of communications between patient-care staff and administration is one where all communications are submitted in writing and the expected time of response is usually a matter of days or weeks, then to establish a face-to-face mode of interaction in the treatment setting with an expectation that the shortest time lapse possible between request and response is desirable will require extra effort on the part of those in the treatment setting. Often, a subtle variation of this common theme is the further expectation that top-to-bottom response is expected to be slower than bottom-to-top response, again contributing to patients' sense of disqualification. Having to be the point of discontinuity or the resistance in a larger system process is stressful and contributes to staff burnout. Staff who transmit toxic administrative processes to clients are unhelpful.

Models of conflict management are also important in a therapeutic milieu. Underground or unacknowledged conflicts among the administrative group of a program invariably raise the tension level for all those under them, and the conflict often gets played out by other levels of staff or by the client group. It is as though every layer provides a possible way of seeking a solution. Unresolved conflicts between administrative subgroups will be played out by subgroups at other levels and echoes will take place between staff and clients. The axiom in systems is that a more powerful echo effect takes place from larger system to smaller, with an amplification along the way. Resolution at the highest layer paves the way for all layers below to work out similar issues. Trying to affect upper levels of a system by shifts at lower levels is much more difficult.

The ability to articulate and acknowledge what is sensed but not spoken is as effective at a larger system level as at a personal level. The degree to which speaking the unspoken is supported at a general system level will allow individuals to begin to feel it in the air, and observe and experiment for themselves. Speaking the unspeakable, articulating what is taking place, naming feelings, and making space for differences are all powerful medicine. Experiencing one's impact supports a sense of realness and potency. All of these processes and norms develop and persist when introduced and supported through administrative style, staff policy, and procedures, rather than as process discontinuities that frontline troops have to maintain in the face of the larger system influences.

Developing a process consciousness is not easy. Prerequisite is leadership that can conceive of the system as tool, and can notice the echoes of process at intrapsychic, interpersonal, and larger system levels. A second requirement is careful staff selection and training. It is also necessary to establish this therapeutic environment within the bounds of a larger system that will at least tolerate the milieu and, better yet, can echo some of the most important factors. Ongoing attention to the health of the milieu must be the major task of some small group of people since, without such vigilance, the environment will revert to the major processes of the next larger environment.

A hallmark of particularly effective healing environments is that they rarely survive for long periods of time. The stress of trying to maintain small utopias embedded in the larger inflexibilities of bureaucracies makes healthy treatment milieus rare in the public service delivery sector. The fact that they continue to be born, live for a while, and subside speaks to the intuitions of individuals and sensitive small groups about healing and health. The larger crazinesses of our current culture do not support the maintenance of subsystems that behave with integrity. Initiation of a truly therapeutic milieu requires strong leadership and clear vision, along with a skill in managing complex factors. The individuals who can provide this leadership often move away from the work because of career opportunities or personal factors that compete, or because the function of being the barrier between the subsystem and the larger system is a role fraught with burnout.

SUMMARY

A combination of therapeutic interventions is likely to be the most effective with most people in trouble. Individual treatment, involvement in interaction within a small group setting, and belongingness in a larger culture, all of which build on strengths, notice nonproductive patterns, and offer opportunities for learning without shame, can together be a most powerful healing force. In the development of therapeutic tools, attention has been paid to developing psychosocial treatment modalities, but the interrelationship of Gestalt thinking with this arena has not been explored as much.

The Gestalt-based principles of organism in environment, equal emphasis on process and content, health as figure, and power to learn in the present experience are all supportive of the design of the therapeutic milieu. Developing and maintaining such an environment for healing is a little like being a logger driving logs down the river in an eternal balancing act, which of course requires a good deal of flexibility. An effective milieu is a living, breathing thing that requires tending. The reward for tending can be small miracles in the form of human dignity, respect, and change.

REFERENCES

Bateson, G., Jackson, D. D., Haley, J., & Weakland, J. (1954). Toward a theory of schizophrenia. *Behavioral Science, 1*, 251–254.

Becker, E. (1969). *Angel in armor, A post Freudian perspective on the nature of man*. New York: Free Press.

Enright, J. B. (1976). Gestalt awareness strategies in the training of people helpers. In J. Downing (Ed.), *Gestalt awareness*. New York: Harper and Row.

Goffman, E. (1961). *Asylums: Essays on the social situation of mental patients and other inmates*. Chicago: Aldine Publishing.

Goffman, E. (1963). *Stigma: Notes on the management of spoiled identity*. New York: J. Aronson.

Jacobs, A., & Spradlin, W. W. (Eds.). (1974). *The group as agent of change*. New York: Behavioral Publications.

Jones, M. (1953). *The therapeutic community*. New York: Basic Books.

Jones, M. (1968). *Beyond the therapeutic community: Social learning and social psychiatry*. New Haven, CT: Yale University Press.

Kraft, A. M. (1966). The therapeutic community. In S. Arieti (Ed.), *American handbook of psychiatry*. New York: Basic Books.

Merry, U., & Brown, G. L. (1987). *The neurotic behavior of organizations*. New York: Gestalt Institute of Cleveland Press/Gardner Press.

Nevis, E. (1987). *A Gestalt approach to organizational consulting*. New York: Gestalt Institute of Cleveland Press/Gardner Press.

Paul, G. L., & Lentz, R. J. (1977). *Psychosocial treatment of chronic mental patients: Milieu versus social-learning programs*. Cambridge, MA: Harvard University Press.

Perls, F. (1973). *The Gestalt approach*. Palo Alto, CA: Science and Behavior Books.

Perls, F. S., Hefferline, R., & Goodman, P. (1951). *Gestalt therapy: Excitement and growth in the human personality*. New York: Dell.
Smith, E. W. L. (1976). The roots of Gestalt therapy. In E. W. L. Smith (Ed.), *The growing edge of Gestalt therapy*. New York: Brunner/Mazel.
Stratford, C., & Brallier, L. (1979). Gestalt therapy with profoundly disturbed persons. *The Gestalt Journal, 11*(1).
Zinker, J. (1977). *Creative process in Gestalt therapy*. New York: Brunner/Mazel.

Index